EXPORTING JIM CROW

EXPORTING JIM CROW

Blackface Minstrelsy in South Africa and Beyond

CHINUA THELWELL

University of Massachusetts Press
Amherst and Boston

Printed in the United States of America

ISBN 978-1-62534-517-2 (paper); 516-5 (hardcover)

Designed by Sally Nichols
Set in Alegreya and Bebas Neue
Printed and bound by Maple Press, Inc.

Cover design by Sally Nichos
Cover photo: "Cape Town Coon Carnival 1937."
Courtesy of National Library of South Africa, Cape Town.

Library of Congress Cataloging-in-Publication Data

Names: Thelwell, Chinua, author.
Title: Exporting Jim Crow : Blackface Minstrelsy in South Africa and Beyond / Chinua Thelwell.
Description: Amherst : University of Massachusetts Press, [2020] | Based on the author's thesis (doctoral)—New York University, 2011. | Includes bibliographical references and index.
Identifiers: LCCN 2019044412 | ISBN 9781625345165 (hardcover) | ISBN 9781625345172 (paperback) | ISBN 9781613767665 (ebook) | ISBN 9781613767672 (ebook)
Subjects: LCSH: Minstrel shows—South Africa. | Blackface entertainers—South Africa. | Whites—Race identity—South Africa. | Blacks—Race identity—South Africa. | South Africa—Race relations. | South Africa—Social life and customs.
Classification: LCC GT3650.5.S6 T44 2020 | DDC 791/.120968—dc23
LC record available at https://lccn.loc.gov/2019044412

British Library Cataloguing-in-Publication Data
A catalog record for this book is available from the British Library

An early version of chapter 2 first appeared as "'The Young Men Must Blacken Their Faces': The Blackface Minstrel Show in Pre-Industrial South Africa, 1862–1872," *TDR: The Drama Review* 56, no. 2 (T218) (Summer 2013): 66–85. Copyright © 2013 by New York University and the Massachusetts Institute of Technology. Published by the MIT Press. An early version of chapter 4 was previously published as "Toward a 'Modernizing' Hybridity: McAdoo's Jubilee Singers, McAdoo's Minstrels, and Racial Uplift Politics in South Africa, 1890–1898," *Safundi: The Journal of South African and American Studies* 15, no. 1 (January 2014): 3–28. Copyright © 2014 Taylor & Francis. Reprinted by permission of Taylor & Francis (https://www.tandfonline.com/).

CONTENTS

Preface
vii

Introduction
BURNT CORK NATIONALISM AND THE FIVE WAVES OF MINSTREL GLOBALIZATION
1

Chapter 1
FOUNDATIONS
Blackface Minstrelsy in the United States and across the British Empire, 1830–1862
16

Chapter 2
AN EMPIRE OF BURNT CORK
Blackface Minstrelsy in Preindustrial South Africa, 1862–1872
37

Chapter 3
DIAMONDS, DANDIES, AND DISPOSSESSION
Minstrel Shows during the South African Mineral Revolution, 1872–1889
73

Chapter 4
"SLIPPING THE YOKE"
McAdoo's Jubilee Singers, McAdoo's Minstrels, and Racial Uplift Politics, 1890–1898
96

Chapter 5
BROWN-ON-BLACK MASQUERADE
Cape Town's Coon Carnival
131

Afterword
GLOBAL BLACKFACE
Toward Transnational Minstrelsy Studies
183

Notes
213

Index
265

PREFACE

Exporting Jim Crow is a history of blackface minstrel shows in South Africa. It is a story of America's first popular culture export to Africa. From the 1860s through the 1880s, blackface minstrel shows were the most popular form of entertainment among the British settlers of the Cape and Natal Colonies. The colonists loved watching white people mock black people while smeared in blackface makeup. I focus mainly on the exclusionary racial nationalism of American and British minstrel shows and how those logics were reinterpreted in South African contexts. My research findings are shaped by archival evidence, my disciplinary training, and personal upbringing.

I was born in Massachusetts to activist-scholar parents. My father is Afro-Jamaican, my mother is Japanese American, and I identify as Afro-Asian. During World War II, my Japanese American family members were placed in "concentration camps" (nowadays sanitized as "internment camps") and treated as "alien citizens" by the U.S. government.[1] In the 1960s, my father organized against Jim Crow segregation and racial disenfranchisement as a member of the Student Nonviolent Coordinating Committee during the civil rights movement. Two decades later, my mother started an organization called New WORLD Theater and introduced me to performance as antiracist discourse.[2] In 1990, as a preteen, I watched Nelson Mandela's release from prison on live television. As my family watched the crowds of people lining the streets to welcome Mandela, my parents narrated an age-appropriate description of apartheid. This was an eye-opening moment. I knew something of Jim Crow segregation in the United States but nothing of a global color line. It saddened me to learn of a white supremacist project that stretched far beyond the borders of the United States. Several years later, the New WORLD Theater staged *Sheila's Day,* a story of black female domestic workers living under apartheid, and I was enamored with the political music of the play. My parents named me after the inimitable Chinua Achebe, a friend of my family, giant of African literature, and canonical figure in postcolonial studies, may he rest in peace. All of which is to say I have a responsibility to my family, namesake, and ancestors. I will not contribute to the ongoing normalization of white nationalist politics in this country and abroad by sanitizing one of the most racist forms of entertainment to ever be created in the United States. I foreground the antiblack vitriol in blackface minstrel shows and refuse to whitewash the history like recent college textbooks.[3]

This kind of self-reflection on one's personal background is rarely addressed by scholars who write about blackface minstrelsy. I mention this now because the scholarship on early blackface minstrelsy in the United States is split roughly along racial lines, as a group of white scholars are pushing a narrative of minstrel progressivism, while a group of black scholars are thoroughly critiquing that narrative.[4] I fall firmly on the side of the latter and am critical of recent attempts to portray early blackface minstrels as radical progressives.

For example, an essay published by W. T. Lhamon in 2012 claims the blackface minstrel icon Jim Crow is "the most radical cultural force known in America" because he is a popular-level expression of the idea of universal citizenship, regardless of race or class. Lhamon proposes a performance genealogy connecting Thomas Dartmouth Rice's first rendering of the song "Jump Jim Crow" in 1830 Louisville to Barack Obama's "More Perfect Union" speech in Philadelphia in 2008. In Lhamon's account, Jim Crow and President Obama both function as symbols of an integrated nation: "[Blackface] lore practiced from 1830 Louisville to the present in Philadelphia focuses citizens on a struggle to move toward full union. . . . [T]his lore continually played out the problem of incorporating roguery, black and otherwise." For Lhamon, hierarchical thinking is primarily the preserve of upper-class white legislators, while working-class white people generally harbor feelings of inclusion: "If policies seem to prove that people have believed whites superior to blacks, how could citizens now come to vote for integration, intermarriage, and equality?"[5] When I look backward from 2019, these claims ring hollow. Lhamon placed too much faith in the racially progressive voting patterns of twenty-first-century working-class white Americans. President Obama won only 43 percent of the white vote in 2008 and 39 percent in 2012.[6] Furthermore, in the 2016 election, white people were the main racial demographic who voted for Donald Trump: the "birther" candidate who mobilized xenophobic white populism and ran the most hateful presidential campaign since George Wallace. President Obama's electoral victories should be attributed to the increasing racial diversity of the American electorate rather than some kind of latent Jim Crow populism within the white working class.[7] Minstrelsy studies is greatly indebted to Lhamon because his analysis of cultural exchange in Manhattan's Catherine Market and advocacy for a transnational turn are immensely generative contributions to the field. However, it is dangerous to create overly celebratory narratives championing the "radical" potential of early blackface minstrelsy. If such stories proliferate, minstrelsy studies risks becoming yet another voice in contemporary America explaining away white American racism and normalizing white supremacy.

Revisionist scholarship championing the progressive potential of early blackface minstrelsy in the United States has influenced academic interpretations of blackface minstrelsy in South Africa. Denis-Constant Martin is the most prolific scholar who writes about the Kaapse Klopse (Clubs of the Cape) carnivals of Cape Town's coloured communities. His excellent research has introduced many people inside and outside of South Africa to Klopse carnival troupes who drew much inspiration from blackface minstrel aesthetics during the late nineteenth century. Martin's explanation of blackface minstrelsy's popularity with "all groups of the South African population" relies heavily on the hypotheses of the white American scholars who portray early minstrelsy as interracial, antiauthoritarian class resistance.[8] In turn, several talented scholars who write about Cape Town carnival have recirculated Martin's claims of working-class resistance in the blackface minstrel shows that reached South Africa.[9] When Martin wrote these claims of minstrel radicalism in

1999, it was impossible for him to consider the scholarly criticisms of this narrative that would later be published in the following years. *Exporting Jim Crow* provides an update regarding the ongoing scholarly debates on blackface minstrelsy in the United States. Claims of white minstrel "radicalism" currently occupy a contested place in the scholarship on American blackface minstrelsy, are very debatable, and can be challenged with many primary sources that speak to a virulent racism.

Hopefully, my book will contribute in some small way to an increasing level of mutual understanding between coloured South Africans and African Americans. I believe that coloured Klopse who are interested in a genuine cultural exchange with African Americans should have access to more scholarship that accounts for the racism in early blackface minstrel shows. This way, more carnival participants would understand why the vast majority of African Americans are highly critical of the traditions of blackface minstrelsy. I also believe that African Americans who are genuinely interested in understanding what was previously called "Coon Carnival" must move beyond the shock often provoked by the word *Coon*. Documents from as early as the 1940s prove that coloured people were not using *Coon* in a racial way. Large portions of the coloured community were unaware of the racist origins of that word. Many coloureds reappropriated minstrel aesthetics into a carnival culture that celebrated the end of slavery in the Cape and could create brief emancipatory moments during the holiday season while living in an apartheid state that was even more racist than Jim Crow America year-round. Oftentimes, the popular cultures that Americans export to the world are reinterpreted anew in local settings.

Conversely, sometimes the racist images that Americans export to the world are uncritically consumed by local audiences. I focus on the racial nationalism of blackface minstrel troupes whose target audience was English speakers across the British Empire. The professional minstrels who visited South Africa in the nineteenth century were touring the colonies of the British Empire. The minstrels spoke, sang, and joked in English. When they arrived in the Cape and Natal, they spent most of their time in the cities where many white English-language speakers lived.[10] Given this context, I mainly use English-language sources to flesh out this history. By documenting a history that links the Cape and Natal Colonies to the British and American empires, *Exporting Jim Crow* traces the spread of blackface minstrelsy across the anglophone world.[11]

Many people supported my research during its early stages. Michael Gomez, Jennifer Morgan, Tavia Nyong'o, Nikhil Singh, and Andrew Ross offered invaluable mentorship. Robert Trent Vinson, Veit Erlmann, Denis-Constant Martin, and Dale Cockrell generously shared archival findings and advice. I am also indebted to Arlene Davila, Lisa Duggan, Daphne Brooks, Walter Johnson, Adam Green, Awam Ampka, Marlon Ross, John Higginson, Vivian Bickford-Smith, Shamil Jeppie, Rip Lhamon, Matthew Wittmann, Jill Lane, Doris Abramson, Elinor Boyles, Miles Grier, Steve Fletcher, Miabi Chatterji, Jan Padios, Ariana Camacho, André Carrington, Devin Murphy, Vivek Bald, Frank Leon Roberts, Marti Newland, Ben Slote, Barry Shapiro, Ian Binnington, Frank Forts, Ken Pinnow, Paula Treckel, Aisha Lockridge, Calion Lockridge, Max Maxwell, Riki Hing, Akemi Kochiyama, Alwin Jones, Lisa Coleman, Joseph Schloss, Gerald Gill, Chip Gidney, Addison Hazard, Eddie Bustamante, Marcus Pinn, Josh Pressman, Muhammad Al-Bilali, Ruth Hannival, Craig, Desiree, Ian, Noreen, Cindy, and François Josias.

During the latter stages of my project, I received help and useful information from Kevin Gaines, Penny Von Eschen, Catherine Cole, Tracy Davis, Andrew van der Vlies, David Kramer, Danielle Roper, Kellen Hoxworth, Francesca Inglese, Douglas Jones Jr., Peter Limb, Robert Edgar, Nadia Davids, David Coplan, Mia Bay, Jay Cook, Paulina Alberto, Gerald Early, Brian Willan, Willemien Froneman, Gavin Williams, Jonathan Hicks, Roger Parker, Andy Fry, Matthew Morrison, Steven Pond, Grant Farred, Siba Grovogui, Catherin Appert, Bradley Shope, Stephen Johnson, Rosamond King, Sonya Donaldson, Eng-Beng Lim, Uri McMillan, Alisha Gaines, David Leonard, Emmett Price III, Portia Maultsby, Lance McCready, Dingani Mthetwha, Seth Markle, Robin Crigler, Gladys Jiménez-Munoz, Yeidy Rivero, Danika Medak Saltzman, Maya Berry, Leonard Brown, Kim Clark, Petra Rivera-Rideau, Josslyn Luckett, Furaha Norton, Theresa Delgadillo, Rafia Zafar, Valerie Weinstein, and the anonymous reviewers who thoroughly vetted my manuscript. I am thankful to everyone at the University of Massachusetts Press and am especially grateful for the editorial advice of Brian Halley, Clark Duggan, Rachael DeShano, and Annette Wenda.

Colleagues at William & Mary are a constant source of support: Francis Tanglao-Aguas, Leisa Meyer, Hermine Pinson, Artisia Green, Fred Corney, Cindy Hahamovitch, Kate Conley, Joel Schwartz, Virginia Torczon, Leah

Glenn, Joanne Braxton, Jody Allen, Jacqui McLendon, Iyabo Osiapem, Michael Blakey, Admasu Shiferaw, Gayle Murchison, Mei Mei Sanford, Suzette Spencer, Olaocha Nwabara, Bené Nightchild, Deenesh Sohoni, Stephen Sheehi, Gérard Chouin, Hiroshi Kitamura, Jeremy Pope, Eric Han, Josh Hubbard, Scott Nelson, Kathrin Levitan, Hannah Rosen, Richard Turits, Betsy Konefal, Michael Butler, Melvin Ely, Paul Mapp, Fabrício Prada, Nick Popper, Ron Schechter, Lu Ann Homza, Laurie Koloski, Ayfer Karakaya-Stump, Simon Middleton, Carol Sherrif, Chandos Brown, Tuška Beneš, Phil Daileader, Adrienne Petty, Jerry Watkins III, Andrew Fisher, Melvin Ely, Karin Wulf, Matthew Franco, Chitralekha Zutshi, Josh Piker, Maria Galmarini-Kabala, Christopher Grasso, Charles McGovern, Brad Weiss, Neil Norman, Bill Fisher, Magali Compan, Steven Hanson, Arthur Knight, Lynn Weiss, and Max Katz.

I appreciate the help of staff members at the National Library of South Africa, Western Cape Archives and Records Service, Centre for Popular Memory, Hampton University Archival and Museum Collection, W. E. B. Du Bois Library, New York Public Library, Beinecke Library, Harvard Theater Collection, and William & Mary: Daneene Kelly, Latasha Simms, Najwa Hendrickse, Melanie Geustyn, Leonard Benjamin, Emily Walhout, Adrienne Sharpe, Donzella Maupin, and Andreese Scott.

This research was supported by generous grants from the Ford Foundation, Andrew W. Mellon Foundation, and Northeast Consortium for Faculty Diversity. Funding was also given by several units at William & Mary, including the School of Arts and Sciences, History Department, Wendy and Emery Reves Center for International Studies, Asian Pacific Islander American Studies Program, Lemon Project, and Africana Studies Program.

I cannot thank my family enough: Michael, Roberta, Andrew, Emily, Mikiko, Quincy, and Koa.

EXPORTING JIM CROW

Introduction

BURNT CORK NATIONALISM AND THE FIVE WAVES OF MINSTREL GLOBALIZATION

In 1926 Prince Edward (later King Edward VIII) of England toured South Africa to much acclaim. In each city, large crowds turned out to welcome and celebrate him. In Johannesburg and Pretoria, the song sheets to "Dixie," "My Old Kentucky Home," "The Old Folks at Home," and other American blackface minstrel tunes were distributed among the crowds and sung for the prince.[1] I argue that these songs were shared reference points connecting the royal family to a group of British settlers who lived far away from Buckingham Palace. Furthermore, this welcoming rally is one example of blackface minstrelsy's widespread circulation across the Atlantic world. In the middle of the nineteenth century, dozens of white American and British minstrels traveled abroad in search of new audiences. As blackened entertainers danced across newly formed international circuits, they popularized a set of aesthetic formulas for representing black people and colonial subjects. Indeed, by 1926, a transnational exchange of minstrel songs, sketches, and dance moves had been playing out for nearly a century.

The first person to export American blackface minstrelsy across the Atlantic was Thomas Dartmouth (T. D.) Rice, widely considered to be one of the founders of this performance genre.[2] Rice brought his "Jump Jim Crow" song and dance to England in 1836 and immediately enjoyed sensational popularity. The resulting Jim Crow mania was not confined to the British metropole. Over the next decade, "Jump Jim Crow" spread to several urban centers across the British Empire, as colonists in Calcutta, Sydney, and Natal performed amateur renditions.[3] In 1848 a puppeteer in Cape Town included the "Character of Jim Crow" who could "dance a Jig and sing a Comic song" among his "automaton figures."[4] Rice's tours of England and the ensuing popularization of the American minstrel show abroad mark the first moment when "New World" performance culture was shipped back to the "Old World" on a large scale. Before minstrel shows were exported outside of the United States, cultural influence between the Old and New Worlds was unidirectional, as European and African cultures poured into North America. This one-way exchange and the originality of American blackface minstrelsy were not missed by American commentators, as *Putnam's Monthly* observed in 1854: "The only places of Amusement where the entertainments are indigenous are the African Opera House [minstrel theaters], where native American vocalists, with blackened faces, sing national songs, and utter none but native witticisms."[5] An undeniably racist genre for representing black people was the first homegrown popular culture export of the United States.

South Africa has a long and complex relationship with blackface minstrel shows. From 1862 to the late 1880s, blackface minstrelsy was the most popular form of entertainment for the British settlers of the Cape and Natal Colonies.[6] Minstrels popularized racial slurs as *nigger, Jim Crow, darkie,* and *dandy* were regularly used in the diamond fields of Kimberley in the 1870s. Zine Magubane relates: "It was largely due to the popularity of minstrelsy that Africans who worked in the fields were often called 'nigger.'"[7] Decades after the diamond rush in Kimberley, several iconic South African activists and writers responded to the enduring legacy of minstrel speech. Nelson Mandela and Peter Abrahams were highly critical of the word *nigger,* and Sol Plaatje described it as a slur of "opprobrium and contempt."[8] Wide-eyed minstrel caricatures appear in the advertisement sections of twentieth-century Cape Town newspapers.[9] During the apartheid era, Cape Town hosted many carnivals that were influenced heavily by blackface minstrel aesthetics, as thousands of coloured carnival goers blackened up and paraded through the streets and stadiums of the city. Traditionally advertised as "Coon Carnival," the "official" name for the event has changed several times. In the early 2000s, it was renamed the "Minstrel Carnival," and right now it is called the "Cape Town Street

Parade."[10] The cultural influence of blackface minstrelsy in South Africa is undeniable, yet relatively few works of scholarship have been published on the topic. *Exporting Jim Crow* tells a history of blackface minstrelsy in South Africa and the global arena and is intended as a jumping-off point for anyone who is interested in blackface imagery in transnational settings.

As the title of this introduction chapter suggests, burnt cork nationalism is a central part of my discussion. *Burnt cork nationalism* refers to the cork that was burned to create the blackface makeup and to the exclusionary racial nationalism in the repertoire of minstrel images, jokes, songs, and sketches. I argue that the patriotic humor of minstrel shows often portrayed black characters as noncitizens, unfit for democratic participation in a white "racial state."[11] In the mid-1840s, many minstrel shows in the United States comprised two sections: first, an opening of "refined music" where performers appeared in formal American concert attire with no blackface makeup and, second, the featured presentation of blackface minstrelsy. In the blackface minstrel portion, the stage characters were billed as "Southern Darkies," "Plantation Darkies," or "Dandy Darkies," while in the formal music section the nonblackened performers were described as "citizens."[12] This two-section structure is a perfect example of burnt cork nationalism: the white citizen juxtaposed against the blackened "alien." This binary was not lost on antislavery activists of the 1840s. Frederick Douglass portrayed minstrel shows as spaces of racially exclusionary white civic participation when he condemned "the filthy scum of white society" who "have stolen from us a complexion denied to them by nature, in which to make money, and pander to the corrupt taste of *their white fellow citizens*."[13] Several present-day scholars have described the binary oppositions in blackface minstrel songs and sketches: black-white, low-high, chaos-order, body-mind, emotion-intellect.[14] *Exporting Jim Crow* foregrounds the minstrel dichotomy of white citizens and black "aliens."

The blackface mask, with its accompanying exaggerations—jet-black paint, large lips, wide grins, and the occasional woolly wig—was a visual symbol of the racial "alien" and crucial component of burnt cork nationalism (see figure 1). My analysis of minstrel masking builds on previous interpretations of blackface as an antiblack caricature. Ralph Ellison believed the function of "[the blackface mask] was to veil the humanity of [black people]," Michael Rogin described the mask as "grotesque, demeaning, [and] animalistic," and Nathan Huggins criticized "[minstrel] faces

Figure 1. Dick K. Knowles. Courtesy of Houghton Library, Harvard University (MS Thr 1848).

made up in the most grotesque burnt-cork caricatures of [black people], with painted-on huge red clownlike lips."[15] In my opinion, each of the aforementioned qualities contributed to a visual minstrel imaginary in which black people were portrayed as noncitizens and considered inherently inferior to whiteness.[16]

In the Cape and Natal Colonies of nineteenth-century South Africa, blackface minstrels reinforced supposed differences between British setters and black racial "others." During the mid-nineteenth century, many British settlers across the empire believed that Anglo-Saxons were the only race capable of self-governance.[17] The blackface caricatures of minstrel stages contributed to this mentality by offering examples of incompetent black citizenship. These caricatures reinforced ideas of who should be included and who should be excluded from civic participation. Tellingly, when one minstrel troupe staged a "whiteface" performance without makeup in Kimberley, a local newspaper described them as "gentlemen singing in a gentlemanly way."[18] In the Cape Colony, notions of respectability and gentility were often deployed across racial lines, and "gentleman" status was reserved for British men.[19] Therefore, only by taking off the blackface mask could white minstrels claim "gentleman" status. Blackface was the visual bedrock of a transcolonial cultural imaginary in which notions of citizenship, race, gender, and social status were thoroughly entwined.

In the United States and South Africa, the imaginary of burnt cork nationalism also advanced a fantasy of black "aliens" who eagerly contribute labor to the white racial state despite their position as noncitizens. The faithful servants and slaves who appeared in minstrel shows happily work all day to increase the profits of white citizens. These imaginary black subjects sang sad songs lamenting the death of "kindhearted" slave masters and did not protest for equal rights. Such depictions, I argue, carried special weight in South Africa, where local economies were heavily dependent on maintaining a large, cheap, expendable, and disenfranchised African labor force.

My interpretation of the blackface minstrel shows that were exported to the Cape and Natal Colonies brings the extractive logics of blackface minstrelsy and Western colonial states into a comparative framework. Whereas minstrels expropriate "black" skin, song, and dance as commodifiable resources, "colonial states . . . facilitate the extraction of raw materials and 'native' labour power."[20] This kind of materialist interpretation of blackface minstrelsy brings us closer to engaging Catherine Cole's suggestion: "Could a transnational appraisal of blackface lead us to conclude that blackface, rather than being a quintessentially American form, is rather a quintessentially colonial one?" I argue that blackface minstrelsy was indeed "quintessentially colonial," because its extractive cultural logics mirrored the extractive economic logics of the settler colonies. Although David Harvey's notion of "accumulation by dispossession" was created to describe imperial economies, it can also be applied to the cultural logics of early blackface minstrel shows. Tavia Nyon'go's concept of "primitivist accumulation" is also instructive, as it describes a two-pronged process whereby black cultural capital was expropriated as stage commodity and simultaneously imagined in fantastical form. By engaging the material reality and discursive ramifications, this framework helps scholars acknowledge the colonizing logics of blackface minstrelsy.[21] Many British settlers in the Cape Colony of the nineteenth century advanced an ideology of "accumulation and dispossession."[22] Given this worldview, how exciting it must have been for these settlers to watch a touring minstrel troupe and realize that "black" culture was one more part of the colonial landscape that could be "owned." As proponents of critical race theory have observed, white settlers often invested in whiteness as a form of exclusive property.[23] Meanwhile, they imagined blackness as being thoroughly commoditized, unmoored, and available for pillaging. In the colonial settings of the Cape and Natal, blackface minstrel shows offered fantasies of resource expropriation.

One such fantasy played out in January 1931 when, as reported in the *Cape Times*, the city hall of Cape Town hosted a minstrel-inspired "Plantation Ball." Makeshift decorations transformed the hall's interior into a southern American cotton plantation during the slavery era in the United States. Ball organizers created "a striking background for the dancers," with "hand-painted panels" of "coal-black mammies" and "piccanins" (a racial slur referring to black children) filling baskets with "cotton from the fields." A group of "cotton picker" musicians wearing "appropriate garb" serenaded the dancers with minstrel songs. Real baskets of cotton scattered across a log cabin porch added "further realism" to the scene, "as if the pickers had just left their work to make merry among the dancers."[24] Here is a white supremacist fantasy born of the minstrel imaginary in which tireless black slaves happily pick cotton all day and make music for the white American aristocracy at night. Indeed, the American plantation, with its attendant power dynamics and methods of coercion, directly facilitated the extraction of black music and labor, as many white American plantation owners ordered enslaved Africans to sing and dance under the threat of violence.[25] White South Africans attending the Plantation Ball could imagine themselves as white American slave owners dancing to the music of their "property." This foray into white supremacist nostalgia was especially comforting to white Capetonians at the time, who were seeing their standard of living decrease during the Great Depression. African migrants to South African cities were increasingly viewed as economic competition, taking jobs away from white people.[26] Therefore, the Plantation Ball offered a racial fantasy of simpler times when happily enslaved black people did not "steal" jobs from white people but instead worked for them for free. Ball attendees further celebrated their exclusive status as white citizens as they partied in a building that represented the Cape Town municipal government. By the time of the ball, the union of

South Africa was a well-established racial state, distributing resources and democratic rights along racial lines: in 1930 the African population outnumbered the white population, but Africans made up only 1.2 percent of eligible South African voters.[27] In response to the economic downturn, state officials revamped a decades-long public discussion on white poverty, and "poor whites" received assistance from the racial state. State-run relief efforts were not mobilized for hungry Africans.[28] For burnt cork nationalists at the ball, it was very clear whom the citizens were and who carried the mark of disenfranchisement.

THE FIVE WAVES OF BLACKFACE MINSTREL GLOBALIZATION

Catherine Cole's aforementioned comment describing blackface minstrelsy as "quintessentially colonial" is also speaking to the transnational circulation of minstrel shows. She is calling for a "transnational appraisal" because there is a scholarly tendency to keep the analysis on blackface minstrelsy bounded within the confines of the United States. There is good reason for this approach, as minstrel shows have made an enduring and profound impact on the American cultural imaginary. Blackface minstrel shows were the most popular form of American entertainment from the 1840s to the 1890s, at which point vaudeville took center stage.[29] Minstrel aesthetics did not die out in the 1890s; instead, blackface acts were incorporated into vaudeville variety shows.[30] As the technologies of representation advanced, the blackface muse continued to influence generations of white entrepreneurs. Michael Rogin argues persuasively that four of the most innovative early American films, *Uncle Tom's Cabin* (1903), *Birth of a Nation* (1915), *The Jazz Singer* (1927), and *Gone with the Wind* (1939), "were founded on blackface."[31] Meanwhile, the early American animation industry was obsessed with blackface, pumping out several characters who were inspired by the minstrels, including Bosko, Mickey Mouse, Felix the Cat, and Bugs Bunny.[32] The popular early radio show *Amos 'n' Andy* was thoroughly saturated with minstrel dialect and song.[33] Indeed, several American popular culture industries are heavily indebted to the minstrels. Less is known about the role of blackface minstrelsy in the international arena. Recent scholarship has begun filling in the gaps by focusing on the blackface minstrel troupes who traveled outside of the

United States.[34] *Exporting Jim Crow* contributes to the transnational turn in minstrelsy studies.

I argue that the global dissemination of blackface minstrelsy played out during five successive waves. The first wave began when T. D. Rice visited England in 1836 and ended roughly around the 1848 London tour of George Pell's Ethiopian Serenaders. At this point, few professional acts moved outside of the axis of the United States, Canada, and England. The next wave expanded the geographic terrain of professional minstrelsy when an unprecedented number of American, British, and Australian minstrel troupes toured multiple hemispheres in search of new audiences between the 1850s and 1880s. This is when professional minstrelsy was introduced to South Africa. During the third wave, the minstrel parade slowed to a trickle, as vaudeville eclipsed minstrelsy as the most popular form of entertainment in the United States, and a relatively small number of American vaudeville performers brought blackface acts abroad between the 1890s and 1915. In the 1890s, a "coon-song craze" (syncopated music that trafficked racial stereotypes and slurs) swept through the United States, England, and Australia, keeping the minstrel machine rolling, but the general story across the anglophone world was one of relative decline.[35] During the fourth wave of minstrel globalization, live performers in blackface makeup no longer needed to physically travel abroad to spread minstrel-inspired imagery. Instead, new technologies facilitated global exchanges in blackface iconography. Images of white actors in blackface were shipped abroad to international audiences via Hollywood films. American print media advertisements and comic book illustrations also exported blackface aesthetics. This wave began in 1915 with the release of the film *Birth of a Nation* and ended in the 1960s when blackface became taboo in the United States and Hollywood stopped making uncritical blackface cinema. Currently, we are living through the fifth wave of minstrel globalization. After the gains of the civil rights movement, blackface became taboo in the American entertainment industries. In most American "mainstream" venues, it is no longer socially acceptable to perform in blackface. Instead, several American movies and television shows present a self-aware blackface that shifts the object of ridicule from African American people to naive individuals who foolishly blacken up. These self-conscious and self-critical examples of blackface comment on the racism of early blackface minstrel shows. Meanwhile, examples of contemporary blackface harking back to the traditional racism of early minstrel shows have recently shown up in several countries. *Exporting Jim Crow* describes a history of minstrel globalization that stretches back to the nineteenth century.

Minstrel troupes were well suited for the nascent international touring circuits of the nineteenth century because they had few performers (the smallest minstrel troupe who toured South Africa had only three members) and carried a small number of props. Many of the second-wave minstrel troupes who visited the Cape and Natal Colonies were touring a route I have dubbed the "Anglo-colonial circuit" running from England to South Africa, India, and Australia. The larger markets of India and Australia offered the most lucrative stops on the circuit. The minstrels followed the trends of imperial commerce, were quick to visit rapidly expanding economies fueled by mineral rushes, and preferred territories with relatively large populations.

After the discovery of gold in the 1850s, Australia became a popular touring stop, as American minstrel troupes began chasing miners who were chasing gold rushes. American minstrel troupes forged a Pacific circuit that ran from California to Australia and included stopovers in Honolulu and Tahiti. By the 1860s, the Pacific circuit expanded to include Batavia, Singapore, Manila, and Hong Kong.[36] The story of blackface minstrelsy in South Africa is partly about imperial triangulation and competing cultural metropoles, because the Anglo-colonial circuit of London-based minstrels and the Pacific circuit of the American minstrels converged in the Cape and Natal. South Africa was a minstrel nexus linking the Atlantic, Indian, and Pacific Oceans.

In the 1860s, the Anglo-colonial minstrel circuit was superimposed over an already existing imperial network linking the British metropole to the colonies. Settlers, capital, technology, and ideas were disseminated across this imperial web.[37] Steamship and telegraph technology increased the speed of distribution. In order to participate in the imperial network, one had to be a white British subject and indigenous people from the colonies were excluded. The British imperial networks, like the colonies they fed, were racially exclusionary systems of "power and domination."[38]

BLACKFACE AND THE RACIAL STATE

Exporting Jim Crow also narrates a story of exclusionary settler colonies maturing into bureaucratically advanced racial states. My narrative of white racial politics in South Africa foregrounds the British nationalism of the nineteenth century, a jingoism Robert Ross describes as "the prime nationalism of South Africa, against which all the subsequent ones, whether Afrikaner or African, reacted, either directly or at a remove."[39] As several scholars have argued, many of the policies of the apartheid state can be traced back to the Cape and Natal Colonies of the nineteenth century.[40] In turn, the politicians and intellectuals of the Afrikaner colonies played a central role in imagining apartheid. All of which is to say the four European colonies of South Africa, whether run by British settlers or Afrikaners, were exclusionary racial states from the outset. The racially discriminatory logics of these colonies became more legally refined in 1910 when the Union of South Africa was founded and even more bureaucratically advanced in 1948 with the creation of apartheid.

Apartheid was state-sanctioned racial privilege, violently enforced segregation, a marvel of bureaucratic biopower, "the ultimate racism of the world."[41] The apartheid state masqueraded as an anticolonial project by using the concept of "independent nations" to justify racial segregation. The Afrikaner and British populations were lumped into a single "nation," while African ethnic groups were siphoned into several such units. This formula allowed the architects of apartheid to claim the white "nation" as the largest.[42] Meanwhile, the African majority was squeezed into "Bantustans": the least productive farmlands, an area that collectively constituted only 14 percent of the available land. A logic of "separate development" claimed each "nation" was free to advance economically on its own terms. In reality, the Bantustans were intentionally underdeveloped peripheral zones supplying cheap labor to the developed core regions of South Africa's economy, the white areas where profits were repatriated.[43] White people maintained a standard of living on par with the global North, while Africans and coloureds were intentionally impoverished.

The United States propped up the apartheid government as a Cold War ally. During the 1950s, considerable American investments fed the apartheid economy. In 1960 apartheid police shot dozens of antiapartheid protesters in what has come to be known as the Sharpeville Massacre. The international backlash was swift, as billions of Rands were disinvested from the country. The U.S.-backed International Monetary Fund (IMF), World Bank, and a group of private American investors helped stabilize the apartheid economy by giving loans to South Africa totaling around $190 million.[44] Decades before, when the Mixed Marriages Commission convened in South Africa in 1939, the first act was to send a representative to the U.S. Library of Congress to study American precedents. The search uncovered well over a hundred antimiscegenation statutes in thirty-seven states.[45] Here is a moment when Jim Crow laws were literally imported into South Africa. Indeed, Jim Crow America and apartheid South Africa were kindred burnt cork nations, sharing capital and white supremacist methods across the Atlantic Ocean.[46] Many white citizens in both countries expressed a simultaneous love of blackface minstrel aesthetics and caustic hatred toward black citizenship.

Both South Africa and the United States were legally sanctioned racial states for the vast majority of their existence. It is therefore not a coincidence, I argue, that both countries share histories of burnt cork nationalism in which blackface caricatures often represented the racial "alien": that black other who was incapable of democratic participation. Moreover, it is also not a coincidence that blackface minstrelsy became taboo in mainstream American media outlets during the last decade of legal Jim Crow segregation and the blackface mask was removed from Coon Carnival at roughly around the time when apartheid ended. Aesthetic interpretations alone cannot explain such remarkable shifts in the cultural imaginary. Instead, we must consider the rise of relatively empowered black citizens who demanded control over the iconographies of blackness. When racial states give way to multiracial democracies, the blackface mask is rendered outdated. In this new climate of expanded racial citizenship, blackface recedes into relative obscurity because the symbols of white racial states do not reflect the ideals of multiracial democracies.

RESEARCH METHODOLOGY, CHAPTER SUMMARIES, AND KEY TERMS

While researching this book, I collected approximately thirty-five hundred South African primary source documents on blackface minstrelsy and related subjects: memoirs, photographs, diaries, nineteenth- and twentieth-century English South African newspapers, African newspapers and magazines,[47] coloured newspapers and literature, Afrikaner newspapers, and interview transcripts from the Centre for Popular Memory.[48] These sources reveal a large sample of minstrel songs and sketches that were performed in South Africa. In several U.S. archives, I found the lyrics for 248 songs and scripts to thirty-five short plays that were presented to South African audiences. Close textual readings of the songs and scripts reveal the messages of blackface minstrelsy in South Africa. Although there is a strong chance much of the material performed in South Africa deviated from the original published texts, this is the most effective research method available to scholars who are interested in the messages that minstrel shows disseminated in South Africa.[49] I also employ theoretical frameworks, data, and insights from South African history, performance studies, American studies, critical race theory, postcolonial studies, black Atlantic history, and whiteness studies to interpret primary sources and build my narrative.

My analysis of minstrel music foregrounds the important role that song lyrics played in reinforcing notions of racial difference. Furthermore, I draw insights from scholars in ethnomusicology and sound studies to arrive at an essential point: even when accounting for the sensory pleasures and aesthetic affectations of minstrel music, scholars are describing a racializing genre of performance.[50] Indeed, the British colonists of South Africa often heard blackface minstrelsy as racial music. Their descriptions of minstrel music included the following language: "nigger melody," "nigger minstrelsy," "nigger style," "nigger songs," "Necromantic Operetta," "plantation song," "plantation solo," "Ethiopian minstrelsy," "Ethiopian song," "negro melodies," "negro delights," and "songs . . . of nigger life."[51] I believe the music (instrumentation and vocalizing) was the aesthetic packaging that made the racist messages of the song lyrics more appealing. Minstrel shows offered more entertainment value than the average proslavery lecture or phrenology speech. As such, minstrel shows pioneered a highly aestheticized form of racist commentary that has enjoyed a long-lasting presence in many countries.

Chapter 1 begins with a transnational history of blackface minstrelsy from 1830 to 1862. The story starts in the United States with a quick primer on early minstrel history. Following that, I describe the Anglo-colonial and Pacific circuits of the blackface minstrels: midcentury touring routes connecting the United States to England, Australia, India, and South Africa. The chapter ends with a brief overview of European colonialism in South Africa. Because the European colonists were the main audience for minstrel shows, their history is part of the backstory explaining minstrelsy's introduction to South Africa. Western colonialism laid foundations that cleared the way for the global dissemination of blackface minstrelsy.

Chapter 2 focuses on the 1860s, the decade when professional minstrelsy was introduced to South Africa. The blackface minstrel show was a bidirectional discursive practice, simultaneously imagining fantastical black caricatures while drawing boundaries around white British settler identity. Blackface minstrelsy helped preserve and strengthen a white British settler identity that had achieved coherent form by the middle of the nineteenth century. In the 1860s, blackface minstrels performed at events celebrating connections between colony and metropole. Minstrels made appearances at queens' jubilees and royal family birthday celebrations. Minstrel shows also created stronger imagined links between the major areas of British settlement, as newspaper articles in Cape Town and Port Elizabeth tracked the movements of minstrel tours through the cities and towns of the colonies. Such tours strengthened the sense of a shared cultural community, as British settlers from one colonial city understood they could watch a show that was recently performed in another colonial city. The cultural and geographic distance between colonies shrank as British settlers imagined a global community connected through burnt cork and minstrel songs.

Chapter 3 examines the cultural and discursive influence of blackface minstrelsy in South Africa during the mineral revolution decades of the 1870s and 1880s. The discovery of diamonds in the late 1860s led to industrialization, urbanization, violent colonial expansion, and a parade of professional British and American minstrel troupes. The Cape and Natal became valuable natural resource colonies, deemed worthy of economic and military investment from the British metropole. Most of the remaining independent African civilizations were violently brought into the orbit of a newly invigorated British imperial state. Meanwhile, blackface minstrels followed the scent of capital and dispossession. As the British colonies expropriated diamonds for its mineral revolution, minstrels expropriated blackness on colonial stages. Racial segregation is another key theme in this chapter. Many strategies of social control—pass systems, segregated schools, and closed-compound housing for African workers—were institutionalized during the mineral revolution. For several historians, these measures represent the opening salvos of South African apartheid.[52] Chapter 3 brings blackface minstrelsy into the discussion on apartheid's nineteenth-century origins.

Chapter 4 shifts to the 1890s, when the first troupes of African American performers toured South Africa: the Virginia Jubilee Singers (1890–92, 1895–96) and later McAdoo's High Class Coloured American Minstrel Vaudeville Company (1897–98). The manager of both groups was Orpheus McAdoo, an African American entrepreneur and baritone vocalist. He championed an uplift-politics agenda by portraying African Americans as civilized, refined, and deserving of first-class citizenship. His performers did not wear blackface. This was not the incompetent citizenship of traditional minstrel show caricatures. McAdoo's troupes challenged the established orthodoxy of burnt cork nationalism.

Chapter 5 examines the early history of Coon Carnival, an annual holiday celebration of coloured working-class communities in Cape Town. I focus specifically on carnival troupes who identified as Kaapse Klopse. The Klopse troupes of the early twentieth century were heavily influenced by the minstrel troupes who toured in the nineteenth century. Many early carnival participants were consciously portraying African Americans and native Africans. The chapter comments on these brown-on-black masquerades.

The afterword situates South Africa's minstrel history within a larger story describing the five waves of global blackface. Encapsulating a narrative that stretches from 1836 to the present, it traces the spread of American blackface minstrel shows in the British Isles, continental Europe, Africa, the Caribbean, Central America, South America, and Asia. Scholars are just beginning to develop an understanding of the global reach of blackface minstrel aesthetics. This chapter describes common themes in the available English-language scholarship and identifies directions for future research.

I use several key terms throughout this study. The ideology of "race" erroneously suggests humanity can be broken down into several subgroups that naturally have different personality traits and varying levels of intellectual and physical ability. The academic consensus is that "race" is a myth and social construct lacking scientific and biological validity. "Black" is a socially constructed racial category describing people who trace their ancestry to Africa. In South Africa, African Americans, the African diaspora, and most indigenous Africans are widely considered "black." Indigenous South Africans who are counted as "black" include the Xhosa, Zulu, Swazi, Pondo, Matabele, Sotho (Southern Sotho, Pedi, and Tswana), Venda, and Tsonga. "White" is a socially constructed racial category referring to people who trace their ancestry back to Europe. This includes but is not limited to white Americans, white Europeans, British South Africans, and Afrikaners/Dutch South Africans. In South Africa, "coloured" is a socially constructed racial category commonly referring to mixed-race people of European, African (Khoekhoe and San, collectively known as Khoisan), or Asian descent (another racial construct). In South Africa, since the late nineteenth century, "coloured" and "black" are usually treated as separate racial categories. All of these imaginary categories are made very real through human practice. *Exporting Jim Crow* is about that practice.

— Chapter 1 —

FOUNDATIONS

Blackface Minstrelsy in the United States and across the British Empire, 1830–1862

Some things are known as categorical truth: T. D. Rice toured several American cities performing a song and dance called "Jump Jim Crow" during the 1830s. Some things are the stuff of legends: many commentators have tried to explain the inspiration behind Rice's act. In one account, Rice was traveling in Louisville (in some versions it was Pittsburgh or Cincinnati) when he saw an elderly black man with a deformed right shoulder and a rheumatic left leg doing a song and dance. Rice learned the routine, added additional verses, and began touring.[1] A different version located Rice in Pittsburgh when he learned the song from a black stevedore.[2] Another account claimed Rice paid a black stable hand to "sing the song over to him until he had learned it."[3] In another telling, Rice completed the outfit for his first show by borrowing the clothes of a black man named Cuff. A near-naked Cuff waited by the side of the stage as Rice stirred the audience into a frenzy. Cuff overheard the sound of an approaching steamship, wanted to carry the luggage of the embarking passengers, and needed his clothes back. He tried unsuccessfully to get Rice's attention. Exacerbated and naked, Cuff ran onstage, and the audience roared in laughter.[4] Recently, revisionist scholars argue that Rice did not need to travel to the American South or frontier cities in the Midwest to find Afro-diasporic music and dance. Instead, Rice would have found ample exposure to black culture while living in the relatively integrated communities of lower Manhattan.[5]

I am more interested in the discursive work of these stories than the actual veracity of the claims. One narrative presents Rice as an interloper in black culture and mocker of the disabled. Another offers a metaphor for the dispossessing cultural logics of early blackface minstrelsy: a black man stripped naked onstage. A different telling insinuates an equal exchange of money for song. Another presents blackface minstrelsy as a by-product of cultural exchanges between lower-class black and white people in an apparent attempt to downplay the uneven power relations. Because origin narratives are largely about laying the discursive foundations for framing a particular kind of story, here I engage an origin narrative that is central to this book: the birth of burnt cork nationalism.

Consider Rice's curtain speech at the Holliday Street Theater in Baltimore in 1837:

> Before I went to England, the British people were excessively ignorant regarding "[American] free institutions." (hear) *They were under the impression that negroes were naturally equal to the whites,* and their degraded condition was consequent entirely upon our "institutions"; but *I effectually proved that negroes are essentially an inferior species of the human family, and they ought to remain slaves.*—(Some murmurs of disapprobation from the boxes, which was quickly put down by the plaudits of the pit.) You will never again hear of an abolitionist crossing the Atlantic to interfere in our affairs.—(Tremendous applause). I have studied the negro character upon the southern plantations. The British people acknowledged that I was a fair representative of the great body of our slaves, and [British actor] Charles Kemble attested the faithfulness of my delineations.—(Three Cheers) Ladies and Gentlemen: It will be ever a source of pride to me that, in my humble line, *I have been of such signal service to my country.*[6]

If burnt cork nationalism is a repertoire of blackface minstrel conventions and aesthetics that emphasize the distance between white citizens and black "aliens," T. D. Rice is a founding father of the burnt cork nation.[7] In this speech, Rice comfortably wears the skin of a proslavery patriot. The country he "serves" is the United States of the 1830s, where the enslavement of African people was legal and naturalized citizenship was restricted to "free white person[s]," to use the phrasing of the 1790 naturalization act. According to the census of that same year, 20 percent of the country was enslaved.[8] The United States is a prime example of a white racial state that unevenly distributed resources and democratic privileges along racial lines. Through acts of blackface performance, T. D. Rice simply brought the concept of racially exclusionary citizenship into the theatrical arena. His patriotism for the white racial state was not lost on his contemporaries. In 1841 a white American U.S. ambassador was greeted by a brass band rendition of "Jump Jim Crow" in Mérida, Mexico. The welcoming committee seemed to believe "Jump Jim Crow" was the national anthem of the United States.[9]

SAMBOS AND DANDIES: EARLY BLACKFACE MINSTRELSY IN THE UNITED STATES

The earliest available playbill listing "Jim Crow" on the program is from Louisville, Kentucky, on September 22, 1830. The song and dance was an instant success, and from 1830 to 1836 Rice toured major American cities in the East, West, and South.[10] In June 1836, Rice embarked on a triumphant yearlong tour of England that included a brief stop in Paris. In 1837 Rice returned to the United States and eventually made it to Baltimore, where he delivered the aforementioned speech on slavery and white racial superiority at the Holliday Street Theater. In the following decades, he appeared in minstrel shows and *Uncle Tom's Cabin* dramas in the United States and London.

In recent years, revisionist scholars Dale Cockrell and W. T. Lhamon have reinterpreted Rice as a progressive champion for working-class people of all races. According to this perspective, white audiences of early blackface minstrelsy were attracted to the genre because it was "as much about healing as about wounding" and "slashing back at the pretensions . . . of authority more than at blackness." Later, in the 1840s, the minstrel show was reconfigured as a vehicle for expressing antiblack racism when elite commercial interests co-opted the culture in the aftermath of the economic panic of 1837.[11] However, as Douglass Jones Jr. has pointed out, T. D. Rice's proslavery speech about black racial inferiority is noticeably absent from such scholarly narratives.[12] Revisionist scholars also do not consider the mobs of white American Independence Day revelers who broke into several Manhattan properties known for hosting abolitionist meetings on July 4 and July 9, 1834. One group of burnt cork nationalists entered the Chatham Street Chapel, vandalized the space, staged a mock "bobolition meeting," and enthusiastically sang "Jim Crow."[13] As these events suggest, Jim Crow often represented exclusionary white racial nationalism. This observation is further supported by the actions of white railroad workers.

In the late 1830s, railroad companies in Massachusetts forced black travelers to ride in segregated, dirty, and overpacked luggage cars. When black abolitionists such as Frederick Douglass refused to move from first-class accommodations, white railroad workers forcefully dragged them to these cars. The railroad workers christened the segregated cars "Jim Crow." According to Elizabeth Pryor, this naming practice was a deliberate response to black activists who demanded equal rights and citizenship status. Furthermore, "[white] workers asserted their own sense of national belonging by brutally enforcing segregation."[14] Thus, it is not a coincidence that the term *Jim Crow* would later describe the system of de facto and de jure racial segregation in the American South. The burnt cork nationalism of T. D. Rice was recycled in the American lexicon as a signifier for systems of racial exclusion and segregation.

Several years after Rice popularized the blackface solo act, the Virginia Minstrels introduced the blackface ensemble. In February 1843, the Virginia Minstrels opened in the Bowery Amphitheater of New York City. The ensemble of Dan Emmett, Billy Whitlock, Frank Brower, and Richard Pelham enjoyed immediate success and toured Boston, Liverpool, and London by the end of the year. The original Virginia Minstrels was a short-lived troupe because members branched off to pursue other opportunities. Still their influence is undeniable, as countless imitators began forming ensembles, donning blackface, sitting in semicircles, and calling themselves "minstrels."[15] Decades later, "Dixie," a song popularized by Dan Emmett, became the de facto national anthem of the Confederacy: a white racial state founded on racial slavery.[16]

The original Virginia Minstrels troupe was formed in response to the economic depression following the panic of 1837. Many New York–based entertainers struggled to make a living. Dan Emmett claimed the troupe was created in an ad hoc attempt to "browbeat" the manager of the Bowery Amphitheater into a paying gig.[17] Responding to this origin narrative, Eric Lott astutely suggests that "the minstrel show appears to have taken form most immediately as a response to unemployment."[18] Also worth noting are Virginia Minstrel playbills claiming to offer "songs, refrains, and ditties as sung by the southern slaves at all their merry meetings."[19] This was "primitivist accumulation," as black cultural capital was simultaneously produced as stage commodity and fantastical image.[20] The Virginia Minstrels were four unemployed white entertainers who breathed new life into their careers by trafficking "authentic" blackness.

Christy's Minstrels (sometimes called "Christy Minstrels") were an influential early troupe whose songs and sketches were rendered by many professional and amateur minstrels. Managed by Edwin Pearce (E. P.) Christy and starring comedian George Christy (born George Harrington), this troupe began performing in Buffalo, New York, in 1843 and was originally known as Christy's Plantation Minstrels.[21] After touring several American cities, E. P. Christy's Minstrels settled in Mechanic's Hall in 1846 and enjoyed a decade-long run in Manhattan.[22] They collaborated with songwriter Stephen Foster and originated several canonical songs of the early minstrel repertoire. Mel Watkins describes Christy's as "the most successful minstrel act in antebellum America."[23]

The three-part minstrel show format took coherent shape in the late 1840s. Minstrel shows began with an ensemble piece known as the "walkaround." After this song-and-dance segment, the interlocutor (master of ceremonies) called for order with the statement "Gentlemen, please be seated," and the troupe members arranged themselves in a semicircle facing the audience. The interlocutor was a parody of high society: a bombastic upper-class white man who corrected the language of other characters and often spoke in "standard English." Tambo and Bones were rendered in blackface by the most "talented" comedic actors of the company, and these characters were named after the instruments they played: the tambourine and bones (handheld percussive instruments made of animal bones or wood). They wore ragged, sometimes oversized cloths in a grotesque portrayal of plantation slaves, sat at the ends of the semicircle, and were also known as "end men" or "cornermen." The semicircle portion was a comedy show in which the minstrels bounced jokes off one another. Oftentimes, the grandiose language of the interlocutor was comedically juxtaposed against the mispronunciations and "poor grammar" in the "slave dialect" of Tambo and Bones. The first part of the show was followed by an olio and afterpiece. The olio was variety entertainment in the form of solo songs, group songs, dance solos, and stump speeches. The afterpiece was a comedy sketch usually set on a southern plantation that often ended with a company-wide song and dance.

Other stock blackface characters strutted across minstrel stages alongside Tambo and Bones. The "urban dandy" or "zip coon" was an unassimilated free black man who dressed in fancy outlandish clothes and tried to speak English with upper-class pretensions, only to come off as foolish and ridiculous. The racial messaging was clear: black people were unassimilable and could not successfully blend into the upper echelons of northern society. The prima donna was a man in drag who appeared in select minstrel shows in the late 1840s. By the 1860s, this female character was a featured part of many American blackface minstrel shows.[24]

Minstrels drew cultural material from a wide range of sources, including southwestern frontier humor (Davy Crockett folktales), Anglo-American folklore, folk music of the British Isles, the Irish jig dance, and Afro-diasporic music, dance, and folklore. The major instruments used in minstrel shows also came from diverse sources: the banjo and jawbone were of West African origins, while the fiddle, bones, and tambourine can be traced to Irish roots.[25] Some blackface minstrel troupes also staged burlesque European operas and Shakespeare plays.[26] The actual origins of minstrel culture notwithstanding, the genre was racially coded "black." Lott offers a useful description of the uneven power relations at play: "Partly shared, partly black cultural practices were circulated as authentically black, with whites profiting outright . . . while obstructing the visibility of black performers."[27]

The popularity of minstrel shows is undeniable. Although Manhattan was the epicenter for professional minstrelsy prior to the Civil War, several troupes enjoyed multiyear runs in New York, Philadelphia, and Boston.[28] The minstrels followed three North American touring routes, moving through the North (including lower Canada), South, and Midwest and West.[29] Blackface minstrels entertained miners in the goldfields of California. They also performed in the White House in 1844, for the "Especial Amusement of the President of the United States, His Family and Friends."[30] It was not until decades into the minstrel era that black performers gained access to such elite spaces. In 1859 a pianist named Thomas Greene Bethune (Blind Tom) became the first black musician to perform in the White House.[31] A grotesque parody of blackness reached the White House long before actual black artists. This is what happens in a burnt cork nation built to advance the interests of white men.

William Henry Lane and Thomas Dilward were the first African Americans to perform in blackface minstrel troupes. Lane was an ingenious dancer with lightning-fast feet who was widely known as "Master Juba." His style combined West African juba dancing with the Irish jig.[32] Several scholars describe Lane as the founder of American tap dance. In 1844 he beat John Diamond, a renowned white minstrel jig dancer, in a series of challenge dances. By the end of that year, Lane was touring with a minstrel troupe in which he was advertised as the headliner and marketing himself on playbills as the "greatest dancer in the world." In his signature routine, the "Imitation Dance," he verbally called out the names of the best white minstrel dancers, mimicked their dance moves, and ended the set with a showstopping display of his own virtuosic style. According to a playbill, this routine demonstrated the "vast difference" between Lane and "those that have heretofore attempted dancing." James Cook argues that the "Imitation Dance" was not simply a display of dance superiority; it was a commentary on the racial appropriations of the minstrel show. Here was a black person mocking the white people who were trying to dance like black people.[33] Thomas Dilward began performing in George Christy's minstrel troupe in 1853. Although he was a skilled dancer, singer, and violin player, his talents were probably not the main attraction. He was a little person who stood somewhere between twenty-three and thirty-six inches tall. His stage name, "Japanese Tommy," contributed to an "exotic" stage persona. Robert Toll speculates Dilward was included in George Christy's minstrel troupe as a counterpart to Tom Thumb, a famous little person who performed in P. T. Barnum's circus.[34] If this was true, Dilward's inclusion in the minstrel show can partly be attributed to the popularity of "freak shows" during this period.[35] Dilward and Lane were the only black people who performed alongside white minstrels in the antebellum era. A black person had to be physically "abnormal" or exceptionally skilled to break into this exclusionary industry. The minstrel troupes of this era resembled the American body politic because they were composed almost entirely of white men.

Several scholars describe the racial vitriol of early blackface minstrelsy.

According to Alexander Saxton, many "founding" minstrel figures, including Stephen Foster, were closely connected to a hawkish and proslavery Democratic Party led by Andrew Jackson.[36] Douglass Jones Jr. thoroughly situates blackface minstrelsy within the white identity politics of the Jacksonian era. According to Jones, "Whites' refusals to collaborate with actual African Americans in early minstrelsy undermine the claim [of revisionist scholars] that the form's producers and publics sought social and political accord with their black counterparts." Tavia Nyong'o questions the "increasingly orthodox division of minstrelsy into an early radical phase followed by its co-optation by commercial and middle-class interests," offers several accounts of black abolitionists who were critical of blackface minstrelsy, and suggests that revisionist scholars have created a romanticized portrayal of an inclusive white working class. Saidiya Hartman argues convincingly that "donning the blackface mask reiterated racial subjection" instead of breaking down racial barriers.[37] All of which is to say the racism in early blackface minstrelsy is well established, despite some scholars' recent attempts to downplay the antiblack messages and foreground a supposed "progressivism."[38] In the following paragraphs, I briefly discuss several examples of burnt cork nationalism as a gendered discourse of exclusionary citizenship.

In antebellum America, a man's willingness to effectively serve in the military was often thought of in relation to his level of fitness for citizenship. The "ideal of the citizen-soldier" was flipped on its head in blackface minstrel songs in which untrained black soldiers cowardly flee the battlefield at the first sign of danger.[39] One early example, first published in 1835, is a song called "Jim Brown." This "comic song" portrayed an incompetent black military band leader. The humor relied heavily on urban dandy logic by mocking the pomposity of the title character.[40] This version of early minstrel humor became especially pronounced during the American Civil War. The cover art for a song called "Raw Recruits" portrayed a group of incompetent black soldiers who were unable to stand in military formation (fig. 2). In the popular song "Black Brigade," minstrel caricatures vow to join the Union army "by word ob mouth," while actual military service "am quite annular story." In one joke, Sambo described his retreat from the Battle of Bull Run: "Some struck for der country, but dis chile he struck for home."[41]

Burnt cork nationalism was patriarchal. In the 1850s, many minstrel

Figure 2. Raw Recruits. Courtesy of Houghton Library, Harvard University (TCS 82 [Bryant's Minstrels]).

stump speeches parodied women's rights lectures. One such minstrel speech from 1853 lampooned Elizabeth Oakes Smith, an advocate for women's suffrage on the northeastern lecture circuit. Such speeches reinforced the exclusionary belief that women could not be responsible citizens. Another speech offered the following pun: "Dese womans all want to be Captains, when ole Human Nature formed em spressly for Mates!"[42]

Many blackface minstrels were "unwavering patriot[s]," advocating imperial expansion on multiple fronts. Minstrels fervently endorsed manifest destiny.[43] One troupe encouraged the U.S. Army to conquer "yellow skins" in Mexico and take the land.[44] Other minstrel songs looked to Texas, Oregon, and Cuba as future conquests and imagined a day when "de Yankee boys will has de flag ob almost every nation."[45] Originally published in 1848 by Stephen Foster, "Oh! Susanna" was the first minstrel song to sell several thousand copies of sheet music. Months after the original was released, minstrel composers published eight new versions, reimagining the tune as an anthem for western pioneering, imperial expansion, and the California gold rush.[46] Black skin and culture were not the only targets for dispossession, as land figured prominently in the imaginary of burnt cork nationalism.

JIM CROWS AND COURT MINSTRELS: BLACKFACE MINSTRELS STORM THE BRITISH METROPOLE

In 1836 the first wave of minstrel globalization began when British people of all classes embraced T. D. Rice's Jim Crow act. In response to his popularity, a cottage industry of spin-off products sprang up. Jim Crow hats, pipes, and cigars helped British consumers indulge beyond the ephemerality of the live-show version. Publishers printed a book of children's songs called *Jim Crow's Alphabet* and a "mock autobiography" titled *The Origin of Jim Crow*.[47] Rice enjoyed successful return visits in 1838 and 1843. Implausible stories proliferated. According to an Australian newspaper, Prince Albert bought a parrot who could sing the "first verse of 'Jim Crow' and afterwards whistle and jump in a most ludicrous manner."[48]

In 1843 the Virginia Minstrels brought a three-part minstrel show to England and introduced the stock characters of Tambo and Bones. Three years later, the Ethiopian Serenaders presented a "refined" minstrel show by wearing formal clothes, using less "plantation" material and featuring harmonized singing. They inspired local performers to develop distinct forms of British blackface minstrelsy intended for upper-class consumers. Several of these British minstrel troupes focused more attention on harmonizing, "refined" musical arrangements, and songs from the British Isles. Some British minstrel troupes tried to further appeal to the tastes of elite British audiences by performing with an orchestra and conductor. One group of British blackface minstrels called the Coloured Opera Troupe dressed in eighteenth-century court dress and powdered wigs.[49] By the end of the 1850s, at least fifty homegrown professional blackface minstrel troupes were making a living in Great Britain.[50] Although most British minstrels were men, several women donned the burnt cork mask as well.[51]

During the 1850s, the British public became enraptured with another American import: *Uncle Tom's Cabin.* Although it is uncertain whether Harriet Beecher Stowe saw a minstrel show, scholars have argued that she drew inspiration from minstrel character tropes when she wrote the novel. Some of its most famous scenes, in which Topsy interacted with Miss Ophelia, closely mirrored the end man–interlocutor exchanges of minstrel shows.[52] In turn, blackface minstrels drew inspiration from *Uncle Tom's Cabin,* staging multiple stage adaptations on both sides of the Atlantic. Between 1852 and 1855, at least twenty *Uncle Tom's Cabin* productions were staged in England.[53] Uncle Tom songbooks, almanacs, and wallpaper were sold in British markets, and "Topsy dolls won the tender care and affection of little English Evas" as "Uncle-Tom Mania" swept through England.[54]

Several factors contributed to the immense success of *Uncle Tom's Cabin* in England. The minstrel shows of the 1840s popularized the conventions of blackface minstrelsy and readied the British public for the caricatures in *Uncle Tom's Cabin.* Furthermore, abolitionist renditions of *Uncle Tom's Cabin* invoked a sense of British moral superiority over their former colony. They imagined England as a land of freedom where slavery was abolished, while the United States was a backwater bastion of archaic ideals. Whereas American dramatizations of the novel cautiously negotiated the tensions of the volatile political climate of the 1850s, British adaptations went so far as to imagine the overthrow of slavery in the United States.[55] Meanwhile, several British minstrel shows presented critiques of American slavery. Such criticisms conveniently glossed over England's historic role as a leading player in the transatlantic slave trade.[56]

Burnt cork nationalism was highly adaptable, as British minstrels quickly realized that blackface minstrelsy was a perfectly suitable conduit for celebrating British national identity. In 1928 a London-based manager of local minstrel troupes made the following claim: "Although of American origin, the minstrel business was brought to its highest state of perfection in this country."[57] Early British minstrel songs voiced a similar patriotism. A British version of "Jim Crow" contained the following lines:

But, say de jolly Englishman
It is my firm belief
No country like the country
Of plum pudding and roast beef.[58]

In order to better understand the racial nationalism in these lyrics, I try to picture a blackface caricature singing them. When doing this, I see an unscrupulous sycophant praising a nation that was heavily invested in slave trading as the greatest country in the world. The burnt cork nationalist imaginary neutralizes the "threat" of antiracist critique by presenting black caricatures who grovel at the feet of "white" nations. Similarly, a British minstrel song called "Niggermania" (1847) proudly stated:

Everything's done brown
As far as art of man goes
Nothing now goes down
But blackeys, bones, and banjoes.

The song described John Bull (the personification of England) as "being in a state of nigger effervescence."[59]

During the nineteenth century, because relatively few Afro-diasporic people were living in the British metropole as compared to the United States, the supposed "threat" of black freedom and equality was not as pronounced. Still, the British minstrel show managed to maintain a large degree of racist posturing. Michael Pickering, the preeminent historian of British minstrelsy, argues that blackface minstrelsy was "the major source of knowledge of the 'negroid' type" for a majority of British Victorians.[60] Furthermore, British minstrel scripts and song lyrics circulated notions of "British superiority" over racialized "savages." Such hierarchical orderings in turn reinforced Britain's global "ideology of imperialism."[61] The concept of race was central to the imperial project, and the ubiquity of race thinking in Victorian England is well documented. According to Patrick Brantlinger, expert on Victorian race relations, "racism informed virtually all aspects of . . . Victorian culture."[62] In such a context, blackface minstrel entertainments reinforced notions of British racial superiority. Black visitors to England made similar observations. In 1885 a black officer in the

First West India Regiment named A. B. Ellis claimed that minstrel shows made it difficult for black soldiers to be treated respectfully in England, because "the popular idea in Great Britain of the negro is that he is a person who commonly wears a dilapidated tall hat, cotton garments of brilliant hue, carries a banjo or concertina, and indulges in extraordinary cachinnations at the slightest pretext." He believed these minstrel images were just "as far from the truth" as the stereotypes advanced "by the vivid fancy of Mrs. Beecher Stowe." Two years later, when Frederick Douglass revisited England in 1887, he attributed a palpable increase in racial hostility against black people to blackface minstrels "who disfigure and distort the features of the Negro and burlesque his language and manners in a way to make him appear to thousands more akin to apes than to men."[63] Douglass and Ellis understood the racist potential of blackface minstrel exports.

BABU AND JIM CROW: BLACKFACE MINSTRELS TOUR THE BRITISH COLONIES

After the popularity of blackface minstrel shows was firmly established in the British metropole, minstrel entrepreneurs set their sights on the British colonies. During the 1850s, American minstrels contributed to the second wave of minstrel globalization by forging a Pacific circuit that ran between the gold rush towns of San Francisco and Melbourne. Honolulu and Tahiti were midoceanic connecting nodes, as minstrels made their way between larger markets in California and Australia. Honolulu was a profitable tour stop where blackface minstrelsy became the most popular form of commercial entertainment, and several professional troupes enjoyed extended stays performing for multiracial audiences.[64] Meanwhile, the settler colony of Australia was the real prize of the Pacific circuit, boasting a relatively large amount of English-language speakers and the pockets of miners who were prospecting for gold. A steady parade of professional white American blackface minstrels toured the gold-mining towns during the 1850s, including the New York Serenaders (1851), Rainer's Original Ethiopian Serenaders (1852), Totten's Harmoneons (1854), the Backus Minstrels (1855), and the San Francisco Minstrels (1857). According to the historian Richard Waterhouse, London-based Christy Minstrel troupes took the minstrel mantle from the Americans in the 1860s, claiming the "most important and influential" Australian tours of the decade. These British troupes made it to Australia via another second-wave route, an Anglo-colonial circuit that reached Australia via South Africa and India. The Australian colonies were thus a nexus point where the Pacific circuit connecting San Francisco and Melbourne overlapped with an Anglo-colonial circuit that stretched back to London. The professional Australian minstrel scene of the 1860s bore the influence of these overlapping imperial networks, as the stage material oscillated between American "plantation" and British patrician styles of blackface minstrelsy.[65]

Minstrel language was incorporated into the British settler lexicon. By the 1840s, *nigger* was a common racial slur in Australia, used to describe indigenous people. According to Richard Waterhouse, "The prism through which Australians viewed Aborigines was . . . cut by the minstrels." Waterhouse offers similar observations regarding Chinese caricatures that appeared in minstrel shows. Several of the American minstrel companies who toured Australia in the 1850s sharpened their repertoires in San Francisco mining towns, where anti-Chinese hostility ran high. American minstrels quickly learned that anti-Chinese material was popular in Australia, where white miners also felt threatened by Chinese competition.[66] Originally created in antebellum-era America, the blackface minstrel show offered an adaptable set of aesthetic conventions, able to comment on race relations in multiple colonial contexts. India was another such location.

After the American Revolution (1765–83), India became the center of the British Empire. Newly established trading networks ran through India and repatriated large amounts of wealth back to the British metropole.[67] In 1838 a well-received rendition of "Jem Crow" [*sic*] was staged by British colonists in Calcutta.[68] In 1851 the New York Serenaders were probably the first professional minstrel troupe to visit. Throughout the 1850s, British military bands on the subcontinent played "negro tunes" from sheet music that was likely inspired by blackface minstrel songs.[69] By the 1860s, professional blackface minstrelsy enjoyed a strong presence in several major cities. An American named Dave Carson was the most successful minstrel of this era. Carson's San Francisco Minstrels arrived in India 1861 via the Pacific circuit and toured between Calcutta and Bombay for the next five years. Because India was not a large British settler colony, minstrels depended on the patronage of local Indians.[70] Carson's repertoire blended "plantation" material with local references, songs, accents, and languages. Oftentimes, he portrayed local ethnic groups. His most popular character was "Bengalee Baboo" (Bengali Babu), a Bengali man with aspirations of upward mobility whose futile attempts to imitate British high society were intentionally laughable and absurd. The "Bengalee Baboo" is a perfect example of the adaptability of minstrel caricatures, as Carson reinterpreted the urban dandy to speak to the local sensibilities of British colonial administrators and Westernized Indians. Carson's comedy reinforced colonial hierarchies and even targeted audience members who refused to stay in their place. During one performance, two Parsi men declined Carson's request to change seats when they were double-booked with a British colonial administrator. According to a white audience member, Carson altered his "Bengalese Baboo" routine to include a "scathing side hit" of the Parsi men that probably made them "[feel] exceedingly small." Not long after this incident, Carson premiered a Parsi caricature called "Davejee Carsonbhoy."[71] In total, Carson enjoyed a lucrative twenty-year career in India, returning several times with new troupe lineups. A contemporary of Carson claimed he "made $100,000 by singing nigger minstrel songs in broken Hindi English in oriental dress."[72]

So far my treatment of second-wave minstrel globalization has focused on professional American minstrels who entered the Pacific circuit via San Francisco. However, the story is not complete without discussion of the aforementioned contemporaneous Anglo-colonial circuit that ran from England to Australia and made stops in India and South Africa. Nish's Christy Minstrels pioneered this circuit in 1862 when they boarded a London steamship headed to Cape Town. The foundations of this tour date back to 1857, when two white Americans named J. W. Raynor and Earl Pierce brought a Christy's Minstrels troupe to England. This was the first troupe to perform in London while claiming the Christy Minstrel moniker. Raynor probably felt he earned the name while performing alongside E. P. Christy in one of the early Christy Minstrel ensembles.[73] After a successful run at the St. James Theatre and a tour of the provinces, Raynor returned to America in 1860.[74] A troupe member named Anthony Nish assembled a new Christy Minstrel outfit with the intention of touring Australia.[75] In 1862 Nish's troupe of American and British performers embarked on a trailblazing tour of British colonies that went straight through South Africa. Nish's Christy Minstrels forged an Anglo-colonial circuit spanning across the Atlantic, Indian, and Pacific Oceans. The Cape and Natal Colonies served as profitable relay points, connecting this network of British colonies across hemispheres. Blackface minstrelsy was shipped to South Africa via an already established imperial network. Therefore, the story of blackface minstrelsy in South Africa must be contextualized within a broader history of Western colonialism in this region.

"WE'RE BRITISH. . . . WE'LL RIP THE CANDY FROM YOUR MOUTHS": COLONIES AS RACIAL STATES

The Cape Colony was founded in 1652 as a refresher station for the ships of the Dutch East India Company (Vereenigde Oostindische Compagnie) on their way from Amsterdam to the VOC colonies in Asia.[76] Located in Table Bay, the Cape Colony provided fresh water, food, and supplies to ships that were headed eastward. Company employees, known as free burghers, farmed food for passing ships. Over the course of several decades, people from Madagascar, India, and Indonesia were shipped in as enslaved workers. Eventually, the settlement was named Cape Town.[77]

Crucial to this history is the VOC's relationship with the native inhabitants of South Africa, particularly the Khoekhoe herders and San hunter-gatherers (collectively known as Khoisan) of the Western Cape. The colony expanded by waging a series of resource wars. Colonists violently expropriated native lands in a recognizable pattern of "conquest and dispossession."[78] After losing several wars, many Khoisan were subjected to a process of proletarianization.[79] The cycle began with a resource war, as colonists used scorched-earth tactics targeting livestock. After depriving the natives of traditional means of subsistence, colonists forcibly incorporated them into the colonial system as landless laborers. This pattern of conquest, dispossession, and forced proletarianization defined material relations between the colonies and several native groups for the next several centuries.[80]

The VOC quickly established the legal foundations for racial hierarchy in the Cape. Five legal categories were recognized: company employees (administrators of the VOC), free burghers, Khoisan, slaves, and free blacks (nonwhite individuals who were not Khoisan and not enslaved). Rights were distributed unevenly across racial lines. Only the company employees, free burghers, and free blacks could own land or hold political office in the colony. Free blacks were the outliers as the only nonwhite people who had rights. However, this relatively small population was unable to exert much influence in the colony. The vast majority of nonwhite people were legally denied two major avenues for social advancement: political office and landownership. Notions of status were coupled with skin color, as the enslaved population tended to be a darker hue.[81]

When the British took over the Cape Colony in 1806, they kept the legal racial hierarchy intact. During the first two decades of British rule, colonial administrators continued to observe the five legal categories. Timothy Keegan notes, "British influence tended to harden the hierarchies of race rather than dissolve them."[82] For example, the Caledon Codes of 1809 introduced the first "pass system," forcing Khoisan to carry a document naming their Cape Colony employer. Khoisan who were unable to produce a pass could be detained and forced to sign a labor contract. British colonial administrators created new strategies for maintaining the racialized labor force of the colony.

Although the commitment to racial hierarchy continued, the British implemented several relatively progressive changes. An 1807 ban on the slave trade originated in the British metropole and was extended to the colonies. This made life marginally better for Cape slaves, as most slave masters had to rely on natural population growth, were not able to buy new slaves, and could not afford to beat their "property" to death. Later, in 1828, Ordinance 50 gave Khoisan the same rights as white settlers. A transnational network of British missionaries pressured the metropole to pass this law.[83] However, Ordinance 50 did little to disturb the established racial order. By 1828 white settlers had claimed almost all the available land in the colony, and newly empowered Khoisan found few opportunities for economic advancement. A third progressive change came when the British metropole announced the end of slavery in 1834. This was followed by a four-year "apprenticeship" period that was slavery by another name and the actual ending of slavery in 1838.

For many Dutch settlers, now self-identifying as Afrikaners, Ordinance 50 and the abolition of slavery were the final indignities.[84] According to this perspective, British rule posed a direct threat to what Afrikaners saw as the "natural" racial order. In 1836 large groups of Afrikaners left the Cape Colony and traveled north in search of new lands to claim as their own. In the late nineteenth century, Afrikaner intellectuals retroactively named the emigrants "Voortrekkers" and their journey the "Great Trek." The Great Trek was a pivotal moment in South African history, as Europeans left the coastline and began moving into the interior, violently uprooting black African civilizations. Two Afrikaner states were founded: the Transvaal Republic in 1852 and the Orange Free States in 1854. The constitution of the Transvaal Republic established the boundaries of a racial state: "The people are not prepared to allow any equality of the non-white with the white inhabitants, either in Church or State."[85]

In the 1830s, a group of Voortrekkers traveled eastward with the intention of creating a port city. After winning a series of military victories against the Zulu, they established the short-lived Natalia Republic in 1839. In 1843 the British Empire forcefully annexed the young country, renaming it the Colony of Natal and establishing the city of Durban. The British settler elite felt threatened by the sizable African demographic majority and over the course of the nineteenth century developed new strategies to extract labor and maintain political dominance. Theophilus Shepstone, secretary of native affairs for the Natal Colony, developed the "Shepstone System," which forced Africans to live in "locations"—a euphemism for the least productive lands in the colony. This was arguably the first large-scale system of racial segregation in South Africa.[86]

The economies of the Cape and Natal limped through the decades, showing slow to negative growth rates well into the 1860s. When the Cape was acquired by the British Empire in 1806, the vast majority of colonists practiced subsistence agriculture, and few products were created for export. A half century later, although British rule opened transnational trading networks, most colonists continued to grow crops for sustenance.[87] In 1820 a state-aided settlement scheme brought four thousand British immigrants and helped grow the white settler population, but still the economies sputtered along. Aside from the merchant elites who controlled the wool and wine export trades, few settlers enjoyed large amounts of wealth. There were no discernible natural resources for export, and as late as 1860, ox wagons were the main method for bringing goods to markets.[88] The Cape Colony struggled through a severe depression in 1865, when the price for wool plummeted after the end of the American Civil War.[89] The British colonies of South Africa were relatively small markets compared to India and Australia. Nonetheless, South

Africa was a major node in the Anglo-colonial circuit as a steady stream of minstrels visited the colonies.

The economic problems of the colonies can partly be explained by a failure to secure a sufficient amount of unskilled, low-wage laborers needed for growth in a capitalist system. Slavery had been abolished in 1838, and British colonists experimented with a number of coercive techniques that attempted to produce a black proletariat underclass over the next thirty years. In Natal colonists reached out to India after learning that local Africans did not want to work on the newly created sugar plantations. In 1860 the first indentured South Asian workers arrived in Natal. Meanwhile, in the Cape Colony, colonists increasingly viewed the Xhosa as a major source of cheap labor.

The first resource war between Cape colonists and Xhosa broke out in 1779, initiating a hundred years of intermittent conflict.[90] A series of wars put serious strains on Xhosa economies, as the scorched-earth tactics of British settlers decimated cattle reserves and agricultural production. British settlers justified the expropriation of Xhosa lands with a language of racial and cultural superiority.[91] During the 1850s, a catastrophic event sped up the process of proletarianization. An exceptionally lethal European cattle disease killed off much of the Xhosa's livestock. Cattle was a major part of Xhosa economies, and some chiefdoms lost more than 80 percent. Several Xhosa prophets suggested "witchcraft" as the source of the problem. They believed a massive sacrifice of the remaining cattle and grain would cleanse the land of witchcraft and resurrect Xhosa casualties from the past half century of colonial warfare. The ancestors would bring cattle, help defeat the British, and reclaim the land. The resultant "Cattle Killing" of 1857 further devastated the Xhosa economy, leaving large amounts of people without a means for subsistence. Facing starvation, many Xhosa began pouring into the Cape Colony in search of employment. Cape officials realized this situation could be exploited and took steps to make "servitude" or "public work" a precondition for famine relief. In 1857 the Cape parliament passed the "Kaffir Employment Bill," which enforced five-year nonnegotiable contracts of indentured servitude for Xhosa in the colony. By the end of the year, almost thirty thousand Xhosa were registered as workers, and it is estimated that around the same number had entered the colony unregistered.[92] Governor George Grey commented on the situation: "A restless nation, who for years have harassed the frontier, may now, to a great extent be changed into useful labourers."[93]

For the first time in the history of the colony, large numbers of Xhosa traveled to the Western Cape to find work. The timing of blackface minstrelsy's popularization in the 1860s is a remarkable coincidence. Just when British settlers were beginning to interact with Xhosa contract laborers on an unprecedented scale, they were introduced to the black slaves and servant characters of professional minstrel troupes.

The most recent frontier war, known as the Kat River Rebellion of 1850–53, further contributed to the entrenchment of racial attitudes in the Cape. The colonial government established the Kat River settlement as a haven for displaced Khoekhoe and a buffer zone between the colony and the Xhosa chiefdoms to the northeast. Missionaries had very different hopes for the area, believing a successful settlement would demonstrate how Christian teachings could "civilize" the Khoekhoe. For these missionaries, the Kat River settlement would prove that human difference could be bridged by a shared Christianity. However, during the Kat River Rebellion, many Khoekhoe sided with Xhosa rebels and attacked the colony. The alliance between the Xhosa and Khoekhoe was portrayed in the British settler press as a declaration of race war. Elizabeth Melbourne relates: "The notion of ineradicable racial difference gained considerable currency in the wake of the war."[94] When professional blackface minstrelsy reached the Cape Colony in the 1860s, missionaries advocating a shared humanity had lost what little influence they had in the first half of the nineteenth century. Indeed, by 1862 British settlers were ready for a new language of racial difference. Much of this language was provided by traveling minstrels in blackface paint.[95]

When professional minstrelsy arrived in 1862, the Cape Colony, on a superficial level, was marginally more democratic than Natal. Natal colonists disenfranchised the African majority. By contrast, when representative government was granted to the Cape in 1853, the constitution did not exclude voters on the basis of race. However, in practice the Cape property requirements restricted access, nonwhite voters never constituted more than 15 percent of the total electorate, and white settlers maintained a monopoly over the machinery of the colonial state.[96] Any intellectually responsible explanation for the popularity of blackface minstrelsy must acknowledge the highly racialized worldview of the Cape and Natal colonists.[97] The burnt cork nationalism in minstrel shows offered racial fantasies that meshed neatly with the exclusionary race thinking of many colonists.

In the 1860s, the Cape and Natal Colonies were lucrative way stations for British and American minstrels traveling between the larger markets of London and Australia.[98] The blackface minstrel story in South Africa overlaps with that of the Dutch East India Company. Both used South Africa as a convenient way station as they traveled across the Atlantic and Indian Oceans. A comprehensive list of "things" mimicked by the minstrels must include the colonial circuits of Western empires.

— Chapter 2 —

AN EMPIRE OF BURNT CORK

Blackface Minstrelsy in Preindustrial South Africa, 1862–1872

In 1862 a wealthy resident of Port Elizabeth advertised the sale of a large and expensive piece of property. The property included an elaborately furnished main house, a coach house, rooms for servants, horse stables, and a six-thousand-gallon water tank. It also included an inn "known to everyone" as the "Jim Crow."[1] T. D. Rice, the creator of the Jim Crow character, had passed away two years earlier, never having performed in South Africa, and has been portrayed by revisionist scholars as a symbol of pan-Atlantic working-class culture.[2] Nonetheless, his popularity among British colonists throughout the world was so great that even upper-class settlers in the Eastern Cape made references to his most famous character. Two decades later, a building in Kimberley was named "Uncle Tom's Cabin."[3] The names of iconic minstrel characters were etched into the built environment of the major cities of the Cape Colony. Such acts of "imperial ornamentation" were not unique to South Africa; British settlers across the empire renamed streets, monuments, and places with anglophone monikers.[4] What is unique about the aforementioned examples are the ways in which British settlers used minstrel references to mark colonized spaces. This development is not surprising because the British settlers of South Africa often used blackface minstrelsy to articulate the logics of empire.

This chapter examines the first decade of professional minstrelsy in the

Cape and Natal Colonies of South Africa, a time when blackface minstrel shows contributed to the race thinking of the British colonists. Blackface minstrel shows were shared cultural spectacles enjoyed by British settlers of all classes, genders, and ages. In these shows, Anglo-Saxon whites were presented as ideal colonial citizens. Professional minstrel troupes circulated variants of burnt cork nationalism by portraying black caricatures who were undeserving of equal access to the economic and civic privileges of the white settler colonies.

Three professional blackface minstrel troupes toured South Africa in the 1860s. In August 1862, Nish's Christy Minstrels began the first professional minstrel tour of the British South African colonies. The troupe was a mixture of American and British minstrels identified in the local press as Nish, Joe Brown, Washington Norton, Charles Steele, Melvyn, T. Rainford, and Stewart. They enjoyed instant success, performing binightly for packed houses and waking to glowing reviews in the local newspapers. They sold Christy Minstrel songbooks and shaped the direction of blackface minstrelsy in the colonies for years to come, as the songbooks continued to circulate long after their departure, showing up in sheet music form in music stores in major cities such as Cape Town and Port Elizabeth. Nish's Christy Minstrels left South Africa in late November 1862 and traveled east to India and Australia. In 1865 a second group, Leslie's Christy Minstrels, toured the Cape and Natal. During this tour, an American comedian named Harry Leslie appeared alongside Charles Steele and J. R. Taylor (fig. 3).[5] The third and longest professional tour of the 1860s played out between September 1868 and April 1869, when Norton's Christy Minstrels came to South Africa. This act included Washington Norton and Charles Steele—two performers with whom the Cape public was already well acquainted—and two new minstrels named Norman Coyle and Rayner. The three professional minstrel troupes who toured the Cape and Natal in the 1860s spent the vast majority of their time in four major cities: Cape Town, Port Elizabeth, Durban, and, to a lesser extent, Grahamstown.[6]

Also of interest are the British settler amateur minstrels who blackened up and took to the stages of the Cape and Natal Colonies. Although local colonists presented several scattered blackface performances during the 1840s and 1850s, the popularity of amateur blackface minstrelsy increased dramatically when the professional troupes visited in the 1860s.[7] Cape Town was the site of a thriving minstrel scene as the Young Men's Insti-

Figure 3. Harry Leslie. Courtesy of Houghton Library, Harvard University (MS Thr 1848).

tute Christys, Juvenile Christy Minstrels, 86th Royal Downshire Minstrels, Catholic Young Men's Society Christy Minstrels, Amateur Coloured Troupe, and Original Cape Town Christys staged staggered and sporadic performances in the 1860s.[8] Amateur performers tried to satiate the public demand for minstrelsy during moments when professionals were not touring the colonies.

The question of how blackface minstrelsy contributed to the race discourse of the British colonists is central to this chapter. To answer this, I turn to Michael Omi and Howard Winant's notion of a racial project. They define a racial project as "simultaneously an interpretation, representation, or explanation of racial dynamics, and an effort to reorganize and redistribute resources along particular racial lines."[9] The British settler colonies of South Africa in the nineteenth century fit this definition. These colonies implemented a number of laws that worked to distribute wealth and political power along racial lines. But in order for a racial project to be effective, there must be an element of race discourse, some kind of discursive mechanism working to explain racial difference. In South Africa during the 1860s, blackface minstrelsy functioned as an important part of that mechanism. Indeed, it was one of the major discursive sources working to preserve boundaries of racial difference in the British colonies of South Africa during the last decade of the preindustrial era.

Minstrel portrayals of black servants in a U.S. plantation context could easily be reinterpreted to fit the discursive needs of a South African colonial system of labor that relied heavily on African proletariats. Over the colony's history, settlers employed several methods of labor coercion, including slavery, apprenticeship, indentured servitude, and "Masters and Servants" laws. In both the United States and South Africa, black subservience was a necessary component of the "natural" racial order, and minstrelsy often provided hyperbolic images of what that racial order could look like. In most instances, British settlers believed the minstrel caricatures were accurate representations of people of African descent. In other moments, minstrel images provided a template for British settlers that described not necessarily what they believed Africans to be, but an ideal of what Africans could become with the "proper disciplining" and "civilizing" influences. Many British settlers believed that Africans could be transformed to fit the labor needs of the colonies through coercive state mechanisms. Furthermore, the American blacks in minstrel songs had supposedly benefited from generations of white tutelage, whereas recent Xhosa arrivals to the Cape Colony had not. A large portion of the blackface minstrel songs presented in South Africa in the 1860s portrayed African American workers as happy, carefree, and subservient. Many British settlers wanted to turn these fantasies of black labor into reality.

British settlers especially appreciated the racial humor in minstrel shows. Several days before Nish's Christy Minstrels left the Cape, colonial authorities presented a "twelve-point star medal of gold" to Washington Norton to "recogni[ze] . . . the great pleasure" he brought to the "Cape people" with his "humorous and clever delineation of negro character."[10] The troupe members who specialized in instrumentation or sentimental song were noticeably absent from this award ceremony. Although the varied repertories of the Christy Minstrel troupes who toured South Africa included "plantation songs" and folk music from the British Isles, the racial commentary was the most appealing part of the show. While the musical packaging contributed to the popularization of blackface minstrelsy, for many British settlers in the Cape the racial comedy was the main attraction.

REPRESENTATIONAL STRATEGIES: MINSTREL CARICATURES AND BRITISH SETTLER DISCOURSE

Many British settlers believed minstrel caricatures were accurate representations of African people. One of the first reviewers of Nish's Christy Minstrels claimed their show was based on "broad caricature, with a recognizable basis in fact. . . . [S]o essentially true to life—especially African life . . . are the 'sketches' of these clever impersonators of negro character, that they could scarcely fail to please." A few months later, another review of the same troupe stated: "Messrs. Brown and Norton are delineators of Nigger character, and they are most accomplished actors. Even at the Cape, where the Nigger character is so well understood, the caricatures of these performers created a perfect furore." As the decade progressed, other reviewers commented on the supposed realism of minstrel shows. An article from 1865 claimed: "Mr. Leslie came next in the eccentric dance and song, 'The Essence of Old Virginia,' in which he again displayed his great power as a delineator of negro character, in the impersonation of which all that is comic is brought out in so natural and artistic a manner as to secure the immediate sympathies of his hearers." Similarly, the *Eastern Province Herald* described Ginger Blue, the main black character in the minstrel play *The Virginia Mummy* as "a nigger shoe-black, [who] is evidently a simple, good-natured fellow, with only just so much of the instinct of his race as betrays itself in love of money, brandy, good living, and mischief." The same article claimed Harry Leslie's portrayal of Ginger Blue was "pleasing and extremely life-like." A Durban-based reviewer suggested the "negro oddities" were "as true to life as possible" and was particularly impressed that "so large an amount of local knowledge could have been acquired in so short a time."[11]

The prima donna character, the white male in drag portraying a black woman, was brought to South African shores by Norton's Christy Minstrels in 1868. According to one newspaper: "[Mr. Norton's] prima donna was inimitable. The affected negro lady was personated so admirably—so naturally to the life, that had it not been announced that Mr. Norton would sustain this character, the audience would have believed that a veritable negress was before them; the voice, the gestures, the dress, was all in all."[12] Another described Norton's prima donna as "most life-like."[13] Relatedly, a *Cape Argus* review portrayed minstrel music as "genuine nigger melodies."[14] The actual origins of the songs notwithstanding, reviewers and audience members often believed they were being exposed to the authentic folk music of enslaved Africans from the American South. Clearly, many British settlers saw a large amount of "accuracy" in these shows. But what exactly was being portrayed on minstrel stages? The minstrel troupes who toured the Cape and Natal Colonies used several representational strategies.

Midway through an 1865 tour of the Cape and Natal Colonies, Leslie's Christy Minstrels merged blackface minstrelsy with ethnological show business by displaying an "8 Feet High . . . 400 lbs African Giant" during an intermission. I did not find postshow descriptions of this act and suspect the "giant" was a stage trick created by the minstrels.[15] Nevertheless, the purported "Giant" is worthy of mention because the minstrels who advertised it were clearly reproducing a foundational convention of the minstrel formula. Minstrel shows relied heavily on the trope of hyperbolic blackness: exaggerated and outlandish portrayals of black physical appearance, song, dance, speech, and supposed character traits. Minstrels portrayed black characters as racial others whose excesses marked them as different from whiteness. As in the United States, in the South African colonies whiteness was the normative subject position whose qualities and characteristics stood for moderation, control, and responsible citizenship. Meanwhile, blackness was associated with overindulgence, disarray, and noncitizen status. According to this racist logic, the white median was the yardstick by which black surplus was measured, and black surplus served as a marker of racial distance. When minstrels took the stage with blackened faces and wide grins, the audience knew something "black" was about to happen. In such a minstrel context, presenting an "African Giant" made perfect sense.

Hyperbolic blackness spilled from minstrel stages when curtains rose to burnt cork faces grinning widely into the audience. The pitch-black minstrel mask is the most visceral example of minstrel hyperbole. This mask was designed specifically to isolate and exaggerate two physical traits that were attributed to black people: large lips and dark skin. Here, Mark Twain's description of minstrel lips is instructive: "thickened and lengthened with bright red paint to such a degree that their mouths resembled slices cut in a ripe watermelon." Burnt cork completed the embellishment with a jet-black face paint. White skin was the standard of normativity against which the burnt cork mask was measured. Relatedly, one nineteenth-century commentator in the British metropole observed: "With white faces the whole affair would be intolerable. It is the ebony that gives the due and needful colour to the monstrosities, the breaches of decorum, the exaggerations of feeling, and the 'silly, sooth' character of the whole implied drama." A British settler in Natal made a similar suggestion: "Coloring the skin justified a breadth of treatment in representing the grotesque, which would not otherwise be obtainable. What would seem silly and distorted in an actor of our race, loses its insane aspect when done by a mock ethiopian."[16] For minstrel enthusiasts, the mask was a vital part of the spectacle, a necessary visual effect completing the onstage "monstrosities."

Hyperbolic blackness was often expressed as frenetic corporality, as minstrels used fast movements and eccentric gestures to mark blackness as nonnormative. The minstrel imaginary presented black bodies that were exceptionally dexterous, energetic, and capable of extraordinary physical feats. Hans Nathan's description of the black caricatures portrayed in the first performance of the Virginia Minstrels is a useful representation of this imaginary: "When they could force themselves to remain seated, they would stretch out their legs toward their audience in rowdy fashion and bend their feet and their toes at the sharpest possible angles." Relatedly, in 1846 a British reviewer described the "savage energy [animating]" a minstrel musician in blackface whose banjo playing "nearly wrung him off his seat. His white eyes rolled in a curious frenzy."[17] The trope of frenetic corporality also appears in the British settler press of the Cape. One description mentioned a tambourine player who "appears to have pledged himself to the demolition of parchment and the utter annihilation of his boot-leather." Meanwhile, the "imperturbable Bones" had "knuckles the whole length of his fingers, and could, I positively believe, play with his feet."[18] If "black" bodies were capable of such extreme physical feats, it did not take a large leap in logic to picture energetic African workers attending to the labor needs of the colony. Indeed, a review of a minstrel show in Port Elizabeth praised one performer for "literally work[ing] like a nigger."[19]

In the burnt cork nationalist imaginary, obedient black servants happily worked to increase the profits of white citizens. Many American minstrel songs performed in South Africa advanced this imaginary. A song called "Tapioca" was a popular example of this logic:

> When I used to work upon the levee,
> Many happy darkies there I see
> Cotton coming in so very heavy
> O golly there was lots of work for me
> Black man hauling in the cargo
> Sun am very hot upon the head
> When I'm done I dance a jolly gargo
> Rumtum on the banjo then to bed[20]

Similarly, a song called "Down the River" portrayed jolly oarsmen traveling across an unnamed channel:

> There's plenty on board for de darkies to eat
> And there's something to drink and to smoke;
> There's de banjo, de bones, and de tambourine,
> And de song, and de comical joke
> Oh the river is up, and the channel is deep
> And the wind blows steady and strong
> Let the splash of your oars the measure keep
> As we row the ole boat along[21]

In the song "Angelina Baker," a blissful work regiment is disrupted by a heartbreaking woman. The enslaved protagonist sings,

> Way down on the old plantation. . . .
> Oh, den I work, and den I sing, so happy all the day
> Til Angelina Baker came and stole my heart away.[22]

In these minstrel fantasies, black people hew wood and draw water with cavernous smiles.

No fantastical minstrel plantation was complete without a rendering of "benevolent" slave masters. Later, in the twentieth century, the Zulu servant who faithfully sacrifices his life to save the master would become a common trope in early South African film.[23] Such cinematic fantasies can be traced back to the plantation odes of the minstrel shows of the 1860s. In "Beneath the Weeping Willow," a black slave offered to trade his life for that of the master:

> O'ver Massa's grave the willow's weeping,
> And I weeping too;
> Under the green sod he is sleeping,
> Oh, bitter, bitter woe.
> He gave me my freedom 'ere we parted;
> What use that freedom now to me?
> Oh, darkies, I'm almost broken-hearted,
> Massa I never more shall see.
>
> Chorus—
> But if it could have been my lot,
> To sleep on earth's cold pillow
> And dying, rest in mass'as stead
> Beneath the weeping willow
>
> O'ver massa's grave, the children kneeling,
> Lipsing a prayer;
> Cruel and painful is the feeling,
> To look upon them there.
> So good and kind was dear old Massa,
> Better a man could hardly be;
> Tear upon tear comes falling faster,
> Each time I look upon that tree.
> Chorus[24]

The chorus of a popular minstrel song called "Massa's in the Cold Ground" mourned the death of a "benevolent" slave master:

> Down in the corn-field
> Hear that Mournful sound;
> All the darkeys are a weeping
> Massa's in the cold, cold ground.[25]

The minstrel shows of South Africa expressed much sentimentalism for the American plantation. The protagonist of "I Long for My Home in Kentucky" sings nostalgically for the "[green] field whar [he] labor'd," the "old cabin home," and "massa who lives in his own handsome halls."[26] The dying elderly slave in "Old Potomac Shore" describes a riverside plantation where "all was mirth and glee." He supposedly takes solace in knowing he will "rest [sweetly]" in a plantation grave on the banks of the Potomac River.[27] Indeed, minstrel sentimentalism was itself a racial discourse that portrayed black men as "unmasculine" others. In the Cape Colony of the mid-nineteenth century, masculinity was constructed as "loyal, brave, and active," while femininity represented the "spiritual, sensitive, and vulnerable."[28] In such a context, British settlers would have interpreted minstrel caricatures as "creatures of feeling" who lacked the "manly" qualities of white citizens.[29]

Masculinity was also measured in democratic fitness and one's ability to competently contribute to the civic life of the colonies. Blackface minstrels often presented irrational caricatures, reinforcing the concept that black people were unfit for democratic participation. Many of the minstrel jokes that reached South Africa relied heavily on a variant of minstrel humor I call black illogics. Such jokes portrayed black thought as comically nonsensical. In such portrayals, illogical black characters were often juxtaposed against white rationality. British settlers got the message. For example, one settler newspaper described "nigger chaff and nonsense" as a "usual" part of blackface minstrel shows.[30]

An early minstrel play called *The Virginia Mummy* relied heavily on black illogics humor. *The Virginia Mummy* was first written by T. D. Rice in 1835 and was a featured part of many minstrel shows in South Africa.[31] The plot focuses on the courtship of a white couple, Captain Rifle and Lucy. Because Lucy's father, Dr. Galen, does not approve of Rifle, Rifle creates a scheme to distract Dr. Galen while he meets with Lucy. Rifle reads an advertisement posted by Dr. Galen in a local newspaper, offering money for an authentic mummy corpse. Then Rifle pays a black shoe shiner named Ginger Blue to impersonate the mummy. While Ginger Blue distracts Dr. Galen, Rifle, disguised as an Egyptian, convinces Lucy to elope.

The sketch is filled with black illogics humor. In the opening scene of *The Virginia Mummy*, Rifle pays Ginger Blue to fetch a letter from the post office. Upon Ginger's return, Rifle asks, "Well, did you get any letters for me?" to which Ginger replies, "No, dar wasn't any for you; but here's an armful I buy'd for wrapping paper. Will any ob dem do?" A frustrated Rifle responds, "No! Was there ever such a perfect stupid ink bottle?" In many black illogics jokes, white characters are annoyed by the irrational incompetence of black characters. Later in the scene, Rifle asks Ginger, "Well, what does the paper say?" to which Ginger responds, "I doesn't know; he habn't spoke a word yet." Another example comes later when Rifle tries to turn Ginger into a mummy: "No, no; come here to me. I want you now to make folks believe you are a mummy," to which Ginger responds, "Whose mommy?" In the comedic climax of the sketch, Ginger is dressed as a mummy. He is being paid more than one month of wages to stay still and quiet to maintain the facade. Yet he is unable to do either, as he speaks and runs around the room. Ginger repeatedly forgets the basic idea that mummies, in Rifle's words, "are dead, and never eat." Throughout the play, Ginger constantly misunderstands Rifle and responds with non sequiturs. Ginger is black illogics personified, while Rifle represents the rational thought of white male spectators. After enduring a long sequence of black illogics, an exacerbated Rifle seems to speak for the white audience: "I can't get any information from this fellow."[32]

Newspaper columnists in Port Elizabeth agreed with Rifle's assessment of Ginger and its implied judgments about black people. The *Eastern Province Herald* reported, "There will also be represented the comic interlude of the 'Virginia Mummy,' in which Mr. Harry Leslie will personate Ginger Blue, an oddity of a nigger." Three days later, the *Port Elizabeth Telegraph* chimed in: "Mr. Harry Leslie as Ginger Blue, certainly surpassed his former efforts. Through his inimitable delineation of negro character, the audience from first to last were kept in a perfect roar of laughter."[33] Relatedly, James Thayer, a sailor in the U.S. Navy during the Civil War, also viewed *The Virginia Mummy* as a commentary on race. For him, the play was about the "childlike" qualities of black people.[34] These testimonies cut directly against revisionist claims that *The Virginia Mummy* was making fun of "wacky science and quack Orientalism" rather than Ginger Blue.[35] Nineteenth-century commentators in South Africa and the United States, saw racial difference as the main comedic focus of *The Virginia Mummy.*

Many minstrel stump speeches were heavily dependent on black illogics, as they portrayed aspiring black orators stammering out malapropisms, unintended puns, and inaccurate historical and topical references.

One telling example, titled "Or Any Other Man," was performed in many professional and amateur minstrel shows in South Africa.[36] The speech used black illogics humor to portray an audacious urban dandy caricature.[37] The speaker talks with a stutter, misquotes "Shakspere," and cannot accurately recount historical facts. His speech begins with a malapropism: "Feller Citizens. Correspondin' to your unanimous call I shall now hab de pleasure ob ondressin' ebery one of you." He conflates the Rocky Mountains with the Allegheny Mountains: "rockyganey mountains." He speaks of strife between "de Norf" and "de Souf" and worries about dissidents who might "tear up dat magnificent and maniglorious American flag." He claims he was there when "General Cass" signed the "Decliclumption ob Dependence." Cassius Clay, a politician who was well known in the United States, was born in 1810, well after the actual signing in 1776. The speaker dreams of being "president of dis glorious unicorn." British settlers easily dismissed these presidential aspirations as impossible because the speaker's meandering thoughts were too disjointed, irrational, and counterfactual. Taken in total, "Or Any Other Man" implied all citizens were not equal, and so-called illogical racial others were unfit for democratic participation.

Professional and amateur minstrels who performed in South Africa likely adapted this speech to make local references while still maintaining the comedic focus: the notion that black "aliens" were unworthy of civic participation. Tellingly, Leslie's Christy Minstrels advertised "Or Any Other Man" alongside the following notice: "with new local allusions."[38] This troupe definitely continued the tradition of presenting illogical black speakers. The *Natal Mercury* described a "parliamentary stump oration" by Harry Leslie as "the art of saying much about nothing. . . . It was a very clever specimen of pure nonsense . . . and bounded in local references which showed a great amount of study."[39] Another Leslie's Christy Minstrels stump speech called "Burlesque History of England" included a "grotesque mingling of historical facts with local allusions."[40] They also featured a speech called "Aunt Chloe's lecture on the rights of woman" (an apparent reference to the character Aunt Chloe who appears in *Uncle Tom's Cabin*) that was described by the local press as "an amusing specimen of a feminine stump."[41] This speech likely followed the formula of other stump speeches by relying heavily on black illogics humor. Tellingly, a British settler amateur minstrel stump speech from 1866 was an incompetent commentary on the economic troubles of the Cape Colony. Here are some representative lines: "Breddern and Sistern, wid yur approbashun . . . Allow me, Brudder Jack, dis bobservashun . . . trajidies from Shokespoke's page . . . Bredren, I hab a heap more to say. On de umportant toothpics ob de day . . . Look at de Agrimcultural Eximbishun! Does dat Show show wer'e in a bad cumdishun?"[42] British settler amateur minstrels quickly applied the black illogics formula to local circumstances.

The blackface sketches and songs that were performed in the Cape and Natal Colonies were filled with another kind of minstrel joke I call crooked gluttony humor. Sketches of this type portrayed blackface caricatures with unquenchable appetites. According to these jokes, black people fed their appetites by stealing food and quickly wolfing down the evidence. Minstrel jokes about black thieves criminalized black "aliens" who refused to respect property rights like "ideal" Cape and Natal citizens. In "Who Stole the Chicken," performed by the Amateur Coloured Troupe in 1869, two black slaves accused each other of stealing the master's chickens, only to realize that both were aspiring chicken thieves who failed to get the prize.[43] In *The Virginia Mummy*, Ginger Blue stole and drank an entire bottle of brandy during a short window of opportunity when the other characters left the room. The song "The Sly Young Coon" portrayed a black man who stole food from a barnyard. According to a song lyric, "he eat so much, he yearned for sleep." Crooked gluttony jokes made comedy of black poverty, ridiculing black people for being hungry. In South Africa, black gluttony was portrayed as a racial attribute, while the racial projects that contributed to black hunger—decades of scorched-earth tactics targeting livestock and agriculture—were conveniently left out of the story.

The minstrel shows of the Cape and Natal Colonies were also packed with comedic violence. The aforementioned black man in "The Sly Young Coon" was caught by the authorities after stealing the food. According to the song,

> De dog bit him in de back . . .
> He cried, "oh, my!
> 'Tis up wid I;—
> I'll die! I'll die!"
> And dat was de last ob him
> Den was not he a foolish coon[44]

In the "Challenge Dance," an enslaved character speaks of a master who was like a father to him: "In de most confectionery manner, he'd cotch me be de frote when I axed for my meals, and dat's what he called givin' me a collar-egiate eddicatium."[45] In "The Rival Lovers," Aunt Hetty catches Jumbo trying to steal two portions of pay and strikes him in the back with a wooden stick. Later, Jumbo's first instinct is to "run a pick fork fro dem" when he learns of rival suitors.[46] A minstrel sketch called "The Young Scamp" mixed minstrel sadism with black illogic humor when Uncle Ephram teaches his son how to handle bullies: "Hit em wid a brick! Kill 'em! Get a big knife and carve 'em, but don't neber fight."[47] The protagonist in the original version of "Oh! Susanna" brags about killing "five hundred nigga."[48] In a song called "Gal Wid the Blue Dress On," a black women scarfs down a table of food so fast, "she choaked to death wid a tater."[49] During a sketch called "The Coopers," Workman gives Pete an ultimatum: pay a two-dollar debt or fight. Pete kills Workman with a handsaw, hides the body, "and covers him over with shavings." Instead of preparing for the law, the other characters break into song and dance. One character explains the situation: "Hang us! . . . And now, while I feel in the humor, we'll have a jolly good blow-out, and dance till we get tired." The murder of a black man is trivialized, as blackfaced caricatures rejoice while a fresh corpse cools in the next room.[50] Indeed, as Saidiya Hartman observes, minstrel violence contributed to the maintenance of racial hierarchy: "Beatings, blows, and brawls reestablished the identity of those who defied the boundaries of race and status. . . . [C]haracters like Sambo Johnson, Doctor Quash, or Merikey . . . put on airs and, more important, strove to be something greater than they were and thereby trespassed the racist logic of suitable placement. In the end, however, these vain aspirations were punished and blacks returned to their proper stations. Whenever Zip Coon slipped out of place, he was brutally returned there."[51]

Hartman's comments allude to a form of minstrel humor I label the failed facade: a minstrel joke in which black characters try to disguise themselves as something else but are exposed as frauds. In the essentializing worldview of minstrel shows, black stayed black, the few black performers of early minstrelsy played only black characters, and black characters failed miserably when trying to impersonate something else.[52] Meanwhile, white actors enjoyed the freedom to try on racial and ethnic identities like different-colored hats.

Two of T. D. Rice's earliest plays, *The Virginny Cupids!* and *The Virginia Mummy,* contributed to the popularization of failed-facade humor in the United States and South Africa.[53] In *The Virginny Cupids!* two male characters, Cuff and Sambo Johnson, compete for the affections of Rose. The story starts with Sam Johnson on route to meet Rose while Cuff is already in her living quarters. In an effort to maintain the peace, Rose hides Cuff in the cupboard. In a way, Cuff is impersonating the cupboard. He knows he must stay quiet to maintain the illusion but is unable to restrain himself from singing along to Sam Johnson's song:

> Johnson
> I'd laugh to tink if you was mine, my dear, my lub, my rose,
> I'd gib you eberyting dat's nice, de Lord above knows,
> Dar's possum fat an' hominy, and sometimes—
>
> Cuff [sings out from the closet]
> —*Rice!*
>
> Johnson
> Cowheel an' sugarcane an' eberyting dat's
>
> Cuff [sings out from the closet]
> —*Nice!*[54]

Cuff's "blackness" takes the form of an uncontrollable desire to contribute to song. His singing exposes the facade, and he is discovered by Sam Johnson. Failed-facade jokes worked to essentialize blackness by presenting black caricatures who were doomed to fail when trying to be anything else.

The entire plot line of *The Virginia Mummy* revolves around failed-facade jokes. Both Rice's version of the play and later iterations make it clear that Ginger Blue's imitation of a mummy was intended to be interpreted with racial undertones. In the Charles White version, after putting on the mummy costume, Ginger Blue delights in the possibility of switching races: "I'll swear *black* is *white,* I is a mummy!"[55] In the T. D. Rice version, Ginger Blue is more clear about the racial messaging: "Massa, put plenty of turpentine wid de white paint so it won't rub off. I like to make 'em believe I'm a white man, too."[56] Somehow Ginger maintains the facade into the closing moments of the play when Ginger's real identity is exposed. After ingesting an elixir that is supposed to bring mummies back to life, Ginger moves, and the following conversation ensues:

GALEN: See! It winks! It moves!

RIFLE: Give it more.

GALEN: See!—It walks—It moves. Look! Look! (he runs about the stage, Ginger following)

ALL: It lives! 'Tis brought to life—it lives!

GALEN: Now, Mr. Egyptian (Rifle); ask me for anything—everything—you shall have it

RIFLE: The hand of your ward.

GALE: Take her, and all her fortune. Likewise, a bottle of this elixir, which I will prepare. The world shall now acknowledge me! Most reverend [*sic*] mummy, what shall I order for your dinner?

GINGER: I isn't hungry, 'cause I eat up all de breakfast

CHARLES: (seizing him) Curse me, if it isn't Ginger Blue; the nigger at the hotel.[57]

Ginger's failed attempt to maintain the mummy facade and "make 'em believe I'm a white man" was an early example of failed-facade humor. In this play, Captain Rifle's successful impersonation of an Egyptian trader was juxtaposed against Ginger Blue's unsuccessful charade. Whereas whiteness was mutable, blackness was bounded. Tellingly, one Port Elizabeth reviewer believed the piece succeeded mainly because of the failed facade:

> It is now that the merit of Mr. Leslie's performance is seen. With the change of circumstances, in other and less artistic hands, [Ginger Blue] would be little less than an exhibition of mere buffoonery. . . . But Mr. Leslie does not go beyond the shoeblack. . . . *He is Ginger Blue in a character foreign to himself, and it is the contrast of the "make-up"—which is that of a veritable mummy—with his retention of his individuality, that constitutes the excellence of this performance. Were he for one moment to ape what he conceived to be the manners of a mummy, the illusion would be dispelled, and the artistic touches, which now render the character pleasing and extremely life-like, would be lost.*[58]

Another example of failed-facade humor appeared in a sketch presented by amateur minstrels in Cape Town called "The United States Mail." Lucy hides a black postal worker named Sam in a bag of potatoes because she does not want her suitor, Mr. Wagner, to find her in the presence of another man. After some conversation, Lucy and Wagner decide to play music and dance. Wagner suggests music "in the Old Virginia Line." Sam delivers a quick side speech: "I hope dey won't play dat; kase if dey does, I neber can keep still, and dat will spoil every ting."[59] Once the "plantation music" begins, Sam is unable to contain himself, and he begins dancing. Wagner notices the bag moving, and after some stage business Sam is discovered. Sam's "blackness" becomes visible when something deep down in his bodily design forces him to dance to the banjo. Ultimately, failed-facade jokes expressed an essential minstrel logic: the minstrel color line could be traversed in only one direction. A color line allowing for multidirectional movement might undercut the bonds between whiteness and citizenship, blackness and servility.

Blackface minstrel shows in the South African colonies provided a forum for British settlers to laugh at the supposed "exotic" and "natural" characteristics of black people in the United States and Africans in South Africa. Because all people of African descent were lumped together into the same essentializing racial category, it was not a large interpretive leap for British settlers to liken the behaviors of onstage "negro Americans" to those of local "Bantu Africans." As such, the British settler press described the "niggers" of minstrel stages as "fact[ual]," "true to life," "lifelike," and "veritable."

British settlers believed minstrel show caricatures to be accurate because the racial images of blackface minstrelsy neatly coincided with the racial worldview of British colonists. In the 1830s, elite British settlers began articulating a racial dichotomy that projected the negative aspects of their own culture onto indigenous Africans. In their view, the Khoekhoe and Xhosa were all the British elite were not: disrespectful of authority, hypersexual, and unorganized. In the wake of labor shortages following the abolition of slavery in 1834, two specific stereotypes dominated the race thinking of the colonists: the African thief and the lazy African. The Vagrancy Ordinance of 1834 tried to solve these "problems" by giving colonial authorities the power to arrest any poacher, squatter, or unemployed person. Later acts such as the 1841 Masters and Servants Ordinance and the exceptionally coercive Masters and Servants Act of 1856 were designed with similar goals in mind. The latter increased the penalty for desertion and defined insubordination, neglect, and the "use of abusive or insulting language" as criminal acts.[60] The important point to keep in mind is that images of lazy, stealing Khoekhoe and Xhosa directly supported the passing of policies designed to force indigenous Africans into positions of subordinate labor. The racial discourse of British settlers was intended to meet the needs of an emerging form of "racial capitalism" that was heavily dependent on African labor. Significantly, most of the supposed characteristics of Africans outlined in British settler race discourse—unorganized, disrespectful of authority, hypersexual, and prone to theft—were regularly included in the minstrel shows that swept through the colonies between 1862 and 1872.[61] This correspondence helps to explain the widespread belief on the part of British settlers that minstrel caricatures were accurate representations of Africans.

The relationship between minstrel show caricatures and nineteenth-century British South African race discourse was mutually reinforcing: each lent credence to the veracity of the other. Many minstrel songs and sketches performed in the Cape and Natal offered images of thieving, disorganized, and hypersexual black characters.[62] Thus, commentators who enthusiastically wrote about the "realism" of minstrel caricatures did so because British settlers in South Africa already saw Africans in these ways. In other words, minstrel caricatures were understood as realistic because they reflected many of the preestablished race discourses of the time. At the same time, the explanatory power of these preestablished race discourses were reinforced, as white settlers saw them repeatedly acted out onstage. Much of the laughter created by minstrel shows in South Africa can be described as a laughter of recognition: British settlers were amused by minstrel caricatures who supposedly reflected the "nature" of local Africans.

Blackface minstrelsy became popular in the Cape and Natal largely because of its durability as a discursive system that could comment on people of African descent on both sides of the Atlantic. When minstrel discourse did not neatly coincide with British settlers' stereotypes of Africans, it provided idealized fantasies of black workers. British settlers who complained about "unreliable" African workers saw an ideal to strive for in the minstrel caricatures of happy and obedient African American slaves. In this way, blackface minstrelsy was able to speak to the racial projects of the British colonies in South Africa because much of its original material provided ideological support for racial projects in the United States that attempted to relegate African Americans to the bottom of various rural and urban economies. The economy of preindustrial South Africa, just like large portions of the antebellum United States, was heavily dependent on a subordinate black labor force. The blackface minstrel shows of the Cape and Natal provided frameworks for imagining an obedient black labor force that might one day be like that of the antebellum United States.

Several histories of South Africa suggest that the roots of twentieth-century racial oppression stretch back to the preindustrial period of the mid-nineteenth century when British settlers attempted to sustain a racially stratified labor system in the aftermath of the abolishment of slavery.[63] It is important to account for the role performance culture played in the maintenance of this racial hierarchy. As one of the most popular forms of entertainment for British settlers during the 1860s, blackface minstrelsy was one of the major discursive institutions working to preserve the boundaries of racial difference during the last decade of the preindustrial era. However, I make this point while observing Robert Ross's caveat: "I would not want to argue that pre-industrial social relationships and ideologies determined what happened thereafter, only that they provided a legacy on which the makers of twentieth-century South Africa, of all backgrounds, could and did build."[64] Minstrel shows provided forums where British settlers could come together to laugh at the so-called true-to-life qualities of Africans. This public forum contributed to the race thinking of a society that would go on to create the system of racial apartheid some eighty years later.

"RESERVE YOUR MONEY FOR THE REAL CHRISTY MINSTRELS": AMATEUR MINSTRELS, SURROGATION, AND BURNT CORK NATIONALISM

The version of blackface minstrelsy that reached South Africa in 1862 had moved a long way from the genre's lower Manhattan white working-class origins. W. T. Lhamon and Dale Cockrell have argued that blackface minstrelsy first emerged in the 1820s as a cultural expression of the racially diverse working-class neighborhoods of lower Manhattan. Many of the early performers came from the infamous Five Points neighborhood in Manhattan and had ample opportunity to observe black culture in the saloons and markets they frequented. According to this perspective, early

American minstrel culture blended European music and dance forms with Afro-diasporic performance traditions to articulate working-class sensibilities that critiqued the upper classes, bragged about comically hyperbolic displays of strength in the tradition of American frontier humor, and portrayed menial labor.[65] As mentioned previously, the argument that early blackface minstrelsy carried a large amount of "progressive" potential is very debatable. Less debatable are the ways in which the class orientation of the genre shifted in the 1840s. By 1847 the major New York–based minstrel troupes were moving toward more "respectable" entertainment, minimizing "vulgarity" as minstrels sought to broaden their class appeal and reach a larger audience base.[66] Historians of the British minstrel show have demonstrated that the genre had a much larger middle- and upper-class audience in England than it did in the United States.[67] The London-based Nish's Christy Minstrels troupe who reached South Africa in 1862 reflected these developments. Their first performance in Cape Town was under the patronage of the governor of the Western Cape. The stalls were the most expensive seats in the house, followed by seats in the amphitheater, then finally seats in the gallery, the upper section where small-scale farmers and contract workers could afford to watch the show.

Not long after their first appearance in the colony, the minstrels performed at the Commercial Exchange, an elite club paid for by the subscription fees of its members where the major merchants and traders of the town came together to talk about the economic issues of the day.[68] The *Cape Argus* suggested the show would be staged so "the elite of the city may have an entertainment all to themselves without being disturbed by the noise of the gods above" and speculated that "everybody [who] is anybody is going." Furthermore, the *Argus* predicted Nish's Christy Minstrels would adapt their program to the tastes of elite spectators: "Of course, at the Exchange there will be less 'kicking up behind and before'; part singing will be the staple of the entertainment."[69] The line "kicking up behind and before" was a quote from the chorus of a popular comedic minstrel song called "Old Joe."[70] The *Argus* believed part singing, rather than dancing and comedic business, would appeal to the "refined" tastes of the audience at the Commercial Exchange.

There is only one brief eyewitness account of the Commercial Exchange performance, left by a second-generation British settler named John Rose. Rose was a classically trained violin player and a regular on the Cape

Town stage. According to Rose, "The Christys' Minstrels gave a delightful entertainment at the Commercial Exchange this evening, to a crowded house, and I scarcely ever enjoyed an evening more. The Governor & Mrs. Wodehouse were present. . . . The violoncello solos are the finest that have been heard at the Cape."[71] This account suggests Nish's Christy Minstrels were able to successfully adapt their show to fit the tastes of upper-class British settlers. The violoncello was not a traditional instrument of the American minstrel show.

Later in the decade, minstrel troupes published several advertisements in local newspapers, boasting about the elite patrons who attended their shows. In 1865 Leslie's Christy Minstrels published one such list: "Her most gracious Majesty the Queen, His Royal Highness the late Prince Consort, The Prince of Wales, and all the Royal Family; The Emperor and Empress of the French; The Archduke and Archduchess Maximilian of Austria . . . [and] leading members of the [British] nobility."[72] This troupe's first performance in Cape Town was carried out "under the distinguished patronage and presence of his Excellency Sir P. Wodehouse, Lady Wodehouse, and Suite, who have kindly signified their intension of being present."[73] Amateur minstrel troupes in South Africa also used this marketing technique. In 1869 a local troupe with upper-class pretensions called the Royal Downshire Minstrels, ran a series of advertisements, claiming many luminaries had attended their shows: "The Royal Downshire Minstrels . . . Patronized by H.R.H. the Duke of Edinburgh and Officers of H.M. St. Galletes, General Sir Richard Airey, K.C.B., Lady Airey, General Crutchley and Staff, Nobility and Gentry of Gibraltar, Colonel Lowe, C.B., and Officers of the 86th Royal County Down Regiment, also by the Mayor and Inhabitants of Port Elizabeth."[74] Later that same year, a local newspaper reporting on a performance by the Amateur Coloured Troupe stated: "Each section of the hall was crowded, the President of the Free State (under whose patronage the performances were given), with Lady Brand and family, and several members of Parliament, were amongst the occupants of the reserved seats."[75] The minstrel shows of the Cape and Natal were a cross-class affair, and this reality brings very real consequences for the "progressive" potential of the genre.

The case study of South Africa offers scholars an example of early blackface minstrelsy that varies from the early American context. As mentioned earlier, several scholars claim that early American minstrels often expressed working-class attitudes and tried to subvert elite values. But in South Africa in the 1860s, elite Anglophones were consistent participants, either as amateur performers or as audience members. Perhaps this is why moments of race or class subversion rarely show up in the English-language South African press. The working-class sensibilities and cross-racial camaraderie that some scholars see in early American minstrelsy were absent from the version that reached South Africa. Instead, the burnt cork nationalism of early American minstrelsy, mediated through the British metropole, was reinforced and adapted within a British settler South African context.

In December 1862, the *Grahamstown Journal* published advertisements selling the "sounding board, drop scene, and stage fittings of [Nish's] Christy Minstrels."[76] The Christy Minstrels had performed in Grahamstown two months prior and left the Cape Colony in late November. The public demand for minstrelsy continued in their absence. In the aftermath of Nish's Christy Minstrels tour, a parade of amateur British settler minstrels filled the void created by the departure of the professionals. Perhaps some of these amateurs bought the material in this advertisement for their own onstage impersonations. This advertisement provides present-day researchers with a reminder that cultural reproduction in a new location is never a guaranteed outcome. In order for a performance culture to catch on with a new population, a kind of cultural literacy must be first established. The local population must have access to the skill sets needed to reproduce the culture. Language barriers, if they exist, must be broken down. Content originally created to comment on the happenings of another location must be adapted to fit local sensibilities. And finally, as this advertisement suggests, the technology needed to re-create the culture must be available.

The economic downturns of the 1860s made it difficult to earn consistent profits from amateur minstrel shows. The amateur troupes of the Cape and Natal did not become professional minstrels. The British South African colonies never produced homegrown professional minstrel troupes, largely because they were relatively underpopulated and had considerably less wealth than other British territories.[77] Nonetheless, during the 1860s, many British settlers devoted much time and energy toward staging a performance genre that offered relatively few material rewards. It was not easy to stage a minstrel show. Scripts had to be memorized, dialects imagined, and comedic timing practiced, and there was music to be learned. When taking these time-consuming factors into consideration, the question becomes: What made amateur minstrelsy so appealing to British settlers? One account from a British settler amateur minstrel sheds some light on this question:

> Have you ever been an amateur Christy Minstrel? Once on a time before "the enemy" had begun to silver my locks and ere the gravity becoming to the "shady side of fifty" had settled on me, in a weak moment, I consented to perform in an amateur Christy Minstrel entertainment. I never could sing; like Artemus Ward, I am saddest when I sing; so are they that hear me; they are sadder even than I am. "But," said the charmer, "all you'll have to do is bang a tambourine about." The eventful day arrived, the hour approached, and we proceeded to black. . . . The curtain rose and the concert commenced. All went well for some time, and we began to warm up to the spirit of the thing. The way I assaulted that tambourine was a marvel. I seemed to be possessed with an ardent desire to drown the other music, and I succeeded so well that I was continuing long after the others had finished. But what of that? The audience cheered, and I was happy. The more they cheered the more phrensical [*sic*] I became, until I conceived the happy idea of performing on the head of banjo, who sat next. I did it once, the audience cheered and laughed. I did it again; once more there was a laugh, but I didn't hear it. I was told afterward that the way the banjo descended on my cranium drew forth shouts of applause.[78]

In this passage, a first-time minstrel describes intense feelings of happiness as he hears the cheers of the audience. The applause was an enabling mechanism, encouraging him to act without common decency or civilized restraint. As the applause grew louder, he became "more phrensical" as he began to access the frenetic corporality convention of minstrel shows. In this account, frenetic corporality took the form of rowdy, and "possessed," "assault[s]" on the tambourine. Indeed, frenetic corporality was not simply a commentary on black physicality; it was a gateway ticket granting access to an imaginary form of premodern play. Later in the passage, the wild beating of the tambourine progressed to the literal beating of another cast member as frenetic corporality transitioned to minstrel sadism. The crowd greatly appreciated the smashing of instruments over the heads of the performers. This passage suggests amateur minstrelsy was a popular pastime partly because it provided opportunities to act without social constraint. Victorian codes of conduct could be publicly transgressed when performers hid behind the blackface mask. By creating spaces where appropriating "uncivilized" black bodies was acceptable, amateur minstrelsy helped British settlers move outside the restraints of Victorian society.

Amateur minstrels were also displaying their class privilege. To be an amateur minstrel was to have leisure time to dedicate to the craft. They even went so far as to announce their class identity in local newspapers. In 1868 Norton's Christy Minstrels performed in Port Elizabeth alongside some local amateurs. One newspaper stated, "It should be borne in mind that nearly all these gentlemen [amateur minstrels] are engaged in mercantile pursuits in the day time; and that the rehearsals had to be conducted between the hours of 5 a.m. and breakfast time."[79] Relatedly, many amateur shows were staged for charity rather than personal profit, as amateurs represented their forays into blackface minstrelsy as philanthropic endeavors.

Amateur performers used print culture to learn minstrel songs. They purchased songbooks from professional minstrels during the intermissions of shows.[80] Afterward, they probably re-created the music by blending interpretations of the songbooks with their memories of the professionally rendered versions. They also bought minstrel sheet music and songbooks from music stores in Cape Town and Port Elizabeth.[81] Tellingly, many songs that appeared on the playbills of amateur troupes were not on the professional minstrel programs I was able to find. These songs were probably not introduced to South African audiences by professional minstrels. Instead, amateurs bought them in local stores. As such, professional minstrels were not the only vessels spreading the culture in South Africa. Shopkeepers played an important role as well.

That being said, amateur minstrels drew much of their inspiration from the performances of the professionals. Because no professional minstrels took permanent residence in the colonies, minstrel culture had to be remembered and reproduced through a process Joseph Roach calls "surrogation." For Roach, surrogation is essential for understanding the ways in which "circum-Atlantic cultures" were remembered and re-created by various communities across historical time. Circum-Atlantic cultures were in a state of constant reproduction, as key carriers of the culture either died or moved away. In order for the culture to continue thriving, new members of the community had to fill the voids created from departures by becoming substitutes for the original performers. Significantly, the process of surrogation is often messy, as the community was not always in agreement over who had the necessary talent or the level of "authenticity" needed to fill in for the originators. Indeed, the process of choosing a surrogate elect had everything to do with the ways in which communities defined their own identities.[82] The process of surrogation would have been especially significant for settler communities like the ones found in South Africa during the 1860s. Because British settlers in the Western Cape lived far away from the metropole, issues of origins and "authenticity" were especially important to them. In this context, staging blackface minstrel shows and working through the question of who had the right to be surrogates of the original Christy Minstrels became a means of performing and preserving a kind of British settler identity in South Africa.

Roach argues that circum-Atlantic communities often participated in heated debates about issues of authenticity and origins as they tried to establish who would be the legitimate surrogate elects of the originators. This kind of conflict certainly played out in Cape Town. Two months after the first performance of Nish's Christy Minstrels, the *Cape Chronicle* ran the following article:

> The Christy minstrels have set everybody mad, and nothing now goes down but burnt cork, and Pompey's jokes. At Grahamstown they have been arranging some entertainments in aid of the distressed Lancashire Operatives, and of course nothing could do but the young men must blacken their faces, and don exaggerated shirt-collars. They must further be termed the "Graham's Town Minstrels" in imitation of their recent illustrious visitors, and are tossing of course, the airs the "originals" have rendered famous. We must, I suppose, pardon this presumption in consideration for the good object for which it is assumed.[83]

The first sentence was a deliberate attempt to flaunt minstrel knowledge by referencing a lyric from the aforementioned patriotic British minstrel song titled "Niggermania": "nothing now goes down / But blackeys, bones, and Banjoes."[84] Next, after establishing a certain degree of minstrel knowledge and cultural authority, the commentator called out the "presumption[s]" of a group of amateurs who were trying to perform blackface minstrelsy in the tradition of the Christy Minstrels. The offended writer nevertheless concluded the Graham's Town Minstrels were not a complete insult to the originals because they were performing for charity. One week later, the *Cape Chronicle* published a more aggressive critique of amateur minstrelsy: "A daring correspondent of one of the local papers is desirous of hearing the counterfeit Christy's, supposing these to be the originals and imagines that the result would be gratifying. Subside into insignificance, rash man, or the maddened Capeites will certainly maltreat you for thus libeling their idols."[85] The Graham's Town Minstrels were the first South African amateur minstrel troupe to perform after Nish's Christy Minstrels left the colony. Some commentators publicly criticized their legitimacy and were not ready to accept amateur performers as surrogates of the originals. As the 1860s progressed, the issue of surrogate authenticity reemerged multiple times.

In 1865 Leslie's Christy Minstrels toured the British colonies of South Africa. They entered from the eastern port of Natal. As they performed in Natal, another group of professional British performers, known as the OIO Christy Minstrels, landed in the southern port of Cape Town and commenced a short season. In response, Leslie's Christy Minstrels ran an advertising campaign in the Cape Town newspapers. On September 5, 1865, they published a statement in the *Cape Argus:* "Reserve your money for the *Real Christy Minstrels,* who are now at Port Elizabeth and will arrive at Cape Town in about fourteen days' time." A few weeks later, they published a more aggressive advertisement, directly naming the OIO Minstrels: "The world renowned and only original Christy Minstrels from 444 and 472, Broadway, New York, organized in 1842 by E .P. Christy . . . have the honour to state that the O.I.O. minstrels having proceeded to Cape Town and there copied [the Christy Minstrels'] Business, which they attempt to place on the Stage. [The Christy Minstrels] have determined to proceed to Natal prior to visiting Cape Town."[86] Leslie's Christy Minstrels tried to police the boundaries of the culture by discounting the legitimacy of a group of potential surrogates. They undoubtedly had entrepreneurial motives for doing so. Most important for my purposes, they used the concept of "authenticity" to persuade the Cape Town public not to support the OIO Minstrels. One narrative that was circulating throughout the

Atlantic world during this period claimed that E. P. Christy initiated the first minstrel ensemble in 1842.[87] By recirculating that origin narrative in their promotional material, Leslie's Christy Minstrels tried to discount potential surrogates and position themselves as the only legitimate heirs of the original Christy Minstrel troupe. The OIO Minstrels disbanded a few weeks after arriving in Cape Town. A bad review in a local newspaper did not help their cause. Furthermore, the smear campaign of Leslie's Christy Minstrels might have dissuaded potential customers. For minstrel fans in Cape Town, the issue of surrogate authenticity weighed heavily. It mattered little that Leslie, Steele, and Taylor were not part of the original Christy Minstrels ensemble and were also surrogates.[88] Their claims of "authenticity" appealed to the sentiments of British settlers.

The advertising campaigns of two separate festivals also placed much value on the concept of the original Christy Minstrels. In June 1864, plans were made to celebrate Queen Victoria's birthday in the town of George. According to a local newspaper, "invitations were sent round a day or so previous, which also announced that the Christy Minstrels would perform the second part of the entertainment. Rumours circulated that the Minstrels had arrived from England by the last mail and would appear at George for the first time; and sure enough, when the time came, there they were, but not 'imported.'"[89]

Later in November 1870, a grand fete was planned in the central gardens of the city of Cape Town. An advertisement in a local newspaper claimed the following: "For the amusement of those who prefer broad fun, the Directors, utterly reckless of the expenditure which it has entailed, have imported per several Mail Steamers. St. James' Hall, Piccadilly, and The Original Christy Minstrels. To say one word as to what these world-renowned and eminent Artists can do would be utterly superfluous. They have distanced every other Candidate for public favour, and on the Night of the Fete they will surpass themselves."[90] St. James Hall and Piccadilly Street were two well-known landmarks in central London. The organizers who printed this advertisement were insinuating that when the Christy Minstrels came to town, they brought London with them. By attending the fete, British settlers could enjoy the latest trends from the mother country. Interestingly enough, no professional London-based Christy Minstrel troupe participated in the 1864 or 1870 celebrations. The organizers made disingenuous claims in an attempt to use minstrel authenticity to populate their events. Festival organizers who tried to publicize their events by evoking the original Christy Minstrels were appealing to a British settler perspective that tended to prefer professional performers who were imported from the metropole over local surrogates.[91] For many British audiences in South Africa, the minstrel show was a fresh infusion of metropolitan culture. By participating in minstrel spectacles, as audience members or performers, British settlers strengthened their connection to the metropole.

A British settler identity in South Africa had taken coherent form by the middle of the nineteenth century. This identity owed its cohesiveness to several factors, including a capitalist ideology that brought settlers together under a common set of economic goals, the invention of a shared settler history, the articulation of a defined group of settler characteristics, and an increased role of women as teachers of British culture and values to the younger generation. According to Alan Lester, British settler identity was largely a response to the "collective anxiety" of colonists who lived "in an insecure frontier space."[92] Ultimately, the burnt cork nationalism of minstrel shows helped assuage the "anxiety" by defining white British settlers against black Africans. Blackface caricatures discursively supported a specific kind of imagined community, a racially homogenous settler colony. This imagined community was trying to hold on to British culture and tradition, maintain political and economic connections with the metropole, and incorporate the local Africans as workers but not equal citizens, all while sketching out a living in an "unstable" frontier zone. British settlers of all classes, genders, and ages could participate in this shared minstrel culture.

During the 1860s, many minstrel shows linked settlers in South Africa back to the British metropole. From 1861 to 1865, Northwest England was devastated by what has been retroactively named the Lancashire Cotton Famine. The British textile industry went into severe depression after Union blockades of the Confederate states cut off its main supplier of cotton. Halfway through Nish's Christy Minstrels' tour of 1862, the troupe dedicated the proceeds of several shows to a Lancashire relief fund.[93] The British settlers who attended these shows could feel reassured, knowing their laughter was aiding their fellow countrymen in Lancashire.

The blackface minstrels of the Cape and Natal often celebrated the British royal family. In 1863, when Prince Albert of England married Alexandra of Denmark, an extravagant festival blending patriarchy with patriotism was staged in the botanical gardens in the center of Cape Town. British settler women were not allowed in the parades and could attend only as onlookers.[94] During the festivities, a group of amateur minstrels had their own tent.[95] One of their offerings was a British settler parody of an American minstrel song called "The Other Side of Jordan." American versions of this song spoke down to Cubans, "Irishmen," and Louis Napoléon, claiming "the Americans will show them what they will do / on this and the other side of Jordan."[96] The British settler adaptation appropriated the song as a vehicle for expressing transnational British identity. This version celebrated the union of the royal family and voiced an admiration that stretched across the ocean: "[The] little Queen . . . is truly loved on de oder side ob Jordan."[97] As the decade progressed, blackface minstrels also appeared in events celebrating Queen Victoria. In June 1864, a group of local minstrels performed at a birthday event for the queen in the town of George in the Western Cape.[98] Entire minstrel shows in honor of the queen's birthdays were staged in Cape Town.[99]

Several minstrel songs directly engaged British culture and history. The most obvious examples were the minstrel burlesques of Shakespeare, a tradition that began in the 1830s with the performances of T. D. Rice. During the 1860s, burlesque performances of *Romeo and Juliet, Macbeth, The Merchant of Venice,* and *Othello* were staged in the British colonies. One popular song titled "The Queen's Letter" was described by a local newspaper as having "words which cannot be listened to by the subjects of Her Majesty without emotion."[100] The *Port Elizabeth Telegraph* claimed the song was "founded upon the autograph letter of sympathy addressed by Queen Victoria to her brave army whilst fighting in the Crimea."[101] In 1868 Norton's Christy Minstrels regularly performed "Beautiful Isle of the Sea," the first verse of which reads:

> Beautiful Isle of the Sea
> Smile on the brown of they waters
> Dear are your mem'ries to me;
> Sweet as the songs of your daughters.
> Over your mountains and vales,
> Down by each murmuring river,
> Cheer'd by the flower loving gales,
> Oh, I would wander for ever.[102]

For British settlers of the Cape and Natal, this song probably invoked much nostalgia for the British Isles. One stump speech titled "Burlesque History of England" included a "grotesque mingling of historical facts with local allusions."[103] A song called "God Bless the Prince of Wales" was performed during a minstrel show in Port Elizabeth in 1872.[104]

Most tellingly, "God Save the Queen" was often sung at the end of minstrel shows. In each of the programs that list "God Save the Queen," there was no intermission between the blackface sketches of the third act and the performance of this patriotic anthem. Thus, there may have been no time for performers to wash off the burnt cork so they could perform this song in whiteface. If indeed "God Save the Queen" was sung in blackface, we are presented with a particularly striking image born of the imperialist imaginary: the racial "others" of South Africa as loyal Christian colonial subjects, loving and caring for the health of the queen. Blackface minstrel shows that included patriotic songs, performances in honor of the queen's birthday, and the festival celebrating the marriage of the Prince of Wales all created a similar effect. This kind of colonial imaginary in which Africans kneel at the feet of the British royal family can be thought of as a cultural response to the many violent clashes between British settlers and colonized peoples in South Africa and throughout the empire in the nineteenth century.

From 1811 to 1851, British settlers fought a series of frontier wars against the Xhosa chiefdoms in the Western Cape. Several midcentury uprisings by "subject peoples" across the British Empire contributed to the anxieties of the period. News of events such as the Indian "Mutiny" of 1857, Maori uprisings in New Zealand in 1860 and 1863, and the Morant Bay Rebellion of 1865 in Jamaica were readily available in South Africa.[105] The minstrel image of dark-skinned colonial subjects singing in honor of the royal family could have functioned as an imperial fantasy of African subjectivity that alleviated fears that local Africans would rise up against the British colonies. This was especially significant in South Africa during this period because it was unclear whether the metropole would deem the Cape and Natal Colonies economically profitable and worthy of imperial military support. Fears of being abandoned by the metropole might have been alleviated when colonists imagined the local African civilizations that surrounded them to be loyal subjects of the queen.[106]

Blackface minstrelsy also introduced a set of anxieties to the Cape and

Natal Colonies; one of these was a fear on the part of white settlers that by attending minstrel performances and participating too enthusiastically, one ran the risk of becoming a blackened British person. A settler community is certainly invested in processes of intergenerational transfer, in which the values and traditions defining their identities are passed on to children. White women in the Cape and Natal Colonies were given the task of teaching white children the norms, values, and culture of British society.[107] In this social scheme, children must be protected from contaminating influences. One telling newspaper review of an 1866 minstrel show for children in Cape Town commented on the enjoyment of the young audience: the children were "anything but niggardly in encouraging the performers with all the applause that their tongues, hands, and feet were capable of expressing."[108] This punning on the word *niggardly* can be understood as an example of the influence of minstrel aesthetics in local newspaper reporting, but, more important, underneath the joyful tones of this quote lies an anxiety around the contaminating influences of "black" culture. The writer was insinuating that children who clapped along to the rhythms of "black music" were not in danger of "going native." Instead, children who watched blackface minstrel shows were "anything but niggardly," a statement reflecting the binary racial thinking that dominated the colony during this period.

This observation is complicated by the fact that whiteness was not a homogenous category in the Cape and Natal during the 1860s. The onstage antics of minstrels also helped contribute to the maintenance of a British settler hierarchy of whiteness. Blackface minstrels who performed in the United States often portrayed white ethnicities, and South Africa was no different. For English colonists in the 1860s, the two major groups of ethnic white others were the Dutch, and to a much lesser extent the Irish, who had begun immigrating to the colonies as early as 1820.[109] Portrayals of Dutch characters were common in South Africa. For example, one 1865 review stated "Mr. Leslie['s] . . . dialogue in which he introduced his experience of life and manners amongst the Dutch farmers was received with frantic bursts of laughter. His imitation of the Cape Dutch was beyond all praise, and shows that a wonderful talent for mimicry he possesses."[110] On multiple occasions, the Amateur Coloured Troupe performed a song called "Malingo Hoy, the Cape Town Coolie," which seems to be a parody of the language that would later be known as Afrikaans. The song lyrics were described by the troupe as "Dutch-Mozambique lingo."[111] In 1870 the Amateur Coloured Troupe performed a minstrel sketch called "The Rival Lovers" in which one of the characters was jokingly described as "Dutchy."[112]

Portrayals of Irish people were also a common part of blackface minstrel shows, appearing in the songs "The Irish Lilt," "When Johnny Came Marching Home," and a sketch called "The Irish Tutor."[113] In 1868 one reviewer claimed the highlight of a minstrel show was an "irresistible [Irish shanty]; the strange effect of the Irish comic song being warbled by 'niggers' caught the popular fancy, and the audience was kept in a roar during the performance."[114] This song, in which impersonations were stacked in layers, attests to the ways in which multiple ethnic and racial others could be discursively produced through minstrel performance. In this song, normative whiteness imitated blackness imitating Irishness, and the crowd laughed heartily as they celebrated their high social standing as white English settlers.

The minstrel show became such a clear signifier of British/English cultural identity in colonial South Africa that some Africans interpreted it as such. Although the surviving evidence of how black South Africans responded to mid-nineteenth-century minstrel shows is slim, one newspaper article suggests the reaction was both visceral and astute. In November 1872, a professional minstrel troupe known as Harvey-Dougherty-Leslie-Brahim Minstrels began promoting their show in Port Elizabeth. They used a standard blackface minstrel advertising strategy by posting across the city pictures of themselves in Victorian formal wear with no makeup above pictures of themselves in "plantation" clothes and blackface. A white newspaper correspondent overheard the "nigger complaints" of three Africans who saw the advertisement. The Africans spoke in Dutch, and the correspondent relayed the conversation in that language. The critique translates as "So is it with the damn Englishman. We must by him work, work all days of our life, and therefore he stitch us on the wall just for a mockery. The Englishman is the worst race under the heavens."[115] The usage of the term *mockery* is instructive, for it demonstrates that Africans who were exposed to minstrel imagery understood they were being ridiculed by the performers. The quote also articulates an understanding of material relations and cultural expropriation: the Africans understood that those who control the means of production often have free rein to expropriate and mimic the identities of subordinate groups. The word *therefore* suggests a direct connection between the expropriation of blackness on minstrel stages and the expropriation of black labor in Port Elizabeth. Put differently, the Africans knew this was a spectacle of black dispossession. But most striking for scholars who study race discourse is the way these Africans used minstrel imagery as a springboard to comment on British/English people. In this instance, the racializing process of the minstrel show worked in multiple directions: the Africans understood the minstrel image not simply as a cultural practice that provided commentary on blackness but also as a cultural practice that revealed much about whiteness. In this moment of discursive reversal, the imagery of blackface minstrelsy was used to place the British at the bottom of an African racial hierarchy that used morality as its organizing logic. For these Africans, this advertisement was proof that the English were "the worst race under the heavens."[116]

British settlers continued to use minstrel references to celebrate an imagined connection to the metropole long after the 1860s. Here, W. T. Lhamon's concept of "blackface lore cycles" is instructive. For Lhamon, popular culture works in lore cycles such that the various expressions, songs, and gestures of a popular culture may go underground for long periods of time, only to resurface during moments when the social functions that were originally central to the operation of the culture become central issues in society once again.[117] The aforementioned visit of the Prince of Wales in 1926 offers a case in point. In Johannesburg and Pretoria, the song sheets to many minstrel classics were passed among the welcoming crowds and sung for the prince.[118] In this telling moment of burnt cork nationalism, British settlers sang songs whose protagonists were black slaves in order to welcome their prince to South African shores. Blackface minstrel songs were part of the shared cultural repository linking the British colonists to the metropole. In British South Africa, the connection between colony and metropole was oftentimes imagined through and against the bodies of black men and women.

CONCLUSION: AN EMPIRE OF BURNT CORK

In September 1862, right when Nish's Christy Minstrels were enjoying a run in Cape Town, the *Grahamstown Journal* published the following: "The Christy Minstrels, I am glad to find, are getting on in [Cape Town] like a house on fire, and I hope they will be induced, by-and-by, to pay us a visit in the far east."[119] When professional minstrel troupes toured the Cape and Natal, newspapers from the major cities often tracked their travels. One article from the *Port Elizabeth Telegraph* described the scope of Norton's Christy Minstrels' 1868 tour: "Between the 7th of September and the 7th of March [the Christy's Minstrels] have given 100 performances in the colony, and have travelled over 2,000 miles of ground in this province and the Free State."[120] The three professional minstrel troupes who toured in the 1860s helped British settlers think in spatial terms, bridging the long distances between the major areas of British and European settlement. Settlers in one city knew the show they just witnessed was recently performed in other cities. Furthermore, settlers could use newspaper articles to track the tours of the professional minstrels. The notion of a shared cultural event is one we take for granted in today's thoroughly globalized world, where culture moves across national borders in a matter of seconds via high speed Internet. By contrast, the British South African colonies of the 1860s did not have access to the technology of the present and could not financially support many professional performers. As a result of these conditions, shared cultural events were relatively rare spectacles. The visit of a professional troupe with the stature of the Christy Minstrels was a major public event. Settlers in one city could know they were witnessing the same cultural event as settlers in another city. One illuminating primary source provides a glimpse of the ways in which popular music could be combined with new technologies to shrink the imagined geographic distance between areas of British settlement. In 1879 a reporter for Kimberley's *Diamond News* newspaper excitedly described a scene he witnessed at the telegraph office:

> It is not often that one man is able to converse with another, when they are separated by a hundred miles of South African country, but this pleasure I experienced the other afternoon. . . . I went to the telegraph office. . . . Operations had already commenced, and as I entered a small wooden instrument was handed to me, which, when placed to my ear, sang "Juanita" in very good tones. At least, by doing as directed, I heard the song, and was then told that the singer was in Fauresmith. Applying the instrument to my mouth, I requested that the music be kept up, when a popular ballad was whistled. A gentleman present then sang a song, which was encored from the other end, and so a very pleasant hour was passed. To elucidate this, let me explain that for the nonce the

> telegraph was converted into a telephone line. . . . For a hundred miles the voices travelled, and so rapidly that conversation could be carried on almost as easily as if the parties conversing were face to face.[121]

The British settlers who were testing the communications technology sang popular songs to one another. This experiment applied the concepts of constants and variables. The constant was a shared cultural text, a song called "Juanita." Both parties involved knew how the song was supposed to sound. "Juanita" was a romantic ballad that did not originate from minstrel shows. However, it was included in minstrel shows in Cape Town. The variable was the telegraph machine, which they hoped would present the song in a clear and tonally accurate way. The song came through in "very good tones," and the new technology passed the test. In this moment, a popular song was used to bridge the geographic distance between colonial settlements.

Such bridging was one of the many functions of the minstrel show in colonial South Africa. As the most popular form of entertainment among British settlers in mid-nineteenth-century South Africa, the minstrel show contributed to the maintenance of a British settler cultural identity, connecting British people who lived in cites separated by hundreds of miles. Here was a burnt cork nation expanding across the South African colonies.

These imaginings of extended communities did not end at the borders of the British colonies of South Africa. British settler newspapers continued to follow the tours of the professional minstrels as they traveled to other parts of the world. In 1863 the *Port Elizabeth Telegraph* published two letters from Nish's Christy Minstrels in Australia, saying the tour was going well and that they planned to return to the South African colonies soon. In 1864 the *Port Elizabeth Telegraph* described the packed houses the Christy Minstrels were enjoying in Australia. In 1865 the *Cape Argus* ran an advertisement informing the public of the Christy's successful tours of India, China, and Mauritius. At the tail end of the tour of Leslie's Christy Minstrels, the *Natal Mercury* claimed they were planning to head to India next. Two articles in 1866 excitedly reported on the successful shows of Leslie's Christy Minstrels in Australia. In 1868 a Cape Town newspaper happily announced, "A christy's troupe that has been performing at St James Piccadilly hall in England is about to arrive in the colony." Finally, at the end of the tour of Norton's Christy Minstrels, Cape Colony newspapers described their future itinerary: they would leave Cape Town and head to the British Crown colony of St. Helena and later Rio de Janeiro, Brazil.[122]

By following the travels of the Christy Minstrel troupes, British settlers developed an understanding of a globalized world connected in ways that were not possible prior to the proliferation of the steam engine in the 1860s.[123] The same minstrel show performed in Cape Town could potentially take place a couple of weeks later in places as far away as London, China, Australia, and even Brazil. For the first time in human history, people on opposite ends of the world could witness the same event weeks after one another and develop an understanding of the global scope of the event. For the British settlers of the Cape and Natal, touring blackface minstrel troupes were a window into a global community of British colonists who were connected by a love of burnt cork.

— Chapter 3 —

DIAMONDS, DANDIES, AND DISPOSSESSION

Minstrel Shows during the South African Mineral Revolution, 1872–1889

> The hall was crowded from floor to ceiling, and from ceiling to floor again. The rafters and beams of the roof were crowded with people, as well as the chairs and forms. . . . Long before the hour of performance the doors were thronged, and when the doors were opened the people came in with a rush, and the ticket-takers had more work than they had counted upon. . . . The conundrum of the evening was, "Why is a drunken nigger like our Government? Because he is Giddy at the head." There were cheers for [treasury general Richard] Giddy upon this.
>
> —*Diamond News*, July 27, 1872

During the mineral revolution years in South Africa, blackface minstrelsy was the main form of popular entertainment for British settlers in Cape Town, Natal, and the newly established mining city named Kimberley. As such, references to blackface turned up in the blue-collar poetry of the diamond fields. Many supervisors at diamond mining companies believed their profits were threatened by theft. They responded by offering commissions on any diamonds turned in by African workers. One company in Du Toit's Pan mine realized that the practice of offering commissions was so profitable they could afford to pay a 25 percent reward. A local newspaper brought this practice to the public's attention with a comedic poem voicing the angst of white workers. Here is a representative verse:

I wouldn't be a secret-
ry nor a manager,
To be a toiling Overseer
I'd very much demur;
I wouldn't build a crusher,
Nor such paltry things invent;
I'd rather be a nigger, and
Get 25 per cent.

The refrain "I'd rather be a nigger, and / Get 25 per cent" appears at the end of each stanza. The penultimate stanza switches to prose format to deliver the punch line: white workers should blacken up and cross the color line to get a fair deal. "[No, ladies and gentlemen, many and many a time my mother has said: ''arry, my angel-hearted boy, don't let nothing never persuade you to be a Prime Minister of the Cape Colony, or a digger, or an England's Only General. . . . No, my beaming boy,' said the old lady, bless her heart! 'You be a Christy Minstrel, and go work in the claims for your wages and 25 per cent.' I took the old lady's advice, and—all together, if you please, gentlemen]." This poem, where black skin leads to a life of privilege and undeserved wealth while white workers are left in the cold, was regularly recited in the diamond fields of Kimberley.[1] Because, as Eric Lott has observed, "cultural expropriation is the minstrel show's central fact," it makes perfect sense for blackface to appear in a poem about the distribution of income across racial lines.[2] During the mineral revolution, local aspiring poets had ample opportunities to watch blackface minstrel shows as the burnt cork nation violently extended its borders into the diamond fields.

Indeed, the cultural logic of blackface minstrelsy reflected imperial values. As David Harvey has argued, imperial projects function as resource-based projects that are most interested in capital "accumulation by dispossession."[3] Blackface minstrelsy was also a form of dispossession; however, instead of focusing only on traditional targets for the taking, like land or natural resources, the minstrel show claimed black cultural capital through acts of "primitivist accumulation."[4] In the imperial imaginary, almost everything in the colonial landscape is extractable, including the indigenous inhabitants. In the context of colonial South Africa, when white performers appeared in blackface they claimed a kind of imperial ownership over black people. Thus, readers should not be surprised to learn that blackface minstrelsy took root in the diamond fields and that the minstrels voiced support for imperial expansion. During the mineral revolution era, most of the remaining independent African civilizations were subjected to colonial rule, as the imperial regimes implemented more extreme techniques of labor coercion. As the colonies violently expanded and brought more African workers into their orbit, blackface minstrels continued to draw lines around colonial citizenship and champion the concept of a white racial state.

Many materialist historians believe the mineral revolution decades were crucial to the formation of the South African racial order and the institutionalization of segregation.[5] Most of these materialist histories privilege economic explanations for social and political power over all others. As a result, the ways in which expressive cultures contributed to the creation and maintenance of South African race and gender hierarchies are rarely acknowledged. This chapter foregrounds the role of performance culture. Minstrel shows provided discursive support for the racial order of an industrializing South Africa.

Between 1872 and 1890, an unprecedented number of professional minstrel troupes and variety companies starring blackened performers toured the Cape and Natal Colonies. A partial list includes the Harvey-Dougherty-Leslie-Brahim Minstrels (1872–74), the Ashante Dwarf Minstrels and Punch and Judy (1874), the Australian Variety Company featuring a little person billed as the "Australian Tom Thumb" (1875),[6] Harvey's Grotesques (1877), Baby Benson and the Benson American Troupe (1877), the London Minstrels (1879), the Victoria Loftus Troupe (1881–82), the Anglo-American Minstrels (1883–84), the Georgia Minstrels (1884),[7] Washington Norton and the Merrymakers (1885), the Wheeler Comedy Company (1885–86), DeVere's Comedy Company (1888), and D'arcs Marionetts (1890). This played-out during the second wave of minstrel globalization (1850–80s), when an unprecedented number of minstrel troupes were touring internationally. Many of these troupes visited South Africa because they were chasing mineral rushes. This strategy brought them to California in the 1850s, Australia in the 1860s, and South Africa in the 1870s and 1880s.[8]

Several relevant social developments coincided with the minstrel tours of the 1870s and 1880s. During these decades, the relatively small subsistence-based agriculture economies of the Cape and Natal expanded through industrialization processes. The chief export changed from wool to diamonds as the colonies transformed into natural resource economies. This led to greater integration with the economy of England and, by extension, the world economy. Excess capital from the diamond fields and large investments from England sparked rapid industrial and urban growth. The new economy was dependent on a low-wage labor force greatly surpassing that of the preindustrial era. British colonists created new strategies for securing and controlling African labor.

A few months after the founding of the city of Kimberley, white prospectors hastily moved to re-create the established racial order in the diamond fields in an effort to secure control over future profits. In March 1872, they drew up a list of demands, one of which proposed that "no Kafir or other colored person" would be given a digging license unless they were backed by fifty white claim holders. The desired goal was to create a white monopoly of the diamond claims and incorporate Africans as cheap expendable workers. The miners also called for the creation of a pass system that made it possible to fine and arrest any Africans in the mining camps who did not have documentation stating who their employer was. Another demand would give all "employers and constables" the right to search African workers for diamonds anytime they felt the need to do so.[9] A few months later, Cape governor Sir Henry Barkly issued "Proclamation 14," and the aforementioned demands became law.[10] As the 1870s progressed, a clear trend of structural racism emerged in which skilled white workers were brought in from Europe to operate the heavy machinery, white overseers were recruited from the local settler population, and Africans performed a majority of the backbreaking and oftentimes life-threatening mine labor, with limited access to the profits their labor generated. Leonard Thompson summarizes the situation: "Step by step, the working class was split into two strata, white and black: the white, privileged, well paid, and free; the black, unprivileged, poorly paid, and unfree."[11] The Cape and Natal Colonies were shameless racial projects designed to distribute resources and rights along racial lines.

During the recessions of the 1860s, the British Colonial Office had reason to doubt the potential profitability of the Cape and Natal, but the discovery of diamonds greatly expanded their interest. The previous reluctance of the imperial metropole to fund expansionist wars in the Cape and Natal Colonies vanished, and England began investing military resources in South Africa. The colonists hoped that expanded territorial control would help secure more African labor and more access to mineral wealth. In 1871 the British high commissioner announced the annexation of the diamond-rich territory approximately five hundred miles northeast of Cape Town that would come to be known as Griqualand West, with a capital city named Kimberley. In the late 1870s, England launched a series of imperial wars in South Africa to repress local populations and further expand its territory. Between 1877 and 1879, British armies conquered and subjugated the Xhosa of the Cape's eastern frontier, the Pedi, and the Zulu.[12] The process of colonial expansion continued into the 1880s. William Worger relates: "The British government, acting in response to pressures generated by the rise of the diamond industry, intervened in the subcontinent and conquered most of those black societies hitherto independent . . . a fundamental change in Kimberley's rural hinterland, as formally independent black producers were transformed in many cases into largely landless proletarians."[13]

The imperial project was greatly contested. At times, Africans responded to the incursions of British and colonial forces with successful military tactics. For example, the Zulu handily defeated large imperial armies on a number of occasions, and the Sothos' guerrilla warfare campaigns eventually broke down British settler morale and paved the way for the creation of a semiautonomous state known as Basutoland.[14] However, these moments of successful resistance were overshadowed by an encroaching colonial order with too much technological, discursive, and military backing to be outright defeated. Scorched-earth tactics laid waste to pastoral economies, as British soldiers slaughtered the cattle and burned the crops of local populations. The general trend was one of racial subordination, and many Africans had little choice but to become low-wage workers. As such, they had to endure a number of coercive mechanisms restricting their individual freedoms.

When the diamond rush was in its infancy, the government of the Cape Colony passed new labor laws intended to regulate the power relations between black workers and white employers. The Masters and Servants Act of 1873 tried to preserve the absolute authority of white employers. It enabled "masters" to define a wide range of behaviors of "servants" as misdemeanors, including "careless work," "neglect," or "bad language." Offenders could be punished with fines or three months of imprisonment. The definitions of misdemeanors were taken from the Cape Slave Codes and were used with the intention of establishing a racial order mirroring that of the preindustrial period.[15] Furthermore, African workers were regularly singled out for corporal abuse from white overseers.[16]

White workers who gleefully recited poetry about donning blackface and collecting a 25 percent commission would instantly regret this decision if they were to actually switch places with Africans in real life. And as the burnt cork nation feasted on diamonds and black labor, minstrel shows stoked feelings of white superiority, offered imperial fantasies of racialized dispossession, and defined colonial citizenship in racially exclusionary terms.

OF DANDIES AND DISPOSSESSION: MINSTRELS TAKE THE DIAMOND FIELDS

During the first decades of the mineral revolution, British settlers of all classes continued to frequent minstrel shows. Many minstrel shows, just like in the 1860s, offered three different prices of admission and split the audience into three separate economic strata. But some minstrel shows were staged solely for the elites. One of the first performances of the Harvey-Dougherty-Leslie-Brahim Minstrels (henceforth referred to as "Harvey Minstrels") was advertised as a "Grand Fashionable Night" and staged for Governor Barkly and his wife. One newspaper correspondent was fascinated by the sight of Cape Town's upper class enjoying the performance:

> His Excellency and Lady Barkly and a numerous suite occupied the gallery, and the body of the hall was literally crammed with what we were going to call a highly fashionable audience, only that they unbent, and laughed, and enjoyed themselves as thoroughly as if they were but made of common clay like the rest of us. . . . The faces of the audience—now rapturously intent on the exquisite notes of Mr. Leslie and the rich vocal strains of Mr. Braham, or the deep organ tones of Mr. Truro, and at another in contortions of laughter at the excruciating comicalities of Mr. Dougherty and the rich nigger humour of Mr. Harvey—was almost as amusing a study as the appearances on the stage itself.[17]

Here is a snapshot of wealthy Capetonians thoroughly enjoying a blackface minstrel show. Members of these elite audiences contributed directly to the colonial projects of the period. Governor Barkley oversaw the annexation of the diamond fields and the passing of racially exclusionary legislation during the 1870s. His appreciation of blackface minstrelsy did not translate into a modicum of respect for the rights of local Africans. A burnt cork nation looks out only for its own.

In the 1870s and 1880s, minstrel shows continued to celebrate British settler identity. Alan Lester has argued that many late-nineteenth-century British settlers attempted to preserve their cultural heritage by staying up-to-date with the latest fashion trends from England. British settlers learned about new trends by reading English publications and communicating with friends and family. They tried to hold on to that which made them British by re-creating the new metropolitan trends in the Cape and Natal.[18] The minstrels who graced the stages during "Grand Fashionable Night[s]" were not the only visual stimuli in the theater. Such events provided spaces for British settlers to come together while sporting the latest elite fashion trends from the metropole. The Harvey Minstrels understood the appeal of the British metropole and presented themselves as importers of the newest trends.

In March 1873, an article in the *Diamond News* described how the Harvey Minstrels "speak in glowing terms of the English feeling of Queenstown—the English people of Queenstown, and the thoroughly English reception given at Queenstown." A couple of months later, the minstrels were in Kimberley, where they "assembled at Duncombe's Hotel [for] a festive gathering in honour of Her Majesty's birthday. In addition to the Minstrels . . . there were forty and fifty gentlemen present, and champagne flowed freely. Mr. Duncombe having been voted to the chair, proposed the health of the Queen, which was most enthusiastically received, and followed by the national anthem, sung by the Minstrels. The health of the Prince of Wales, proposed by Mr. Harvey, also met with a hearty response, the Minstrels singing 'God bless the Prince of Wales,'" several other toasts and songs followed."[19] The Harvey Minstrels contributed to a British settler variant of burnt cork nationalism. "God Bless the Prince of Wales" was sung during their shows.[20] They also performed the patriotic songs "Down among the Dead Men," "Beautiful Isle of the Sea," and "God Save the Queen." Furthermore, Dougherty's stump speech on Henry Stanley's expedition to find David Livingston in central Africa celebrated a widespread story of British imperial exploration (fig. 4).[21] On at least one occasion, the minstrels went so far as to fly a Union Jack in front of the stage.[22]

Figure 4. Huey Dougherty. Courtesy of Houghton Library, Harvard University (MS Thr 556 [52]).

In turn, British settler newspapers described blackface minstrelsy as a fresh metropolitan import: "Mr. Dan [*sic*] Rice was seen by us many years ago in his famous 'Jim Crow' assumption at the Surrey Theatre, London, when the whole metropolis was placarded with 'Jim' in the well known attitude delineated at the conclusion of each verse. It was not long before every street corner had a 'Jim Crow.' All the boys 'blacked up,' and took to amateur 'Jim Crowing.'"[23]

One reviewer claimed the music of the Harveys was "equal to anything of the kind we have heard in the old country."[24] Later, when the London Minstrels toured in 1879, they mentioned a theater season at London's St. James Hall in their advertisements. One local paper responded to the advertisement: "The London Minstrels . . . are from St. James' Hall, and no higher certificate could be produced by a Minstrel troupe."[25] By mentioning St. James Hall as their previous venue, the London Minstrels presented their show as a fresh injection of metropolitan culture (fig. 5). A year later, a solo performer named Bertie Phillips began a short season in Kimberley. Phillips's variety show featured the "GREAT IMITATION SONG of London

Figure 5. Lew Simmons and Frank White. Simmons was a member of the London Minstrels. Courtesy of Houghton Library, Harvard University (MS Thr 1848).

Actors . . . the Moore and Burgess Minstrels (who never perform out of London)."[26] The Moore and Burgess Minstrels were one of the most successful British minstrel troupes in the latter half of the nineteenth century.[27] In this advertisement, Phillips claimed to be their surrogate. By restating the Moore and Burgess catchphrase, "[we] never perform out of London," Phillips was reminding Kimberley audiences of their peripheral position. Indeed, Phillips was insinuating that his show was bringing a rare metropolitan spectacle to Kimberley and hoping these claims would lead to packed theaters. Later in 1883, the Anglo-American Minstrels performed in Kimberley. One reviewer wrongly attributed the Moore and Burgess catchphrase to the Christy Minstrels: "The part-singing was so delightfully rendered that we thought of the days of 'Auld lang syne' when we were in dear old England and used to listen to the Christy Minstrels who 'never perform out of London.'"[28] Most important for our purposes is the reviewer's description of the sensation of being transported back to England through minstrel music. The American signifier in "Anglo-American minstrels" was swept by the wayside as the reviewer heard London in their music.

Blackface minstrels further advanced the imaginary of burnt cork nationalism by singing war songs and donating to patriotic causes. In 1876 amateur minstrels performed in Cape Town for the benefit of the "Soldiers Widow and Orphan Fund."[29] Two years later, minstrels continued to support the war effort when British imperial and colonial forces invaded and annexed several Xhosa-controlled territories.[30] As the campaign unfolded, Harvey's Variety Troupe was performing a "new colonial war song" called "our brave artillery" that "evokes great enthusiasm every evening."[31]

The Anglo-Zulu War of 1879 offered much inspiration for blackface minstrels in the colonies. In 1878 relations between Cetshwayo kaMpande's Zulu civilization and the colony of Natal deteriorated. In previous decades, the Zulu, and the Afrikaner republic of the Transvaal, had been involved in a series of territorial disputes. At the time, these disputes never escalated to all-out warfare because Natal acted as a mediator, maintaining an unstable peace. However, the political relations between the three territories changed in April 1877 when the Transvaal was annexed to Natal. Not long after the annexation, in response to pressure from Afrikaner leaders, Theophilus Shepstone decided to invade Zululand. In January 1879, a combined army of colonial and imperial forces moved into Zululand. The first phases of this British military campaign were unsuccessful, as the colonial and imperial forces lost several battles during the first month of the war. The most devastating defeat was in Isandlwana, where on January 22 they suffered sixteen hundred casualties. The colonial army spent the greater part of the next two months regrouping and waiting for reinforcements. Meanwhile, in February, two concerts were staged in Cape Town by a bandmaster referred to in the local papers as Mr. M. Curry, with local amateur minstrels playing central roles. The first concert ended with a portrayal of "the Capture of King Cethwaye [*sic*] and the Fall of Zululand."[32] Because the fighting was far from over, this imagining of what the capture of Cetshwayo and the fall of Zululand might look like was a colonial fantasy intended to assuage the fears of British settlers who might have been losing confidence in their prospects for victory. The second concert was also connected to the war; it was carried out for the "Relief of Widows and Orphans and Widows of Soldiers Killed in Zululand."[33]

A few weeks later, the London Minstrels came to Cape Town for a three-week run. Afterward, they left Cape Town and went to Natal, presumably to be closer to the front lines. Before leaving they performed a piece called "The Runaway Zulu," which was likely inspired by the war. They also dedicated one show to the "aid of the Zulu and Native war sufferers' relief fund."[34]

Other patriotic minstrels focused on the Twenty-Fourth Regiment at the battle of Rorke's Drift, in which a small amount of British soldiers defeated a large Zulu army. In May 1879, the *Cape Times* mentioned a song called "The Nobel [*sic*] 24th" that was being sung by "Mrs. Paulton in Maritzburg, and . . . one of the Christy's in Durban."[35] Two months before the *Cape Times* published this article, the Twenty-Fourth Regiment had left Pietermaritzburg for the front lines. Interestingly enough, they marched out of the city as a band played "I'm Leaving Thee in Sorrow, Annie," a song that appeared in many minstrel shows.[36] Another example comes four years after the conclusion of the Anglo-Zulu War, in November 1883, when the Anglo-American Minstrels performed in Kimberley. A local newspaper reported, "An interesting feature of the entertainment, as relating to the recent historical past of South Africa, will be the production of the 'Rorke's Drift March,' or 'Honor to the Brave,' with full band and chorus."[37] The battle at Rorke's Drift was widely celebrated throughout the British Empire as an example of extreme bravery in the face of overwhelming odds. On January 22, 1879, a few hours after the British army's devastating defeat at Isandlwana, a hundred British soldiers successfully defended a garrison at Rorke's Drift from a series of attacks by around two thousand Zulu warriors. Thus, the Anglo-American Minstrels performed their patriotism by honoring Rorke's Drift. Indeed, minstrel performers and composers contributed to the imperial imaginary of the British colonists in South Africa by creating a patriotic soundtrack for the Anglo-Zulu War. With their blackface performances, minstrels offered a unique spectacle: "black" people celebrating the war victories of the British Empire. These patriotic caricatures were not formidable Zulu warriors who challenged British hegemony. Instead, they were depicted as pacified Africans rallying for the British Empire—assimilated Africans who sang in English, the disenfranchised and dispossessed dregs of a burnt cork nation.

Sometimes British soldiers went so far as to blacken up as amateur minstrels. A photograph of British volunteer soldiers posing with blackface makeup, eccentric attire, and musical instruments can be found in the Western Cape Archives (fig. 6). The soldiers depicted in the photograph

Figure 6. Duke of Edinburgh's Own Volunteer Rifles. Courtesy of Western Cape Archives and Records Service (AG 13327).

were part of the Duke of Edinburgh's Own Volunteer Rifles: a volunteer regiment of reserve soldiers who were active during the late nineteenth and early twentieth centuries.[38] The image is a stark visual reminder of the connections between blackface minstrelsy, colonial violence, colonial expropriation, and settler patriotism.

In the 1870s and 1880s, professional minstrel troupes continued to portray white ethnic others and contribute to understandings of normative whiteness. The Harvey Minstrels' repertoire included two offerings featuring ethnic white characters, a one-act play titled *Johnny Schmoker*, and an "Irish comic song" called "Tim Finagan's Wake."[39] In 1875 a Kimberley newspaper praised Jerry Wood of the Australian Variety Company as "one of the finest rollicking Irish boys that ever whirled a shillelah [*sic*] or was chased by a policeman or danced a jig." An 1877 description of Cheever's and Kennedy's Great American Entertainment Troupe included "German, Irish, and Nigger [acts]." A few months later, the Benson American Troupe was performing in Kimberley when a child performer named Baby Benson presented an "Irish Act" called the "Jolly Irish couple," in which she played a "Wild Irish Boy."[40] Furthermore, the Benson American

Troupe often sang a song called "The Jolly Irishman" that described a series of drunken brawls:

> They fought and dhrank,
> And dhrank and fought,
> And fought and dhrank,
> They dhrank and fought,
> Bowld Irishmin wur they![41]

One of Baby Benson's signature songs was titled "The Dutch Broom Girl" and was likely understood by British settlers as a commentary on the local Dutch population.[42] The last example from the 1870s comes in the form of a one-act sketch called *Poor Paddy,* which was performed in 1877 by Harvey's Variety Company.[43] In total, Irish people received the brunt of the white ethnic humor in the 1870s. Moving to the next decade, in 1881–82 the Victoria Loftus Troupe presented several one-act plays: *Uncle O'brieans, Fritz! Our Cousin German,* and *Those German Emegrants* [*sic*]. They also staged an "Irish drama" known as *Wicklow Wedding.*[44] One member of their troupe presented a set of "origional [*sic*] Dutch specialties."[45] Later, during an 1883 tour, the Anglo-American Minstrels dedicated entire nights to Scottish song and were praised in the local press: "The rendering of national ballads by a Minstrel troupe with blackened faces is a new departure."[46] White ethnic characters were also a central part of the Wheeler Comedy Company's repertoire in 1886–87. Frank Wheeler portrayed Irish characters named "Barney the Baron" and "the Irish Boy." Irish characters also appeared in other Wheeler Comedy Company sketches: the "Irish Farce," "Brian O'linn or the Irish Mormon," and "The Shaughraun."[47] One publication claimed that Wheeler specialized in "Anglo-Dutch characters."[48] A particularly glowing review observed, "Mr Wheeler is very good in negro character but last night he proved that in German character sketches he was just as good, his Jacob Schmidt being inimitable."[49] During the Wheeler Comedy Company's rendition of "Alladin," one member of the company had "the superb impudence to play the part of a Chinese Emperor with an Irish Brogue."[50] In this moment, an Irish accent was used to convey Chinese foreignness. Like depictions of black characters, these representations of white ethnic others also helped solidify normative British/English settler identity.

From 1862 to the late 1880s, minstrel shows provided a forum in which

Cape and Natal colonists could come together and celebrate British settler identity. Many minstrels proudly claimed England as the previous stop on their tour in order to capitalize on settler desires for a connection to the home country. Likewise, at minstrel "Grand Fashionable Night[s]," upper-class settlers dressed in the latest metropolitan fashions while watching a cultural import they imagined to be from the metropole. Songs celebrating British culture, the royal family, and Britain's imperial wars were regularly included in minstrel shows. Minstrel representations of white ethnic characters also worked to further solidify local understandings of who was British and who was not. Indeed, for British settlers in the Cape and Natal, participating in minstrel culture was a means to hold on to that which made them British. In this way, the British South African colonists developed their own uses for blackface minstrelsy.

In the United States, the blackface minstrel show expressed a "peculiarly American structure of racial feeling," to quote Eric Lott.[51] It was next exported to England in the 1830s and 1840s, where it was quickly popularized. In the following years, minstrel shows reached South Africa, and British settlers used the culture to maintain connections with the British metropole. In the Cape and Natal, the culture acquired new social functions greatly removed from its original antebellum American context. Like a traveler collecting mementos, blackface minstrelsy took on new social meanings while dancing across the Atlantic world.

Although blackface minstrelsy had moved far from its original antebellum contexts, the genre continued to spread antebellum-style racial imagery. During the mineral revolution era, British settler reviewers continued to praise the so-called authentic portrayals of minstrel performers. E. H. Harvey of the Harvey Minstrels received a large amount of praise. One reviewer glowingly labeled him "a photographer of negro life."[52] Another claimed that his rendition of "Hamfat Man" was delivered in "true nigger style."[53] Harvey was also described as "a true nigger dandy."[54] Tellingly, one reviewer went so far as to compare him to a local African:

> The only true nigger in the company is the Tambo, Mr. E. H. Harvey. We once had the pleasure of knowing a nigger in this city of Cape Town, he played the banjo of home manufacture, consisting of a piece of wood with holes pieced in it for the screws, and a preserved meat tin for the sounding board. Upon these were stretched pieces of simple cord for strings. Many a time and oft, by the uncertain light of a tallow candle,

> have we listened to him play and sing, his eyes glistening with merriment, rolling about on his seat, and, at intervals, uttering explosions of laughter. Harvey with the cork on, is exactly his counterpart. Nothing but careful study of nigger characteristics, their light hearted merriment, their peculiar ode of word clipping, could have secured the power Mr. Harvey has of delineating nigger dance and song.[55]

The reviewer used the minstrel convention of frenetic corporality ("rolling about on his seat, and, at intervals, uttering explosions of laughter") to describe the mannerisms of the African musician in this passage. Here is another example of British settlers portraying local Africans through a minstrel lens.

Years later, the belief that stage performers were able to represent authentic blackness continued. In 1877 one reviewer described Tom Benson as "unquestionably the best delineator of Negro character," with the exception of Hugh Dougherty of the Harvey Minstrels.[56] One particularly telling review described Victoria Loftus's portrayal of the character of Topsy: "Undoubtedly the best played part in the piece was Topsy. Miss Victoria Loftus in this character gave a really powerful psychological study of the untutored child of nature, that would but for the touches of humour have been almost painful in its intensity."[57] The reviewer was commenting on a rendition of *Uncle Tom's Cabin* that included a scene called "Topsy's Ignorance."[58] It is clear from the review that Victoria Loftus portrayed Topsy as "primitive" and "premodern."

According to Vivian Bickford-Smith, during the mid-1870s and early 1880s, many British settlers in Cape Town began questioning if it was possible to "civilize" local Africans: "The view that it would take Africans a long time to become like 'us' became an explicit part of the discourse of Englishness in Cape Town between 1875 and 1882. Journalists on the *Cape Times* and *Lantern* wrote numerous racist articles about African intelligence and the difficulty of inculcating 'civilized' (i.e. English) values."[59]

Such viewpoints were also a mainstay in the minstrel shows of this time period. The urban dandy character was a commentary on the many "humorous" ways in which black city dwellers failed to understand the nuances of modern city life. The South African press often praised E. H. Harvey for his representations of urban dandies.[60] The black illogics humor of minstrel shows also contributed to the idea that black people were premodern and incapable of rational thought. Take, for instance, the following description of a Dougherty stump speech caricaturing a black politician: "Sometimes when he philosophizes . . . you follow him for some time as if his philosophy was to lead to some rational conclusion, but the climax [results in] well feigned perplexity upon his part, which is irresistibly ridiculous."[61] Dougherty's illogical stump speeches inspired local adaptations. A British settler writing under the pen name "Lawks" published a meandering statement filled with malapropisms titled "Dougherty Beaten" that offered a hyperbolic example of this representational strategy.[62]

Many failed-facade jokes appear in the minstrel shows of the 1870s and 1880s. Such humor reinforced the concept that local Africans were not able to change and by extension assimilate. Failed-facade jokes were featured in multiple sketches, including *Siamese Twins, The Virginia Mummy, The Virginia Cupids!,* and *Napoleon Hemmed In.* The latter featured a scenario in which a black servant tried to disguise himself as a painting. The white characters instantly spot the ruse, observing how the painting "looks very much like our servant, Napoleon."[63] As in other failed facades, the message here was clear: black people who tried to be anything other than black were doomed to fail. Minstrel shows of this period continued to reinforce notions of unchanging blackness and contributed to widespread beliefs that Africans could not participate responsibly in modern society.

In the Kimberley diamond fields, minstrel caricatures portraying black thieves carried special ideological significance. In the early 1870s, many small claim owners competed for African labor. This high demand for African labor contributed to a rare situation in which Africans had a certain amount of agency to negotiate for high wages. If one claim owner offered relatively low wages, Africans could leave and find work with a different employer. After unsuccessful periods of prospecting, some claim owners were unable to pay their workers, and this often resulted in desertion. In most cases, claim owners did not view desertion as a response to their failure to pay wages owed or as a predictable outgrowth of a competitive labor market but instead "were convinced that the major cause was diamond theft. If an African stole a diamond he would not need to work and could live on his illicit earnings in the warren of tents and tin shanties that made up the camps. The frustration at poor finds was often put down to wholesale theft. Colonial newspapers reported lurid stories of Africans, suspected of theft, being beaten to death by their masters."[64] Claim owners looking for "evidence" of African thievery could find it in the minstrel shows of Kimberley, where many crooked gluttony jokes portrayed black people as thieves. Such race discourse onstage contributed to real-world consequences. As the above passage mentions, some of the Africans suspected of theft were beaten to death. This kind of violence was encouraged in burnt cork nations where the lives of racial "aliens" did not matter.

During the 1870s and 1880s, minstrel caricatures and British settler race discourse were locked in a mutually reinforcing relationship. British settler stereotypes about African characteristics were reinforced on minstrel stages, and, in turn, minstrel representations were understood to be authentic because they reflected British settler race discourse. Minstrel shows also reaffirmed British settler notions of African inferiority and unassimilable difference. However, one section of the audience may have been learning these concepts for the first time. During this period, blackface minstrels regularly offered weekend matinee shows for children. As a result, young British settlers who were just beginning to learn the social logics of British settler identity were exposed to the racial logics of the minstrel imaginary.

Descriptions of children's shows are rare, and none of the programs were published in the local newspapers. However, some details have survived. According to one account, children responded to the "comicalities of . . . Dougherty and Harvey" with "shrill laughter."[65]According to another account, a minstrel show for children was also attended by "anxious" African nursemaids who were probably uncomfortable with the grotesque caricatures: "Crowds of pretty children, with half anxious and half merry-looking nurses of every shade of colour from European white to African ebony, filled the hall, and the shouts of shrill laughter from the little ones, their sparkling eyes and joyous clapping of hands, were fitted to thaw the heart of the most inveterate old bachelor that ever abominated children."[66]

Benson's American Troupe gave several Saturday matinee children's shows in 1877. British settler children were enamored with Baby Benson, a white American child performer who specialized in ethnic and racial impersonations. One advertisement described her as a "Negro Comedian" who will "black her face" and sing "favourite songs" like "Old Black Joe" and "Old Mother Gum."[67] Other accounts mentioned the popularity of a "pathetic ballad" titled "Old Negro Dying." As one advertisement put it, Baby Benson "imitat[ed] an old nigger, seventy-nine years of age."[68] Furthermore, she also presented a spectacle of instant race changing as described in this advertisement: "The Wonderful Dream of BABY BENSON . . . HER DREAM has left so vivid an impression upon her mind, that she has persuaded the Manager to allow her to perform a feat never before attempted by a living Artist, . . . AN INSTANTANEOUS LIGHTNING CHANGE From a Black Face to a White Face! This astonishing change will be effected in two seconds, and the audience will scarcely lose sight of the Artiste. SEE LARGE POSTERS!"[69]

According to theater historian Virginia Mason Vaughn, "quick changes" in which performers moved between two different social positions were a common technique in British theater during the early modern period: "These quick changes are calculated to amaze the audience. Pleasure emanates from the sudden realization of the actor's legerdemain. Like the spectator's sigh of satisfaction when a talented female impersonator takes off his wig and reveals that he is 'really' a male, these theatrical moments please most when the audience is made aware of the differences between the actors and the role he plays. The greater the perceived difference between performer and persona, the more wonder and pleasure we feel."[70] Baby Benson's "instantaneous lightning change" was calculated to awe the audience by making visible the great distance between the black characters she played and her white American self. This distance was measured in terms of race and age.

Baby Benson may have inspired British settler children to blacken up. Benson's American Troupe left Cape Town in late May 1877, and in August of that year newspapers reported that a "Juvenile Negro Minstrel Troupe" gave a "private entertainment" in Cape Town.[71] For some British settler children, participation was not limited to spectatorship. These children blackened up and rendered their own minstrel shows. In South Africa, as was the case with the rest of the world, the concept of race was not a natural idea. Because British settlers were not born with a racial consciousness, they had to be taught how to see, hear, and categorize race.[72] British settler children were introduced to racial concepts in the formal schools of the Cape Colony.[73] Minstrel shows supplemented their school curriculum with a playful and informal pedagogy on race. Indeed, minstrel shows molded the minds of the next generation of burnt cork nationalists.

Blackface minstrel shows filled several social functions during the first decades of the mineral revolution. Minstrelsy championed a binary of burnt cork nationalism juxtaposing British settler identity against black "alien" otherness, contributed to notions of a shrinking world,[74] offered a cultural imaginary in which blackness could be dispossessed and owned, and taught racial hierarchy to settler children. Furthermore, some minstrel songs rendered African life expendable. A popular song called "Ten Little Niggers" was a troubling example of minstrel sadism humor:

> Ten little niggers, going out to dine
> One choked his little self, and then there were nine
> Nine little niggers, crying at his fate
> One cried himself away, and then there were eight
>
> Chorus
>
> One little, two little, three little, four little, five little nigger boys
> six little, seven little, eight little, nine little, ten little nigger boys
>
> Eight little niggers, slept until eleven
> One over slept himself then there were seven
> Seven little niggers, cutting up sticks
> One chopp'd himself in halves, and then there were six
>
> Chorus
>
> Six little niggers, playing with a hive
> A bumble bee kill'd one, and then there were five
> Five little niggers, going in for law
> One got in chancery, and then there were four
>
> Chorus
>
> Four little niggers, getting going out to sea
> A red herring swallow'd one, and then there were three
> Three little niggers, walking in the zoo
> A big bear cuddle one, and then there were two
>
> Chorus
>
> Two little niggers, sitting in the sun
> One got frizzled up, and then there was one

One little nigger living all alone
He got married, and then there were none
One little nigger, with his little wife
Liv'd all his days a happy little life
One little couple, dwelling by the shore
Soon raised a family of ten nigger more

Chorus.[75]

The song "Ten Little Niggers" voiced a large amount of racial malevolence during a period of increased hostility. The 1870s and 1880s were decades of constant warfare between the British colonies and neighboring African civilizations. Popular songs devaluing black life legitimized the violent expropriations of land and resources that were being carried out during the period. By trivializing black life as comedically expendable, minstrel shows assuaged possible feelings of guilt. Indeed, one of the minstrel show's more pernicious effects was its devaluation of black life during years when many black lives were taken under the guise of colonial expansion and patriotic nationalism.[76]

"APPETITE AND FORCE": WHEN RACIAL PROJECTS GROW FANGS

Kimberley passed its first labor law in 1872.[77] Proclamation 14 created harsh penalties for diamond theft and attempted to control black workers by establishing a pass system. All Africans in Kimberley had to carry passes stating who they worked for and the duration of their contracts. If an African traveler was unable to present a pass and was "found wandering or loitering without being able to give a good and satisfactory account of himself," he could be fined or arrested for up to three months.[78] Rudimentary in form, this system later evolved into one of the major mechanisms for controlling black workers during the apartheid era.

Other strategies of labor control that later became instrumental to apartheid were also implemented during this period. In 1876, for example, British colonists considered creating "locations" for Africans in Griqualand West. Worger relates: "Colonel Lanyon proposed the establishment of a series of rural locations for blacks, each location small enough so that it could not be self-sufficient, all carefully dispersed throughout the countryside in such a manner that they could be used as labor reserves for the newly established white farmers, and with white magistrates in control so that the power of chiefs could be curtailed."[79] In the late 1870s and early 1880s, the vast majority of Africans in Kimberley and the surrounding Griqualand West area were placed in the locations. The locations were designed to expedite the process of turning Africans into a migrant labor force. This preference for African migrant labor would later become a stated goal of the apartheid regime.

By the middle of the 1880s, Kimberley miners implement a closed-compound system, which was designed to exert total control over African labor. African workers were housed in enclosed compounds surrounded by fences and watch guards. At the beginning of the day, workers were brought directly from their living quarters to the mines and were funneled back to the enclosed compounds after the workday was completed. This system was designed to prevent theft and maintain viselike control of African labor. According to John Cell, Kimberley's closed compound system spread quickly throughout the British and Afrikaner territories of South Africa: "The compound system was widely imitated. On the railways and docks, on farms in white areas, in fledgling industries, comparable labor patterns took root throughout the country. . . . The exploitation color bar became the basis of South Africa's political economy."[80]

In Cape Town, new practices of racial segregation developed in response to a measles outbreak in the early 1880s. City officials attributed the outbreak to the "uncivilized" and "dirty" practices of African urbanites. Bickford-Smith relates: "The racialisation of problems of poverty in Cape Town furthered the emergence there of a dominant-class ideology of social separation for the 'races.' This ideology promoted the view that exclusionary segregation alone was not enough to protect White bourgeois supremacy. The social separation of all Blacks from all Whites was required. . . . Discriminatory social practice was necessary. It would help control Blacks while preventing the degeneration of poor Whites." In the 1890s, Cape Town elites opted for segregation, as special schools, railway cars, and locations were created for Africans.[81]

The opening salvos of apartheid certainly would have been fired even if Nish's Christy Minstrels had not landed in Cape Town in 1862 and started a minstrel craze that lasted for several decades. That is, practices of segregation in the Cape Colony and the location system of Natal developed primarily as a response to local circumstances and exclusionary economic interests. Nonetheless, racial projects are both material and discursive. Blackface minstrelsy contributed to the discursive component of the British colonial project by strengthening British settler ideas about unbridgeable and insurmountable racial difference on a popular level. These ideas were central to systems of labor expropriation and racial segregation, and blackface minstrels happily gave much discursive ammunition to these projects. Blackface minstrelsy was obviously not the final deciding factor contributing to the creation of segregation in South Africa; however, minstrelsy nurtured attitudes of racial difference in a society that would later go on to create apartheid: one of the most bureaucratically advanced and ruthlessly violent racial state projects of the twentieth century.

How successful was the burnt cork nation at extracting diamonds for its mineral revolution? Consider Cecil Rhodes, a patriotic citizen of the British colonies who spent no time blacking his face for Kimberley audiences. But like the minstrels, he benefited from a project of dispossession. While the minstrels danced in Kimberley, Rhodes was cashing in on the civic privileges of whiteness and building a company named De Beers Consolidated Mines. By 1884 he owned the De Beers mine, and by 1889 his company had monopolized the entire South African diamond industry. A white American named Gardner Williams served as De Beers's chief mining operations officer. Williams was educated at Yale's Sheffield School and the Colorado School of Mines, where he learned to extract as much ore as possible for the lowest possible cost. Williams's technical skills in metallurgy, mineralogy, and what is today called "management" helped streamline Rhodes's project of accumulation by dispossession.[82] Rhodes imagined an Anglo-Saxon empire enveloping the entire world.[83] In 1890 he became prime minister of the Cape Colony and began advocating racial empire on a statewide level. He wanted to create a Cape-to-Cairo train line: an infrastructure of expropriation that would run across the entire African continent. When he died in 1902, many believed him to be the wealthiest man on the planet. I view his storehouses of diamonds as the privatized fruits of a racial project whose canine teeth had grown into fangs. If resource expropriation was the minstrel show's central fact, Cecil Rhodes was the culmination of the minstrel dream in South Africa.

But some people protested. Consider the following account of a Harvey Minstrels show in Natal in 1874: "At the second night's entertainment a shower of stones thrown in from the outside through the windows caused some disturbance."[84] Someone's brazen rocks disrupted the most popular professional minstrel tour of the 1870s. Scholars will probably never know who threw the stones and for what reason(s). Perhaps a group of rival entertainers? Or British colonists who had gotten into a disagreement with the minstrels? Or maybe some Africans who were offended by the mockery of the blackface mask? The concrete details are unknown, but what is most important is the simple fact that someone disrupted this performance. Someone hurled stones through the windows of the blackface minstrel institution. Later, in the 1890s, sources reveal another discernible intervention. This more substantial and better-documented example arrived on the shores of Cape Town as a band of African American performers whose manager was named Orpheus McAdoo.

— Chapter 4 —

"SLIPPING THE YOKE"

McAdoo's Jubilee Singers, McAdoo's Minstrels, and Racial Uplift Politics, 1890–1898

On September 17, 1897, a Cape Town newspaper reviewed a show by Orpheus McAdoo's High Class Coloured American Minstrel Vaudeville Company:

> Mr. Orpheus M. McAdoo and his minstrel, entertainments indeed . . . have been calculated to make even a misanthrope smile. By the way, how is it that when the house is convulsed with laughter at the antics of the corner men the remainder of the troupe presents such an extraordinary degree of gravity. One of the features of the entertainment to my mind is the extraordinary contrast between the ridiculous behavior of Tamboes and Bones and the sedate solemnity of the remainder of the company, who seem to silently protest against the foolery taking place under their noses.[1]

This writer offers a brief glimpse of the onstage personas of the noncomedic performers in McAdoo's troupe and a window into the covert ways they tried to counter the degrading logics of minstrelsy while staging the minstrel genre. To borrow a phrase from Ralph Ellison, McAdoo's troupe changed the joke and slipped the yoke of traditional blackface minstrelsy.[2] They were the only troupe of African American minstrels who toured South Africa.

Orpheus Myron McAdoo was born in slavery in Greensboro, North

Carolina, in 1858. His mother was the only literate enslaved person on the plantation. She taught him to read and helped him excel academically. He graduated from the Hampton Institute for former slaves and Native Americans (now known as Hampton University) in 1876 and taught at that school for almost a decade.[3] McAdoo began a professional music career in 1885, when he joined Frederick Loudin's Fisk Jubilee Singers, a troupe of African American vocalists that included several members of the original Fisk Jubilee Singers.[4]

McAdoo learned the repertoire and sensibilities of the original Fisk Jubilee Singers while touring with Frederick Loudin's company. In the 1870s, the original Fisk Jubilee Singers toured the United States, the British Isles, and Europe, raising money for Fisk University (an institution of higher learning for African Americans founded in 1868). The Fisk Jubilee Singers pioneered and popularized a new genre of music that would come to be known as jubilee singing. Jubilee singers specialized in "concert spirituals," African American folk spirituals transcribed and arranged in Western notation. Folk spirituals were created by enslaved African Americans during the antebellum era. These were communal songs with biblical references commenting on the injustices of American slavery. Some folk spirituals included hidden messages for how to escape on the Underground Railroad.[5] Concert spirituals continued to circulate the antislavery themes of folk spirituals. As such, concert spirituals were an early form of African American protest music. McAdoo eagerly trained in these traditions of protest as he toured Europe, East Asia, Australia, and New Zealand with Frederick Loudin's company.

In 1889 McAdoo left Loudin's troupe and returned to the United States to put together his own ensemble, which he called the Virginia Jubilee Singers, or the Virginia Concert Company. This troupe arrived in Cape Town in June 1890 and performed for their own benefit. After touring South Africa for nineteenth months, they went to Australia. In June 1895, McAdoo returned to South Africa for another long tour. Early in 1897, McAdoo went to the United States to recruit new artists. In June of that year, he introduced a new act to South African audiences: McAdoo's High Class Coloured American Minstrel Vaudeville Company (henceforth referred to as "McAdoo's Minstrels"). This troupe, in addition to singing concert spirituals, also offered "Buck and Wing Dancing, Banjo Playing, Scenes from Slave Life, Juggling, Burlesque, and Comedy."[6] Altogether,

McAdoo and his troupes spent almost five years in South Africa. They were pioneering contributors to Afro-diasporic cultural formations in South Africa.

In 1976 Josephine Wright published the first scholarly work on McAdoo in which she observed, "[McAdoo is a] now forgotten black musician who helped to introduce the secular and sacred songs of black America to international audiences."[7] Since then, several researchers have increased scholarly understanding of McAdoo's legacy by tracing the influence of McAdoo's tours on the development of black South African music and addressing the ways in which McAdoo's troupe challenged and reaffirmed dominant colonial-era race discourse.[8] This chapter offers further analysis of McAdoo's contributions by focusing on his uplift politics and his attempts to circulate counternarratives undercutting the race thinking of British and Afrikaner colonists in South Africa. Ultimately, I argue that McAdoo challenged the minstrel logic of burnt cork nationalism by advocating for black citizenship.

Two major late-nineteenth-century social developments impacted several aspects of McAdoo's tours. First, gold was discovered in the Witwatersrand in 1886, and the resulting gold rush created the densely populated city of Johannesburg. Johannesburg was merely thirty miles south of Pretoria, the capital of the Afrikaner Transvaal Republic. Together, Johannesburg and Pretoria formed a new northern node in the South African entertainment circuit of the 1890s. The addition of these two cities to the circuit allowed South Africa to support longer tours. Of additional significance is the solidification of coloured racial identity by the late 1880s. According to historian of coloured identity Mohamed Adhikari, in the period between emancipation and the mineral revolution, mixed-race former slaves and Khoisan oftentimes saw themselves as two separate groups. However, a collective identity was formed in response to the social changes of the mineral revolution. Many black Africans were moving to the Western Cape. The resulting competition for jobs between these newcomers and the relatively Westernized Khoisan and mixed-race descendants of former slaves resulted in the creation, on the part of the latter, of a coloured racial identity. Adhikari relates: "[Mineral revolution] developments drove acculturated Africans to assert a separate identity as Coloured people, in order to claim a position of relative privilege in relation to Africans on the basis of their closer assimilation to Western culture and being partly descended from European colonists."[9] The new meaning of the term *coloured* was quickly incorporated into the South African lexicon. As will be discussed shortly, McAdoo tried to use this middle racial category to his advantage.

McAdoo's troupes pioneered an original variant of racial uplift politics in South Africa. African American racial uplift politics first developed in the postbellum era as a middle-class African American response to notions of black "backwardness." During this period, black reformers and institutions advanced notions of upward social mobility and "improvement" of the race. Advocates of racial uplift believed that discourses portraying black people as incapable of fully participating in modern democratic nations could be challenged if upwardly mobile African Americans actively disseminated images of black civility and refinement. They hoped this strategy would contribute to the removal of social barriers to black citizenship. While he was in South Africa, McAdoo continued this line of thinking by presenting himself and the members of his troupe as upper-class, highly "civilized" performers. Kevin Gaines has demonstrated that racial uplift advocates in the United States often tried to challenge the degrading stereotypes of blackface minstrelsy.[10] Given this context, a surface-level analysis might come to the conclusion that McAdoo contradicted his own politics when he transitioned from jubilee singing to minstrelsy. I doubt this was the case. Instead, McAdoo found ways to continue championing uplift politics by creating a new kind of minstrel show. McAdoo's Minstrels challenged some of the traditional conventions of the minstrel show and thereby altered its racial discourse. McAdoo offered a minstrel show that was new to South Africa because his performers were actual black people who did not blacken up, and their characters were deserving of first-class citizenship status.

McAdoo's Minstrels were the most popular troupe to visit South Africa during the third wave of minstrel globalization (1890–1915), an era when few blackface minstrels were touring international circuits. They brought a fresh infusion of minstrel culture during a relative dry spell. However, McAdoo's Minstrels differed substantially from the blackface caricatures of previous decades because they refused to consciously reproduce the exclusionary logics of burnt cork nationalism.

THE SPECTACULARLY OPAQUE UPLIFT POLITICS OF THE VIRGINIA JUBILEE SINGERS

> Ladies and gentlemen, let's not forget why we are here. Our purpose is not to liberate the natives from their oppression. Much as we might empathize with their predicament. No! Our mission is to provide an outstanding example of what the freedman, that's us, can be, given the opportunity.
>
> —Orpheus McAdoo as represented in David Kramer's *Orpheus in Africa*

Orpheus McAdoo was dedicated to a kind of racial uplift politics project that advanced images of black civility and bourgeois refinement to white South African audiences. McAdoo had direct access to people who were schooled in the Fisk Jubilee model of racial uplift politics. The first group he toured with included several former members of the Fisk Jubilee Singers. During this tour, he was exposed to the racial uplift model for presenting black culture. George White, musical director of the original Fisk Jubilee Singers, created concert spiritual adaptations with the hopes of "display[ing] the artistic merit of the music."[11] The original Fisk singers were trying to elevate the status of black folk music to "art music." The Fisk troupe performed in Victorian formal dress and were trained in upper-class decorum. For example, while the group was on a ship headed for England, George White "read to the troupe from a manual on shipboard decorum: 'how to dress, and how not to over-eat.'" Furthermore, according to Maggie Porter, a soprano in the Fisk troupe, "[we] didn't sing in Negro dialect; always in good English."[12] In Europe one audience member said the Fisk singers were "not as black as we expected nor dressed in the gay colours which are falsely supposed to distinguish the negro taste. They are simply eleven young Christian *ladies and gentlemen.*"[13] All of these elements (formal wear, formal musical arrangement, "proper" upper-class decorum) were consciously presented by the troupe in order to create an aura of respectability and refinement.

McAdoo's Virginia Jubilee Singers followed the formula of the Fisk Jubilee Singers. They were well dressed and "well mannered" when singing concert spirituals onstage. In the advertisements for the performances of the Virginia Jubilee Singers in South Africa, McAdoo often described the ensemble as "Coloured Ladies and Gentlemen." He also published a list of distinguished patrons who had watched the troupe perform: "The

Jubilee Singers have been honoured by appearing before her Majesty Queen Victoria, the Prince and Princess of Wales, the King and Queen of the Netherlands. Seven Crowned Heads of Europe. Governors in Australia, Sir Henry and Lady Loch, Six Presidents of the United States (Including President U.S. Grant) President Kruger, Transvaal Republic, and other celebrated personages."[14] This advertisement was a clear attempt by McAdoo to package his jubilee show as "legitimate art." A review of a classical music concert in Pretoria in 1891 that coincided with a concert by McAdoo's ensemble suggested that McAdoo achieved this goal: "The entertainment [at the classical music concert] was very poorly attended, probably in consequence of the great attraction of the Jubilee Singers."[15] Apparently, Pretoria's classical music audience opted for the Jubilee Singers over local renditions of Western classical music.

British settlers praised the "refined" quality of the Jubilee Singers' music but sometimes did so in racially derogatory ways: "The airs sung are the inspirations of nature, and in a curious degree resemble the melodies which are frequently to be heard amongst the aborigines of South Africa. As a matter of course the harmonies that have been added are the result of a more advanced musical education, and they are so skillful that they in no way overshadow or obscure the peculiarities of the original tunes."[16] According to this perspective, Afro-diasporic music was the result of "natural," uncultivated abilities rather than "proper" Western musical training. For this reviewer, McAdoo's troupe was successful because they were trained in Western music and were able to perform the songs in an organized and "proper" way. A similar review claimed: "These singers must be heard in order to get an adequate idea of what high artistic and finely cultivated taste can do with the palliative old plantation melodies."[17] Another commentary suggested:

> The words in themselves are of a less moment. They are repetitions of an ecstatic phrase of consolation that crooned or sung or shouted was a world of comfort, but when uttered with the natural musical instinct of the negro voice takes an artistic side which it is the work of the Jubilee singers to present to the public. And this they do with remarkable skill. Themselves . . . trained in pure music, they retain all the characteristics of the melodies, but deliver them with the perfection which does justice to the original by adding the superior qualities of cultured execution.[18]

For these reviewers, McAdoo's troupe was proof of the educational benefits of the Western "civilizing" mission. Training in Western music had allowed McAdoo's troupe to cultivate their "primitive" music into a more "sophisticated," more "organized," and ultimately "superior" format. Such statements demonstrate how McAdoo's version of uplift politics often did little to disturb the cultural racism of the period.

McAdoo's presentation of self was also a racial uplift project. McAdoo cultivated and projected a Victorian-style upper-class image of himself. According to a profile of McAdoo from the Hampton Institute's *Freeman Journal:* "He is prosperous, and an Australian by adoption. He was a classmate of Booker T. Washington. In his accent he is decidedly English. He dresses well in the style of the English upper class. . . . He wears a few diamonds within the bounds of propriety. . . . From all indications he is a thorough gentleman from tip to tip."[19] His use of a British accent, upper-class wardrobe, and ornamentation all contributed to the cultivation of a sophisticated, elite, Westernized persona.

McAdoo also advanced his uplift politics during moments of public speaking. Whether in the medium of newspaper print or a public lecture, his acts of public speaking were intended to demonstrate that he and the members of his troupe were refined, upper-class, civilized professionals. In one interview for a local newspaper, McAdoo claimed his musical product was the result of a large amount of disciplined practice:

> Referring to the performances of his Company, he remarked that they must practice constantly to enable them to keep up the pitch they have attained. He replied, "Yes. We rehearse on every opportunity. We have had two hours hard practice this morning." "Do you occasionally add to your present extensive and varied repertoire?" "Oh yes! And we vary our own special pieces with compositions of the popular masters. For instance, we are now working up the prison scene in *Il Trovatore.* The part of *Maurico* written for Mario, the great Italian Tenor, will be sung by Miss Mattie Allen, and as the singer is not visible, the audience may well imagine that it is a man singing." "She has a wonderful voice." "Yes! It excited great interest wherever we perform." . . . "When will you sing the prison scene in public?" "Not before I am satisfied with it. We shall practice a great deal yet."[20]

In this interview, McAdoo presented himself and his troupe members as hardworking professionals with very high standards who "practice" and "rehearse" often in order to perfect their craft. Furthermore, McAdoo mentioned the Italian opera *Il Trovatore* with the intention of demonstrating his knowledge of "highbrow culture." McAdoo cultivated an image of industrious, cultured, and articulate professionals.

McAdoo often used the intermissions of his jubilee concerts as opportunities to talk about the history of his troupe, the Hampton Institute, and the history of the Civil War and Reconstruction.[21] In doing so, McAdoo continued the original Fisk Jubilee Singers' tradition of mixing song with public speaking.[22] McAdoo also used the lecture format to address moments of discrimination he and his troupe experienced. During an intermission of a performance in Durban in November 1890, McAdoo talked about the ironies of having performed for "crowned heads and leading men of England and the Continent" and still finding it difficult to secure a hotel accommodation in Durban:

> In Durban [the troupe] had . . . unpleasant experiences. The agent came to Durban more than a week in advance, and arranged for their reception at the Clarendon Hotel, where after they had been shown to their rooms, the proprietors appeared to think she had made a mistake, and told them they could not stay, as they were blacker than she expected, and exception had been taken to their presence by, amongst other boarders, an American, who was, said Mr. McAdoo, evidently well out of his own country. For two hours, on a wet evening he [Mr. McAdoo] walked about Durban, trying to find a place to receive his people, and at last was accommodated at the Belgrave hotel. He spoke very warmly of the feeling thus shown to people of a different colour, though their souls might be white. He was, however, greatly pleased with the reception accorded him and his friends by a Durban audience, and hoped to be able to satisfy them each evening.[23]

Sometimes the racialized commodity speaks back.[24] This act of describing an example of discrimination, purposefully located during the intermission of a well-received show, was an attempt to tell Durban audiences that their right to hear this imported music was contingent on the ways in which they treated the troupe. In this speech, McAdoo was claiming the right to have equal treatment based on the fact that he was exchanging a rare cultural commodity in South Africa. In a way, McAdoo was educating the audience about the proper way to treat visiting coloured artists. That night, McAdoo's racial uplift politics depended heavily on his ability to demonstrate his control over European language. The *Natal Mercury* observed that "Mr. McAdoo spoke in excellent English."[25] By demonstrating mastery over the English language, McAdoo was subtly claiming he had assimilated into European culture and was deserving of equal treatment. His oratorical interludes contrasted starkly with the caricatures of black politicians rendered by white performers in blackface in the many minstrel stump speeches performed in South Africa during the previous three decades.

During other examples of public speaking, McAdoo disciplined rude members of the audience. One newspaper article commenting on a show in Cape Town stated that "Mr. McAdoo, the Manager, had to rebuke the rowdy element [in the balcony], and that element finding the audience had no sympathy with it was contented to behave itself more agreeably."[26] At the end of another show, "he again spoke, saying that the gallery audience in Durban was the quietest they had ever seen in any part of their travels, a plume in the cape of the 'gods' they were not slow to acknowledge."[27] McAdoo claimed a position of authority in which he could comment on the theater decorum of white audience members. I suspect that McAdoo was able to make such comments largely because much of the audience categorized him as "coloured" rather than "negro." The audience understood him as coloured because he identified as such, and this was a strategic act of self-classification that I believe to be an example of spectacular opacity.

Daphne Brooks coined the term *spectacular opacity* to describe the antiessentialist performative acts of black Atlantic pioneers who could not be easily placed in racial categories. She defines it as "the opaque performances of marginalized cultural figures" that "confound and disrupt conventional constructions of the racialized and gendered body."[28] The spectacular opacity of the Virginia Jubilee Singers becomes especially clear when we examine the strategy of racial classification deployed by McAdoo in English South African newspapers.

In one of the first advertisements McAdoo published in Cape Town, he described the Virginia Jubilee Singers as "Ten Coloured Vocalists from U.S., America."[29] McAdoo was not using the term *coloured* in the way it was generally used in the Anglophone world at that time, a generic term for describing all people of African descent. Instead, McAdoo advanced a South African definition of *coloured:* a biologically mixed racial group positioned between white and indigenous African on the South African racial hierarchy. Evidence attesting to McAdoo's understanding of the South African meaning of *coloured* can be found one month into his first tour, when he placed an advertisement in the *Daily Independent,* announcing "a concert for Natives and Coloured People."[30] McAdoo understood the stigma of native African status and understood that the relatively light skin color of some of the members of his troupe could be used to his advantage. McAdoo was not trying to pass as coloured South African. He was presenting himself as a coloured American and hoping the colonists would view him as mixed race.

McAdoo knew that the three-tiered racial classification system of South Africa differed from the two-tiered system in the United States. In South Africa, the "one-drop" rule of the United States did not apply, and there was a somewhat ambiguously defined middle group. Perhaps for the first time in his life, McAdoo was presented a choice between two different racial classifications. To use a contemporary analogy, he had a pencil and two boxes in front of him. One box was marked "negro" and the other "coloured." He checked the box marked "coloured" because he wanted to gain access to the social and cultural capital of that racial designation, and he felt confident that he and other members of his troupe could play the role convincingly. As coloured people, McAdoo and his troupe members could claim to have a certain amount of white ancestry. McAdoo believed that white settlers would take his music more seriously if they thought his performers were mixed-race professionals. In this way, McAdoo advanced an original form of racial uplift by stepping outside the social position of "negro" in order to make claims for rights. McAdoo's "spectacular opacity" was both antiessentialist and essentialist, as he demonstrated that racial borders could be transgressed while simultaneously using the logic of racial hierarchy to gain access to cultural and social capital that gave him certain advantages.

The available archival evidence suggests McAdoo succeeded in his spectacularly opaque movement between racial categories. Most local newspapers did not question McAdoo's claims of being a coloured American. The *Daily Independent,* one of Kimberley's leading newspapers, provided one example: "Considerable curiosity is evinced amongst the community generally to hear these Coloured artists. . . . [H]ere are half a score of Coloured young men and women going through a programme."[31] Another article paraphrased a McAdoo speech: "Mr. McAdoo gave the audience particulars of his concert company, and explained that although not posing entirely as philanthropists, a certain amount of the money earned by his company was devoted to the foundation of scholarships and for the education of the Coloured race at Hampton Va."[32] According to another account, "It was a novelty to see Coloured people singing at the theatre."[33] A majority of British settler theater reviewers accepted McAdoo's claims of being coloured.[34]

The relatively light skin color of McAdoo and some members of the troupe made the racial hybridity narrative more believable and attracted the attention of some local commentators. One newspaper article was especially interested in a troupe member named Mattie E. Allen, "whose complexion is so much farer [*sic*] than the rest that she would almost pass for an English girl."[35] Troupe members who could be visibly labeled as mixed race provided further legitimacy to McAdoo's claims of coloured identity. Mattie Allen's mixed-race appearance helped British settlers accept McAdoo's racial identity narrative (fig. 7).

McAdoo was not able to create full consensus, however. A few writers voiced skepticism of McAdoo's claims of coloured identity. According to a newspaper from Pretoria, "The artists engaged are all *more or less coloured people from the United States.*"[36] Years later, a Johannesburg newspaper advanced the same wording: "Nearly all the performers are Americans, and *more or less coloured,* so their portrayals are genuine representations of plantation life."[37] Other reviews went a step further by not even acknowledging McAdoo's claims of coloured identity and using the term *negro* to describe the troupe. For example, one article described a song "in which the wild free music in the negro nature is admirably shadowed forth."[38] Another article called the troupe "a little band of freed negroes."[39] Reviewers who used the term *negro* to classify the troupe or labeled the troupe as "more or less coloured" were relatively rare. The vast majority of available newspaper articles accepted McAdoo's racial identity narrative. By claiming coloured identity, McAdoo's troupe made claims for rights that were not available to native Africans.

Racially discriminatory laws and practices in the South African colonies made the strategy of classifying the troupe coloured American a very logical maneuver. By the 1890s, pass systems had been established in Natal, Kimberley, Cape Town, and the Transvaal Republic. If local authorities believed

Figure 7. Cabinet card photograph of Mattie Allen and Orpheus M. McAdoo, circa 1895. Courtesy of Orpheus M. McAdoo and Mattie Allen McAdoo Papers, Yale Collection of American Literature, Beinecke Rare Book and Manuscript Library, Yale University (JWJ MSS 60, box 1, folder 3).

McAdoo and his troupe members were native Africans, their individual freedoms could be severely limited. Knowing this, McAdoo made advanced preparations for his trip to the Transvaal Republic by having the American consul in Cape Town write a letter to President Paul Kruger: "To the bearer of this letter, Mr. McAdoo, who is a Director of a Singing Association, together with 10 members, both male and female, are natives of Virginia in the United States of North America. . . . They have asked for my cooperation in asking Your Highness for an uninterrupted pass to be free to go to their homes safely, after the time fixed for the natives. . . . Request for an uninterrupted pass for a specific period for the singing group McAdoo (coloured people from America)."[40] The usage of the phrase "coloured people from America" suggests an understanding of the stigma of native African status and a hope that mixed-race American citizens could secure better treatment. Years later, McAdoo commented on his experiences in the Transvaal and an "incident" of discrimination in a newspaper interview:

> Before crossing the borders into the territories belonging to the South African Republic, Mr. McAdoo . . . says he was very careful to find out whether he and his fellow singers would be obliged to be indoors before nine o'clock in the evening, and whether they would be forbidden to use the sidewalks, and generally whether they would be treated as Kafirs [*sic*]. Fortunately, with the assistance of the American Consul in Cape Town (for the singers are all American citizens), they were not only promised all the ordinary privileges of white people, but a welcome into the bargain. "This," says Mr. McAdoo, "we have received everywhere without exception." . . . "The only unpleasant incident of any consequence which I have yet experienced occurred at Middleburg," continued Mr. McAdoo, "when we stayed at the Transvaal Hotel. I was told that a complaint had been made to the Landdrost that coloured people were staying at the same hotel as white persons and so I had to go and see the Landdrost. I explained to him how we stood, and showed him our credentials, and he said he was very sorry and expressed himself satisfied that we were within our rights.[41]

These attempts to distance the troupe from "Kaffirs" must be thought of as a response to the violent and debilitating modes of social control that had developed in South Africa. McAdoo's letters to the Hampton Institute described an exclusionary racial order in the British and Afrikaner colonies:

> [We] opened in Cape town on June 30th, to the most fashionable audience. Every one seemed captivated with the singing; never heard such singing in all their lives, they said, and "just to think that black people should do it." The latter remarks will give you some idea of a feeling of prejudice; well, so it is. There is no country in the world where prejudice is so strong as here in Africa. The native to-day is treated as badly as ever the slave was treated in Georgia. Here in Africa the native laws are most unjust; such as any Christian people would be ashamed of. Do you credit a law in a civilized community compelling every man with a dark skin, even though he is a citizen of another country, to be in the house by 9 o'clock at night, or he is arrested? Before I could go into parts of Africa, I had to get out a passport and a special letter from the Governors and Presidents of the Transvaal and Orange Free State or we would have all been arrested. Black people who are seen out after 9 o'clock must have

> passes from their master. Indeed, it is so strict that natives have to get passes for day travel. In places we have visited I have often hear the City Hall Bell ring promptly at 9, warning every black person to be inside. I met a few colored men, Americans living here. One opened a business in Johannisburg [*sic*] and before he could open he had to get a white man to allow him to use his name, because no Negro is allowed to have his own business. These laws exists in the Transvaal and [the] Orange Free States, which are governed by the Dutch, who place every living creature before the native. I have so much good and bad to tell you about Africa.[42]

In March 1898, a member of McAdoo's troupe learned about the discriminatory practices of Natal from the inside of a jail cell. Dick Collins was at the Inchanga Railway when a policeman classified him as a native breaking curfew and promptly arrested him. Here is the most detailed description of the incident:

> What appears to be an unpardonable piece of blundering on the part of a member of the Natal Police was perpetrated at Inchanga on Tuesday by the arrest, as a native, of Mr. Dick Collins, of the McAdoo Minstrels. . . . It does not appear quite clear whether or not he was drinking, but as he was standing in the bar he was approached by a member of the Natal Police (Trooper L'Estrange), attired in plain clothes who addressed him in Kafir. Feeling annoyed no doubt, at being mistaken for a native, and at being addressed in the native language, Mr. Collins reply is stated to have been not exactly a polite one. At the same time, however, he gave the policeman to understand, in English, that he had no knowledge of the language in which he was addressed, and that he was an American citizen. The policeman appears to have refused to accept the explanation, and arrested Collins on the spot. The latter was detained in the lock-up for several hours, and was then liberated on bail of L5. On Collin's [*sic*] behalf the American Consul in Durban was immediately communicated with, and as the result of the intervention of the gentleman the Attorney-general, recognizing that a serious mistake had been made, immediately quashed all the proceedings.[43]

McAdoo's claims of coloured American identity may have been a strategic response to an extremely oppressive racial order. There were real practical reasons why McAdoo chose to distance himself from the label "negro" and, by extension, "native African." Tellingly, although McAdoo distanced himself from Africans while navigating colonial cities, he found ways to connect with Africans in other settings.

McAdoo used different strategies when presenting to different publics. In his advertisements in the English-language press and during his performances for majority white audiences McAdoo claimed a mixed-race American identity and distanced himself from native Africans. But during moments when he was beyond the white gaze, McAdoo and his troupe members reached out to black South Africans in significant ways. One example can be found in a letter to the Hampton Institute written by Eugene McAdoo, Orpheus's brother and a member of the troupe. According to the letter, the troupe left Grahamstown in November 1893 and traveled for three days to visit the Lovedale Institute, a school for Africans that Eugene admiringly dubbed "the African Hampton." The highlight of the visit came when McAdoo's troupe exchanged songs with the Lovedale students: "We sang for them for nearly a couple of hours, and then they favored us with some of their songs, which we thoroughly enjoyed, for their voices were indeed good."[44] By organizing this event, McAdoo facilitated an Afro-diasporic cultural exchange.

Many black Africans and coloureds embraced McAdoo's cultural project. In the early 1890s, two "African Choir[s]" composed of native black South African ensembles modeled after the Virginia Jubilee Singers toured England, Canada, and the East Coast of the United States.[45] The African activist and journalist Sol Plaatje saw the Virginia Jubilee Singers perform on two occasions in Kimberley in 1895. A year later, Plaatje delivered a baritone solo during a "Grand Vocal Concert" in Kimberley. The event included many renditions of concert spirituals and, according to Plaatje biographer Brian Willan, was an example of McAdoo's cultural influence in Kimberley.[46] Similarly, Heather Hughes's biography of John Dube (the founding president of the African National Congress [ANC]) suggests Dube was inspired by McAdoo's 1895 visit to Pietermaritzburg. Dube was likely influenced by McAdoo when he contributed lyrics to *Amagama abantu*, the first printed collection of nontraditional secular Zulu songs.[47] One song, called "Amaqabuqabu" (Innovations), urged Africans to "abandon your old ways" because "progress has arrived" and voiced an uplift politics assimilationist mentality. Nearly a century later, during the 1980s, a veteran *isicathamiya* (Zulu choir–singing) singer named Thembinkosi Phewa mentioned McAdoo's troupe as a major cultural influence: "Our oldest brothers, the first to sing isicathamiya, were the Jubilee Brothers. That was in 1891."[48] More recently, in Cape Town in 2015, coloured playwright David Kramer staged a musical about McAdoo titled *Orpheus in Africa.*

McAdoo was also interested in facilitating an educational exchange with black South Africans. In 1891 McAdoo sent a group of letters to the *Southern Workman,* the journal of the Hampton Institute. The letters were written by Africans who had spoken with McAdoo about Hampton. They described a lack of educational opportunities in South Africa and expressed hopes of attending Hampton. They also asked for the creation of a scholarship that would help pay the transportation fees of Africans who could not afford the trip across the Atlantic. The editors of the *Southern Workman* responded positively: "It might be a good thing to help some over for the sake not only of themselves but to show the unbelieving Dutch boers and other colonists what American practical education can do for the natives to-day as in the past."[49] The same issue of *Southern Workman* included an announcement of McAdoo's seventy-dollar scholarship fund for an African named Titus Mbongwe to attend Hampton and a statement from McAdoo claiming:

> [In South Africa there] is no sympathy between the whites and blacks. There is as much prejudice here regarding the natives as there is in Georgia. They don't believe in the blacks being educated. I informed you of my hope to send a native to Hampton to be educated. It was taken up here in the press, and I received a call from a committee, asking me if I were singing to educate Negroes, or was it my own enterprise. One said, (he was a minister:) "If it is to educate the Kafirs and Zulus, you will never succeed in Africa." I told them it was my own enterprise and when once I got the money, like, any else, I could do what I liked with it.[50]

While on route to Hampton, Titus Mbongwe died in a tragic train wreck in England. However, McAdoo had sparked a fire, and in the following years about a dozen black South Africans received formal education at Hampton.[51] McAdoo's approach to philanthropy was a clear departure from those of the white minstrel troupes who toured South Africa in previous decades. The white minstrels were more interested in donating to the "Lancashire" and "Native war sufferers relief" funds than helping indigenous Africans.

African press outlets responded enthusiastically to McAdoo's uplift politics project. Josiah Semouse, a black African clerk who worked in Kimberley's post office, responded to the Virginia Jubilee Singers with a kind of nascent black nationalism: "Hear! Today [African Americans] have their own schools, primary, secondary and high schools, and also universities. They are run by them without the help of the whites. They have magistrates, judges, lawyers, bishops, ministers and evangelists, and school masters. Some have learned a craft such as building etc. When will the day come when the African people will be like the Americans? When will they stop being slaves and become nations with their own government?"[52] Semouse was clearly impressed by the Fisk and Hampton models of education and hoped similar institutions would be created by black South Africans. John Tengo Jabavu, editor of the African newspaper *Imvo Zabantsundu,* also saw McAdoo's Jubilee Zingers as a model for emulation: "It would strongly savour of presumption for a native African of this part to venture a critique on his brethren from America, who are now visiting this quarter of their fatherland, and whose position socially, is being deservedly pointed at on all hands as one that Natives here should strive to attain." Moreover, Jabavu believed that McAdoo's success directly refuted stereotypes about Africans: "Already [McAdoo's troupe] has suggested reflection to many who, without such a demonstration, would have remained skeptical as to the possibility, not to say probability, of the Natives of this country being raised to anything above remaining as perpetual hewers of wood and drawers of water."[53]

Years later, in 1897, *Imvo-Zabantsundu* described McAdoo's minstrel ensemble as "our countrymen."[54] McAdoo's troupes presented a model of black modernity that was embraced by local Africans. They did so while walking a trapeze tightrope between coloured American and negro American. By using the term *coloured,* McAdoo claimed a mixed-race identity in an attempt to increase the chances that his troupe would be viewed as "refined," "civilized," professional artists. South Africa, because of its three-tiered classification system, was the only stop on McAdoo's tour where such a strategy could be deployed. In 1898, when McAdoo's High Class Coloured American Minstrel Vaudeville Company left South Africa for Australia, they changed their name to McAdoo's Georgia Minstrels and Alabama Cake Walkers.[55] McAdoo's decision to remove the word *Coloured* from the troupe's name was probably a response to the different racial classification system in Australia. In Australia there was no middle category in between white and aborigine that was comparable to the coloured classification in South Africa. Instead, *coloured* was used as a generic term for describing nonwhite people. McAdoo had little to gain by identifying as coloured in Australia. South Africa was the only country on McAdoo's tour where including the term in his troupe's name could benefit him. For McAdoo, identifying as coloured was a strategic, calculated decision, intended to influence the ways in which his troupe was received.

MINSTRELSY AND UPLIFT POLITICS

> What is this obsession with minstrelsy. Why would you have me paint a black mask on a face that is already black?
>
> —Orpheus McAdoo as represented in David Kramer's *Orpheus in Africa*

While touring South Africa in the early 1890s, the repertoire of the Virginia Jubilee Singers consisted mostly of concert spirituals, with few songs of minstrel origins. Tellingly, even though the material of the first tour was very different from that of a traditional minstrel show, the press still read minstrelsy into the performances. For example, one reviewer stated, "To a certain extent the performance is of the form of the Christy Minstrel entertainments, but are devoid of the vulgarities and forced humour of that class." The reviewer went so far as to describe the troupe as "Christianized Christies."[56] Although the Virginia Jubilee Singers tried to present black music in ways that diverged from the conventions of blackface minstrelsy, some white settlers continued to interpret their shows through the prism of minstrelsy.

The original Fisk Jubilee Singers also encountered moments of misclassification when they first toured in the 1870s. American and British audiences often believed they were a traveling minstrel troupe. African Americans who toured the Atlantic world in the late nineteenth century were retracing performance circuits that were thoroughly saturated with minstrel imagery. Minstrel frameworks were easily read into their performances by audiences whose schema for interpreting black culture was constrained by minstrel monocles. The Fisk Jubilee Singers established techniques for presenting African American music that were "in explicit opposition to minstrelsy" by creating "an aura of seriousness around their activities."[57] They called their shows "services of songs" instead of "concerts." They sang in "standard English" because the use of "negro dialect" might encourage comparisons to minstrelsy. They also stood still while singing onstage and did not dance.[58] Indeed, the name "Jubilee Singers" was purposefully chosen to distinguish the Fisk troupe from blackface minstrels.[59] Years later, as mentioned above, the uplift politics of McAdoo's Virginia Jubilee Singers drew heavily from the Fisk model. For these reasons, McAdoo's decision to head back to the United States halfway through the second tour and put together a minstrel troupe seems on the surface level to be a significant departure from his earlier modus operandi.

Veit Erlmann offers a useful explanation for why McAdoo made this change to minstrelsy, stating, "Until February 1897 the program remained unchanged, but a saturated market must have induced McAdoo to give the jubilee hymns 'a well-earned repose.'"[60] It is also important to consider blackface minstrelsy's widespread popularity in the British colonies of South Africa at the time. During McAdoo's travels his troupe undoubtedly would have learned about the professional minstrel troupes who successfully toured South Africa during the previous decades. McAdoo read the reviews of his shows and knew that the label "Christianized Christies" did not appear out of thin air. A sensitive manager with a knack for gauging the local scene, McAdoo would certainly have noticed a public demand for minstrelsy in the South African colonies that could be tapped into. In doing so, McAdoo faced the same dilemmas that many Afro-diasporic performers were forced to engage during the nineteenth and early twentieth centuries: how to make a living in an entertainment market so saturated with minstrel aesthetics that blackface antics were the safest and easiest route to a steady paycheck. How could one establish and maintain one's humanity while traversing a burnt cork economy so dedicated to the denial of black humanity? If McAdoo was going to present minstrelsy, it had to be on his own terms. He would continue the uplift politics project even as he transitioned from jubilee singing to minstrelsy. McAdoo found ways to transform minstrelsy into a vehicle for expressing uplift politics. This was an abrupt departure from the burnt cork nationalism of traditional minstrel shows.

When McAdoo returned to South Africa with a minstrel show in June 1897, his spectacular opacity reached a new level of complexity. He continued to self-identify in advertisements as mixed-race American, claiming his troupe was composed of "High Class Coloured American" performers.

However, unlike in previous tours, he began using the term *negro* in his advertisements to refer to some sections of his program. He renamed the cakewalk the "Negro Minuet."[61] He began using the phrase "Negro Sketch Artistes" to describe his comedic performers.[62] He added a new "Negro Sketch" called "Trilby's Wedding; or, Life on the Mississippi."[63] Finally, McAdoo began using the phrase "twenty ebony eminent entertainers" in many of his newspaper advertisements.[64] The term *ebony* was chosen partly for alliteration, but also for its racial connotations. Because the word *ebony* describes an intensely dark shade of blackness, British settlers likely associated it with black African identity instead of mixed-race coloureds. All of this suggests McAdoo continued to label the troupe coloured while also including insinuations of "negro" identity when he switched from jubilee singing to minstrelsy.

These developments suggest two possible strategies of representation. First, McAdoo was trying to present a racial narrative in which the mixed-race members of his troupe impersonated "pure negroes" during specific sections of the program. Conversely, and perhaps more likely, McAdoo labeled some members of his troupe as "negro" and others as "coloured" in order to access the social capital that each category allotted. By claiming coloured identity for some members of the ensemble, McAdoo could continue to present an image of his troupe as "civilized" and "refined." Meanwhile, by describing other troupe members as "negroes," McAdoo may have been trying to bolster the racial "authenticity" of the company's minstrel portrayals. McAdoo understood that "negro" identity carried special value when trafficking in the minstrel genre.

The strategy of using the concept of racial "authenticity" to increase interest in black minstrelsy was nothing new. According to Robert Toll, early black minstrels who were performing during the American Civil War knew "their principal appeal was their authenticity as black men." One group, for example, toured New York and Massachusetts and billed themselves as "SEVEN SLAVES just from Alabama, who are EARNING THEIR FREEDOM by giving concerts under the guidance of their Northern friends."[65] Black vaudeville stars Bert Williams and George Walker offered a more contemporaneous example. They performed in blackface and billed themselves as "Two Real Coons" around the turn of the century. In an article for *Theatre Magazine*, George Walker described the appeal of black minstrelsy: "Bert and I watched the white 'coons,' and were often much amused at seeing white men with black cork on their faces trying to imitate black folks. Nothing about these men's actions was natural, and therefore nothing was as interesting as if black performers had been dancing and singing their own songs in their own way."[66] McAdoo's contemporaries believed that audiences were interested in "authentic" blackness. Perhaps, McAdoo's frequent uses of the word *negro* were calculated attempts to use the logic of racial "authenticity" to fill theater seats.

If McAdoo consciously used authenticity to increase interest in his troupe, the available evidence suggests his strategy succeeded. During the 1897 tour, South African newspapers praised the authenticity of McAdoo's Minstrels. The *Transvaal Advertiser* stated: "The choruses were entered into with that happy abandon which only the American negro is capable of."[67] The *Standard News* of Johannesburg argued that McAdoo's troupe was more authentic than white minstrel performers: "There is a peculiar charm about the manner in which the Americans render their choruses, a charm which has been frequently remarked, and upon which several more or less successful attempts at imitation have been based; but it may safely be said that these lineal descendants of the originators of the old slave melodies and negro songs are still unexcelled by any of those who bestow on them 'the sincerest form of flattery.'"[68] Another article linked authenticity with nationality by claiming the realism of McAdoo's troupe was tied to their American origins: "The Vaudeville class of entertainment is a distinctly American form of amusement, and, needless to say, Mr. McAdoo's talented company can display all the artistic effects in *true native* style."[69] One article commented on the "unique realism" of the company.[70] Another appropriated minstrel speech: "The eccentricities of the real 'cullurd brudder' of the United States are portrayed to the life, because it is the real 'cullurd brudder' who performs."[71] According to another reviewer: "Nearly all the performers are Americans, and more or less coloured, so their portrayals are *genuine representations of plantation life.*"[72] Finally, one article compared the portrayals of the "coloured artists" in McAdoo's troupe to native Africans: "In addition to his original company, Mr. McAdoo added a very strong male quartette of Coloured artists of most versatile talent . . . [T]he first part of the programme is of the well-known Christy Minstrel type, but there is the addition of novelty and character that stamps the performance with a uniqueness and interest all its own, and through it all one recognizes that mode of mirth and actions that is peculiar to the African native; a proof of the influence of heredity rising to generations of separation and new environment."[73] The author's belief that a "mode of mirth" could be passed between generations of Africans to finally settle in McAdoo's troupe members was clearly grounded in notions of racial essentialism. Such interpretations were partly possible because of rare moments when McAdoo's Minstrels reproduced the essentializing proslavery logics of minstrelsy.

In January 1898, McAdoo sang "Massa's in the Cold Ground" and added one more voice to a long parade of performers who presented songs about "benevolent" slave masters on South African minstrel stages. A correspondent for the *Cape Times* believed it was "finely rendered" and did not suggest the song was interpreted ironically.[74] A few days later, one of the troupe members performed a rendition of "I'se Gwine Back to Dixie," another song that was thoroughly saturated with sentimental nostalgia for the southern plantation:

I'se gwine back to Dixie,
No more I'se gwine to wander,
My heart's turned back to Dixie,
I can't stay here no longer,
I miss de ole plantation,
My home and my relation,
My heart's turned back to Dixie,
And I must go.

Chorus

I'se gwine back to Dixie,
I'se gwine back to Dixie,
I'se gwine where de orange blossoms grow,
For I hear the children calling,
I see their sad tears falling,
My heart's turned back to Dixie,
And I must go.

Verse two

I've hoed in fields of cotton,
I've worked upon the river,
I used to think if I got off,

I'd go back there, no, never.
But time has changed the old man,
His head is bending low,
His heart's turned back to Dixie,
And he must go.[75]

As these examples suggest, black performers who tried to reinterpret the minstrel show in progressive ways were working with a restrictive repertoire filled with proslavery songs. Such moments, when McAdoo's troupe fell back on proslavery minstrel show conventions, were far from the norm. The most complex theatrical offering presented by McAdoo's Minstrels was titled *Good Old Georgia in '49*. This title conveyed a great deal of sarcasm because this play did not nostalgically celebrate southern plantations like traditional minstrel shows. *Good Old Georgia in '49* was advertised as a "great pathetic plantation drama" and "the sequel to Uncle Tom's Cabin."[76] The following is one of the longest and most informative reviews of the piece:

> The story runs to the effect: Eph. Jackson, an old negro slave, ran away from bondage seventeen years ago, and went to the North to try and earn enough money to buy the freedom of his wife and children. Not having succeeded, and feeling that his days were numbered, he starts back to his old Southern home. The scene opens with Eph on the road, having walked nineteen miles from the station. He has four more miles to walk, but being tired and weary, he lies down by the roadside to rest, and there falls asleep. He is discovered by his two sons and carried to his old home, where, after conciliation with his young master, he passes away to his everlasting rest. The piece was excellently played and staged, and is full of alternating pathos and humour. The scene where poor old Eph., after being thrashed by his masters, takes a pathetic farewell of the slaves, was extremely affecting. . . . As old Eph. Jackson Mr. W. Smith played with great power, and acted the poor broken down slave in a manner which left little to be desired.[77]

Good Old Georgia in '49 was not a traditional blackface minstrel farce. Eph's escape to freedom and attempts to buy the freedom of his family cut directly against the happy-worker minstrel trope. Additionally, the "benevolent" master construct was flipped upside down by the portrayal of a violent beating Higgins gave to Eph. This one-act play offers a serious representation of the violence that enslaved black people had to endure. In doing so, it provided a somber reflection on the violence of slavery that diverged significantly from minstrel sadism humor. Furthermore, *Good Old Georgia in '49* offered an alternative to the failed-facade humor of minstrel shows from previous eras.

The previously quoted review goes on to describe each individual performance. The following statement is particularly noteworthy: "Colonial Higgins was represented by Luis Love in the most approved melodrama way."[78] Colonial Higgins and Mrs. Higgins were white characters who were portrayed by Louis Love and Mattie Allen. Years before, as quoted earlier, the *Natal Mercury* described Allen as having a "complexion . . . so much farer [*sic*] than the rest that she would almost pass for an English girl," and in a way she was passing for a white women in *Good Old Georgia in '49*.[79] The members of McAdoo's troupe were even able to impersonate white people. *Good Old Georgia in '49* was performed in every city that McAdoo's Minstrels visited, and newspaper reviews in each city commented on the great performances of the members of the troupe who played the black characters. Interestingly enough, the above description of Luis Love's performance comes from the only newspaper article that ventured a comment on the quality of the actors who played the white characters. The notion of non-white people playing white people may have been perplexing and difficult for British settler reviewers to describe. If we contextualize Louis Love's and Mattie Allen's representations of whiteness as coming at the tail end of thirty years of minstrel shows in South Africa in which failed-facade humor was a major theme, we can arrive at a possible explanation for why most British settler newspapers did not mention their impersonations. McAdoo's Minstrels imagined a more permeable color line that could be moved across in multiple directions, as black actors had the agency to portray white people and not be exposed as fake. In other words, the impersonations in *Good Old Georgia in '49* were so unconventional, they were indescribable. Other unconventional moments abound when McAdoo's Minstrels advanced an uplift politics agenda.

Racial uplift projects were class-based interventions in racial thinking that offered images of "refined" and prosperous African Americans who could comfortably blend into the upper stratums of society. McAdoo continued this line of reasoning when he described his new troupe as "High

Class . . . Refined . . . Minstrel . . . Company."[80] Other terms such as *clean, wholesome,* and *artistic* were often also used in his advertisements. By employing such language, McAdoo was trying to distance his troupe from the lowbrow reputation of minstrelsy. One newspaper reported that "the printed programme contains the following unusual announcement: 'Mr. McAdoo will feel obliged to any person who will point out any item in the programme which they may consider objectionable.'" The writer went on to say, "After the unqualified success which attended Saturday's performance Mr. McAdoo . . . would do well to omit this remark, because even the most fastidious could not find the least objectionable feature in such an excellent representation."[81] Another article expressed confidence in McAdoo's ability to stage a "tasteful" minstrel show: "Mr McAdoo having personally selected the different performers, is a sufficient guarantee that the performances given will be of a high-class order."[82]

Turn-of-the-century black performers often tried to distance themselves from the stereotypes they played by cultivating images of professionalism. Karen Sotiropoulos relates: "[Bert Williams and George Walker] played 'darkey' roles, but they made clear they were not that which they performed; instead they presented themselves as salaried actors benefiting from the new leisure culture—in short, as skilled professionals."[83] The available archival material suggests McAdoo's troupe used a similar strategy while performing minstrelsy in South Africa, by printing advertisements emphasizing artistry in local newspapers. In turn, the British settler press often described the troupe as artists. Here are some examples: "Highly artistic entertainment"; "Every one of the Company is an artist"; "The company consists of the best coloured artists obtainable in America"; "Each member of [the company] is an artist in the truest sense of the word"; "McAdoo's company of coloured artistes"; "Mr. McAdoo's artistic company"; and "real artistes."[84] Another review called the troupe "the finest combination of coloured professionals that ever left the shores of America."[85] McAdoo presented his minstrels as examples of black professionalism.

An opera singer named Susan B. Anderson (sometimes listed in South African newspapers as "Susie") was one of the more revealing additions to McAdoo's troupe. Concert programs and the local press described her as the "Black Melba," a direct reference to an internationally renowned white Australian opera singer known as Nellie Melba.[86] Anderson expanded the musical repertoire of the company and helped McAdoo maintain the appearance of respectability he so enthusiastically coveted. In January 1898, McAdoo ran an advertisement in the *Cape Times* announcing a variant of the three-part minstrel format that blended high- and lowbrow culture. The first part was a presentation of "American minstrels," the second was a "grand olio," and the third consisted of "thirty minutes of Grand Opera. Scenes and Choruses from 'Bohemian Girl.'"[87] The British settler press was quick to praise the opera portion of the program, stating that Susan Anderson, Mattie Allen, and Jeannie Robinson were "able and versatile artistes," deserving of "a very high [ranking] as operatic singers."[88] Another reviewer claimed Susan Anderson's thirty minutes of grand opera "proved that art knows no colour."[89]

The cakewalk gave McAdoo another opportunity to package his material as high art. Several newspaper reviews mentioned the cakewalk as the high point of the performance:

> The long programme concluded with "The Grand Cake Walk, or *the Negro Minuet,*" which created the greatest amount of interest. The performance was unique and Saturday's performance was said to have been the first out of America. The members of the company advanced in pairs towards a large cake, which was placed on the platform, and the responsibility of awarding the cake to the most graceful couple was thrown upon the audience. After a good deal of competition the cake was awarded to Miss Shirley and Mr. Willard Smith. Mrs. McAdoo and Mr. Love being a close second.[90]

McAdoo's description of the cakewalk as a racialized minuet was an attempt to challenge a system of thinking that linked race to class. The minuet carried upper-class significations as a former court dance of the French monarchy and popular ballroom dance for European elites. In advertisements McAdoo described the cakewalk as a "graceful and artistic American novelty." McAdoo chose to not present the cakewalk as a folk dance that enslaved Africans performed in slave quarters. Instead, he positioned it as "highbrow" art: a black version of an aristocratic European dance.[91]

Just as important as the repertoire of McAdoo's Minstrels are the traditional parts of minstrel shows that were purposefully left out. In anticipation for the first performance of McAdoo's Minstrels in South Africa, the *Cape Argus* predicted that stump speeches would be included in the program.[92] However, the available archival material suggests McAdoo's

Minstrels did not perform stump speeches. The inaccurate prediction on the part of the *Cape Argus* is understandable, given that stump speeches were a standard part of most minstrel shows. Why did McAdoo exclude a proven part of the minstrel formula? The answer lies in the object of ridicule of most stump speeches. Stump speeches caricatured black public speakers unable to "properly" speak upper-class English. McAdoo's troupe did not include stump speeches because stump speeches lampooned the uplift politics project they were trying to realize.

Of similar importance is the fact that McAdoo's Minstrels performed only one coon song during their time in South Africa.[93] Coon songs were a particularly degrading variant of minstrel music often featuring the zip coon, also known as the urban dandy character. This was a free northern African American, who dressed in ostentatious clothing and attempted to speak upper-class English. His attempts to assimilate always failed, as his ridiculous clothing and incorrect English ultimately exposed his black "backwardness." Historians of the late-nineteenth-century minstrel show label the 1890s as the decade of the "coon-song craze" in the United States, England, and Australia.[94] McAdoo's Minstrels refused to bring the coon-song craze to South Africa. McAdoo probably chose to exclude coon songs because, like the stump speeches, they too caricatured the type of assimilationist racial uplift project he was trying to manifest.

McAdoo's Minstrels did not blacken up. Newspaper reviews suggest the absence of blackface. One reviewer described their show as "genuine negro minstrelsy (without the aid of black cork)" and preferred McAdoo's troupe over traditional blackface minstrelsy, writing, "as previously stated, it is the genuine article, not the spurious, which, however realistically served up, lacks the charm that attaches to the former." Another reviewer compared McAdoo's ensemble to a popular white British troupe known as the Moore and Burgess Minstrels: "It is a Moore and Burgess with black men instead of the burnt cork imitation." A third reviewer used quotation marks to suggest an absence of burnt cork: "In the first part of the programe is presented what might reasonably be regarded as the acme of negro minstrelsy, displaying every favourable characteristic of the most accomplished 'burnt cork' artistes."[95] Furthermore, a portrait of one of McAdoo's troupes in stage attire did not include blackface (fig. 8). By choosing not to wear burnt cork, McAdoo's Minstrels refused to

Figure 8. The Georgia Minstrels and Alabama Cake Walkers. Courtesy of Hampton University Archives.

circulate the minstrel show's most enduring visual image regarding black citizenship. Blackface marked the black "alien" who could not responsibly participate in modern democratic nations and, as such, had no place in the uplift politics project of Orpheus McAdoo.

As mentioned above, a surface-level interpretation might come to the conclusion that McAdoo rejected the Fisk Jubilee model of presenting black culture as art when he transitioned to the minstrel show. However, a close examination of the archival material reveals the ways in which McAdoo's troupe continued to practice uplift politics even when performing in the minstrel genre. In doing so, his troupe advocated a politics of upward mobility for black people while working in a genre that traditionally presented black people as "natural" inhabitants of the lower rungs of society. McAdoo's troupe refashioned the minstrel show into something that was consistent with their worldviews. Moreover, they challenged the standard representational logics of minstrel shows by portraying white characters. McAdoo's Minstrels were in the business of turning social and aesthetic conventions awry. For them, racial categories were outfits that could be worn to amass social capital. Orpheus McAdoo, a self-described Australian by adoption who spoke with a British accent, may have understood that race was more of a performative social category than a fixed biological reality.

BLACK MUSIC FALLS ON DEAF EARS: DISENGAGED ENGAGEMENT AND THE PROBLEM OF UPLIFT POLITICS

In February of 1891, the Virginia Jubilee Singers were touring the Afrikaner Transvaal Republic. President Paul Kruger attended one of their performances. A local newspaper described Kruger's reaction to the show: "His Honour was evidently greatly pleased with the cordial reception accorded him, and greatly enjoyed the entertainment. . . . In place of item no. 3 an old slave song, 'Nobody knows the trouble I have seen,' was substituted, and so plaintive was the melody that tears could be seen stealing down the rugged features of the President."[96] This article provides present-day researchers a brief glimpse of an emotional response to African American music by one of the most powerful politicians in late-nineteenth-century South Africa. Kruger may have cried for the Voortrekkers, the Afrikaners who left the Cape Colony in the 1830s in an attempt to escape the relatively progressive racial policies of the British colonists, re-create a racial order premised on Afrikaner racial superiority, and establish an independent Afrikaner Republic. Or perhaps it was the Slagtersnek rebels and those Afrikaner farmers who believed they were oppressed by the British rulers of the Cape Colony. The tears could have been for Piet Retief and those white settlers killed by the Matabele, Zulu, or Sotho, or for those white burghers who gave their life in the 1880 resource war between the Transvaal Republic and the British Empire. Kruger may have refracted the suffering in the song away from the black American protagonists and into his own nationalist project. Indeed, by the late nineteenth century, an incipient nationalism was gathering momentum in the Transvaal and Orange Free State. The nationalists believed that the Afrikaner people were caught in a constant state of siege, the first antagonist being British imperialism and the second being the African masses. The song appealed to Kruger because he and his people knew what "trouble" looked like. It came in the form of harsh terrain, British laws, British bullets, and African assegais (spears).[97]

Another viable interpretation accounts for the possibility of real sympathy. For at least the duration of one song, Kruger may have genuinely empathized with the suffering of the enslaved protagonists of the song. The African American concert spiritual tradition made many references to the enslaved Israelites of the Old Testament, a body of stories the Afrikaners were deploying toward their own nation-building projects in South Africa. Perhaps this was a moment when African American music about slavery and the hardships of living in a society in which one was treated as an inferior race was heard enthusiastically and empathically by people who were authority figures in a society that operated with its own racial hierarchy. But this empathy did not translate into concrete policy changes. There was no campaign to remove exclusionary and segregationist policies in the Transvaal Republic directly following the performances of the Virginia Jubilee Singers. Similarly, in the British cities of Kimberley, Cape Town, and Natal, the great popularity of the Virginia Jubilee Singers did not result in a sustained effort to end discriminatory practices against black Africans. Kruger did not wipe the tears from his cheek, then rush home from the theater to begin scripting a new plan to remove the pass system and give Africans full rights in the Transvaal. The tears seem to convey a genuine sympathy for the enslaved protagonist of the song, but no concrete political action followed. How can we explain this seemingly contradictory reaction to the music of the Virginia Jubilee Singers?

Jon Cruz's study of the ways in which African American spirituals were received by missionaries, antislavery activists, and early folklorists in the United States provides a useful analytic for explaining Kruger's contradictory responses to African American music. Cruz argues that many northern observers who commented on black music separated the aesthetic qualities of the music from the social and economic contexts that created the music. Cruz introduces the concept of *disengaged engagement* to explain how "the discovery of the spiritual is characterized by a peculiar engagement with black music that also disengages aesthetic and culturalist interests in black music from the plight of blacks during the decades after the Civil War."[98] This fostered a situation in which white listeners wholeheartedly enjoyed black music but failed to translate this enjoyment into a concrete interest in improving the social situation of former slaves. Put simply, *disengaged engagement* describes listeners who enthusiastically engage the aesthetics of black music but disengage from the politics. Paul Kruger's tears and his subsequent return to business-as-usual racial exclusionary politics represent a clear example of disengaged engagement in South Africa. British settlers and Afrikaner statesmen responded positively to the aesthetic qualities of African American music but failed to follow this response with a sincere examination of the ways in which the racial systems they created worked to discriminate against local Africans.[99] Unfortunately, this variant of *disengaged engagement* was made all the more possible by McAdoo's claims of mixed-race identity.

The Virginia Jubilee Singers claimed a coloured mixed-race identity and deployed a spectacularly opaque variant of racial uplift politics. McAdoo used the three-tiered racial classification system to his advantage, while also legitimating distinctions between black and coloured that had negative implications for local Africans. By claiming a coloured American racial identity, he distanced himself and the members of his troupe from the social position of negro American. This movement away from the social position of negro American contributed to an atmosphere of reception in which white settlers would take his music more seriously. However, McAdoo's strategy unintentionally created opportunities for settlers to interpret his music as an accomplishment of mixed-race coloureds rather than black Africans. Unfortunately, this may have allowed for a kind of *disengaged engagement* to play out, as "coloured" American music was publicly appreciated but concrete actions to improve the situation of local Africans did not materialize.[100]

These responses to McAdoo's troupes are indicative of some of the broader problems of racial uplift politics. Kevin Gaines argues that uplift politics often worked to support racial hierarchies rather than subverting them: "Black elites who spoke of uplift opposed racism by calling attention to class distinction among African Americans as a sign of evolutionary race progress. . . . With the advent of Jim Crow regimes, the self-help component of uplift increasingly bore the stamp of evolutionary racial theories positing the civilization of elites against the moral degradation of the masses." Likewise, Karen Sotiropoulos is critical of the uplift project: "Reformers often redeployed power relations by categorizing working-class or southern behavior as 'too black,' that is, too close to stereotypes and in need of reform. . . . By distancing themselves from the larger black population, and often from leisure activities deemed 'too black' like ragtime music and dance, middle-class proponents of racial uplift actually reinforced the prevailing ideology of racial hierarchy."[101] Racial uplift projects, although providing significant counternarratives to class-based racial stereotypes, oftentimes stumbled onto a kind of social Darwinist logic that measured black people in terms of progress on an evolutionary scale. Indeed, the belief that black people should concentrate on "self-improvement" often assumes a previous dysfunctional state and leaves institutional and structural obstructions to advancement undercriticized.

McAdoo's uplift politics could be appropriated to fit the needs of progressive and conservative racial projects in South Africa. As was discussed earlier, John Tengo Jabavu, editor of the African newspaper *Imvo Zabantsundu*, believed the Virginia Jubilee Singers proved Africans did not have to be "perpetual hewers of wood and drawers of water." Jabavu's sentiments directly clashed with a response from the conservative *Grahamstown Journal*, which was published alongside Jabavu's article in *Imvo Zabantsundu*. The *Grahamstown Journal* article is a remarkable example of race thinking that is worthy of being quoted in full:

> The advent of the Jubilee Singers to this continent has suggested some interesting and valuable lessons to the Journal. We are naturally drawn to the conclusion that there is an immense possibility of improvement in the aborigines of this part of the world—when we see what American life and education have been able to do for the descendants of West African slaves. It is true that the parallel is somewhat complicated by the fact that some of our recent visitors were of mixed descent; but also some of them, we presume, were not so and thus the inference we would suggest appears to hold good,—namely that the Kafir, Fingo, and Bechuana races, which are naturally not inferior to the negro races, should be capable of being developed into an equal aptitude for music and song, and an equal power of industrious application and of civilization generally. This view, however, appears to contradict our experiences of the Native tribes. At all events we can fairly say that the progress made by the aborigines of South Africa during nearly a century of British control has been so slow as to be disappointing. The races of this country have only been the objects of instruction for two or three generations; which America has had the negro in hand for several centuries. From this point too, we see that the rough discipline of slavery was not without its beneficial effects in inuring the negroes to that habit of regular toil which seems very foreign to the aboriginal African mind. When we see in Natal and Zululand nearly half a million of stalwart people spending their lives in almost absolute idleness, while the Colony is obliged to import coolies to till the soil, there is a strong temptation to wish that we could apply some moderate pressure to such laggards, to make them work. But every one sees that that is out of the question. We can only go on as we have begun, but more diligently, in endeavoring to indoctrinate the natives into enlightenment, sobriety, and industry. Our work will be done more successfully, if we ourselves are shining examples in these respects. Time is in our favor, and the multiplication of the native population will assuredly drive the next generation to

> work. Our fixed policy should be to prepare them for it by industrial and educational training, by breaking up the despotic tribal governments, and by abolishing the superstitious and embruting [*sic*] customs of heathenism. We cannot afford to let the natives stagnate in their immemorial barbarism. Their welfare and ours alike require that we should be continually seeking to elevate them. The task will tax all our prudence, skill and patience; but the rewards will be ample. There is a mine of wealth in the native labour of South Africa, far exceeding in value all the gold and gems its soil contains; though like those hidden treasures, it will require much toil and skill on our part to bring it to light and utilize it.[102]

It is not clear why this *Grahamstown Journal* article was uncritically republished by the editors of *Imvo Zabantsundu,* especially since it clashed directly with Jabavu's suggestion that McAdoo's troupe proved Africans were capable of being more than manual laborers. The journal article was a troubling response to McAdoo's racial uplift politics that employed a Darwinist logic, placing negro and mixed-race Americans higher on an "evolutionary" time line than Africans. Here, McAdoo's presentation of a "civilized" troupe only supported the author's idea that more "diligent" methods of coercion could "discipline," "civilize," and Christianize the African "heathens." For the editors of the *Grahamstown Journal,* the hard-working Virginia Jubilee Singers reaffirmed the mid-nineteenth-century discourse of African idleness.

Years later, a coloured writer also expressed a similar sentiment. In 1897 the *South African Citizen,* a newspaper for coloured people in Kimberley, South Africa, claimed, "Mr. McAdoo's Minstrels . . . showed the superiority of the American coloured people over the South African."[103] Unfortunately, McAdoo's claims of coloured identity encouraged Afrikaner, British, and even coloured observers to separate the accomplishments of the troupe from that of native Africans.

Following McAdoo's tours of the 1890s, the South African colonies continued on a path toward racial segregation and racial stratification. This was to be expected. McAdoo's troupe members knew there was little they could do to disturb the racial projects of the South African colonies. They were not so naive as to believe that a small band of performers could significantly alter the direction of a society so rooted in racial hierarchy. Nevertheless, McAdoo's performers continued to speak back in the best way they knew how. Approximately six years after Kruger's attendance and public tearing up at a Virginia Jubilee Singers performance, McAdoo's Minstrels were performing in front of a British audience in Pretoria when Tambo turned to Bones and asked, "After you die, where would you like to be buried?" Bones responded, "In a Dutch cemetery." Tambo asked, "Why is that?" to which Bones replied, "Because a Dutch cemetery is the last place the devil would go to look for a black man." A British settler newspaper claimed this was "perhaps the most successful gag ever perpetrated in the President Theatre" and went on to say that "a more cutting fling at boer negrophobia could hardly be uttered, and the audience roared."[104] This joke succeeded largely because it positioned the British audience as open-minded progressives when compared to "negrophobe" Afrikaners. But most important, the greater significance of this joke lies in the ways it spoke back against racial discrimination. McAdoo's troupe offered counternarratives that challenged British and Afrikaner race thinking.

In order to maintain a racial order, those in power often assimilate and depoliticize potentially subversive counterdiscourses. This is why two newspaper articles that covered the last performance of McAdoo's Minstrels in South Africa are especially noteworthy. Although this was a performance of McAdoo's Minstrels, both reviews made reference to McAdoo's earlier jubilee troupe, confusing the two genres. The first article was titled "McAdoos Jubilee Singers" but described a "huge reception" for "McAdoo Minstrels at the Metropolitan Hall last evening."[105] The second article was titled "McAdoo's Minstrels" but claimed "the programe showed the Jubilee Singers at their best."[106] This conflation of jubilee singing and minstrelsy was another one of the unintended consequences of McAdoo's decisions. That is, by switching from jubilee singing to minstrelsy, McAdoo inadvertently created discursive space for British settlers to fuse the two genres together. The original Fisk Jubilee Singers were adamantly against this kind of logic. However, by 1898, British settlers in South Africa had been exposed to thirty-six years of professional minstrel troupes and only one ensemble of American jubilee singers. By conflating the two genres, British settlers rendered the unfamiliar familiar, and the complexity of McAdoo's troupes was boiled down to minstrelsy. In this way, British settlers assimilated the potential threat of McAdoo's uplift politics into a form that was more palatable.

McAdoo's troupes tried to challenge the prevailing forms of race thinking in the South African colonies. However, by the 1890s, South African race discourse was an ocean tanker with too much weight and momentum to be turned around by one band of performers. Furthermore, jokes and songs do not fare well when pitted against guns, laws, and prisons. The South African racial projects of the nineteenth century continued largely unhindered on a path toward an apartheid century.

— Chapter 5 —

BROWN-ON-BLACK MASQUERADE

Cape Town's Coon Carnival

The Kaapse Klopse Carnival, also known as Coon Carnival, Minstrel Carnival, or Cape Town Street Parade, is an annual holiday celebration for coloured Capetonians. It is primarily the cultural heritage of the Kaapse Klopse, or Clubs of the Cape, troupes of holiday revelers who were influenced heavily by minstrel aesthetics during the early years of organized carnivals. The celebrations traditionally play out on January 2, or "Tweede Nuwe Jaar," a day that was and is often associated with the abolition of slavery in South Africa. Although slavery officially ended on December 1, 1834, formally enslaved communities honored their ancestors by celebrating on January 2, one of the few days of the year when slaves were granted a holiday. The emancipation celebrations started in the nineteenth century and have continued through the apartheid era up to the present moment, all the while changing with the times. For many past and present participants, the event doubles as a New Year's celebration.

Throughout this book, I use the word *Klopse* as an abbreviated version of *Kaapse Klopse*. Furthermore, I also use the word *Coon* to describe the performers. This is standard practice among present and past participants. For reasons that will be explained shortly, the words *Klopse* and *Coon* are interchangeable in this setting. Because my study is about blackface minstrelsy, I focus on the Klopse/Coon troupes. However, it is important to note that Christmas Bands (bands of instrumentalists who traditionally perform on Christmas Eve, also known as Christmas Choirs) and Malay Choirs (choirs of singers who specialize in Afrikaans- or Dutch-language songs) also contribute to the holiday traditions of coloured people in Cape Town.[1]

During the 1870s and 1880s, blackface minstrel conventions were brought into the celebrations. At that time, several social clubs served coloured communities in Cape Town, and these clubs often celebrated in the streets of Cape Town on New Year's Eve. One group of New Year revelers was called the Pumpkin Darkies and another the Highborn Coons. These club troupes were cultural predecessors of the Klopse.[2] The first organized carnival was held at Green Point Track in 1907. By that year, a large portion of revelers were blackening their faces and incorporating minstrel-inspired clothes, song, and dance. Between 1907 and 1968, a relatively stable set of carnival traditions emerged. On January 1, a carnival competition was held in a stadium sporting venue in Cape Town. On January 2, Klopse troupes paraded between two predominantly coloured neighborhoods, District Six and the Bo-Kaap (Above the Cape) on a route that purposefully went through the center of Cape Town.[3] Talented dancers called Voorlopers ("front walkers," anglicized as "drum majors") and homosexual men cross-dressing as women known as "moffies" often marched at the front of each troupe (fig. 9).[4] After the parade, Klopse marched back to their respective neighborhoods and celebrated deep into the night. During the following Saturdays, Klopse competed in the major stadiums and sporting grounds of Cape Town. The competitions evaluated participants in several categories, including singing, marching, band play, dancing, and quality of dress. Carnival boards organized the competitions by recruiting troupes, advertising the event, booking space, hiring judges, negotiating with the Cape Town municipal government, and buying trophies, among other tasks. The boards were traditionally controlled by middle-class coloureds. A small handful of white people also ran carnival boards. The mid-twentieth-century carnival was a unique spectacle: hundreds of blackface performers singing and dancing in the streets and sporting venues of Cape Town.

According to newspaper reports, thousands of spectators paid to see the early carnival competitions. The audience comprised mostly coloureds, white South Africans (including members of the city government), and

Figure 9. A Voorloper leading marchers during Cape Town Coon Carnival, 1957. Courtesy of the National Library of South Africa, Cape Town.

white tourists. Beginning in the early 1920s, some carnival boards provided reserved seating at a relatively high cost for "European" spectators. This practice created controversy that became especially pronounced during the middle of the twentieth century. Several middle-class coloureds and antiapartheid activists wrote opinion articles critiquing the segregated seating as a variant of apartheid thinking. One common complaint claimed the Coons allowed themselves to be used by the propaganda wing of the apartheid state as evidence that coloured people were happy with the system. A related criticism portrayed the comedy of the Coon troupes as "buffoonery" that reinforced stereotypes about coloureds for white spectators.[5] Other middle-class coloureds appreciated the Coons for creating a space to showcase talented performers.[6] All of which is to say the Coon troupes were not universally celebrated by coloured people in Cape Town.

That being said, the apartheid state was the main adversary of carnival. In 1966 the apartheid government rezoned District Six as a whites-only neighborhood. Sixty thousand inhabitants were forced to leave their homes and move to neighborhoods on the far outskirts of the city. In 1968 Green Point was also declared a whites-only area, and it was made illegal for coloured Klopse to perform there. In 1976 Klopse were further banned from marching in the center of Cape Town. This ban lasted until 1989. After the ban was lifted, Klopse created a new parade-route tradition. In this new tradition, Klopse were and are bused on January 2 from different areas of the city to Keizergracht, a street on the outskirts of the neighborhood that used to be District Six. For many Klopse, this tradition functions as a kind of "homecoming" and memorial to District Six. After gathering on Keizergracht, Klopse parade into the center of the city on a route filled with meaning. The path moves past the old Slave Lodge, a building where the Dutch East India Company kept enslaved people. Klopse march by central Cape Town landmarks, including Adderley Street and city hall, and end the parade in the Bo-Kaap.[7] Several astute commentators describe the postapartheid street march as a symbolic claiming of the city. As John Mason observes, the carnival march creates "an ideal, if imaginary, Cape Town—A Cape Town without apartheid and forced removals, without exclusion and humiliation." For coloured playwright Amy Jephta, the parade is a "necessary reclamation of Cape Town as a post-apartheid city." According to Francesca Inglese, Klopse memorialize "the past" while "assert[ing] contemporary access to the city and perform[ing] their claim to citizenship."[8]

The Klopse troupes of Cape Town function in similar ways to the "Krewes" of New Orleans's Mardi Gras and the "Clubs" of Trinidadian carnival. Klopse troupes follow an internal hierarchy, at the top of which are the "captain" and his "lieutenants." They organize practice times, handle the finances, choose the costumes, hire tailors and musicians, and assign roles to the participants. The troupe members make up the majority of participants and are primarily working class.[9] Troupes can range anywhere from forty members to well over a thousand. Although the carnival has traditionally been a male-dominated space, women have participated in small numbers from the beginning. More recently, in the 1990s, relatively large numbers of women started marching alongside the men.[10]

In apartheid-era Cape Town and Jim Crow Mississippi, the word *Coon* often carried different meanings.[11] Many Capetonians used the word in a nonracial way. Instead of using it to refer to black people, it described carnival participants or Kaapse Klopse. Thus, in Cape Town, to be a "Coon" was to perform with a Klopse troupe during carnival. The earliest documentation I found employing a local Cape Town definition of the word *Coon* comes from 1940. In January of that year, a debate played out in the columns of a coloured newspaper known as the *Cape Standard* over the traditions of the carnival. During the debate, a supporter of Cape Town's carnival legitimized the culture by comparing it to the "Coon Carnivals" of Vienna, Austria.[12] Similarly, in 1948, a correspondent for a coloured newspaper called the *Sun* claimed that "many Oriental countries" open the New Year with "Coon Carnivals."[13] In both instances, coloured observers advanced expansive definitions of the word *Coon* by applying it to carnival revelers in Vienna and Asia who were not using blackface. Over the following decades, several commentators advanced a deracialized definition of the term by using it to describe Cape Town carnival participants who were masquerading as Native Americans rather than African Americans. In 1954 the *Cape Times* described "Wild American Masqueraders—those [C]oons with the feathered headdresses and hatchets—are perhaps the most colourful of all the New Year Carnival revelers of the Cape."[14] Similarly, in 1968 *Drum* magazine (a black-run magazine based in Johannesburg) described "Coons" who "were got up as Red Indians and were plenty wild."[15] Another source from the 1960s suggested, "[Coons] get their name from the backwoods animal, the raccoon, with the white rings around its eyes."[16] These sources from the middle of the twentieth century suggest that by this point, the word *Coon* was deracialized in the context of the Cape Town Carnival.

In the postapartheid era, coloured carnival goers continue to use the word *Coon* in a nonracial way.[17] In 1994 a coloured songwriter and carnival organizer named Taliep Peterson described the situation: "The Americans come and they don't want us to use the word Coon because it's derogatory for the people. Here Coon is not derogatory in our sense. For us the minute you talk Coon, he sees New Year day, he sees satin and the eyes and mouth with circles in white, the rest of the face in black, like the American minstrels."[18]

This new definition of *Coon* partially explains why many carnival participants proudly identified as "Coon." The term was also used to celebrate a carnival culture the apartheid government tried to suppress during the 1970s and 1980s by banning the participants from marching in the center of Cape Town. In the 1990s, several carnival participants told

Denis-Constant Martin, "My father was in the Coons, I am in the Coons, my children will be in the Coons." Within such a context, performing "the Coon" was an act of defiance, refusing to let the apartheid state snuff out the carnival culture.[19]

The American definition of *coon* may have been lost in translation. During the twentieth century, many coloured Capetonians spoke Afrikaans and English but preferred to use Afrikaans as their home language (defined as a language spoken among a community or family).[20] The Afrikaans phrase "Kaapse Klopse" translates as "Clubs of the Cape."[21] During the early years, most coloureds used the word *Klopse* to describe carnival participants.[22] At some point, *Klopse* might have been translated into English as *Coon*. During this process of translation, the nonracial connotation of *Klopse* was probably carried over to *Coon*. Future research using Afrikaans-language sources might test this hypothesis. For now, we can settle with the observation that cultural symbols often change meanings as they move across national borders. This point provides an entry way for understanding how many coloured people appropriated a genre with racist foundations in order to dream about black modernity and coloured liberation. At the same time, many of the racial meanings of early blackface minstrelsy were retained in the apartheid-era carnival even as the word *Coon* was deracialized. Throughout this book, I spell *Coon* with an uppercase C to convey the Cape Town carnival definition of the word. When I use the lowercase word *coon*, I am referring to the American racial slur.

This chapter describes the influence of blackface minstrelsy in early carnival and offers a racial narrative for understanding carnival. Some present-day discussions on carnival retroactively apply a postapartheid nonracialism narrative onto the apartheid-era carnivals. I argue that primary source evidence of the early history of the carnival tells a different story. The carnival was a playground for performing various racial masquerades. That being said, it is important to acknowledge that carnival revelers infused the event with many meanings.[23] My racial narrative was not created with the intention of imposing an all-encompassing master narrative onto the carnival. Instead, my narrative describes only a portion of the carnival participants. Furthermore, my thinking is influenced heavily by scholars of cultural globalization who argue convincingly that many people around the world have creatively detached American popular culture from its original foundations and injected it with new local meanings.[24] My racial narrative is not an attempt to impose American meanings on the carnival. Instead, I use local sources to argue that carnival offered a space for local South Africans to engage the concept of race. This chapter interprets the brown-on-black masquerades in the apartheid-era Coon Carnival.

My analysis of the racial masquerades in early carnival is informed by perspectives on coloured identity advanced by coloured South African sociologist Zimitri Erasmus. Erasmus interprets coloured identity as a constantly evolving formation produced by cultural mixing in a colonial context. This kind of framework accounts for change over time and is useful for interpreting carnival practices that have transformed dramatically over the decades. Of course, there is no one-to-one correlation between the Klopse and coloured identity. One should not be interpreted as a stand-in for the other. Nonetheless, many Klopse view the carnival as a space where coloured identity and culture can be performed and celebrated. Ultimately, I believe the racial masquerading practices of the early carnival lend further support to Erasmus's observation that coloured identities provide space for some to enact a "privilege[d]" agenda in which Africans are "disrespect[ed]" as racially inferior, while others participate in "liberatory," "anti-racist project[s]" positively identifying with Africans.[25] My interpretation of the apartheid-era carnival engages a spectrum of representations advanced by coloured participants, ranging from celebratory portrayals of black modernity to the antiblack racism of traditional minstrel shows. To be clear, I am not suggesting that positive racial affirmation and antiblack racism were equal parts of the carnival imaginary. Antiblack racism was far from the norm, but it did have a presence that should not be ignored or glossed over. Ultimately, though, most early Klopse were far more interested in accessing an imaginary form of African American freedom than denigrating local Africans.

EARLY CARNIVALS AND BLACKFACE MINSTRELSY

Klopse and local media have circulated several different origin narratives about the carnival. Many claim the carnival celebrations began as a response to the end of Cape slavery in 1834. For example, in David Kramer and Taliep Petersen's *District Six* (2002) musical, one character proudly states: "Today we celebrate freedom. You know why? 'Cuz today is the day that the slaves, our forefathers, were freed more than a hundred years ago."[26] For me, this is a very convincing narrative because it has been repeated by many present-day Klopse and is corroborated by documents from the nineteenth century. A newspaper article from 1834 described large crowds of "Apprentices" accompanied by musicians celebrating manumission in the streets of Cape Town.[27] Decades later, in the 1880s, a Scottish observer described the festivities: "Coloured people . . . are celebrating their emancipation from slavery or serfdom some half-a-century ago."[28] In 1885 the *Cape Times* claimed "hideous noises" (read: music) were coming from the "descendants" of "slaves" celebrating the anniversary of the end of slavery.[29] This last account is a reminder of the condescending English-language newspaper coverage on carnival and the emancipatory logics of carnival. The emancipatory roots of carnival are well established. Meanwhile, the questions of when and how blackface minstrel aesthetics were incorporated into the festivities are still open. This is because several different explanations have accumulated over the years.

One such narrative claimed a white baker in Cape Town named C. J. Cole inspired the first Klopse during the 1890s. He dressed his workers in blackface minstrel attire to advertise his store, and the first Coon troupes saw Cole's workers and imitated them.[30] Several other origin narratives named African Americans as a major source of cultural inspiration for carnival. Some suggested that African American sailors visited Cape Town during the 1890s and that their music and dance were incorporated into the festivities of Cape Town coloureds. Another narrative claimed Orpheus McAdoo's Minstrels came to Cape Town in 1887 and enjoyed instant popularity among the coloured community. Cape Town coloureds got the idea to blacken up and form Coon troupes after watching McAdoo's Minstrel troupe.[31] One narrative presented the carnival as an offshoot of New Orleans's Mardi Gras. Another suggested the festivities first began during the 1860s, after a Confederate warship called the *Alabama* captured a Union ship in the harbor of Cape Town. According to this story, Capetonians saw the battle from Signal Hill and paraded the streets in celebration.[32] Relatedly, some have claimed that enslaved African Americans in the crew of the *Alabama* introduced coloureds to minstrel music when the ship was docked in Cape Town in 1862.[33]

I am more interested in the discursive work of these origin narratives than the validity of the claims. Carnival participants who voice origin narratives are trying to locate what and who is being celebrated in carnival. Furthermore, origin narratives play an important role in shaping the carnival imaginary by attaching a set of meanings to carnival performances. Ultimately, I believe my previous chapters can also be read as a narrative that describes the origins of minstrel aesthetics in carnival, since they show how professional blackface minstrelsy arrived and developed in Cape Town from 1862 to 1898, in the decades immediately preceding the first organized carnivals. This narrative acknowledges decades of British and white American minstrel troupes who came to Cape Town and popularized blackface minstrelsy in the city. Among the many troupes who toured during this period were the Christy Minstrel troupes (1862, 1865, 1868), the Harvey-Dougherty-Leslie-Braham Minstrels (1872), the Australian Variety Company (1875), Harvey's New English Company (1877), the Benson American Troupe (1877), Harvey's Ethiopian Opera Troupe (1878), the London Minstrels (1879), the Victoria Loftus Troupe (1882), Cox's Christy Minstrels (1882), the Anglo-American Minstrels (1883), the Georgia Minstrels (1884), Washington Norton and the Merry Markers (1885), the Wheeler Comedy Company (1886), the Rover Minstrels (1888), Braham's Empire Minstrels (1889), D'arcs Marionetts (1890), and McAdoo's Minstrels (1897). With the notable exception of McAdoo's Minstrels, the vast majority of these troupes used blackface makeup. Therefore, any of them could have inspired the early Klopse to blacken up.

As has already been demonstrated, blackface minstrel shows were regularly staged in Cape Town during the latter half of the nineteenth century. Although few sources document the racial makeup of the audience, there are some newspaper accounts claiming that people who would later be classified as coloured were in attendance. In 1870 the *Cape Chronicle* described a "mixed crowd" at an amateur minstrel show: "Among the audience were representatives of every class of the community, from the highest mercantile and official 'swells' to the most humble among the coloured." In February 1877, a *Cape Times* review of Harvey's Variety Company described "the roars" of "Malay" spectators.[34] A few months later, another *Cape Times* article offered relatively detailed observations about "Malay" theatergoers:

> An interesting feature at the Theatre is the Malay audience to be found every evening in the gallery, and sometimes in the pit, keenly attentive as they are to the proceedings on the stage and interested in the action of the play. It would hardly be expected that these Asiatic-Africans, who rarely use the English language as their vernacular, and who have ideas

> and sympathies of their own, should be so completely absorbed in the passion, the sorrow, the bliss of an English heroine, or so responsive to the drolleries of an English low comedian. But one touch of nature makes the whole world kin . . . and somehow that touch in the case of our Malay friends is strong enough to prove our cousinship. It will be perceived that as appreciative playgoers the Malays do not hesitate to ask a favour from the manager, which we doubt now, he will readily accord.[35]

The timing of these testimonies are consistent with Denis-Constant Martin's observation regarding coloured New Year's revelers who were calling themselves Highborn Coons and Pumpkin Darkies in the 1870s and 1880s.[36] These early predecessors of the Klopse probably watched the professional minstrel troupes who visited Cape Town. Years later in 1941, a coloured writer for the *Sun* observed, "The older [coloured] folk will easily recollect that not very many years ago '[C]oons' as we speak of them today were quite unknown except for the occasional Sambo on the concert stage."[37] Given this information, I believe an expansive origin narrative that accounts for the history of professional blackface minstrelsy in late-nineteenth-century South Africa can help explain the minstrel influence in carnival. The early Klopse repertoire was a repository of forty-some years of collective memory. Many professional blackface minstrel troupes came to Cape Town during the second half of the nineteenth century, and some of the performances were staged for multiracial audiences. The first Klopse troupes were inspired by professional minstrels.

Some South African coloureds have also voiced this perspective. In 2013 the comedy coach of the Fabulous Woodstock Starlets, Moeniel Jacobs, claimed, "It started from many years ago with the Christy Minstrels that were here and when they left, we mimicked them and that is how the [C]oon culture started."[38] M. Cassie D'arcy, a coloured writer born in District Six in 1940, offered a similar origin narrative in *The Coon*. In this young adult novel, a tailor who makes costumes for the carnival troupes and has been following the culture for decades suggests that the carnival "started at the end of the last century when a band of black and white faced minstrels from America came to tour the cape."[39] In order to further flesh out this narrative about the aesthetic influences of professional blackface minstrelsy in carnival, the following pages outline major minstrel retentions in the early carnival.

In November 1906, the organizers of the first organized "Coloured

Carnival" met in Workmen's Union Hall in Cape Town.[40] A *Cape Times* summary of the meeting is a useful window into the thought process of the first carnival organizers. It includes an informative list of the names of some participating troupes. One such group, known as the Woodstock Mohawk Minstrels, took inspiration from a famous British minstrel troupe called the Mohawk Minstrels, one of the most successful London-based minstrel troupes in the late nineteenth century.[41] The decision to name a Cape Town troupe after London's Mohawk Minstrels suggests some local carnival organizers were knowledgeable of blackface minstrelsy's history in England and were consciously referencing British blackface performers. Another group name, the Jolly Coons Masquerading troupe, is also telling. The usage of the term *masquerading* implies participants were aware of the racial meanings behind the blackface mask. Between 1907 and 1968, many carnival troupes and organizers described the festivities as a "masquerade," and blackened carnival participants who self-identified as "masqueraders" understood that blackface was infused with racial connotations. The last sentence of the 1906 *Cape Times* article is also particularly instructive: "After discussion, it was resolved there should be a procession, starting from the parade, and it was further resolved to recommend . . . that prizes be given for the following: best costume; banjo, mandolin, and guitar playing; masquerade (teams); sentimental and comic songs; chorus singing; dancing; cake walk (single and double); brass and string band competitions."[42] Each of these competition categories were inspired by minstrel shows. The banjo was one of the major minstrel instruments, and even today it is still used to make original carnival songs.[43] The two major categories of minstrel music, sentimental and comic songs, were part of the 1907 carnival, and these categories continue in the competitions of present-day carnivals. The cakewalk, a major part of the repertoire of McAdoo's Minstrels in 1897–1898, was also a competition category in the 1907–9 carnivals.[44] Furthermore, this 1906 plan to include a prize for "masquerade" is very revealing. This proposed competition category did not make it into the 1907 carnival or any subsequent carnivals. However, its inclusion in the early planning meetings for the 1907 carnival hints at the intentions of the early carnival organizers to make racial masquerade a central part of carnival.[45]

Newspaper descriptions of early carnival music offer much evidence of minstrel retentions. According to one description, "The Dahomey coons came along soberly, swinging a little to the rhythm of their chorus . . .

Figure 10. Cape Town Coon Carnival, 1937. Courtesy of the National Library of South Africa, Cape Town.

and then went cake-walking along, in an [*sic*] out, with the bones rattling and the guitars and banjos strumming for all they were worth."[46] Another source recounted that "the tinkling of banjoes and guitars, the click of the bones, and the beating of tambourines, went swinging through the streets, to the delight and wonderment of the onlookers."[47] These statements reveal a large degree of minstrel musical knowledge on the part of white Capetonians and early carnival troupes. Indeed, several white reporters argued that carnival music was overly reliant on American minstrel influences (fig. 10).

A *Cape Times* correspondent offered the following description of carnival music in 1908: "With regard to the songs, it was a pity that nearly all of these were of THE AMERICAN COON variety, and that hardly a single Afrikander song was heard *throughout* the afternoon or evening. A little originality in this and some other directions should be attempted next year, for this slavish adherence to American coon methods as portrayed in the pages of half penny comic papers becomes monotonous."[48] This patronizing account manages to include some useful information.

According to this reporter, during the first decade of the twentieth century, it was possible to learn American minstrel songs by reading "comic papers" sold in Cape Town. As mentioned in chapter 2, in the middle of the nineteenth century, minstrel songs were distributed in major South African cities in sheet music form. Early Klopse probably learned minstrel songs via print culture. In 1933 A. B. Mitchell, captain of the Cape Town Hawkers troupe, described this process to the *Cape Times:* "The captain buys the music, usually in the form of the latest popular song albums. . . . One of the members, who can read the music, acquaints the others with the tune."[49] Decades later, this print-culture narrative was corroborated by Achmat Levy, a widely respected Klopse organizer who was the founding director of the Cape Peninsula Coon Carnival Board. In 1990 Levy said that many Coon troupes bought American music from a music shop on Adderley Street in the center of Cape Town.[50] As mentioned earlier, professional minstrel troupes were not the only vessels of dissemination; shopkeepers selling sheet music also played a role.

Returning to the 1908 carnival, a second newspaper article corroborates the claims of American minstrel influence: "The strange feature about the chorus competition was that not a single South African ditty . . . was sung. The [C]oons went everywhere for songs. Piccadilly, the 'tuppeny toob,' 'Yalla Bammer,' and 'Idaho,' but never once did they touch South Africa."[51] Decades later in 1939, a reporter from the *Cape Times* observed, "So far [the Coon troupes] still suppress their own originality and slavishly follow a distorted American pattern. American hits of yesterday are still their favourite songs, the rhythm has become monotonous."[52] I will return to these supposedly "monotonous [rhythms]" shortly. For now, it is important to note that much of the early Klopse carnival songs were drawing heavily from American influences.

Although my discussion of early carnival focuses on the influence of minstrel shows, local cultural traditions also shaped the event. In 1949 comic Afrikaans songs called "moppies" were included in carnival competitions for the first time. Although English-language songs continued to constitute a majority of the Klopse repertoire, this is a noteworthy development.[53] Present-day moppies have one defining rhythmic feature: the syncopated *ghoema* beat (sometimes spelled *goema* or *ghomma*). The ghoema beat was named after the ghoema drum, an instrument created by enslaved people who lived in Cape Town.[54] By incorporating moppies and the accompanying ghoema beat into the trophy competitions, Klopse troupes expanded the carnival competition soundscape to include more of their own distinct music-making traditions. But perhaps some version of the ghoema beat was always a part of the Klopse repertoire, even if it was not mentioned in the English-language press coverage on early carnival.[55] Many descriptions of early Klopse bands did not include drums. However, according to several present-day carnival veterans, during the 1950s the rhythm of carnival marches was rendered with a cello instead of a ghoema drum.[56] Early Klopse may have started this practice by using stringed instruments to render ghoema beats. Relatedly, since the first carnival competition in 1907, a trophy has been given to the carnival troupe who performs the best "Grand March Past" or "Exhibition March Past." In the "Exhibition March Past," Klopse troupes parade into the competition arena with much style and flair. This cultural practice was not inspired by touring blackface minstrels. Newspaper accounts describing the professional minstrel troupes who visited Cape Town did not mention minstrel parades in the streets of the city.[57] Klopse troupes who marched in carnival competitions were channeling the traditions of early Klopse who danced to the beats of ghoema drums in the streets of Cape Town in the late nineteenth century.[58] Perhaps a related cultural practice appeared in the 1909 carnival, when a performance called the "Goomah Dance" was presented.[59] Furthermore, given how frequently today's coloured musicians mention the ghoema beat as a central part of the carnival sound alongside the observation that ghoema is a cultural retention from the era of Cape slavery, it stands to reason that some version of this syncopated rhythm may have always been part of the Klopse repertoire.[60] Perhaps the white newspaper reporters of the late nineteenth and early twentieth centuries who described "monotonous [rhythms]," "hideous noises," and "discordant . . . [and] weird music" did not have the cultural literacy to recognize and appreciate ghoema beats.[61] It is difficult to test this hypothesis without sound recordings of early carnival music. Nonetheless, this speculation is worth considering. I mention it now to make a point that is obvious to veteran participants but not to outsiders of the culture: Klopse drew from several cultural traditions, and blackface minstrelsy was not the only source of inspiration. According to several scholars, creolization (cultural mixing in colonial contexts) was and is a central part of carnival culture.[62]

That being said, I must return to the main issue at hand, the minstrel influence in carnival. Some early carnival songs recirculated the racist stereotypes of black people that appeared in nineteenth-century minstrels shows. A description of two songs from the 1908 carnival recounts the "'the Happy Darkies' soloist told a mournful tale about his having caught a chicken by stealth and then lost it by an oversight" and "the 'white noses' [troupe] proclaimed their desire to gather cotton whilst holding sickles in their hands."[63] This account alludes to the crooked-gluttony and happy-worker minstrel tropes discussed in chapter 2.

Relatedly, the minstrel trope of frenetic corporality also appeared in white and coloured newspapers reporting on carnival. In 1936 the *Cape Standard* described the "tireless" bands who marched through the city streets. The next year, the same paper stated, "Without the least sign of fatigue they continued throughout the long afternoon: their boundless energy, their zest and enthusiasm never flagged in an instant, and in spite of the grease paint and the swirling dust clouds . . . their gusto seemed to be intensified . . . banging tambourines and the clicking 'bones.'" Similarly, the *Sun* described the "boundless energy" of the carnival revelers. An American tourist did not miss the aesthetic: "The darkies all danced on again in an exhibition march apparently as fresh and as gay as when they had started." In 1938 the *Cape Times* described the central stage of the carnival as a busy "beehive." The next year, the same paper described "baby coons" who "gallantly attempted to emulate the 'shimmy-shakes' of the grown-ups and seemed quite tireless."[64]

The reportage of the following decades continued to mention similar instances of frenetic corporality. In 1940 the *Sun* described the "ceaseless contortions and inexhaustible energy" of the participants. Ten years later, the same newspaper observed, "Day and night since Sunday the gaily dressed 'coons' have pirouetted and sung tirelessly in the streets of Cape Town." The *Cape Times* continued this trend by describing performers who "capered madly past the stands" of Green Point Track. A *Cape Times* headline from 1956 reads: "Gay and Tireless Coons Please City Crowds." The next year, the *Times* observed "Coons by the thousands" who "marched and pranced and gyrated, sang and danced endlessly and tirelessly through the streets." One *Cape Times* reporter went so far as to present frenetic corporality as the universal characteristic of carnival: "All the coons had one common characteristic—dynamic energy."[65]

According to Eric Lott, minstrel shows in the United States encouraged white workers to move beyond the constraints of industrial discipline. In order to gain access to a preindustrial imaginary, white workers imagined and appropriated a fantastical racial other who seemed to exist outside of industrial disciplining.[66]

I suspect a similar dynamic was playing out in Cape Town among coloured carnival participants. Carnival participants who accessed the frenetic corporality minstrel trope were creating ephemeral moments of joy, liberating themselves from the tedious constraints of a racially stratified industrial society. Blackface minstrelsy offered a set of enabling performance conventions encouraging carnival participants to act in unfettered ways. Relatedly, the anonymity of the blackface mask allowed Klopse to participate without having to worry about social repercussions. This point was made in Noor Ebrahim's memoir about growing up in District Six. He wrote of joining the "Coons," even though his father disapproved. He believed the blackface mask would shield his face so that no one could report his activities to his father.[67] Carnival participants combined the anonymity of the blackface mask with the trope of frenetic corporality in order to celebrate without social inhibition.

Another minstrel retention can be found in early carnival costumes that were heavily influenced by blackface minstrel stage attire. One observer mentioned "dark blue coats, pink trousers and ridiculously undersized hats—as were many of the others—coloured so as to represent the Stars and Stripes." Another account described the "tightly fitting white habiliments, longitudinally striped with red and blue" of the "Happy Little Darkies" troupe. Another observer suggested that "Joseph's coat of many colours would have looked quite sombre by the side of those worn by many a proud coon." The 1937 carnival similarly included "bright parasols bobbing like poppies in the sunshine, gaudy colours flashing, coat tails fluttering in the wind." Such flashy costumes were drawing directly from the urban-dandy characters of minstrel shows.[68]

The Cape Town carnival mask was directly inspired by the minstrel convention of hyperbolic blackness. In his previously mentioned novel about carnival, M. Cassiem D'arcy portrayed the carnival mask as "white round the mouth and the rest of the face a jet-black." Coloured newspaper reporter George Manuel similarly described "greased faces" with "exaggerated, white-painted mouths." In 1951 a *Cape Times* reporter visited the headquarters of a Coon troupe and watched the carnival preparations. According to this account, the troupe captain created the face paint by using an old minstrel technique: "First they put on a Coon blacking compound of the ashes of burnt cork and petroleum jelly . . . which does not burn their faces." Then, in order to create the full effect, they "apply tubes of white 'nigger paste' (their own description) to their lips, making each one happy in the illusion that he, too, is Al Jolson [a white American movie star who performed in blackface], the Coon's beloved hero, oracle and model."[69] Apparently, some Klopse went so far as to racialize the paint of the carnival mask.

Relatedly, in 1948, a *Cape Times* reporter relayed a short conversation with a carnival participant: "The Coon's make-up was running in the heat. 'What is it?' I asked a tall young man in a silvery top hat and silken 'Tails.' 'It's bleck from the pawt,' he told me grinning. Poor chap, what with soot from the pots mixed with vaseline, lipstick, and white shoe cream decorating his face he was unable to mop his sweating brow."[70]

Similarly, in the 1990s, carnival participants told researchers from the Western Cape Oral History Project (also known as Centre for Popular Memory) about the blacking process used in carnival. An interview with a carnival seamstress revealed the following:

LISA: What was the make-up that they used?

FAGMIEJAH: Black Nuggett. Black Nuggett.

LISA: What's that?

FAGMIEJAH: The Polish. Shoe Polish. . . . They used shoe-polish but then they put Vaseline underneath it and then with the shoe-polish.[71]

During another interview, a lifelong member of the Klopse discussed the centrality of blackface in carnival performance:

LISA: And would you paint your faces [in prison]?

BARTY: We'd paint our faces in prison with the [C]oons, that's right.

LISA: With what?

BARTY: With the . . . sometime you get that . . . charcoal. Sometimes you take that coal out of the stove. . . .

LISA: And is that the same thing you paint your face with outside?

Barty: No. They've got . . . a cosmetic . . . you buy it. . . .

LISA: Oh yes, you know the make-up, is it always a white mouth, are they like smiling or . . .

BARTY: Actually that's a tradition for the [C]oons, everybody must wear

> it. You see, if they judge best-dressed and you are not black in your face I don't know today, today they don't count that, but in those years your face must be black. Because the first day from the competition there was best-dressed, the team with the most beautiful colours on you see. *If you are not black or all of you are not black face with a white mouth . . . you will lose some points you see, because then you are not a [C]oon.*[72]

Blacking up was such an essential part of early carnival that points were stricken from the scorecards of troupes who failed to follow tradition. Photographs, newspaper reports, and testimonies from coloured people all tell a story of jet-black face paint in the carnival. Whether carnival participants used traditional burnt cork, cosmetic makeup, shoe polish, or charcoal, they reproduced the visual aesthetic of hyperbolic blackness.[73]

By accounting for minstrel retentions, we can arrive at an expansive aesthetic origins story. This narrative suggests that early carnival was a repository of collective memory, drawing from forty years of blackface minstrel shows in Cape Town. Furthermore, when the parade of professional minstrels ended, their influence continued via the circulation of print culture and Hollywood films (that is, the fourth wave of minstrel globalization). Blackface films *The Jazz Singer* (1927) and *Dixie* (1943) were referenced frequently in midcentury carnivals. Many carnival participants were drawing from cinema, stage, and print minstrelsy. The next question becomes: Is it possible to practice traditional minstrel aesthetics while rejecting the caustic racism of early blackface minstrelsy?

BROWN-ON-BLACK MASQUERADE

Even though most Klopse advanced a nonracial definition of "Coon," some of the racial logics of blackface minstrelsy survived in early carnival. Carnival provided the imaginative space for participants to move across racial lines. Afro-diasporic people were not the only group to be portrayed in carnival. Privateer carnival troupes (also known as "Privates") portrayed nonblack nationalities from around the world, including Europeans. Here's a description from 1907: "The Princess Escort Masquerading Troupe brought up the rear of the procession in a uniform that was most effective. The suits were excellently finished off, pale blue and silver brocade being utilized in the coats, while the knickerbockers, which were frilled with lace, were of an orange colour. They wore white stocking and shoes, and dainty white slouch hats, with white feathers. The Troupe was the smartest dressed combination on the ground."[74]

One account of the 1908 carnival included the following portrayal of Privateers: "The neatest dressed contingent was the Lord Nelson's Escourts. . . . The leader was a European, evidently from Cockaigne. . . . [T]he American Sporting Club appeared as Indian braves in full war paint. And they were most 'fierce.'"[75] A *Cape Times* article from 1925 described carnival participants dressed as "Indians, Mexicans, and cowboys."[76] Later, in the early 1940s, most Privateer troupes were discontinued. A nostalgia piece from 1949 described their former glory: "There was a time in the early 1920s when there was a great deal of variety in the choice of uniform. There were lusty sailors who had never sailed the Seven Seas, there were Spanish Noblemen displaying their hose and doublets, 18th century Englishmen with powdered wigs and buckled shoes, gay toreadors who had never seen a bull and dashing desert sheiks. There were also feathered 'Redskins' with hatchets and knives."[77]

Here is a partial list of Privateer troupe names that were mentioned in early newspaper accounts of carnival: Wild American Masqueraders, Lord Nelson's Escorts, Spanish Cavaliers, Mexican Outlaws, Portuguese Guards, Irish Princes, Italian Life Guards, and Warriors of Mahratta. Of these options, the Native American troupes were the most popular and were the only group of Privateers to continue past the 1940s. According to George Manual, "It was decided by the various organizers that the 'privates' were too slow and pedestrian for the real spirit of carnival and they were dropped from the programme."[78] The blackface Coon character offered more opportunities for energetic celebrations than the subdued military marching of most privateer troupes. This point helps partially explain why American Indian carnival characters known as "atjas" continue to be a part of carnival in the present day.

Contrast, for example, two accounts from the 1920s portraying "Red Indians" and Privateers:

> The mad, wild prancing of the Red Indians (with black faces) surpassed all from a purely spectacular point of view. Hatches in hand, feathers streaming half-way down their backs, and indulging in all manner of physical frenzy.[79]

> It may be well to explain that these Coloured performers do not all class themselves as "[C]oons." Some are known as "privates"—these being

> troupes which set out to represent something more dignified in the way of fancy dress and ceremonial pageantry with less of the accompanying element of acrobatic dancing so noticeable, among the "[C]oons."[80]

Subdued and "dignified" Privateers were not as enticing as "frenzied" Indians or frenetic Coons. This contrast probably contributed to the dwindling numbers of Privateers and their eventual removal from carnival in the 1940s. Presumably, many Privateers decided to switch troupes for the next year's carnival while standing in formation and watching the unrestrained revelries of the Coon and Wild Indian troupes. Most important for our purposes, the Privateers offer convincing evidence of a carnival culture of racial masquerade. Spectators and participants knew that carnival provided spaces where the boundaries between racial identities could be traversed.

Carnival organizers imagined the event as a space for racial play. In one of the planning meetings for the inaugural carnival of 1907, organizers proposed "[team] masquerade" as one of the competition categories.[81] A few days after the 1907 carnival, D. Baron, the secretary of the New Year's Day Coloured Carnival Board, wrote a letter to the *Cape Argus:* "Sir, I wish to take the first opportunity on behalf of the Executive Committee of the New Year's Day Coloured Carnival, to thank the different *masquerading* and sporting clubs which took part in the procession."[82] A carnival announcement from 1921 also featured "masquerading."[83] A publicity notice from 1933 advanced the following headline: "Grand Monstrous Coon and Masquerade Parade."[84] During the late 1940s, the Western Province Coloured Carnival Board advertised a series of "Grand Coon and Masquerade Parade[s]."[85] The message from the carnival organizers was clear: carnival provided an imaginative space where participants could masquerade as other races.

The English-language press coverage thoroughly racialized the carnival participants. Some white spectators went so far as to use the language and hyperbolic conventions of blackface minstrelsy to describe carnival participants: "A final word about the wee mascot darkie who accompanies each troupe and stands in the foreground during the choruses. A typical young 'sambo'—all mouth and teeth—with head and eyes turned upwards, reminding one of the coon whose mouth could not be made any bigger without putting ears back!"[86] Other articles described a wide range of racial and ethnic impersonations in carnival:

> The first of the solo items was by "Madam Potty," in an indescribable costume, who was later joined by her partner in the dress of a Spanish Gipsy. Later "Professor Fisher from Observatrie" appeared in the garb of a sheik. . . . The major part of the programme was taken up by the Coon bands. Each band wore distinctive dress of the characteristic "darky" type, and the members ranged from the age of four years to 40. Included in the programme was a clog dance by "Richard III.," a song by "Lord Roseberry of Rondebosch" and a desert scena by "Professor Fisher," who was accompanied by his harem.[87]

In 1933 a *Cape Times* reporter observed, "Every year there were new variations—American niggers, cowboys, long rose pink riding coats, white satin trousers . . . and rows of shining top-hats. Most of all I liked the 'Greek King's Euzonoi Bodyguard' in its white pleated tunics."[88] A similar *Cape Times* article from 1937 suggested:

> [The Coons] are internationally minded. For instance, there were the Broadway Gentlemen Singing Coons. . . . Then the Warriors of Mahratta, with bright yellow robes and fierce-looking, curved, scimitars, bringing a breath of the East to Green Point. *They, in turn, were followed by the London Hawker Jubilee Coons. None of them has probably ever seen a London hawker, but that didn't prevent them from very creditably impersonating the "pearlies," complete with "moke" and barrow.* From London to the Blue Danube—the Blue Danube Troubadours, singing plaintively, "Rose of No Man's Land." The troubadours gave way to the blood-thirsty Kikuyu Warriors with knives between teeth, and long, menacing spears. Finally, from Africa to America's Southern States—The Millionaire Darkies, the Alabama Coons, the Dawn Darkies, and the Young Louisiana Coons.[89]

This account offers more evidence of the wide-ranging racial masquerades in carnival and the paternalistic white newspaper coverage. In suggesting the London Hawker Jubilee Coons had never been to London, the article pokes fun at carnival participants while failing to acknowledge the central role of white racial states in facilitating the uneven distribution of resources and opportunities across racial lines in South Africa. By labeling the impersonations of the London Hawkers "credible," the author positions him- or herself as a worldly arbiter with a right to travel that was more available to privileged British South Africans than most coloureds. From these accounts, it is clear that carnival participants were not the only people performing race; white journalists did so as well. Taken in total, the English-language reportage conveyed a white spectatorship that readily recognized the racial symbolism in carnival. It would be patronizing to suggest that Klopse did not also understand the racial connotations of blackface masking.

The names of Coon troupes are valuable racial symbols that can be used to access the racial meanings of carnival in its early decades. In the long history of the Western Cape, coloureds rarely had opportunities to name themselves. In such an oppressive social context, the act of naming the carnival troupes carried special significance in the community.[90] The following table is a list of troupe names that made clear references to diasporic blackness between the years 1907 and 1968. The list includes troupes who identified as "darkie" or "nigger," troupes that referenced African ethnic groups, and troupes who mentioned places in the United States.[91] This is not a comprehensive list because my strategy of using newspaper reports proved unyielding during some years. Moreover, during many of the years I cover in this study, local newspapers printed the names of the competition winners, a small fragment of the troupes who participated. Oftentimes, no troupe names were mentioned at all. As such, the following is only a partial list of the carnival troupes whose names directly referenced blackness (see table 1).

This list of troupe names suggests that racial masquerade was a central part of the early carnival. Participants in troupes whose names made clear reference to diasporic blackness understood something racial was going on. It is hard for me to imagine a nonracial way of performing in blackface in the Mississippi Nigger Minstrels or Happy Little Darkies Masquerading Troupe. Also worthy of mention are the many troupes who did not use racial slurs but claimed areas of the United States in their names. Such troupes were masquerading as African Americans when claiming places like Kentucky, Louisiana, or Virginia. This point is corroborated by carnival origin narratives claiming the first Coon troupes were the product of face-to-face cultural exchanges between coloured people and African Americans.

The most widespread origin narrative linking the carnival to African Americans claimed that McAdoo's Minstrels came to Cape Town in 1887 and inspired the first Coon troupes. The earliest publication of this narrative I was able to find appears in 1947 when the *Cape Times* stated, "Another theory is that [the Coon troupes] started after the Jubilee of Queen Victoria in the last century, when a troupe of American coons which visited the old Opera House was copied by the Coloured people of Cape Town."[92] A few years later, in 1951, an amateur historian named Lawrence Green published a book on Cape Town's history. He gave preference to the McAdoo story over all others:

> The origin which appears to be authentic is based on the visit of an American negro minstrel troupe to Cape Town during 1887, the year of Queen Victoria's Jubilee. Their bright costumes and coon songs made an irresistible appeal to the music loving coloured people. Among those who heard the minstrels and memorized their songs were some Malay singers, members of the Dantu family. Their descendants claim that the Dantus started the coons, and that the first troupes appeared on January 1, 1888, wearing the American minstrel costumes and with the blackened faces seen to this day.[93]

As the decade of the 1950s progressed, multiple sources repeated this story. In 1956, the *Cape Argus* reported: "Among many who heard the Negro minstrels [from America] perform, and who memorized their songs were a Malay family named Dantu. It is believed that the Dantu family were the originators of the Coon carnival, and that the first troupe appeared on January 1, 1888, wearing American minstrel costume with blackened faces."[94] In 1957 *Drum* magazine claimed: "In 1887 a group of Negro Minstrels visited Cape Town during Queen Victoria's Jubilee Year. They performed at the Opera House which at that time was in Darling Street. At the end of their engagement some of the company stayed behind and inspired the formation of the first coon troupe."[95]

Later, in 1980, George Manuel recirculated a version of this narrative, writing, "A fresh impetus was given to the carnival spirit in 1888 when an American Christy Minstrel troupe, the Jubilee Singers, arrived in South Africa." According to this account, several members of McAdoo's Jubilee Singers stayed behind after the tour and joined up with local coloured performers known as the Dantu Brothers to create the first "Cape Coon troupe."[96] Clearly, such origin stories linking the Klopse to McAdoo's Minstrels were widespread during the mid- to late twentieth century. However, in this case, the primary source evidence does not match up with popular memory.

McAdoo's Jubilee Singers arrived in Cape Town in 1890, not in 1887. Because the fiftieth anniversary of Queen Victoria's coronation was on 1887, many jubilee celebrations played out in Cape Town that year. Local Capetonians probably conflated McAdoo's 1890 arrival with the jubilee celebrations of 1887. Furthermore, when McAdoo's Jubilee Singers reached South Africa in 1890, their performances were very different from those of the early Klopse. As discussed in chapter 4, jubilee singing and blackface minstrelsy were and are two very different genres for representing African American music and people. McAdoo's Jubilee Singers did not wear blackface. They sang concert spirituals in "standard English" rather than minstrel songs in "plantation dialect." They tried to establish black music as art, sang songs while standing still, and did not feature flashy dancing. Their presentation of physicality was more similar to the slow marches of Privateer troupes than the fast dancing of Coon troupes. Their cultural influence on the early Klopse troupes was minimal at best. Later, when McAdoo's Minstrels toured in 1897–98, they probably inspired at least one of the traditions of early Klopse by popularizing the cakewalk in Cape Town. As discussed earlier, the cakewalk appeared in the carnival competitions in 1907–9. But McAdoo's Minstrels were aware of the dehumanizing history of the blackface mask in America and did not wear blackface. Thus, they could not have inspired the first Klopse to do so. It is entirely more likely that early Klopse learned most of their minstrel traditions from the white performers who toured Cape Town, not from McAdoo.[97]

Other additional carnival origin narratives placed African Americans at the center of the culture. One such story was voiced in 1948 by Jimmy Allen, founding director of the Western Province Jubilee Carnival Board (sometimes called the Western Province Jubilee Coloured Carnival Board). This was one of the most influential early carnival boards, and Allen's position as founding director makes him widely regarded as an authority on early carnival:

> Mr. Allen referred to the long standing controversy regarding the origin of the carnivals and expressed the opinion that as indicated by the word "coon," they had their roots among the Negro slaves in America who, dressed in a variety of gaudy, cast-off garments, entertained their master's families at the New Year. "I think that Negro slaves who escaped from ships in Cape Town and became absorbed in the population were the originators of the carnivals," he added. "We have gradually

> developed the custom and costumes. The persistently America flavour of the troupe titles, which have been handed down from generation to generation, lends considerable support to the theory that the first carnival coons in South Africa were fugitive slaves."[98]

According to this article, Jimmy Allen knew about the American meanings behind the word *coon* and believed the roots of carnival could be traced back to "authentic" African American culture.

A similar maritime narrative focused on black sailors. The following was told to the *Cape Times* in 1959 by Davey Petersen, founder and director of the Spes Bona Nigger Minstrels: "Davey Petersen . . . says he has heard it from older Coon leaders that the idea was planted here by American Negro seamen, who, while their ships were in port, would gather and sing their songs to the accompaniment of a guitar or banjo. The local lads would gather round and join in, and so the Coons were founded. The explanation seems feasible and would provide the direct link with America which is so obvious."[99] Although this story shows up only once in my archival findings, the fact that Petersen was circulating it makes it significant. Because Petersen directed one of the longest-running troupes of the midcentury carnivals, his social contacts granted him access to a large amount of carnival lore. His choice to foreground this story of black sailors over other possible alternatives suggests this narrative was in wide circulation. Relatedly, years later in the 1990s, Achmat Levy explained the origins of a popular carnival song: "If you say, 'Down in the Cornfield, where the cotton grows,' right, if you think back, likes, when, when the black people, American, black American people and the slaves time of course, they sing what . . . down, they was working on, on the cornfields, that's it! Then they make songs of it."[100]

In 1994 a carnival participant advanced another narrative that also centered African Americans: "When the Americans come from America . . . the Darkies . . . the Negroes like . . . they was working on 'lectric. They started putting 'lectric in Cape Town, so they singing the songs like Dixie songs . . . 'Dixie,' and all these."[101] According to this account, African American electricians who lived in District Six taught the song "Dixie" to coloured people. If this is true, African American expatriates might have found a way to appreciate "Dixie" by detaching the melody from lyrics celebrating the old American South. However, I am doubtful that black expatriates who were probably fleeing American racism would sing the unofficial anthem of the Confederacy. It is far more likely that Klopse drew inspiration from American sheet music that circulated in Cape Town. As mentioned earlier, according to Achmat Levy, many troupe members bought minstrel songs from a shop on Adderley Street. Relatedly, in 2008 I found a book of sheet music titled *The Original Christy Minstrel Song Book* in the National Library of South Africa in Cape Town. A song called "Dixie's Land" (an alternate title of "Dixie") appears in the table of contents, although the lyrics and musical score were not preserved in the archive. A robust trade in minstrel songs played out in Cape Town, and some Klopse probably learned to sing "Dixie" by purchasing minstrel sheet music. Even more learned "Dixie" from American movies. The song was part of the soundtrack of several Hollywood films, including *The Littlest Rebel* (1935), *Gone with the Wind* (1939), and *Dixie* (1943).[102] The latter included white American actor Bing Crosby appearing in blackface with large lips and woolly hair, a parade of blackface minstrels wearing urban-dandy outfits, and a musical finale featuring the song "Dixie." *Dixie* was released to international audiences in 1944, and in 1945 Cape Town carnival troupes started a new tradition by referencing "Dixie" in their names. In 1953 a Klopse named Solly Sahabodien alluded to the film *Dixie* when he described major cultural influences on carnival: "We saw American pictures where minstrels were shown parading the streets. . . . They sang songs from California, Dixieland, ragtime stuff and things, so now we also call our troupes after those names."[103] Years later, Achmat Levy described the influence of foreign movies: "[Here's] . . . how [Klopse] getting the songs. . . . [T]en of them goes in to the bioscope and they sing a song and everyone get [the] words, when they come outside, to the corner, then they start sing the song."[104] Ultimately, the story about African American electric workers is not as believable as other possibilities. However, this claim and similar stories suggesting African Americans taught minstrel culture to Klopse reveal much about the early carnival imaginary and the racial logics it promoted.

During the second half of the twentieth century, many Klopse participants and local media sources advanced the narrative that African Americans taught minstrel culture to coloureds. In these narratives, African Americans willingly share black song and dance. If minstrel culture was given to coloureds by actual African Americans, it becomes safe for participants to assume that carnival practices can be traced back to "authentic"

African American culture given willingly, rather than being a minstrel caricature marred by the issue of cultural appropriation. Although *Coon* was not used as a racial slur by the majority of carnival participants, the widespread origin narratives centering on African Americans suggest that many were aware of the racial play behind the blackface mask and, on some level, tried to justify it. Any potential feeling of guilt about hyperbolic mimicry could be assuaged with the comforting thought that real African Americans taught minstrel traditions to coloureds. Ultimately, I believe early Klopse were most interested in representing three kinds of nonwhite identities: African American, African, and coloured.

Many apartheid-era carnival participants self-consciously portrayed African Americans. The often-repeated origin narratives claiming that interactions between coloureds and African Americans created the foundations of carnival culture support this claim. These origin narratives suggest many carnival participants believed they were performing authentic African American culture. However, the version of African American culture that carnival participants represented was actually several steps removed from "authentic" African American culture. As Robert Toll has pointed out, by the 1870s many white minstrel troupes began moving away from "plantation" material to more variety performances. Historians of the late-nineteenth-century British minstrel show have maintained that many British minstrel troupes did not feature much African American music in their repertoires.[105] My survey of blackface minstrelsy in South Africa during the 1870s and 1880s reflects these changes, as a significant amount of the material performed during this period does not appear to come from (or even claim to come from) African American cultural sources.

When carnival participants performed African American culture, they were actually performing African American culture as it was represented on the minstrel stage. Therefore, some of the major minstrel conventions, like frenetic corporality, became a mainstay in carnival. The blackface minstrel formula, with its emphasis on hyperbolic excess, was a performance aesthetic that meshed well with the holiday celebrations in Cape Town. The blackface minstrel who sang comedic songs, crooned dramatic sentimental songs, and danced with reckless abandon provided a compelling model for the first Coon troupes to imitate. African Americans may have been associated with musical ability and high-speed dancing (both of which were minstrel tropes). These were appealing qualities for holiday revelers to emulate, and in doing so the carnival participants inadvertently reaffirmed many of the caricatures of African Americans that had been promoted on the minstrel stage.

African Americans were also associated with black modernity. For many carnival participants, blacking up was a means to access positive traits that they associated with African Americans but were denied to them by the South African government. Martin relates, "In this other world, an imaginary world indeed, the United States occupies a very special place: it is a land of freedom, of creativity and modernity, a land where people who are not white . . . are accepted as they are, where their talents are recognized. . . . Identifying with the United States is one of the mechanisms used by members of Cape Town's Coloured working class to devise an inner sense of self-identity (as opposed to the identity imposed upon them by South African authorities)."[106] Coloured scholar and playwright Nadia Davids recently offered a similar perspective: "Black America gradually became synonymous in the minds of Black Capetonians with freedom, autonomy, and self determination. . . . Adopting American blackface in some ways could be read as a traumatized community's attempt to create further culture cohesion through an imagined global alliance with another ex-slave community."[107] These perspectives are very important contributions to the discussion on early carnival. I find it hard to believe that a coloured community that included the descendants of many former slaves would consciously and consistently celebrate the proslavery logics of early blackface minstrelsy. Instead, most blackface Klopse were interested in establishing transnational alliances with African Americans. In such a scenario, traditionally exclusionary burnt cork nationalism was swapped out for Afro-diasporic nationalism in blackface: an imagined Afro-diasporic citizenship that moved beyond the spatial constraints of the South African racial state.

For many participants, carnival offered a rare opportunity to imaginatively move outside of the exclusionary borders of segregation-era South Africa. A 1921 carnival troupe called the Black Star Line Coons was an original variant of Afro-diasporic nationalism in blackface. The Black Star Line was a fleet of ships partially owned by Marcus Garvey and Amy Ashwood Garvey's New York–based organization, the Universal Negro Improvement Association (UNIA). The fleet was used to establish commercial relations between Afro-diasporic communities who were scattered across the Atlantic world.[108] If the UNIA's ultimate goal of establishing an independent African nation-state ever came to fruition, the Black Star Line would bring black people to the newly formed country. The UNIA established a strong presence in Cape Town.[109] The members of the Black Star Line Coon troupe understood the emancipatory potential of this troupe name. This group of Klopse celebrated the possibility of a nation-state where African American and coloured people could be first-class citizens free from the constraints of Western colonialism and exclusionary white racial states.

That being said, the Black Star Line Coons appeared in only one carnival, while troupes repeatedly referenced Bing Crosby's *Dixie* and Al Jolson's *Jazz Singer* for many years. Actual black people rarely appeared in these American films about white protagonists appropriating blackness. In fact, *Dixie* was a "biopic" very loosely based on the career of Dan Emmett of the Virginia Minstrels. By incorporating this movie and its music into the carnival repertoire, Klopse were recirculating Hollywood lore about an influential white American minstrel. Indeed, Klopse were influenced heavily by the fourth-wave minstrels who starred in Hollywood movies that were shown in relatively affordable inner-city cinemas in Cape Town.[110] Although many Klopse claimed the honor of being the Cape Town version of several international stars, Bing Crosby and Al Jolson enjoyed an especially large presence within the carnival imaginary. In 1935 a "little Al Jolson" appeared in carnival.[111] During the carnival of 1951, Al Jolson was celebrated because he had passed away in the previous year (fig. 11).[112] In 1956 a Klopse troupe toured Durban, and Al Jolson was the only international star who appeared on the program.[113] A Klopse who was remembered as "Cape Town's Al Jolson" performed with the Zonk Coon troupe in the middle decades of the century.[114] Another claimed to be "South Africa's Bing Crosby."[115] Many Klopse were channeling white American blackface performers instead of McAdoo. Coco Fusco has astutely described a kind of white American privilege to appropriate black culture as a "power to choose . . . power to determine value, and the right of the more powerful to consume without guilt."[116] By putting on the blackface mask and consciously imitating Al Jolson and Bing Crosby, some Klopse were trying to access a form of white modernity in blackface. Relatedly, some Klopse troupes highly valued the category of whiteness. In 1955 *Drum* magazine published a profile on a participant who claimed to be the only white Klopse: a man named David Stephens. At that time, Stephens

Figure 11. A picture from Cape Town Coon Carnival, 1957, showing a banner with an Al Jolson reference and a Klopse musician playing a cello pizzicato style. Courtesy of the National Library of South Africa, Cape Town.

was cocaptain of the Spes Bona Nigger Minstrels and a carnival veteran who had marched with the Klopse for thirty-five years. He claimed he was promoted to captain in each troupe he joined because "the rank and file of the [C]oons respected his color more than anything else."[117]

Consider a carnival picture from 1949. Members of the Young Louisiana Coons carry two banners: one blackface caricature striking Al Jolson's "jazz hands" pose from *The Jazz Singer* and another banner with a Union Jack and blessings to Prince Charles of the British royal family (fig. 12). This imaginary seems to be more interested in accessing transnational whiteness in blackface than transnational blackness. Years ago, Denis-Constant Martin advanced a different interpretation in which the Louisiana Coons were rejecting Afrikaner politics by celebrating a British royal family who "was seen by the Coons as a vestige of Justice."[118] I believe people are seeing different things in early carnival because carnival was a multivalent cultural practice creating space for celebrations of different topics. At the risk of creating two straw men, those who present the

Figure 12. Cape Town Coon Carnival, 1949. Courtesy of the National Library of South Africa, Cape Town.

apartheid-era carnival as simply a racist formation drawing only from the most antiblack traditions of the blackface minstrel show are demonstrably wrong. Those who claim no vestiges of antiblack minstrel vitriol survived in carnival are also missing an essential point, namely, that the early carnival was simultaneously infused with multiple and sometimes contradictory messages. This was largely because Klopse who were celebrating emancipation were working with a minstrel repertoire that offered many opportunities for regressive imaginings. As demonstrated in the previous chapter, even Orpheus McAdoo, a former slave who was thoroughly dedicated to uplift politics, was unable to completely extricate his performances from the proslavery logics of the minstrel repertoire.

One example of this complexity is a carnival advertisement from 1926 that offered a "special area reserved for Europeans" and a "Grand Combined Chorus of Troupes" singing "Massa's in De Cold, Cold Ground."[119] As mentioned in previous chapters, this minstrel song mourned the death of a "benevolent" slave master. One viable interpretation presents this moment as an attempt to sell carnival tickets by appealing to the sensibilities of patronizing white spectators rather than a statement of transnational solidarity with another community of former slaves. But what if we try to see this moment through the perspectives of Klopse who used carnival to observe the postslavery sentiments of "Tweede Nuwe Jaar," the second of January, a day that was often associated with the end of Cape slavery and the carnival? Klopse might have reinterpreted the lyrics into an antislavery song celebrating the death of a slave master. Perhaps the mournful notes were sung with a sense of joking irony. While some Klopse eulogized the "kind" master, others may have feted his passing. Carnival was complicated.

Whenever I present research on the Coon Carnival in the United States, African American academics and undergraduate students encourage me to not gloss over the racial language in early carnival: the "darkies," "niggers," and "nigger paste" that were preserved in archives. At a recent academic conference, I showed the aforementioned picture of the Louisiana Coon troupe to a group of American scholars—most of whom are African American—and heard audible gasps of disapproval. I vividly remember teaching carnival for the first time to a group of undergraduate students in Pennsylvania when an African American student raised her hand and asked, "But if this was celebrating us, why are they using the n-word?" Indeed, many coloureds identified as "better than black."[120] A segment of the carnival community was dancing the racial hierarchies of apartheid.

That being said, we Americans must be careful to not impose American meanings onto a coloured South African cultural pastime. We have to acknowledge the fact that culture changes meanings as it moves across national borders. We must also acknowledge the power relations at play. Coloured people were not privileged first-class citizens of the racial state like white American minstrels. Models of cultural appropriation that so accurately identify the privilege of white American minstrels are grossly inadequate when discussing Klopse who portrayed African Americans.

Moreover, oftentimes the archive is biased. The English-language archive reflects a colonial regime that privileged the perspectives of white settlers over anyone else.[121] The picture of the Louisiana Coons is available for present-day researchers because a British South African *Cape Times* reporter saw a Coon troupe who was celebrating the British royal family and deemed them worthy of preservation. Perhaps the emancipatory traditions that present-day academics and Klopse talk about flew under the radars of the "official" chroniclers of Cape history or were intentionally ignored. Gerald Stone, a linguist who conducted ethnographic research on carnival in the late 1960s, claimed many carnival participants carried a "subtle" slave "consciousness" that was difficult for scholars to "demonstrate" but was present nonetheless.[122] I believe English-language newspaper correspondents who covered carnival were generally more interested in cataloging what they could relate with (Union Jack flags) rather than this subtle slave consciousness.

Many Klopse troupes tried to reinterpret blackface minstrel aesthetics toward more progressive goals. While some Klopse were channeling Bing Crosby and *Dixie,* others looked toward African Americans as a model of freedom and black modernity. For many of the early participants, the carnival was a time to celebrate the ending of slavery in the Cape and imagine transnational alliances.

African Americans were a foreign black population with whom the coloured community had relatively little direct contact and did not compete economically. This is in stark contrast to the relationship between coloureds and Africans, a relationship filled with tension and antagonism. Historically speaking, the apartheid state pitted coloureds and Africans against each other in Cape Town's labor market. For example, the Coloured Labour Preference Policy of 1955 attempted to slow the rate of African immigration to the Western Cape and protect coloured labor from African competition.[123] I believe some of the African masquerades in carnival were conscious caricatures born in response to the material relations between coloureds and Africans.

Muhammad Adhikari has published the most thorough historical monograph on coloured identity.[124] According to Adhikari, coloured identity emerged when "acculturated" Khoisan and mixed-race slave descendants responded to large migrations of Eastern Cape Africans to Cape Town in the late nineteenth century. As a result of the sudden influx, the term *coloured* was used to differentiate the relatively Westernized "black" people of the Western Cape from unassimilated Bantu-speaking African immigrants. During the era of white rule, coloured identity "remained essentially stable. . . . [T]his is not to contend that [c]oloured identity was static or that it lacked fluidity but that the continuities during the period were more fundamental to the way in which it operated as a social identity and a more consistent part of its functioning than the changes it experienced."[125] Adhikari describes several "characteristics" that defined coloured identity. First, many people in the coloured community aspired toward cultural assimilation. This assimilationist mentality was fueled by the hope that adopting European culture would lead to inclusion within the dominant group and full citizenship rights. The second characteristic was an understanding that coloureds enjoyed an intermediate status on the South African racial hierarchy. Coloureds often defended this intermediate status by distancing themselves from Africans. One of the major goals of political organizing in the coloured community was to maintain a position of relative privilege over Africans. Furthermore, intermediate status also played a role in "daily life," where "the most consistent—and insistent—element in the expression of [c]oloured identity was an association with whiteness and a concomitant distancing from Africanness, whether in the value placed on fair skin and straight hair, in the prizing of white ancestors in the family lineage, or in taking pride in the degree to which they were able to conform to the standards of Western bourgeois culture. This 'white-mindedness' as one commentator referred to it, could give rise to . . . an aggressive bigotry toward Africans."[126]

Interviews that were carried out around the time of the 1994 elections (which marked the end of apartheid) provide extreme examples of this "bigotry." In 1993 a coloured working-class woman told Adhikari: "And a kaffir, even if he wears a golden ring, still remains an ape. . . . They have nothing, they say they have a culture, they don't have a culture, they're raw. They say we brown people are mixed masala, but we brown people are closer to white people, than they are to white people. Because our culture and the white people's culture are the same."[127]

Social geographer John Western's scholarship on segregation in Cape Town reveals many examples of what his informants called "Coloured Racism." Western visited Cape Town in the aftermath of the 1994 elections and received a wealth of information on racial attitudes. The following theme came up often during interviews: *swart gevaar redux*, or "our country, not theirs." This perspective claims the Western Cape as a coloured territory rather than an African one. Western further views voting trends during the 1994 elections in which coloureds supported the Nationalist Party instead of the African National Congress as evidence of this worldview.[128] One coloured respondent offered the following rationale explaining why coloureds voted for the party of apartheid: "[W]hat is emerging now is very strong currents of racism in [c]oloured communities, particularly in the working-class areas, your Mannenbergs and Mitchell's Plains and things. . . . There's a perception . . . ah . . . that because the government has committed itself to Affirmative Action, that because there are no longer segregated housing areas, developments, there's a perception that they will lose their jobs and that they will lose their houses, or if they're on some housing waiting list they won't get preference even though they've been on it for all these years."[129] Another coloured informant offered more relevant commentary: "Coloureds of the Western Cape do not see themselves as being black. . . . [They] have an aversion to the 'black' as in 'African.' In fact, my own people are horrified when you try to explain to them that they are also Africans. . . . To compare them to Africans is a big no-no because they do not see themselves as equal to the African but superior."[130]

Western argues that material competition for scarce resources is the major factor contributing to such feelings of racial superiority. It is important to note that this material competition between working-class coloureds and Africans was playing out long before the 1994 elections. As Ian Goldin observed, during the first decades of the twentieth century, many failed worker actions convinced most coloured laborers they could not improve their position in relation to white workers. This development combined with a rapid increase in Bantu-speaking working-class people in Cape Town, as well as an economic depression between 1903 and 1909, led to attempts by working-class coloureds to begin improving their position relative to African workers.[131] What has been called "Coloured Racism" against Africans was a response to economic competition that threatened the intermediate status of coloureds in the Western Cape.

Over the years, many Klopse troupes masqueraded as African people. The inaugural carnival of 1907 included the Dahomey Coon Troupe. One 1907 participant was reportedly "dressed, or rather undressed, like an aboriginal native."[132] A carnival advertisement from 1926 mentioned "Kaffir Dances" among the offerings.[133] In 1939 a "Coons Concert in the City Hall" included "humours, sketches, combined singing, and imitation of native war dances."[134] Furthermore, as table 1 demonstrates, entire Klopse troupes impersonated Africans.

Some of the carnival representations of Africans were cultural articulations of a mentality that positioned coloureds above Africans. Perhaps this is why, apart from a small group of musicians, Africans were not invited to participate in the carnival until 1996.[135] During the apartheid era, coloureds had slightly more access to citizenship and resources than most Africans. When bringing the blackface mask into such an equation, the racial impersonations of Klopse begin to look similar (but far from identical) to the burnt cork nationalism of American minstrel shows in which privileged white citizens reinforced their standing by denigrating the concept of African American citizenship. When people have uneven levels of access to citizenship, comically impersonating a group that is lower on the social hierarchy is often a means of reinforcing one's own social position. Some Klopse who blackened up and presented hyperbolic portrayals of Africans were enacting performative expressions of social power. Studies on blackface minstrelsy in the United States observe how middle groups used minstrelsy as a means to distance themselves from African Americans, "Americanize," and move up the social hierarchy. The Irish performers of early minstrelsy were one example of this trend.[136] The immigrant Jewish performers of early-twentieth-century minstrelsy were another.[137] Some Coon Carnival participants were performing a similar act of distancing, and social climbing, as they signed up for the Matabele or Zulu Warriors carnival troupes. Interestingly enough, in the 1908 carnival, one performer from the Dahomey Coon Troupe reportedly sang the refrain, "Ah'm getting mo' like de white folks ebery day." The encore version of the song included the lyrics "Ah'm shure Ah'm gettin' wusser every day."[138] These lyrics expressed a significant logic: by performing and making visible the cultural difference between coloureds and "savage" Africans, coloureds were subtly making claims toward whiteness and "civilization." Just as blackface minstrels in the United States and England contributed to a racial binary that constructed blackness and whiteness as antithetical, carnival representations of Africans produced another binary. Klopse who performed African masquerades in blackface used a hyperbolic African identity as a vessel for moving beyond "civilized decorum," while reinforcing their status as closer to whiteness than the groups they mimicked. African masquerades highlighted the border that separated the constructs of coloured and African, a border marked by the logics of "modernity" and "primitivism." Tellingly, some Klopse said the Zulu carnival masqueraders "looked like cannibals."[139] Carnival gave participants the freedom to be "African" for a day and delight in a "savage" and "premodern" form of play.

At the same time, African masquerades may have also created space for anticolonial imaginings. Some carnival participants may have celebrated Africans as anticolonial freedom fighters. This might be why African ethnic groups who had a reputation for anticolonial resistance, like the Zulu, Matabele, and Kikuyu, were represented in the carnival.[140] When African and Native American warriors were portrayed in carnival, masqueraders imaginatively enacted romanticized versions of premodern warrior masculinity. These performances of warrior identities may have been carried out with respect and appreciation, as some scholars have argued was the case with the Mardi Gras Indians of New Orleans.[141] Some coloureds may have been imagining an anticolonial alliance with Africans, Native Americans, and others who famously resisted the onslaught of white settlers and imperial soldiers.

While some Klopse portrayed Africans, many more were performing coloured identity. Many carnival troupes used minstrel aesthetics to create hyperbolic representations of coloured people. This interpretation is supported by the many troupe names from early carnival that referenced South African places or products: Cape Town Hawker Coons, Cape Town's Famous Checker Coons, Cape Town Gentleman Jazz Singers, Beaconsfield Darkies, Seven Steps Darkies, Mannenberg Entertaining Minstrels, Athlone Cottonfield Darkies, Woodstock Mohawk Minstrels, Bokomo Cornfields Darkies, Maltabella Planation Darkies, and S. A. Independent Darkies. The frequent usage of the term *darkie* is instructive. It suggests many Klopse applied that term in a positive way, similar to how many African Americans have redefined the word *nigga*.[142]

According to Vincent Kolbe, founding member of the District Six museum and local authority on coloured people and culture, the "Klopse at new year was strictly a jolly thing . . . all the comic stuff you know. Entertainment, humor, self-mockery."[143] In other words, a large portion of carnival participants used the conventions of blackface minstrelsy to represent themselves. These Klopse used minstrel aesthetics to create a joyful and comedic coloured carnival character.

Many Klopse were accessing a carnival imaginary Mikhail Bakhtin has labeled the "carnivalesque." Bakhtin coined the term *carnivalesque* to describe a temporary inversion of social power that plays out in carnivals.[144] Cape Town carnival was the only time during the year when the social world was flipped upside down. For many spectators and participants, the carnival was a rare moment when coloureds could claim control over the center of Cape Town. Coloureds took symbolic control over the city by marching through and claiming central thoroughfares and stadiums. Across several decades, many headlines in local newspapers voiced variations of the theme "Coons Take over the City." But the early carnivalesque was not only confined to spatial logics; race was also a large part of the imaginary.

During the era of legal racial segregation, Klopse troupes performed different variants of racial carnivalesque. This form of carnivalesque encouraged temporary opportunities to move across racial lines during an era when apartheid logics reigned supreme. Tellingly, the 1950s were the decade when the segregation-era carnival enjoyed its greatest popularity. During this decade, a high level of public interest in carnival allowed five carnival boards to secure enough performers, funding, and patrons to thrive at the same time. During the first two weeks of January, multiple separate carnivals were staged by the different carnival boards. A combined carnival in 1957 featured troupes from four carnival boards and is an example of the massive scale of the carnivals from this decade. Six thousand performers participated in the combined carnival.[145]

The post–World War II economic boom is a partial explanation for the increase in participation during this decade. Cape Town's residents had relatively more disposable income. More coloureds were able to afford the carnival costumes, and more spectators could purchase tickets to see the spectacle. However, economic factors explain only part of the story. Apartheid's tyrannical methods of social control must also be considered. In 1948 the Nationalist Party instituted the policy of apartheid. In 1949 the apartheid government issued a "total ban on T.V." by claiming state control over all television broadcasts.[146] During that same year, mixed-race marriages were outlawed by the Prohibition of Mixed Marriage Act. In 1950 the state crusade against "miscegenation" was taken a step further with the passing of the Immorality Act. This law made sexual relationships between people of different races a criminal offense. Also in 1950 the Population Registration Act forced each individual in South Africa to register within four prescribed racial categories: "Black," "Coloured," "Asian," or "White." Finally, the Group Areas Act of 1950 mapped out a policy of residential segregation in South Africa's cities, in which different races were forced to live in specific neighborhoods. The social logic of apartheid was one of state-imposed racial essentialism in which people

Table 1. "Black" references in early carnival troupe names

Year	Generic representations of blackness	African representations	African American representation
1907	1. Jolly Coon Masquerading Troupe 2. Dark Town Fire Brigade	1. Dahomey Coon Troupe	
1908	1. Happy Little Darkies Masquerading Troupe 2. Dandy Coloured Coons (reference to minstrel song titled "Dandy Coloured Coon") 3. Dark Town Fire Brigade	1. Dahomeys Masquerading Troupe	1. Mississippi Sporting Club 2. Mississippi Coons
1909			1. Selma Coons 2. Baltimore Coons
1910–13: No organized carnivals in Cape Town			
1914		1. Dahomey Coons	
1915–19: No organized carnivals in Cape Town			
1920	1. Dusky Dinah Coons (reference to a minstrel song titled "Dusky Dinah")	1. Dahomey Coons 2. Matabele Warriors 3. Egyptian Burglars	
1921	1. Dusky Dinah Coons	1.Dahomey Coons 2. Matabele Warriors 3. Egyptian Burglars	1. Black Star Line Coons 2. Virginia Barn Coons
1923	1. Plantation Coons 2. Dusky Dinah Coons	1. Dahomey Coons	1. Virginia Barn Coons
1927	1. Cotton Field Darkies 2. S.A. Independent Darkies		1. S.A. American Darkies
1930	1. Golden Eye Darkies 2. Weeping Darkies		1. Alabama Coons 2. California Jazz Singers
1932			1. Jubilee Singers (a reference to McAdoo's troupe) 2. Happy Boston Coons
1933	1. White Eyed Darkies 2. Checker Plantation Coons		
1935	1. Dawn Darkies 2. Millionaire Darkies	1. Kikuyu Warriors	1. Alabama Coons 2. American Jazz Singers 3. Broadway Gentlemen Coons
1937	1. Grand Parade Darkies 2. Millionaire Darkies 3. Dawn Darkies		1. Young Louisiana Coons 2. Broadway Gentlemen Coons 3. Alabama Coons

Table 1 (*continued*)

Year	Generic representations of blackness	African representations	African American representation
1938	1. Happy Little Darkies 2. Grand Parade Minstrel Darkies 3. Happy Little Niggers in Town 4. Cotton Field Darkies 5. S.A. Dawn Darkies	1. Zulu Warriors	1. Mississippi Darkes 2. Gold Bar Broadway Gentlemen Coons 3. Kentucky Plantation Coons 4. Happy Little Niggers in Broadway 5. Radio Students of Broadway 6. California Jazz Singing Coons 7. Hollywood Jazz Singers 8. Alabama Coons 9. Happy Boston Coons
1939	1. Happy Little Darkies 2. Happy Little Niggers 3. Athlone Cotton Field Darkies 4. Independent Dawn Darkies 5. Honolulu Darkes	1. Zulu Warriors	1. Happy Niggers of Broadway 2. California Jazz Singing Coons 3. Radio Students of Broadway 4. Happy Bostons 5. Gold Bar Gentlemen Coons 6. Louisiana Gentlemen Coons 7. Kentucky Plantation Coons 8. Independent Broadway Darkies 9. Mississippi Darkies
1940	1. Sunflower Darkies 2. Grand Parade Darkies		1. S.A. Broadway Gentlemen Coons
1942	1. International Cotton Field Darkies 2. Sunflower Darkies		1. Kentucky Victory Coons 2. Hollywood Jazz Singers 3. Gentleman Broadway Coons
1945	1. South African Broadway Dixie Darkies		1. Kentucky Victory Coons 2. Broadway Gentlemen 3. Mississippi Darkies 4. Young Louisiana Coons
1946	1. Original Cotton Field Darkies		1. Broadway Ex-volunteer Darkies 2. Broadway Gentlemen Jazz Singers

Table 1 (*continued*)

Year	Generic representations of blackness	African representations	African American representation
1947	1. Original Cotton Field Darkies 2. Cape Town Ex-Servicemen Darkies 3. Zonk Swing Star Darkies		1. American Jubilee Singers
1948	1. Continental Darkies 2. Sunflower Darkies 3. Cape Town Ex-Servicemen Darkies 4. Coronation Darkies 5. Beaconsfield Darkies 6. Honolulu Dainty Darkies 7. Vienna Darkies	1. Zulu Warriors 2. Young Dahomey Crooning Minstrels	1. Pennsylvania Dandy Darkies 2. Kentucky Minstrel Coons 3. Original Louisiana Coons 4. American Jubilee Jazz Singers 5. United Broadway Serenaders 6. Broadway Ex-Volunteer Darkies 7. Hollywood Serenaders
1949	1. Continental Darkies 2. Enfield Darkies 3. Zonk Swing Star Darkies	1. Young Dahomey Coons	1. Pennsylvania Dandy Darkies 2. Kentucky Minstrel Darkies 3. Louisiana Coons 4. Crooning Dixiana Minstrels
1950	1. Loyal Ex-Volunteer Darkies 2. Beaconsfield Darkies 3. Springbok Darkies 4. Rainbow Darkies 5. Cotton Field Darkies		1. Happy Little Niggers of Broadway 2. Pennsylvania Darkies
1951	1. Honolulu Dainty Darkies 2. Spes Bona Festival Darkies 3. Ragtime Millionaire Darkies 4. Bokomo Cornfield Darkies 5. South African Darkies 6. Rainbow Dixie Darkies 7. Invincible Darkies 8. Rainbow Darkies 9 Star Darkies	1. Dahomey Gentlemen Coons 2. Ethiopian Jazz Singers	1. Louisiana Coons 2. Harlem Darkies 3. Happy Little Niggers of Broadway 4. Original Happy Boston Coons 5. Liberty Philadelphia Minstrels 6. Young Boston Singing Broadcasting Coons 7. Louisiana Happy Little Darkies 8. Pennsylvania Darkies 9. Manhattan Dixie Darkies 10. Swanee River Minstrels (reference to minstrel song)

Table 1 (*continued*)

Year	Generic representations of blackness	African representations	African American representation
1952	1. International Cotton Field Darkies 2. Spes Bona Darkies 3. Ragtime Millionaire Darkies 4. Bokomo Cornfield Darkies 5. Young Diamond Eyes 6. Starlight Minstrel Darkies	1. Ethiopian Jazz Singers 2. Young Dahomey Gentlemen Coons	1. Louisiana Coons 2. Happy Little Niggers of Broadway 3. Liberty Philadelphia Minstrels 4. Famous Young Louisiana Coons 5. New Orleans Minstrel Darkies 6. Manhattan Dixie Darkies 7. Virginia Darkies 8. Harlem Darkies 9. Honolulu Dainty Darkies
1953	1. Spes Bona Nigger Minstrels 2. Beaconsfield Darkies		1. Young Louisiana Coons 2. Famous Pennsylvania Darkies 3. United Broadway Gentlemen Coons 4. New Orleans Coronations Darkies 5. Fabulous Cincinnati Jazz Singers 6. Virginia Surprise Coons 7. Hollywood Panamanians Serenaders
1954	1. Beaconsfield Darkies 2. Dainty Dixie Darkies		1. Manhattan Dixie Darkies 2. Famous Pennsylvania Darkies 3. United Broadway Gentlemen Coons 4. Virginia Crooning Minstrels 5. New Orleans Beaconsfield Darkies 6 Beaconsfield Hollywood Palm Beach Serenaders
1955	1. Starlight Melody Darkies 2. Spes Bona Nigger Minstrels 3. Jolson Jazz Singers 4. Original Grand Parade Darkies	1. Young Dahomey Darkies 2. Ethiopian Jazz Singers	1. Young Louisiana Coons 2. Harlem Darkies 3. Fabulous Cincinnati Jazz Singers 4. New Orleans Minstrel Darkies 5. Famous Pennsylvania Darkies

Table 1 (*continued*)

Year	Generic representations of blackness	African representations	African American representation
1956	1. Beaconsfield Darkies 2. Spes Bona Nigger Minstrels 3. Seven Steps Darkies		1. New Orleans Minstrels 2. Louisiana Coons 3. Fabulous Cincinatti Jazz Singers 4. Pennsylvania Darkies
1957	1. Seven Steps Darkies 2. Cape Town Nigger Minstrels		1. Broadway Gentlemen Coons 2. Pennsylvania Darkies
1958	1. Meadow Cotton Field Darkies 2. Starlight Melody Darkies 3. Spes Bona Nigger Minstrels 4. Famous Invincible Darkies	1 Young Dahomey Coons 2. Ethiopian Jazz Singers	1. New Orleans Minstrel Darkies
1959	1. Invincible Darkies 2. Orange Plantation Darkies 3. Maltabella Plantation Darkies 4. Starlight Melody Darkies 5. Spes Bona Nigger Minstrels 6. Meadow Cottonfield Darkies 7. Monte Carlo Millionaire Darkies	1. Young Dahomey Gentlemen Coons 2. Ethiopian Jazz Serenaders	1. Original Philadelphian Liberties 2. Mississippi Nigger Minstrels 3. Canadula Ohio Darkies 4. Yankee Doodle Dandy Darkies
1960	1. Jolson Jazz Singers 2. Spes Bona Nigger Minstrels 3. Duckland Darkies 4. Fabulous Orange Plantation Darkies 4. Five Star Melody Darkies 5. Gold Dollar Gentlemen Darkies	1. Dahomeys 2. Ethiopian Jazz Serenaders	1. Original Colorado Jitterbug Darkies 2. Fabulous Cincinnati Darkies
1962	1. Spes Bona Nigger Minstrels 2. Goodwood Starlight Melody Darkies	1. Dahomey Gentlemen Minstrels 2. Matabele Empire Jazz Singers	1. Golden State Dixies 2. Louisiana Broadway Gentlemen Coons 3. Honolulu Dainty Darkies 4. Dixie Nigger Minstrels

Table 1 (*continued*)

Year	Generic representations of blackness	African representations	African American representation
1963	1. South African Springboks Darkies 2. Spes Bona Nigger Minstrels	1. Zulu Warriors	1. Young Louisiana Gentleman Coons 2. The Young Happy Bostons 3. Alabama Sunflower Darkies
1964		1. Young Dahomey Crooning Minstrels	
1966	1. Spes Bona Nigger Minstrels 2. 20th Century Darkies	1. Young Dahomey Minstrels 2. Ethiopian Hollywood Singers	1. Happy Boston Minstrels 2. Golden State Dixies
1967	1. Spes Bona Nigger Minstrels 2. Young Jolly Jolson	1. Young Dahomey Minstrels	
1968	1. Orient Plantation Darkies 2. Spes Bona Nigger Minstrels 3. Young Jolly Jolson Minstrels (by 1969, they were going by the name Jolly Jolson Nigger Troupe)	1. Ethiopian Jubilee Jazz Singers 2. Young Dahomey Crooning Minstrels	1. Mississippi Nigger Minstrels

were placed in preestablished racial groups. The racial groups were socially, economically, and geographically isolated from one another. Various forms of interracial mixing and border crossing were prohibited. A well-funded police force patrolled the borders between racial identities and violently enforced the policies of separation. In short, the racial state tried to impose a social reality in which racial groups were separate, hermetically sealed, impermeable. Given this constraining social context, we should consider another explanation for the upsurge in carnival participation during the 1950s. That is, carnival offered coloured Capetonians a temporary respite from the essentializing logics of the apartheid regime. During carnival time, coloureds could imaginatively step into the bodies of African Americans, Africans, and Native Americans. Carnival gave participants the power and agency to move outside the predesignated racial identities of the apartheid state. The carnivals of the 1950s advanced a coloured Klopse variant of Bakhtinian carnivalesque foregrounding racial masquerade across colonized groups. This was not the traditional burnt cork nationalism of early minstrel shows in which white citizens reinforced the boundaries of the white racial state. Instead, many participants used minstrel aesthetics to temporarily break the racial shackles of the apartheid state. Nonetheless, by blacking up, some Klopse contributed to a carnival imaginary partly informed by a logic of relative privilege in relation to Africans.

CONCLUSION: POSTAPARTHEID IMAGININGS

In 1939 a Coon troupe was seriously considering a plan to masquerade as Afrikaner Voortrekkers. After some deliberation, "the captain, Mr. J. D. Le Roux, decided to withdraw the items, as a burlesque of the Voortrekkers would hurt the susceptibilities of many Afrikaners. [Afrikaner newspaper] 'Die Burger,' however, states that a number of Afrikaans-speaking people were prepared to hold a meeting in Cape Town protesting against the intention of the [troupe] had they proceeded with their 'Voortrek.'"[147] This story is a reminder of the central role social power plays in delimiting what constitutes socially acceptable masquerade. With talk of Afrikaner protest circulating, the troupe leaders wisely decided it would not be politically prudent to masquerade as a group who occupied a higher position on the social hierarchy of the country. I did not find any moments when Afrikaners were represented in the carnival. For coloured South Africans living in a white racial state, the carnivalesque imaginary was constrained in very real ways. Some social identities were off limits. The whiteness of Afrikaners was a form of exclusive property.[148]

Two decades into the postapartheid era, in January 2010, I saw the carnival in person. I was fascinated by the lack of minstrel retentions. Brass bands were widespread, and I saw only a handful of banjos. Many of the minstrel competition categories remained, such as comic and sentimental singing, but the music drew from contemporary American popular music instead of blackface minstrel shows. The urban-dandy outfit remained as the most obvious minstrel retention. Most important for my purposes, the blackface mask was not part of the carnival I saw in 2010. Klopse continue to wear face paint, but now instead of the minstrel mask they use elaborate multicolor patterns, matching the colors of their respective troupe outfits.[149]

The postapartheid carnival is very different from the carnivals of the early years. Although I believe there is much to celebrate in the early carnivals, the blackface mask was a heavy burden, holding back its progressive potential. Even though many Klopse celebrated black modernity, Afro-diasporic nationalism, and emancipation from slavery while behind the blackface mask, the hyperbolic imagery still carried the potential to be infused with racist interpretations. This was especially evident in the accounts of white newspaper reporters who used dehumanizing terms like *sambo* to describe carnival participants. Addressing such complexities, Denis-Constant Martin has advanced an astute description of the "[blackface] mask of the [Cape Town] Coon" as a "figure of ambivalence."[150] With the discursive baggage and ambiguous potential of blackface removed, the postapartheid carnival mask becomes an empty signifier through which several topics can be celebrated. The new carnival mask can be interpreted as a multicolored mash-up having nothing to do with race. Instead, participants paint their faces to match the colors of their respective troupe outfits and achieve color coordination. Melvin Matthews, chief executive officer of the Cape Town Minstrel Carnival in 2003, stated, "It's not about blackface, you can paint it green or blue or red or white or whatever. . . . It's not about the race."[151] The postapartheid carnival mask can be interpreted as a representation of a nonracialism perspective that has taken hold among some South Africans.[152] Supporting this interpretation is the fact that racial signifiers have been stricken, almost entirely, from carnival troupe names. Ethnomusicologist Francesca Inglese has compiled an informative list of troupe names from the 2012 and 2013 carnivals. Significantly, the list does not mention racial slurs.[153] Similarly, in 2009 photographer Gerald Hoberman published a list of troupes in the Cape Town Minstrel Carnival Association that included no racial slurs.[154] Many participants in postapartheid carnival are celebrating a kind of nonracialism.

Another viable interpretation argues that racial logics have been retained in the postapartheid carnival. In this framework, the multicolored mask represents the Rainbow Nation, the term coined by Archbishop Desmond Tutu to describe South African national identity during the postapartheid era. From this perspective, today's carnival character represents racial inclusion and multiracialism. According to Francesca Inglese, some present-day Klopse describe carnival as "the Rainbow Nation in sound."[155] Furthermore, one interpretation that becomes even more viable when blackface was removed suggests the carnival mask is a symbol of cultural creolization; this is not so much a rainbow, where the colors run side by side, but a mixture of colors—a celebration of creole coloured identity. Now that blackface has been removed, postapartheid carnival participants unambiguously celebrate a myriad of topics: coloured identity, the end of Cape slavery, nonracialism, coloured modernity, black modernity, multiracial democracy, the passing of another year, life, and the survival of coloured creole culture under oppressive conditions.

The postapartheid carnival is a testament to the vibrancy of a creole culture that coloured people refused to let the apartheid regime stamp out. During the apartheid era, the state tried to ban the troupes from marching in the streets. In response, some carnival songs from the era hurled unveiled vitriol at major icons of European colonialism. One song mocked the Dutch East India Company official who was the first commander of the Cape Colony back in 1652, "Hey, Jan van Riebeeck's 'thing' is impotent." Another song cursed a major architect of apartheid: "Verwoerd is gonna die."[156] These songs were created during a time when it was extremely dangerous to openly mock the authoritarian apartheid state. Relatedly, one old *ghoemaliedjies* (drum song) that was sung during carnival time converted "Rule Britannia!" into an anticolonial anthem. The lyrics, translated from Afrikaans to English, read as:

> Come Britannia, the civilizing one
> Make the nations into slaves . . .
> You tyranny will soon humble
> Those that call this land their own.[157]

These were songs of resistance and survival.

The postapartheid carnival is proof of a flourishing coloured carnival culture that is not dependent on blackface minstrel aesthetics to thrive. Few blackface minstrel remnants persist in present-day carnivals. Minstrel-inspired racial slurs have been removed. Blackface makeup has been removed. The only visual retentions are urban-dandy outfits and minstrel-inspired lipstick. But these remnants from blackface minstrel shows are not being used by Klopse to mock black citizenship or physicality. Klopse have decoupled them from minstrel-inspired blackface masking traditions and revised them for a Cape Town carnival context. Similarly, banjos and tambourines are traditional minstrel instruments that still appear in carnival bands. However, by using such instruments to make ghoema beats,

Klopse reinterpreted them as vessels for continuing the music-making traditions of enslaved people in the Cape.[158] Moreover, after Klopse shifted to brass bands in the 1960s, ghoema drums proliferated largely because percussive minstrel instruments were drowned out by the horns.[159] All of which is to say the recent change from "Minstrel Carnival" to "Cape Town Street Parade" offers a more aesthetically accurate way to describe a carnival culture built on local sensibilities rather than minstrel vestiges. The new name, the "Cape Town Street Parade," pays homage to coloured people in the nineteenth century who celebrated the end of slavery decades before blackface minstrel conventions were incorporated into the Tweede Nuwe Jaar festivities. It also accurately describes a postapartheid carnival culture with few minstrel retentions. Today, ghoema beats steadily march forward without the heavy burden of blackface.

When was blackface removed from the carnival? Newspaper evidence from the 1980s demonstrates that blackface was still used in the carnival during that decade.[160] However, photos suggest the tradition of blacking up did not survive into the new millennium.[161] Relatedly, in 1995 a longtime carnival participant named Karriem Thompson described the shift away from blackface: "And the [C]oons you get nowadays . . . they don't use satin anymore. . . . and then you paint your faces white with a black . . . mouth . . . but nowadays you find the guys usually . . . stars or they take apiece of lipstick and just so make up their face."[162] This evidence suggests it was during the 1990s that blackface was removed from carnival. This development poses a necessary follow-up question: Why did the carnival change so dramatically during this decade?

The 1994 election brought sweeping change that fundamentally transformed the social landscape of South Africa. After most coloured voters chose the Nationalist Party over the African leaders of the ANC, many commentators claimed that coloureds voted for the party of apartheid in an attempt to defend their intermediate status. When the ANC won the 1994 election, the coloured community was confronted with a new political reality. Many coloureds believed the ANC government would show preference for Africans in the job and housing markets. According to this perspective, the postapartheid era has brought continued political, social, and economic marginalization for coloureds, as a white power structure was eclipsed by an African one.[163]

If we understand the hyperbolic conventions of blackface minstrel shows as cultural reflections of the power relations in white racial states, the reasons carnival changed in the 1990s become quite clear. The 1994 elections mark one of the most extreme cases of democratic social change in the twentieth century, as an Afrikaner power structure was eclipsed by an African one. Carnival participants could not masquerade as Voortrekkers in 1939, because they did not want to provoke a social group who "outranked" them. In the carnivals of postapartheid South Africa, a similar logic is at work. Now that an African political establishment has been created, hyperbolic representations of blackness are not politically advisable. Thus, the carnival had to adapt to reflect this new postapartheid moment. As we have seen, many of the segregation-era Coon troupes were masquerading as "niggers" or "darkies." In contrast, during the postapartheid era, naming a troupe the "Mississippi Nigger Minstrels" or "Jolly Jolson Nigger Troupe" might incite backlash. Because of these reasons, minstrel slurs and blackface had to be removed from carnival.

In turn, President Nelson Mandela embraced the Klopse in 1996 when he walked into Green Point Stadium wearing a "sequined minstrel style outfit in the colours of the ANC."[164] His speech described a postapartheid national identity narrative in which carnival was "as much a part of South Africa as braaivleis [barbecue] and Zulu dance. . . . *[I]t is us*."[165] Mandela did not wear a carnival mask. He did so as a politician who needed to be easily identifiable if he was going to gain support from a coloured community who overwhelmingly voted against him in the 1994 election. But I believe the decision to not blacken his face sheds light on a more complicated story about the relationship between black Africans and carnival. Mandela was endorsing a postapartheid carnival culture that had discontinued the use of blackface paint and troupe names with racial slurs. Just two years prior to his Green Point Stadium address, he equated the racial slur *kaffir* to *nigger* in his autobiography.[166] It is hard to imagine Mandela endorsing the "Dixie Nigger Minstrels" or "Kaffir dances" of early carnivals. I doubt he would have appreciated the hyperbolic blackface mask that often accompanied the early carnival imaginary. But the postapartheid carnival is a different matter. Now that blackface has been removed from carnival, African people can participate without having to wear a mask that was previously used by white minstrels to dehumanize black people.

American history offers some relevant, albeit extremely different, points of comparison to the early Coon Carnivals. The Mummers Parade of Philadelphia is a white American holiday celebration that plays out on January 1 and traditionally includes large amounts of blackface. One parade character is known as the "mummers wench," a white man in blackface and drag who sports feminine clothes and hairy legs. The usage of blackface in Philadelphia mumming can be traced back to Christmas mumming traditions in England, France, and Ireland when holiday revelers disguised themselves—often in blackface—and walked from house to house to trade comedic skits for food and drink. The tradition of Christmas mumming was brought to Philadelphia by European immigrants in the late 1600s and was practiced throughout the colonial era. Most of Philadelphia's Christmas mummers were peaceful, but from the 1830s though the 1880s, many white working-class mummers put on blackface and physically attacked black people in acts that David Roediger describes as "blackface-on-black violence." Recent white immigrants were also targeted in some of these attacks. Gradually, the local police force and municipal government found ways to regulate the rowdy festivities by shifting the celebrations to New Year's Day and inaugurating an officially sponsored Mummers Parade in 1901. Blackface masking was a large part of the Mummers Parade until the mid-1960s, when the National Association for the Advancement of Colored People (NAACP) and Congress of Racial Equality successfully petitioned the city government to enforce a blackface ban. A small handful of participants continue to blacken up while insisting it as a harmless "tradition," but since 1965 blackface characters rarely appear in the parade.[167]

The social life of *Amos 'n' Andy* is another useful point of comparison. The *Amos 'n' Andy Show* began in 1928 as the brainchild of two white comedians named Freeman Gosden and Charles Correll. Gosden and Correll used minstrel conventions (such as black illogics) to imitate African American speech and song. *Amos 'n' Andy* quickly became one of the most popular radio shows in the United States. During the 1950s, CBS created a television adaptation of the show, which included black actors but continued the minstrel sensibilities of the program. Largely in response to repeated protests by the NAACP, *Amos 'n' Andy* was taken off the air in 1966. *Amos 'n' Andy* represents the last officially sanctioned American entertainment show that can be directly linked to blackface minstrel performance traditions.[168] Its termination marks the end of an era when minstrel-inspired representations regularly appeared in American popular culture. After

1966 most mainstream American media outlets stopped creating portrayals of black people that directly and unequivocally drew inspiration from minstrel shows.

It is not a random coincidence that blackface mummers, *Amos 'n' Andy*, and blackface Klopse were each removed during decades of immense social change when black people gained a larger amount of rights. African Americans and black and coloured South Africans acquired full citizenship status during the 1960s and 1990s, respectively. During the era when white racial states reigned supreme, blackface minstrel conventions often provided a means for relatively privileged people to appropriate the bodies of racialized noncitizens and make visible the distinctions between "modern" citizens and racial "aliens." In these situations, hyperbolic impersonations in blackface often expressed a kind of social power. Groups who have relative social privilege also enjoy the power to mimic the lower groups. When the formally disenfranchised acquire more social and political power, however, the parameters defining what constitutes acceptable racial representation have to change to meet the new social circumstances. The blackface mask was the main visual symbol of exclusionary burnt cork nationalism. When exclusionary racial states such as the United States and South Africa transitioned to multiracial democracies, the blackface mask was rendered outdated and obsolete in mainstream forums. In such multiracial democracies, blackface masking becomes the primary preserve of racist trolls trying to provoke a response, nostalgists who yearn for the cultural aesthetics of the white racial state, antiracist satirists, and those who do not know the ugly history.

That being said, the conservative perspective arguing that the United States and South Africa are multiracial democracies that have successfully moved beyond racist foundations to create "level playing fields" in which all citizens have an equal chance to prosper is categorically untrue. The white racial state is deeply entrenched. Although the legal foundations of Jim Crow segregation and apartheid have mostly been uprooted, the economic hallmark of white racial states, the uneven distribution of wealth across racial lines, moves forward full steam. The racial wealth gap between white and black Americans continues to grow in the United States, while many coloured and black South Africans face increasing levels of poverty during the postapartheid era. These developments cannot be attributed to different levels of intellectual ability, work ethic, "bad" economic choices, or the so-called culture of poverty. Instead, the implementation of neoliberal economics under the Republican Party in the 1980s and ANC in the 1990s facilitated a massive redistribution of wealth upward to the top economic stratum in both countries. The economic ideology of neoliberalism advocates "free markets" without trade tariffs, deregulation in the interest of maximizing corporate profits, the widespread privatization of resources and industries, and a hands-off approach in which the state invests a minimum amount of public funds in education, health care, and the well-being of impoverished people. These policies work in tandem to move resources upward, further increasing the gap between the wealthy and the rest.[169] As such, many white families in both countries who built fortunes during the long era of the white racial state have successfully reinvested their resources and accumulated more wealth during the short decades of multiracial democracy. The ANC did not act alone in their adoption of neoliberalism. They were pressured heavily by the IMF and World Bank to implement a package of neoliberal policies that many commentators describe as the "Washington Consensus." Given these developments, neoliberalism should be added alongside blackface minstrel shows and Jim Crow statutes to a list of American exports designed to empower the powerful. Within this context, Klopse who celebrate working-class resistance, antiracist perspectives, and transnational alliances continue to be as necessary as ever.

Afterword

GLOBAL BLACKFACE

Toward Transnational Minstrelsy Studies

In 1853 U.S. naval captain Matthew Perry began trade negotiations with the Tokugawa Shogunate. At the time, Japan had been closed to outside trade for hundreds of years. Perry's orders were to use "gunboat diplomacy" to open the country to trade with the United States. He sailed his war ships into what is now known as Tokyo Bay, pointed canons at the coastline, and demanded an audience with a Japanese military officer of similar rank. He believed a wide display of American culture, featuring military technology, cuisine, and entertainment, would contribute to successful negotiations in Japan. As such, Perry presented "an exhibition of negro minstrelsy, got up by some of the sailors."[1] According to the program, the minstrels first appeared as "Colored Gemmen of the North" and later as "niggas of the South."[2] A crew member described the event: "The Commodore . . . said the success of his treaty depended upon the success of the entertainment, so we did our best. . . . [The Japanese] commissioners . . . were brought back on deck to witness a performance by the Ethiopian band of the *Powhatan*, who styled themselves 'Japanese Minstrels.'"[3] Another crew member remarked: "When the sable gentlemen made their appearance . . . a murmur of astonishment arose among our simple guests. . . . [W]ooly heads, shirt collars of ample dimensions, and black faces contrasting with black and yellow striped coats, ruffled shirts and the usual parts of a darky band were truly new sights to them."[4] I mention Perry's minstrel show to establish several points.

First, blackface minstrelsy informed much of the maritime culture of many American and British sailors during the mid- to late nineteenth century. White sailors escaped the tedium of oceanic travel by amusing themselves with minstrelsy and eagerly presented amateur minstrel shows for locals when they arrived in foreign ports.[5] Second, in my opinion, it is not surprising to find an entertainment form whose cultural logics of expropriation are "quintessentially colonial" rearing its head in this imperial encounter.[6] And, most important for the goals of this essay, Perry's minstrel show can be placed within a larger nineteenth-century story in which the American cultural export of blackface minstrelsy was brought to all corners of the globe.[7]

In 1998 W. T. Lhamon issued a rallying cry for transnational minstrelsy studies, stating that "blackface was the first Atlantic mass culture." Although his book *Raising Cane* is not the first work of scholarship on blackface minstrelsy outside of the United States, its theoretical contributions inspired a shift in minstrelsy studies away from nationally bounded scholarship toward transnational approaches.[8] Since this groundbreaking book, scholars have dedicated more attention to the global dissemination of blackface minstrelsy. The following pages sketch out a broad history of blackface minstrelsy as a popular culture export that was spread across several imperial networks. The chapter expands the discussion on the five waves of blackface minstrel globalization that was outlined briefly in my introduction. In the first wave, T. D. Rice and several American blackface acts went to London and Canada between 1836 and the 1840s, and after "Jump Jim Crow" was popularized in the British metropole in 1836, amateur renditions of the song were presented in Calcutta (1838), Sydney (1838), and Natal (1846).[9] The second wave comprised professional American, British, and Australian minstrel troupes who toured several international oceanic circuits from the 1850s to the 1880s. During the third wave, a relatively small number of blackface vaudeville acts traveled abroad from the 1890s to 1915. The fourth wave of blackface imagery was disseminated in Hollywood films, print media advertisements, and American comic book illustrations from 1915 to the 1960s. The last wave, the fifth wave, is best described as a self-aware and ironic form of blackface distributed by American movies and TV shows in the post–civil rights era. This periodization is intended as a general guideline. Many examples of transnational blackface do not fit neatly within these periods. Hopefully, future scholars will help expand this global history.

FIRST- AND SECOND-WAVE BLACKFACE MINSTRELSY

The first wave of minstrel globalization began in England in 1836 with T. D. Rice's tour across the Atlantic and ends with the 1848 London tour of Pell's Ethiopian Serenaders. Whereas previous chapters described the contours of first-wave minstrelsy, here I am interested in locating William Henry Lane (also known as "Master Juba") in this story. Lane joined George Pell's Ethiopian Serenaders in 1848. The original Ethiopian Serenaders had recently disbanded after returning to the United States and facing financial difficulties. Although their "refined" and "polite" minstrel show was a big hit with British audiences in 1846–47, their act might have provoked a "backlash" when they presented it to American working-class audiences.[10]

When Pell's Ethiopian Serenaders arrived in London in the middle of 1848, William Henry Lane was often marketed as the main attraction. Advertisements for the troupe featured a description of Lane's dancing that Charles Dickens wrote when he toured the United States in 1841: "Single shuffle, double shuffle, cut and cross-cut; snapping his fingers, rolling his eyes, turning in his knees, presenting the backs of his legs in front, spinning about on his toes and heels like nothing but the man's fingers on the tambourine; dancing with two left legs, two right legs, two wooden legs, two wire legs, two spring legs—all sorts of legs and no legs—what is this to him?" At the time, Charles Dickens was well respected in London as a writer with cross-class appeal. His endorsement of Lane's dancing probably helped Pell's Ethiopian Serenaders build a wide audience in the city.[11] Lane was a central contributor to the success of Pell's recently reconstituted Ethiopian Serenaders troupe. Most important for scholars who are interested in the history of transnational blackface minstrelsy, according to Stephen Johnson, Lane did not use blackface during his performances. Lane did so in order to prove to the audience he was a black man as advertised.[12] Furthermore, as with Orpheus McAdoo, I believe this choice was a conscious rejection of the dehumanizing blackface mask. Lane was aware of the racist problematics of blackface minstrel aesthetics, and he found ways to navigate the culture while maintaining his humanity. He danced in Great Britain for the next four years and died in London in 1852, at the young age of twenty-seven. Michael Pickering believes he "literally danced himself to death. Years of poor diet and irregular sleep only exacerbated his physical breakdown."[13] Lane's career is especially noteworthy because he was the only black person to appear in a first-wave minstrel show. He had to display extraordinary talents in order to do so.

The second wave of minstrel globalization ran from the 1850s to the 1880s, when professional minstrels from the United States, England, and to a lesser extent Australia toured international circuits. England continued to be a lucrative destination. Although white men constituted the vast majority of second-wave minstrels, some were black. In 1866 a white manager named Sam Hague brought a group of African American minstrels to England. They were advertised in the local press as "Hague's Slave Troupe." After American newspapers wrote of their success, white American audiences warmed up to the "revolutionary" idea that actual black people could appear in minstrel shows. Ironically, Hague's Slave Troupe opened doors for African American minstrels in the United States.[14]

In 1881 and 1882, two African American banjo musicians named James and George Bohee toured England with J. H. Haverly's minstrel troupe. When Haverly's troupe left, the Bohee Brothers stayed behind and popularized the banjo in every strata of British society. Toward that end, James Bohee gave banjo lessons to Prince Edward (soon to become King Edward VII). News of the music lessons for the prince quickly spread through high-society circles, and the banjo became a popular instrument among British elites. One contemporary observer remarked, "The [Bohees] took London in a big way. They were wined and dined by society hostesses, patronized by Earls and seduced by Countesses, and engaged to teach the royal infants, including the prodigal prince of wales, to tickle the banjo strings." James and George Bohee chose to spend the rest of their lives in England.[15]

In the latter half of the nineteenth century, many homegrown British minstrel troupes rose to prominence, of which the Mohawk Minstrels and Moore and Burgess Minstrels were among the most popular.[16] When the British minstrel scene was inundated with acts, several troupes went abroad in search of new markets.[17] In 1862 Nish's Christy Minstrel troupe of American and British performers embarked on a tour of the British colonies. They landed in Cape Town in August and toured the British South African colonies. Next, they traveled to India and Australia.[18] Their tour is a watershed moment in the story of minstrel globalization. Nish's Christy Minstrels forged an Anglo-colonial circuit spanning across the Atlantic, Indian, and Pacific Oceans. From 1863 to 1866, Nish's Christy Minstrels toured major Australian cities. Other British-based Christy Minstrel troupes performed in Australia in 1865, 1866, and 1867.[19]

While the 1860s was the decade of British blackface minstrelsy in Australia, the 1870s was America's decade. In the 1860s and 1870s, the American minstrel scene was saturated with acts. In response to increased competition at home, American minstrels went abroad in larger numbers than ever before. Furthermore, steam-engine technology made intercontinental travel more affordable and faster. In 1869 Australia became a relatively accessible designation for Americans when a regular steamship service connected San Francisco with Melbourne and Sydney. By 1870 ten American minstrel troupes were touring what Matthew Wittman calls the "Pacific circuit."[20]

Charles Hicks's Georgia Minstrels toured Australia in 1877. Founded in 1865 by African American manager and performer Charles Hicks, the Georgia Minstrels were the first all-black minstrel troupe to enjoy consistent success in the United States. Eventually, however, Hicks lost control of his troupe to white managers. A discernible pattern emerged: Hicks would start a professional troupe of African American minstrels, build an act and following of fans, only to watch his performers get lured away by white managers with more money. In addition, discriminatory practices made it difficult to book the Georgia Minstrels in major venues. After becoming disillusioned with the minstrel scene in America, Charles Hicks decided to take refuge in Australia in 1877. According to Richard Waterhouse, "[The Georgia Minstrels'] influence and impact [in Australia] were to be even greater than in America."[21] Indeed, the Georgia Minstrels brand was so influential that it was often used synonymously with black minstrelsy in the Australia and the United States. Hicks is an example of an African American entrepreneur who decided to go abroad when the avenues for advancement were blocked off to him at "home." He stayed in Australia from 1877 to 1880 and returned for another three-year run in 1888.

In the 1870s and 1880s, lower-class Irish Australians widely described as Larrikins began frequenting blackface minstrel shows and singing minstrel songs on street corners. According to Melisa Bellanta, Larrikins were drawn to the urban-dandy character of minstrel shows who proudly and flamboyantly claimed public space. In turn, the colonial press disparaged Larrikins as "inhuman savages" or "reincarnated blackfellow[s]." By the end of the 1880s, Australian plays often portrayed Larrikins in blackface. Actual Larrikins seemed to embrace their association with blackness by going to minstrel shows and wearing dandified clothing in self-conscious acts of conspicuous consumption. Still this behavior did not translate into progressive alliances with people of color, as Larrikins were well known for assaulting Chinese Australians. Bellanta astutely concludes, "Larrikins' interest in minstrelsy does not offer us comforting examples of interracial cooperation or healing. . . . And since blackness was a symbolic code as well as a skin colour, the fact that larrikins styled themselves as 'black' did not of itself make them empathise with non-white peoples. . . . [O]ne risks a skewed vision of how minstrelsy operated in placing too much emphasis on its anti-racist potential, especially in the face of manifest examples to the contrary."[22] Indeed, the word *coon,* a minstrel-inspired slur, was used to belittle nonwhite people in Australia in the 1890s. Later, in 1907, when African American heavyweight boxer Jack Johnson arrived in Australia in anticipation for his world championship match against Tommy Burns, the Australian press portrayed him through a minstrel lens. The *Sydney Truth* ran a news story titled "Jaunty Jack Johnson De New Coon Comes to Town" and described Johnson as "a big coon . . . 28 years of age" who was "somewhat babyish looking and of the type of the little coons who may be seen devouring watermelons in a well-known American picture."[23] Months later, during the boxing match, Johnson was heckled by sections of the Sydney audience with taunts of "nigger" and "coon."[24]

Honolulu was a midocean way station in the Pacific circuit, connecting San Francisco to Australia. By the middle of the nineteenth century, blackface minstrelsy was the most popular form of commercial entertainment in Honolulu. In the 1850s, the New York Serenaders made several extended stays (their 1850 run lasted five months) and were followed by the Backus Minstrels and Original California Minstrels. Interestingly enough, in September 1855, King Kamehameha IV invited the Backus Minstrels to his palace to give a private royal performance. Many native Hawaiians went to minstrel shows. According to James Revell Carr, Native Hawaiians likely "identified with the burlesque of plantation life . . . seeing themselves not as ludicrous blackface caricatures, but as trickster figures finding creative ways to 'get over' on the plantation masters."[25]

The blackface clown circus character was exported to Canada, even before the founding of the minstrel show in 1843. Between 1840 and 1843, a group of people identifying as "colored citizens" and some white antislavery activist allies sent four petitions to the city council of Toronto asking for a banning of the blackface clown within city limits. This character often appeared as a "southern plantation slave," spoke in a humorous "slave dialect," poked fun at individual audience members, and specialized in a kind of "self-mockery" that projected incompetence whenever trying to act with the restraint or mental aptitude of a modern citizen. Several of the petitions were an attempt to censor Richard Pelham's blackface act in the touring Bowery Amphitheater Circus (a New York–based circus). They describe and critique "American Actors" who "ridicule" the "African Character" with "songs by the name of Jim Crow and Aunt Dinah." Most unfortunately, two of the petitions claim that real violence against black people was inspired by the blackface smears. The petitions failed to stop blackface acts in Toronto and were left out of the histories of Canadian theater and performance until recently, when Stephen Johnson exhumed them from the archives.[26] How many similar stories about transnational blackface are buried in archives waiting to be unearthed?

Canada was incorporated into the North American minstrel circuit during a relatively early first-wave moment.[27] During the middle decades of the nineteenth century, blackface minstrels performed in all ten provinces of Canada.[28] By midcentury, the Mummers of Newfoundland were using blackface.[29] The influence of blackface minstrels stretched well into the twentieth century, especially in Niagara Falls. Because Niagara Falls is located at the New York–Ontario border, third-wave minstrels from the United States had relatively easy access and visited regularly well into the 1930s. After the parade of professional minstrels stopped, local amateur surrogates picked up the torch as amateur minstrel shows were a regular occurrence from the 1930s to 1960s. Local churches offered amateur minstrel shows for local philanthropic causes. By indulging as consumers or performers, Ontarians could help the local community because "minstrel shows meant good citizenship."[30] Well into the twentieth century, Canadian secondary schools staged minstrel shows, and white children appeared as "pickaninnies." A white Canadian who grew up in Toronto remembers performing in a blackface minstrel show with her fifth grade classmates in 1952.[31]

Blackface minstrels toured several Caribbean locations. Errol Hill's *The Jamaican Stage* finds evidence of blackface performance in the Kingston Theatre in 1840, when a group of amateur performers staged the burlesque "Jim Crow in London." The next year, at the same venue a visiting performer received several encores for his renditions of "Jump Jim Crow." In 1842 a local company performed for an entire season at the Royal Victoria Theatre in Kingston and presented "two short plays, a comic, duet, musical olio, and Negro songs."[32] After a twenty-year hiatus, blackface minstrelsy resurfaces in Hill's narrative in 1865 when a quartet of minstrels led by Frank Hussey traveled from New York to Jamaica. This was the first professional minstrel troupe to visit Jamaica, and their success inspired others to follow, including the Original Georgia Minstrels (1869), Washington Norton's Christy Minstrels (1872), and Edwin Browne's Minstrel and Novelty Company (1884).[33] Blackface minstrelsy influenced two long-lasting performance traditions in Jamaica: singing troupes who wore blackface makeup while rendering Jamaican folk songs and local comedians who performed in blackface deep into the twentieth century.[34]

Donald Hill's *Calypso Calaloo* and Hollis Liverpool's *Rituals of Power and Rebellion* offer histories of Trinidadian carnival that account for the influence of blackface minstrelsy. According to Liverpool, scholars have not reached a consensus regarding the question of when blackface minstrelsy first arrived in Trinidad. Some believe African American expatriates introduced the genre, some suggest traveling professional troupes, and others mention diasporic Trinidadians who came back from the United States. Although the moment of initiation is unclear, the minstrel influence is unequivocal. Both scholars discuss a mid-twentieth-century carnival character with whitened face and an "Uncle Sam costume of scissor-tailed coat, tight striped trousers, white gloves, and tall beaver hat."[35] Liverpool states, "The evidence shows that minstrelsy was an acculturated masquerade that was used by Africans in Trinidad to identify with the sufferings of Africans in the United States. The Carnival revelers, by whitening their faces instead of blackening them, probably showed their resentment of the ills done to Africans in the U.S. Maybe, too, the revelers in Trinidad were taking on the fantasy of power by 'becoming' white."[36]

In 1868 the Teatro Bufo became a very popular form of entertainment in Havana, Cuba. This theatrical genre included much blackface humor and was probably influenced by American minstrel troupes who visited during the 1860s.[37] Teatro Bufo differed substantially from traditional three-part minstrel shows. Teatro Bufo programs oftentimes included fully developed plays with many characters, twisting plotlines, and several acts. According to Jill Lane, the representations of black people in Cuban Teatro Bufo were often racist and exclusionary attempts to define blackness against a nascent Cuban national identity. However, such representations ultimately contributed more so than any other medium to the myth of Cuban mestizaje: a national identity narrative celebrating the blending of European, African, and indigenous people and cultures. Take, for instance, a Cuban anticolonial anthem from 1868, "El negro bueno." The protagonist of the song is a hypersexual, violent, and street-smart black man who in some iterations also happens to be an ardent proponent of "liberty." This was a form of mestizaje discourse in which people of African descent were imagined as contributors to the fight for national independence. I suspect it was precisely because these blackfaced characters were intended to be interpreted as countercultural racial others who did not adhere to the standards of "civilized" decorum that they could voice perspectives that bare-skinned white actors could not. Lane concludes, the "field of performance" was not a space of "reciprocal racial mixing and exchange." Teatro Bufo fed a Cuban mestizaje myth that did not "reflect or create the racial diversity it described." Instead, mestizaje functioned as a discursive "strategy for using, containing, and controlling race in [Cuba]."[38]

Teatro Bufo also traveled. Yeidy Rivero's *Tuning Out Blackness* is a fascinating account of blackface performance in Puerto Rican television and radio that cannot be neatly incorporated into my five waves of minstrel globalization. Rivero stays away from a reductive cultural imperialism approach in which blackface performance in Puerto Rico becomes a "mere copycat version of U.S. minstrelsy." Instead, Rivera focuses on multiple exchanges triangulated between the United States, Cuba, and Puerto Rico. In 1873 the Teatro Bufo was first performed on Puerto Rican stages, after which several Puerto Rican playwrights included the stereotypical "negrito" Bufo character in their works. After these blackface moments in the late nineteenth century, blackface imagery laid dormant for several decades until 1935, when Puerto Rican comedian Ramón Rivero was inspired to blacken up after seeing Cuban Bufo comedian Leopoldo Fernandez stage a play in San Juan in which the main character was "a negrito who stole chickens."[39] From 1937 to 1956, Rivero performed blackface and black voice characters on Puerto Rican radio and television. His characters often critiqued Spanish colonial attitudes and voiced working-class perspectives. For example, Gladys Jiménez-Muñoz remembers the famous greeting of Rivero's signature character, "Diplo," who began each

TV episode with "Xiomara, my sister! This is the greeting of the oppressed masses!"[40] *Diplo* was short for *diplomacia* or *diplomant,* and the character spoke with a Cuban accent that further marked his foreignness. Jiménez-Muñoz and Yeidy Rivero argue Diplo's portrayal of working-class black identity worked to essentialize black people as lower-class foreign objects of ridicule and normalize an upper-class white identity in Puerto Rican media. Ramón Rivero popularized blackface in Puerto Rican media, and after he died in 1956 several Puerto Rican actors and actresses took up his mantle by performing in blackface well into the 1980s.[41]

Blackface minstrels also went to South America. The late-nineteenth-century carnivals of Buenos Aires, Argentina, drew inspiration from blackface minstrel aesthetics. Several minstrel ensembles visited Buenos Aires in the 1860s, most notably a Christy Minstrel troupe in 1869. Around this time, a carnival group called the Dramático-Musical Society Los Negros, composed of young white men from the city's wealthiest families, started blacking up, dancing at balls, and marching double file through the streets. They stopped outside the windows of "decent" young women and serenaded in a caricatured black music. John Chasteen relates, "In song after song they returned to the same theme, dramatizing the love of humble, docile slaves for their masters' untouchable daughters." Imitators followed, and "blackface characterized Buenos Aires carnival for the rest of the century."[42] The white revelers were mocking *candombes,* an Afro-Argentinian carnival practice described by Chasteen as "elaborate pageant[s] with king and queen."[43] Matthew Karusch's comments are instructive: "Unschooled in the intricacies of candombe, [white imitators] performed a crude, mocking imitation of Afro-Argentine dance."[44] Relatedly, in 1902 an elderly black woman who had danced in actual street *candombes* described the blackface imitators who mocked her traditions. Her poignant testimony is very valuable for scholars who refuse to gloss over the power dynamics of blackface masking traditions in racially stratified societies: "In 1870, before the [yellow] fever, young men of good families started dressing up as blacks, even imitating the way we talk. And after a while, there wasn't an Italian in this whole city that didn't dress up as an African, make faces, and do truly ridiculous dances. . . . We had no choice but to shut ourselves up in our houses because we were poor and felt ashamed."[45]

In the 1870s, across the Río de la Plata, in Montevideo, Uruguay, young white men from middle- and upper-class families drew inspiration from blackened Argentinian carnival revelers and began blacking up and taking to the streets to celebrate the Day of the Kings carnival. Overtime, the "negro lubolo," a white person in blackface, became the most enduring carnival character in Montevideo. In the 1870s and 1880s, the blackface carnival troupes were racially segregated groups of white men. Furthermore, they tried to "civilize" the music by foregrounding European melodies and instrumentation and minimizing the African drums. Such troupes often sang comedic serenades to young white women who, according to one song lyric, "will never pay attention / to a negro black as coal."[46]

In the 1890s, working-class people established a stronger presence in Montevideo's carnival. These new carnival troupes reflected immigration trends and included many first-generation working-class European immigrants. Significantly, many of these working-class carnival troupes included actual black participants. Such troupes foregrounded African *candombe* drumming and songs that praised African warrior masculinity. They also danced with mixed-race "morenas," something the white troupes of the 1870s and 1880s were unwilling to do. According to George Andrews, although these working-class blackface troupes presented a kind of rhythmic and sexual portrayal of Afro-diasporic identity that was unlikely to disturb the racial hierarchy, they celebrated a form of Afro-diasporic identity during decades when Afro-diasporic people and culture were being removed from the official narratives of Uruguayan national identity.[47]

THIRD-WAVE BLACKFACE MINSTRELSY

During the third wave of minstrel globalization, from the 1890s to 1915, relatively few blackface minstrel acts toured international circuits. This can largely be explained by developments in the United States, where vaudeville entertainment enjoyed more popularity than blackface minstrel acts. The dwindling amount of blackface acts in the United States accounts for the drop in international tours. Nonetheless, the antiblack sensibilities of blackface minstrel shows continued to circulate in sheet music form. During the 1890s, coon songs were the next major American minstrel export. These songs presented lazy, incompetent, hypersexual, and violent urban-dandy caricatures over the syncopated rhythms of early ragtime music. In the 1890s, hundreds of coon songs were published in sheet music form and distributed throughout the United States.[48] The coon-song craze also swept across England. Eugene Stratton was the most successful British interpreter of coon songs. He reportedly sang his signature song, "The Whistling Coon," in fifteen hundred consecutive shows. Michael Pickering observes how the height of the coon-song craze neatly coincided with "the period of high imperialism" and suggests Eugene Stratton's career demonstrates the connection between "high imperialist racism and the popular music and theater of the time."[49] The craze also reached Australia. In 1888 Charles Hicks began a second three-year tour, during which his troupe popularized coon songs. These songs became a regular part of Australian vaudeville in the 1890s.[50] Scholars have argued that coon songs were the most virulently racist example of blackface minstrel song lyrics. Future research might explore whether the coon-song craze reached other countries outside the United States, England, and Australia.

McAdoo's Minstrels were one of the major troupes to tour abroad during the 1890s. Chapter 4 of this book addresses the ways in which McAdoo's Minstrels creatively reinterpreted the minstrel genre by including uplift politics in their show. In addition, they chose to leave out the more pernicious elements of blackface minstrelsy, including coon songs, stump speeches, and blackface makeup. After enjoying a successful tour of the major cities of South Africa in 1898, McAdoo's Minstrels traveled to Australia. They stayed in Australia for two years and broke up when Orpheus McAdoo passed away in August 1900.[51]

The Golliwog, a grotesque caricature of black people with oversized lips and a ridiculously large head of hair, was introduced to British audiences in 1895 when Florence Kate Upton published a children's book called *The Adventures of Two Dutch Dolls and a Golliwogg*. Golliwogg was modeled after a minstrel doll Upton found at a fair in the United States. Upton was born in America to British parents and emigrated to England in her early twenties. After the success of her first book, she published twelve additional Golliwogg children's stories. Because the character was not patented, several advertising firms used Golliwogs to sell British products. A company known as Robertson's featured a Golliwogg mascot on their bottles of jam for many decades and recently discontinued this practice at the turn of the twenty-first century. Relatedly, Hamleys toy shop of London, the largest toy store in the world, sold Golliwogg dolls up until 2009. They finally decided to stop selling the doll in response to a controversy surrounding journalist Carol Thatcher (daughter of former British prime minister Margaret Thatcher). Thatcher was fired by the British Broadcasting Company (BBC) in 2009 because she called a black tennis player a "Golliwogg" during an off-air conversation. Indeed, the "Golliwogg" character enjoys a long history in England, and many elderly white British people nostalgically associate it with fond childhood memories.[52]

In 1903 black comedians Bert Williams and George Walker brought a three-act musical called *In Dahomey* to London. By this time, the Williams and Walker show was already a major vaudeville act, and *In Dahomey* had been successfully staged on Broadway. *In Dahomey* was a musical satire of the American Colonization Society's back-to-Africa projects of the nineteenth century. The first two acts were set in the United States, and the last was a pantomime in Africa. The final act consciously refrained from presenting Africans as "savage" and Africa as a space of "anticivilization." This portrayal cut directly against conventional British understandings of Africa and confused the opening-night audience. In an effort to restore some semblance of discursive order, the managers of the theater decided to end the show with a makeshift rendition of "God Save the King."[53]

After this fiasco, in order to make the show more palatable to British audiences, Williams and Walker scrapped the original ending and decided to finish with a cakewalk. Camille Forbes comments on this development: "The abandonment of the script not only undermined but overturned the magnificent vision of Africa that *In Dahomey*'s creators had struggled to represent. Audience's expectations foiled the company's attempt at rendering their version of *In Dahomey*. And as the creators submitted to the audience's demands, they took a regrettable step back from their interpretation." Williams and Walker performed in London and the surrounding provinces for a total of eight months. They also staged a private performance for King Edward VII. Their decision to take Africa out of the third act demonstrates the pressure on black performers to conform to British assumptions about Africa. A decade later in 1919, white American entertainer W. C. Fields, described Bert Williams as "the funniest man I ever saw and the saddest man I ever knew."[54] I wonder how much of this sadness can be attributed to the dehumanizing blackface mask Williams wore to advance his career? Williams had to navigate an entertainment landscape that pressured black entertainers to become blackface caricatures in order to make a living. Although, as several scholars have demonstrated, Williams found ways to challenge the race and class hierarchies of his era, I imagine his career to be an emotionally taxing journey.[55] The methodologies of psychology are far beyond the scope of this study. But I would encourage future scholars to seriously consider the psychological toll of the blackface mask.

Blackface minstrels also went to Germany. Charles Hicks brought a Georgia Minstrels troupe to Hamburg in 1870.[56] When Haverly's Mastodon Minstrels toured in the early 1880s, a German audience apparently wanted to see actual black performers and felt deceived by the ruse. Haverly's Minstrels were almost arrested by the police for "a fraudulent attempt to deceive the German public." This setback notwithstanding, minstrel culture enjoyed long-lasting influence in Germany. A "cakewalk craze" swept through Berlin in 1903. Several German composers tried to cash in. A song called "Das Klein Niggergirl" inspired a German biscuit company to trademark the phrase "nigger girl" in 1914. By that point, German advertisers had been printing minstrel caricatures for two decades. One representative example comes from 1903: a trademarked minstrel image with "massively oversized lips . . . kinky hair," and "huge, bare, and deformed [feet]." By 1910 minstrel images were standard practice in the German advertising industry, used to sell shoes, shoe polish, rubber tires, ink, and soap.[57]

Paris was another minstrel hub. According to the art historian Petrine Archer-Straw, minstrel stereotypes slowly filtered into Parisian culture in the late nineteenth century. In the 1880s, many minstrel-inspired posters used "Uncle Sam garb" to signify America. Furthermore, "French advertisements for [black performers] at circuses and burlesque revues" featured "costumes of stars and stripes" referencing "minstrelsy."[58] Later, in the 1920s and 1930s, African American performers were all the rage. Josephine Baker's widespread popularity is well known. Less known are the all-black American variety shows that were so popular in Paris the French critics coined a new name for the genre: La Revue Nègre. As Andy Fry observes, several of these shows featured blackface acts, essentializing portrayals of black identity and primitive sexuality. Mantan Moreland, the African American comedian referenced in Spike Lee's *Bamboozled*, also performed in Paris during these years.[59]

Taken in total, during the third wave of minstrel globalization, a relatively small trickle of blackface acts went abroad. Perhaps vaudeville casts were too large to make international travel a lucrative venture. Or perhaps the existing scholarship on vaudeville focuses too narrowly on the United States. Future research might look for international tours that have not been accounted for. In the early 1880s, the Victoria Loftus vaudeville troupe toured the Pacific and enjoyed a successful stay in South Africa, as discussed in chapter 3. Maybe other vaudeville troupes also traveled abroad.

That being said, even if future researchers find more examples, the 1890s–1915 will probably be remembered as the low point of minstrel globalization. After vaudeville overtook the minstrel show as the most popular form of entertainment in the United States, the amount of international blackface tours declined substantially. Still the minstrel parade continued as early film technology fueled a new wave of minstrel globalization.

FOURTH-WAVE BLACKFACE MINSTRELSY

The fourth wave began when blackface imagery was shipped abroad via Hollywood movies. *Birth of a Nation* was the first feature-length blackface film to be exported outside of the United States. Widely considered a technical masterpiece and social travesty, this film is filled with racist vitriol and blatant historical misrepresentation. Based on a pro-Confederate play titled *The Clansmen* (1905), *Birth of a Nation* proudly regurgitated Confederate propaganda. Set during the Civil War and Reconstruction eras, the movie portrays the relationship between the Camerons, an aristocratic southern family, and the Stonewalls, their northern counterpart. The close friendship between the two families is strained when they are forced to choose sides during the war. In the aftermath of the war, emboldened black legislators try to impose a new racial order on the South. In response, the Ku Klux Klan rises from the ashes of the Confederacy to save the white race from the "threat" of "miscegenation." With the help of the KKK, the Stonewalls and Camerons reconcile, intermarry, and create the foundation for a new white nation. *Birth of a Nation* was the first feature-length film to be shown in the White House. President Woodrow Wilson claimed that "it is like writing history with lightning and my only regret is that it is all so terribly true."[60] The film directly inspired real-world consequences: shortly after its release in the United States, membership in the real KKK increased substantially. The NAACP led an unsuccessful campaign to ban the movie in the United States.

Birth of a Nation's depiction of black citizenship was especially egregious. In one noteworthy scene, black lawmakers in South Carolina during the Reconstruction era eat chicken and sneak swigs of whiskey while imposing a legislative agenda of sexual conquest on "the helpless white minority."[61] Such portrayals of black legislative incompetence were an intentional attempt to dramatize the supposed dangers of black citizenship run amok. Indeed, *Birth of a Nation* is the ultimate cinematic expression of burnt cork nationalism. Director D. W. Griffith, like the early blackface minstrels, understood that blackface caricatures can be used to ridicule the concept of black citizenship. During an infamous scene, a black character, portrayed by a white actor in blackface, tries to rape a teenage white girl. Griffith told the white actor who portrayed the aspiring black rapist to walk with an "animalistic scuttle" and create the effect of foaming at the mouth by gargling with hydrogen peroxide.[62] Such imagery resonated with burnt cork nationalists on both sides of the Atlantic. In England the film's marketing campaign evoked British identity, advertising the movie as "a soul stirring appeal to every Briton."[63]

Birth of a Nation was very popular in England in 1915 and 1916. British reviews of the film were unanimously positive, and many reviewers voiced racial solidarity with the KKK. For example, one reviewer praised Griffin for his "dramatic pictures of . . . that wonderful secret society [the KKK] which, when the Southern States were passing through their troublous times after the war, delivered the white people from the tyranny of the blacks."[64] Sol Plaatje was living in London at the time, and he was one of the few dissenting voices.[65]

Birth of a Nation was exported to several other countries. In the winter of 1915–16, the film premiered in the Teatre de la Opera of Buenos Aires, Argentina. It was shown in that venue more than two hundred times. The film achieved similar success in Chile, Peru, Bolivia, and Uruguay.[66] In 1916 *Birth of a Nation* played in Australia and New Zealand and received positive reviews in the local press. When *Birth of a Nation* came to Canada in 1915, Afro-diasporic communities protested. A black newspaper called the *Canadian Observer* led a failed campaign to ban the movie in Toronto.

The black community in Halifax, Nova Scotia, was more successful. Because of their objections, the movie was not shown in the city.[67]

The film "played to huge emotional audiences" in Germany but was rarely shown in other European countries.[68] In 1916 the movie was banned in France by a newly created government committee whose task was to evaluate potential film imports. Melvyn Stokes believes the film was censored because of its many "violent and dubious" acts. Furthermore, the committee probably did not want to alienate the many black soldiers from the colonies who were fighting for France during World War I. Later, in June 1923, the film was shown in France after a new government committee granted a visa. The film's Paris run was stopped abruptly when Prime Minister Raymond Poincaré rebanned it in August 1923. Melvyn Stokes suggests several factors likely contributed to the prime minister's decision, but most relevant to the current study was a tense racial climate that was created by white American tourists. In the summer of 1923, thousands of American tourists visited France, many of whom were unaccustomed to racial integration and refused to share public spaces with black people. On multiple occasions, white American tourists tried to throw black people out of public bars, restaurants, or nightclubs. The French Ministry of Foreign Affairs issued a statement, reminding white Americans of their status as "guests" and urging them to follow French customs or "sanctions will be taken." According to Stokes, the hostile racial climate stoked by white American tourists was one of the contributing factors leading to the ban of the controversial movie.[69] Here is a telling moment when popular culture was not the main vehicle exporting American racial attitudes abroad. In this moment, white American tourists literally tried to export Jim Crow segregation.

When *Birth of a Nation* was first released, it was not shown in British colonies in the Caribbean or Africa because, as Brian Willan suggests, "the colonial authorities on the ground very likely knew better than to take risks with inflammatory material of this kind." The South African high commissioner in London, W. P. Schreiner, claimed in a letter to a concerned party to have taken "certain unofficial steps . . . [to] prevent the film from going to South Africa . . . [because] it would do harm there." *Birth of a Nation* was not shown in South Africa until 1931, when it came to Johannesburg for a brief four-day run. The film was not received well because the silent-film era was over and it was already outdated.[70]

Because *The Jazz Singer* was the first feature-length film to use synchronized movement and sound, its 1927 release marked the end of the silent-film era. The film established Al Jolson as a major Jewish American movie star. He went on to appear in blackface in several additional Hollywood movies. I am unaware of scholarship that focuses mainly on the reception of Jolson movies outside of the United States. Instead, his influence is mentioned in passing in several studies. According to Kerry Wallach, *The Jazz Singer* was received enthusiastically by many Jewish people living in Germany because it told the story of a family of Jewish immigrants negotiating the tensions between Jewish culture and American culture. Some film reviewers praised the technological innovations of the film. Meanwhile, members of the Nazi Party smeared the film as "pan-Jewish propaganda."[71]

Moritz Makes His Fortune (1931) and *The Flower of Hawaii* (1933) were two German movies that directly referenced Al Jolson. The protagonist of the former was played by German Jewish actor Siegfield Arno. Arno's character was booed offstage after blacking up and lip-synching to an English-language recording of Jolson. Afterward, he was unable to wash the blackface paint off. Wallach suggests this film reflected a tendency in "mainstream Weimar [Republic] circles" to conflate Jewish identity with other racial minorities. Furthermore, Arno's usage of "overacting" may have been a self-conscious attempt to call out and comment on Jolson's hyperbolic racial stereotypes.[72] *The Flower of Hawaii* referenced *The Jazz Singer* and another Jolson movie that was well known in Germany called *The Singing Fool* (1928). The film was set in Hawaii, and native Hawaiians were portrayed in brownface. While riding a ship to Hawaii, several major characters meet Jim Boy, a white American who performs in blackface. According to Valerie Weinstein, Jim Boy's hyperbolic portrayal of blackness exposes the artificiality of the brownface Hawaiian characters. Despite this self-aware irony, Jim Boy's routine reinforces minstrel logics, including the tropes of big mouths and black primitivism. The film's relationship to Jewish identity and native Hawaiians is quite complicated: "By articulating Jewish difference through performances of Hawaiianness, [the movie] challenges Nazi racial anti-Semitism but silences and colonizes a nonwhite colonial Other." Ultimately, Nazi ideologues did not appreciate this movie because it was interpreted as a Jewish film that used the "mongrelized" genre of Jazz music to celebrate cultural internationalism.[73]

Nazi Party leaders believed jazz music represented the dangers of interracial mixing. In 1938 they issued an ineffective ban of jazz on German radio. Adolf Hitler portrayed blacks and Jews as coconspirators trying to corrupt the Aryan bloodline and create a "bastardized and niggerized world." A Nazi propaganda campaign warning against the dangers of "Nigger-Jew jazz" featured brochures with a minstrel caricature playing saxophone through large lips while wearing a Star of David on his lapel.[74] The minstrel caricature on the brochure was clearly referencing Al Jolson. Indeed, Jolson's blackface mask accentuated the lips and probably inspired such hyperbolic imagery.

Al Jolson influenced performance cultures in South Africa and Ghana. As demonstrated in chapter 4, Jolson enjoyed a strong presence in Cape Town's Coon Carnival. Meanwhile, Jolson directly influenced Ghanian concert-party theater, a form of traveling variety theater that was popularized in the Gold Coast (now known as Ghana) in the 1920s and 1930s. Catherine Cole's brilliant study on the concert party includes much valuable information. Concert-party pioneer Bob Johnson appears in stage attire on the cover of his biography, mimicking Al Jolson's "jazz hands" pose from *The Jazz Singer*. During the 1930s, Bob Johnson formed a Jolson-inspired performance troupe called the Versatile Eight. They performed in coastal towns and villages between Sekondi and Axim. Imitators followed, and the concert party became a popular pastime in Ghana.

Cole interviewed many concert-party performers in the 1990s. During her ethnographic research, she "never met anyone, either among performers or spectators, who said that blackface carried any notable ideological weight in terms of race." Respondents said that blackface makeup was intended to create laughter or look "attractive." During the preparation meetings for a Pan-African Historical Theatre Festival, concert party artists offered to perform at the festival in blackface. Cole observes, "[They] seemed entirely innocent about how offensive blackface comedy performed in a former slave castle was likely to be for African Americans, especially those motivated to make a pilgrimage all the way to the Motherland."[75] Ghana's concert-party theater provides a unique example of blackface reinterpreted for West African cultural contexts.[76]

Some of the creators of a popular Mexican comic book character named Memín Pinguín were heavily influenced by American-style blackface imagery. Memín Pinguín is an Afro-Mexican boy with bug eyes, huge lips, and oversize ears who first appeared in 1943. In one story line, Memín travels to Africa to go on an adventure but is kidnapped by a gorilla who thinks he is her son. Dozens of Memín Pinguín comics portray blackness as ugly.[77] According to Sixto Valencia Burgos, one of the main illustrators of Memín Pinguín, the character was partially inspired by the American film and comic franchise *Our Gang* and a black character named "Ebony White" from the American comic series titled *The Spirit.* His account suggests that comic book illustrations were another source of influence contributing to the global spread of blackface-inspired imagery. The example of Memín Pinguín also demonstrates how blackface-inspired imagery can be used to humiliate black people. In 2009 Mexican police officers reportedly beat an Afro-Honduran human rights activist named Ángel Amílcar Colón while taunting him as "fucking black" and "Memín Pinguín."[78]

The Mexican film industry released several blackface movies during the 1940s and 1950s. Most notably, a Mexican film from 1948 called *Angelitos Negros* included multiple blackface moments. Broadly speaking, the plot is largely about bigotry, "miscegenation," and Mexican national identity. A popular brown skin singer named José falls in love with a light-skinned blond woman named Ana. Ana does not know that her lifelong black nanny, Nana, is actually her mother. José figures this out when their first child is born with dark skin. Ana carries a large amount of racial prejudice and promptly rejects her daughter. Nana dies after a slap from Ana sends her falling down a flight of stairs. Afterward, Ana finally accepts her mother and daughter. Throughout the film, José plays the part of the racial progressive who tries to help Ana acknowledge her African background. José's music repertoire includes popular ballads, ranchera, and conga and is meant to represent cultural diversity. José renders several songs while in blackface. According to Theresa Delgadillo, the blackface in *Angelitos Negros* "represents the desire to absorb blackness into the Latin American ideal of *mestizaje*."[79] After the release of *Angelitos Negros,* other Mexican films also included blackface. According to Robert Irwin, "The use of blackface is striking in Mexican cinema in that it is prominent through the 1950s."[80]

In the 1950s and 1960s, Peruvian comic strips began peddling a slew of blackface-inspired characters. Miguel Becerra believes the images were inspired by American movies and television shows. Supporting this claim is a picture from a Lima newspaper from 1952: a Peruvian dancer in blackface. The caption said the dancer "specializes in North American dance."[81] Another possibility is to consider Mexico, a major regional influence, exporting Spanish-language media, blackface movies, and Memín Pinguín comics. Or perhaps Teatro Bufo was exported to Peru? The issue of original influence notwithstanding, Peruvians have developed traditions of blackface representation that I will return to shortly.

One potential avenue of future research could focus on blackface minstrel retentions in mid-twentieth-century radio and television. The BBC ran a radio program called *The Kentucky Minstrels* from 1933 to 1950. According to Michael Pickering, it continued the minstrel traditions of "heavily racialized 'othering,'" "comic ridicule," and musical selections from "plantation darkies." The show trafficked in minstrel nostalgia as the interlocutor often opened with: "Let us turn back the clock . . . and transport you for a few happy moments to the days when minstrelsy was in flower." The mythical idyllic slave plantation figured heavily in this imaginary. Also, *The Kentucky Minstrels* presented a large amount of misogynist comedy, as women appeared as "chatterboxes, nags, spendthrifts, busybodies, self-admirers, and status-conscious consumers."[82] Several years after the end of *The Kentucky Minstrels* radio show, the BBC began a TV show called *The Black and White Minstrel Show*.

Since its first run in 1957, *The Black and White Minstrel Show* enjoyed consistently high ratings. Responding to a climate of increased sensitivity toward racial issues, the BBC eventually ended weekly broadcasts of the show in 1973. Still, many British people wanted it to continue.[83] It was revived for one-off holiday episodes for several years, and the last televised broadcast came in 1978. I have not found any comprehensive scholarly studies on this show.[84] Future research might try to explain why blackface minstrel aesthetics survived in mainstream British media longer than in the United States.

FIFTH-WAVE BLACKFACE MINSTRELSY

The fifth wave of blackface minstrel globalization is better described as a trickle. These are self-aware blackface movies and TV shows in which the comedic focus centers on misguided characters who decide to blacken up. Self-aware blackface often tries to criticize the racist foundations of

American blackface minstrelsy. The most influential example of this is Spike Lee's film *Bamboozled* (2000), a poignant critique of blackface minstrel traditions that satirically criticizes contemporary American popular culture as a "millennium minstrel show." For better or worse, *Bamboozled* ushered in a new wave of self-aware blackface in mainstream American venues. Several American TV shows followed suit: *The Sarah Silverman Program* ("Face Wars," 2007), *30 Rock* ("Believe in the Stars," 2008), *Mad Men* ("My Old Kentucky Home," 2009), and *Always Sunny in Philadelphia* ("The Gang Makes *Lethal Weapon 6*," 2013) have each aired episodes portraying ill-informed white people who blacken up. In such moments, white ignorance, rather than black people, is the main object of comedic ridicule. The controversial movie *Tropic Thunder* (2008) does the same. This new self-aware blackface also circulates internationally. While looking through an entertainment magazine called *Pariscope,* Andy Fry was shocked to see two blackface caricatures staring back at him. It was an advertisement for *The Very Black Show,* the French title for *Bamboozled.*[85]

Liliana Angulo is an Afro-Columbian multimedia artist who deploys a kind of self-aware antiracist blackface similar to that of *Bamboozled.* Danielle Roper has written excellent interpretations of two Liliana Angulo exhibits. In *Mambo Negrita* (2006), Angulo photographed Afro-Columbian women in hyperbolic blackface in order to critique racist traditions of Afro-diasporic representation and decouple notions of black femininity from domestic service. Angulo placed full body mirrors in the exhibit, putting the spectator on display, and breaking the dichotomy of observer and object. In *Negro Utópico* (2003), Angulo painted herself in a thick coat of blackface that rendered her facial features almost indistinguishable. This hyperbolic self-objectification was carried out with the intention of foregrounding and critiquing the hypervisibilty of blackness in Columbia.[86]

Roper found a more traditional example of blackface in contemporary Peru. She watched a blackface performance by Sambos con Sentimiento y Devotion (Sambos of Sentiment and Devotion) during a 2013 festival honoring the Virgin of Candelaria, the patron saint of Puno, Peru. The "Sambos" appeared in blackface, with large bright-red lips and gold chains. They ate watermelon as the crowd laughed heartily. According to Roper, this is an example of "hemispheric blackface: a regional form of racial parody that fuses aspects of US blackface minstrelsy with Latin American traditions of racial parody" and "relies on the myth of racial democracy in

Latin America and the Caribbean to escape critique."[87] Recently, similar examples of purportedly postracial blackface-inspired moments have appeared in several countries outside of Latin America.

After two blackface theatrical productions were staged in Berlin, and a politician appeared in blackface on a billboard alongside a statement "Ick bin ein Obama" (I'm an Obama), a series of heated debates about blackface imagery played out in the German press, online forums, and academic conferences in 2012 and 2013. Defenders of blackface performance in Germany often argue that Germany has no theatrical tradition of blackface racism like the United States and that German blackface works to deconstruct racial identities. Katrin Sieg critiques this postracial blackface narrative and reminds us of the crucial point that blackface performance often reflects power relations: "On a small scale, the blackface . . . debates drive home the point that it requires an enormous amount of effort and risk to challenge the entrenched privileges of small but powerful elites."[88]

Phillip Howard writes about "contemporary Canadian blackface," as blackface incidents have broken out in several Quebec comedy clubs, a few universities, and one secondary school over the past several years. Blackface is often accompanied with representations of dreadlocks and Afro wigs, fried chicken, basketball jerseys, marijuana, and monkeys. In one troubling example, the judges of a Halloween costume competition gave first prize to a duo: a man in a KKK outfit draped in a Confederate flag leading a blackfaced subordinate across the stage in a noose. Defenders of such acts often claim Canada is a multiracial utopia and that Canadian blackface is not racist like American blackface traditions. According to Howard, this "Canadian postracialism" narrative contributes to antiblack racism and relies on "collective amnesia" toward the country's relationship with blackface minstrelsy. Furthermore, many examples of contemporary blackface focus on black people who are not Canadian. Blackface portrayals of African American celebrities, an Ethiopian beauty queen, and many black Jamaicans have appeared in recent years. This form of burnt cork nationalism juxtaposes black foreigners against white Canadian citizens.[89]

Over the past two decades, several blackface incidents came out of the K-pop (Korean popular music) industry of South Korea. These moments are not without historical precedent, as multiple Korean comedians regularly performed in blackface skits with dreadlocks wigs in the 1980s. What has changed is Internet technology that exports blackface caricatures outside of South Korea thus encouraging more international scrutiny. In 2003 blackface was one of the defining features of a K-pop group called the "Bubble Sisters." This foursome believed they were not as attractive as other K-pop stars and needed to highlight their strengths in order to compete. They claimed to sing as well as African Americans while looking as "ugly as African Americans." More recently, a singer from the boy group Beast Is the B2ST appeared in blackface with an Afro wig while eating watermelon. Gil-Soo Han interprets these incidents as examples of "nouveau-rich racism." Foreign workers have been coming into Korea since the 1990s, and the more impoverished the nation the worker comes from, the more xenophobia he or she is likely to face. The recent economic success of the South Korean economy is tied to neoliberal ideologies of economic competition and the idea that "losers" can and should be publicly humiliated.[90]

In the 1990s, Japanese blackface comedians with Afro wigs spewed hyperbolic patois and obscene "Black DJ English" through large red lips during Japanese variety shows. John Russell argues that contemporary Japanese blackface should not be separated from American minstrel traditions, as Japanese audiences were exposed to American blackface through Commodore Perry and the movies of Al Jolson. A less hyperbolic version of Japanese blackface popularly called "black boom" tries to veer towards "realism." A small minority of Japanese youth visited tanning salons and emulated Afro-diasporic hairstyles. According to Russell, this "acceptance of black cultural forms has not . . . led to the acceptance of black people."[91]

In the 1920s, the chief executive of Shanghai's Hawley and Hazel Chemical Company traveled to the United States and was inspired by Al Jolson. The executive believed Jolson's wide smile and bright white teeth would make an excellent logo for a brand of toothpaste. The resulting Darkie Toothpaste brand featured a blackface minstrel caricature complete with top hat and bright-white teeth. The company eventually moved to Hong Kong and established a strong market presence in Japan, China, Malaysia, Thailand, Singapore, and Taiwan. Colgate bought the brand in 1985 and after several years of protest changed the English name to Darlie Toothpaste in 1989.[92] Colgate also whitened the minstrel icon. Still, the Chinese title translates as "Black Man Toothpaste." To this day, "Black Man Toothpaste" is still sold in several Asian countries.

In 2018 blackface appeared in a comedy sketch during a Chinese TV gala celebrating the lunar New Year. A Chinese actress portraying an African women wore blackface and a large fake backside alongside actors in monkey and giraffe suits. International controversy erupted, as many observers outside China took to the Internet to call out the racism in a program that was sponsored by the Chinese state and broadcast to hundreds of millions of viewers.[93] Regardless of whether the producers of this event knew anything of the racist history of blackface minstrel shows (a history that includes much anti-Chinese sentiment), they certainly recirculated the minstrel logic of hyperbolic blackness by creating an African caricature whose "blackness" was marked by an excessively big posterior. They also advanced a patronizing neocolonial logic in which Kenyans were represented as happy recipients of a Chinese built railroad. This episode demonstrates a need for more education on African history and blackface minstrelsy in China. It also illustrates the importance of scholarship on the complex history of racial impersonation in Chinese theater practices.[94] Future research should properly contextualize contemporary moments of blackface in China within this local and transnational history.

The Netherlands hosts a blackface carnival that arguably should not be included in the broader story of blackface minstrel globalization because there is no consensus on its cultural origins. The blackface in question appears in the feast of Saint Nicholas holiday. Every November an imaginary Catholic bishop named Saint Nicholas, or "Sinterklaas," travels through the Netherlands with his blackface "helpers" or "slaves" (depending on whom you ask) known as the "Black Petes" (Zwarte Petes). Capping off the holiday is the exchange of gifts on December 5 and 6. Many white Dutch people argue "Black Pete" has nothing to do with race because his skin is covered in soot after sliding down chimneys. Leaving aside the fact that whiteness is actually a racial category, critics question this miraculous chimney that blackens only Pete's face and not the rest of his body. Critics also point to the Afro wigs, large red lips, and big hoop earrings that often flesh out the character. David Goldberg relates, "No other European society has Sambo as a national teddy bear."[95]

The "Black Pete" debates began in 2011 when a black student activist named Quinsy Gario wore a T-shirt that translates as "Black Pete Is Racist" to a Sinerklaas parade. Police promptly pushed Gario to the ground and kicked him several times while dragging him into a nearby alleyway.

A video of the arrest found its way to YouTube and garnered national and international attention. In 2013 Gario presented his perspective on Dutch television. According to Gario, after the show aired he received online death threats and several tweets with the phrase "ugly nigger."[96] Largely because of Gario's activism, each year the "Black Pete" tradition is debated vigorously in the Netherlands and international press. Defenders of Black Pete believe he is an important part of Dutch holiday tradition, a symbol of Dutch national identity, and harmless holiday fun for the children. English-language scholarship ranges from antiracist[97] to purported neutrality.[98] Meanwhile, in 2015 the city of Antwerp changed the parade tradition by abandoning blackface and advocating the use of black stripes on a white face to signify chimney soot. Some towns have switched to "Coloured Petes" ('Kleurenpieten') who paint their faces in a rainbow array. Still, according to polling data, a majority of the white population continues to hold on to this tradition and adamantly refuses to let go. The 2018 parades were especially ugly. Peaceful protesters critiquing Black Pete traditions were harassed by counterprotesters hurling racial slurs, eggs, and bananas. A few counterprotesters flashed Hitler salutes, and dozens of counterprotesters were arrested and jailed.[99] The Black Pete debates will continue to develop in upcoming years.

CONCLUSION

Because blackface minstrels toured an expansive range of locations filled with many diverse human cultures, it is dangerous to make generalizations about the aforementioned history. Nonetheless, it is important to note that many of the societies where blackface minstrelsy became most popular had preexisting regimes of hierarchical racial thought. Blackface minstrelsy was "quintessentially colonial" because it reinforced a global color line. Furthermore, blackface imagery was used to draw boundaries around white national identity in multiple countries. Although I created the phrase "burnt cork nationalism" to interpret patriotic minstrel shows in the extreme racial states of South Africa and the United States, scholars have applied similar frames of analysis to other countries.

The scholarship on fourth-wave minstrelsy is relatively underdeveloped, and more research is needed on the international reception of blackface films. Furthermore, future research should engage Chude-Sokei's claim that blackface minstrelsy was globalized partly because "colonized black nations and communities" were hoping to "construct a transatlantic conversation between and among different black populations."[100] His hypothesis is heavily based on secondary sources, and future scholarship using primary source documents and ethnographic approaches could further flesh out his fascinating suggestion. Relatedly, researchers who can access non-Anglophone language sources can greatly expand scholarly understanding on the reception of blackface minstrelsy in several understudied locations. I suspect a great many sources have yet to be uncovered.

Consider two South African newspaper articles about globe-trotting blackface minstrels. According to an 1883 article in the *Diamond News,* Frank Hussey performed in California, Rio de Janeiro, Chili, Peru, Hawaii, British Columbia, China, Hong Kong, the East Indies, "Africa," Egypt, Greece, Turkey, Spain, Russia, Germany, Italy, Japan, Canada, Newfoundland, St. Pierre, Ireland, London, Paris, and Australia, and Italy. Similarly, in 1865 a *Natal Mercury* article clamed Leslie's Christy Minstrels were fresh off the heels of a "triumphal tour" of "Australia, the East Indies, China, Japan, the Philipine [*sic*] Islands, the Island of Ceylon."[101] If the claims in these articles prove true, the international touring circuits of the nineteenth century may have included more stops than current scholarship accounts for. However, one pit stop on an international tour does not guarantee long-lasting cultural influence. Future studies can fill in the gaps of scholarly knowledge.

The aforementioned *Diamond News* article was referencing the July 3, 1880, edition of the *New York Clipper.* The *New York Clipper* was the "most influential show business trade paper" in the United States during the late ninetieth century. It even had an international impact, as demonstrated by its appearance in Kimberley.[102] It was first published in 1853, right at the beginning of the second wave of minstrel globalization, and it regularly reported on the travels of blackface minstrels. Richard Waterhouse's well-researched history of minstrel shows in Australia draws heavily from the *New York Clipper.* Future scholars who comprehensively mine this source will likely introduce a large amount of new information to the academic discussions on transnational blackface minstrelsy.

It is not an exaggeration to say that blackface minstrelsy reached each hemisphere of the world and even the most remote places. In March 1902,

British explorer Robert Falcon Scott decided to winter in Antarctica because the ice was too thick for the HMS *Discovery* to pass. His crew raised a shelter on a nearby peninsula and named it "the Hut." A few months later, the crew renamed it the "Royal Terror Theater" and began staging theatrical performances in an effort to pass the time, build morale, and maintain community. According to one crew member, a "nigger minstrel troupe" rehearsed for "many a cold hour . . . in the freezing theatre." The twelve members of the "Dishcover Minstrel Troupe" trudged two hundred yards through the Arctic snows to rehearse in a poorly insulated shack. They crafted makeshift wigs and shabby outfits out of the bits and pieces lying around the ship. On the night of their show, the outside temperature was negative forty degrees Fahrenheit (which converts to negative forty degrees Celsius). After the show, Scott wrote in his diary, "When we got back to the ship after the performance we decided that in spite of the cold we had spent an extremely pleasant evening."[103] The "Dishcover Minstrel Troupe" devoted a large amount of time and energy toward the creation of a "believable" minstrel show. When confronted with a foreign environment, they tried to realize something from home. Commodore Perry's minstrels did something similar. Brian Rouleau observes, "In both instances, and in the many in between, seemingly inhospitable places were rendered cheerful, friendly, and familiar with a few daubs of dark grease and a little dialect."[104] Ultimately, the racial mimicries of the Dishcover Minstrels at the edge of the world raise the following question: If minstrels could reach such remote places, where else might they have gone?

The recent proliferation of digitized archives filled with nineteenth-century newspapers will help the next generation of scholars who study transnational blackface track the movements of minstrel troupes across the globe. *Exporting Jim Crow* is largely based on a primary source collection that I built while researching at the National Library of South Africa in Cape Town. I spent eight months reading microfilm newspapers for thirty to thirty-five hours a week. Today, scholars who study transnational minstrelsy can input keyword searches into online search engines and instantly find relevant primary sources. Unlike library reading rooms, these search engines are available twenty-four hours a day, seven days a week. Kellen Hoxworth's recent dissertation, "Transoceanic Blackface, Imperial Whiteness," is one excellent example of the possibilities that open up when researchers mix the physical archive with the digital archive.[105] Hoxworth began his project by conducting archival research at the National Library of South Africa in Cape Town, the Killie Campbell Africana Library of Durban, the National Library of India in Kolkata, and the British Library in London. Afterward, he searched the "Trove" digital collection of the National Library of Australia, the "Papers Past" digital collection of the National Library of New Zealand, and the World Newspaper Archive to find an impressive amount of sources from several countries.[106] The resulting study is an expansive treatment of transnational blackface that utilizes primary sources from South Africa, India, Australia, Jamaica, London, and the United States. The cost, in both money and time, of traveling to each of these countries to do research in physical archives is very prohibitive. Such brick-and-mortar archives still offer several advantages over Internet databases, including items that are not digitized, face-to-face interactions with knowledgeable archivists, the chance to network with other researchers, as well as opportunities to meet local people and learn more about local cultures. However, in my opinion, the digital archive is the future of transnational minstrelsy historiography. The next generation of scholars will create ambitious projects that employ primary source materials from across the globe. Of course, physical archives, microhistory methods, and ethnographic approaches will not become obsolete. Instead, future scholars can mix the digital archive with traditional forms of onsite research. The new digital humanities offer exciting possibilities for scholars who study transnational blackface.

The issue of access has to be addressed when discussing the great potential of digital archives. The spread of digital archives is not an even process, as many countries in the global South, South Africa included, have yet to digitize large portions of their nineteenth-century newspaper collections. This reality limits the possibilities of scholars who study the first and second waves of minstrel globalization. Furthermore, many digital archives contribute to the monopolization of knowledge because they can be searched only by scholars who are affiliated with universities that can afford the subscription costs. Nonetheless, the possibilities of the digital archive are too enticing to be dismissed. Hopefully, in the near future, more people will have access to affordable Internet and digital archives that are not locked behind subscription walls will become the norm. I am encouraged by the fact that my research trip to the Harvard Theatre Collection was only nine years ago. Today, anyone with an Internet connection can search large portions of this collection online.[107]

I am also encouraged by the efforts of socially conscious scholars who are pushing back against the monopolization of academic knowledge by creating publicly accessible Internet archives on transnational blackface. Stephen Johnson's "Juba Project" is a pioneering example of this kind of open-access digital humanities project. This online database is filled with primary source documents on first-wave blackface minstrelsy in England.[108] In the near future, Kellen Hoxworth also plans to create a digital archive on Dave Carson and the San Francisco Minstrels.[109] I celebrate each of these scholars for trying to make academic knowledge more accessible to the general public and to researchers with limited access to research libraries.

Twenty years after W. T. Lhamon's rallying cry, scholarship on blackface minstrelsy as a popular culture export has grown substantially. Still, there is much more to learn. Blackface minstrels went to Ireland, France, Germany, Sri Lanka, Singapore, Indonesia, China, Hong Kong, New Zealand, Fiji, Tahiti, Jamaica, Trinidad, Panama, Brazil, Peru, and Mexico, among several other understudied locations. They purportedly went to St. Helena, Egypt, Greece, Turkey, Spain, Italy, Russia, Chili, and St. Pierre as well. Indeed, the scholarship on transnational blackface minstrelsy is still in a nascent stage. Here is a story of interest for scholars, intellectuals, and activists who are building a better understanding of the global reproduction of race. Because antiblack racism is a global phenomenon, antiracist thinking must also be global.

NOTES

PREFACE

1. Mae Ngai defines "alien citizens" as nonwhite people born in the United States who technically have formal citizenship but are treated as aliens by the white mainstream. Ngai, *Impossible Subjects: Illegal Aliens and the Making of Modern America* (Princeton, NJ: Princeton University Press, 2004), 8.
2. For more on the New WORLD Theater, see Chinua Thelwell, ed., *Theater and Cultural Politics for a New World* (London: Routledge, 2016).
3. Joseph Byrd, "Whitewashing Blackface Minstrelsy in American College Textbooks," *Popular Music and Society* 32, no. 1 (2009): 77–86.
4. For the first perspective, see Jenna Gibbs, *Performing the Temple of Liberty: Slavery, Theater, and Popular Culture in London and Philadelphia, 1760–1850* (Baltimore: Johns Hopkins University Press: 2014); Christopher Smith, *The Creolization of American Culture: William Sidney Mount and the Roots of Blackface Minstrelsy* (Urbana: University of Illinois Press, 2013); W. T. Lhamon, *Jump Jim Crow: Lost Plays, Lyrics, and Street Prose of the First Atlantic Popular Culture* (Cambridge, MA: Harvard University Press, 2003); W. T. Lhamon, *Raising Cain: Blackface Performance from Jim Crow to Hip Hop* (Cambridge, MA: Harvard University Press, 1998); and Dale Cockrell, *Demons of Disorder Early Blackface Minstrels and Their World* (Cambridge: Cambridge University Press, 1997). Although Eric Lott thoroughly critiques the racism in early minstrel shows, his book *Love and Theft: Blackface Minstrelsy and the American Working Class* (Oxford: Oxford University Press, 1993) should be included in this group. For the second perspective, see Douglass Jones Jr., *The Captive Stage: Performance and the Proslavery Imagination of the Antebellum North* (Ann Arbor: University of Michigan Press, 2014); Matthew Morrison, "Sound and the Construction of Race: From Blackface to Blacksound in Nineteenth-Century America" (PhD diss., Columbia University, 2014); Tavia Nyong'o, *The Amalgamation Waltz: Race, Performance, and the Ruses of Memory* (Minneapolis: University of Minnesota Press, 2009); Saidiya Hartman, *Scenes of Subjection: Terror, Slavery, and Self-Making in Nineteenth-Century America* (Oxford: Oxford University Press, 1997); and Brenda Dixon Gottschild, *Digging the Africanist Presence in American Performance: Dance and Other Contexts* (Westport, CT: Greenwood Press, 1996).

5. W. T. Lhamon, "Turning around Jim Crow," in *Burnt Cork: Traditions and Legacies of Blackface Minstrelsy*, ed. Stephen Johnson (Amherst: University of Massachusetts Press, 2012), 28, 24, 21.
6. Pew Research Center, "Obama's Sweeping Victory," November 5, 2008, www.pewresearch.org.
7. Earl Lewis and Nancy Cantor, eds., *Our Compelling Interests: The Value of Diversity for Democracy and a Prosperous Society* (Princeton, NJ: Princeton University Press, 2016); Steve Phillips, *Brown Is the New White: How the Demographic Revolution Has Created a New American Majority* (New York: New Press, 2016).
8. Denis-Constant Martin, *Coon Carnival: New Year in Cape Town, Past and Present* (Cape Town: David Philip, 1999), 78–79.
9. Francesca Inglese, "Coloured Moves and Klopse Beats: Minstrel Legacies in Cape Town, South Africa" (PhD diss., Brown University, 2016), 35–36; Chanell Oliphant, "The Changing Faces of the Klopse: Performing the Rainbow Nation during the Cape Town Carnival" (master's thesis, University of the Western Cape, 2013), 15; Jane Battersby, "Coon Carnival," in *Encyclopedia of Race and Racism*, ed. Patrick Mason (Detroit: Macmillan Reference USA 2013), 437.
10. In fact, by "1904 only some 40,000 out of a total number of 630,000 Afrikaaners were in the nine major towns in South Africa." David Welsch, "The Growth of Towns," in *The Oxford History of South Africa*, ed. Monica Wilson and Leonard Thompson (Oxford: Oxford University Press, 1971), 2:204.
11. Several minstrel songs were converted into Afrikaans-language folk songs in the middle of the nineteenth century. Veit Erlmann, *African Stars: Studies in Black South African Performance* (Chicago: University of Chicago Press, 1991), 32; Willemien Froneman, "Pleasure beyond the Call of Duty: Perspectives, Retrospectives, and Speculations on Boeremusiek" (PhD diss., Stellenbosch University, 2012), 62–69. Interestingly enough, in 1842, a Cape Town–based newspaper translated the song "Jump Jim Crow" into Afrikaans. *De Verzamelaar*, April 19, 1842, quoted in Kellen Hoxworth, "Transoceanic Blackface, Imperial Whiteness: Performing 'Race' in the Global Nineteenth Century" (PhD diss., Stanford University, 2017), 211–12. Future researchers should further flesh out this Afrikaaner history.

INTRODUCTION: BURNT CORK NATIONALISM AND THE FIVE WAVES OF MINSTREL GLOBALIZATION

1. Michael Rogin, *Blackface, White Noise: Jewish Immigrants in the Hollywood Melting Pot* (Berkeley: University of California Press, 1998), 44.
2. Technically speaking, T. D. Rice was not doing a "minstrel show" because the concept of American ensemble blackface performance was not invented until 1843. However, his popular "Jump Jim Crow" act definitely inspired the blackface comedians who called themselves "minstrels" in the 1840s. This is why I believe the label "blackface minstrel" is an accurate descriptor for T. D. Rice.

Furthermore, it is important to acknowledge the fact that blackface masking traditions existed in England long before the formation of the American republic, and these traditions may have influenced the development of early American minstrelsy. See Robert Hornback, *Racism and Early Blackface Comic Traditions: From the Old World to the New* (London: Palgrave Macmillan, 2018); Kellen Hoxworth, "Transoceanic Blackface, Imperial Whiteness: Performing 'Race' in the Global Nineteenth Century" (PhD diss., Stanford University, 2017); Virginia Vaughan Mason, *Performing Blackness on English Stages, 1500–1800* (Cambridge: Cambridge University Press, 2005); Dale Cockrell, *Demons of Disorder: Early Blackface Minstrels and Their World* (Cambridge: Cambridge University Press, 1997).

3. Hoxworth, "Transoceanic Blackface," 210–12; Richard Waterhouse, *From Minstrel Show to Vaudeville: The Australian Popular Stage, 1788–1914* (Kensington: New South Wales University Press, 1990), 27–28.
4. *Sam Sly's African Journal*, November 9, 1848, quoted in Hoxworth, "Transoceanic Blackface," 218.
5. Eric Lott, *Love and Theft: Blackface Minstrelsy and the American Working Class* (Oxford: Oxford University Press, 1993), 90.
6. Veit Erlmann, *African Stars: Studies in Black South African Performance* (Chicago: University of Chicago Press, 1991), 31.
7. Zine Magubane, *Bringing the Empire Home: Race, Class, and Gender in Britain and Colonial South Africa* (Chicago: University of Chicago Press, 2004), 155. Minstrel slurs regularly show up in British South African newspapers. For the word *nigger* in Kimberley newspapers, see *Diamond Field Advertiser*, September 25, 1874; *Port Elizabeth Telegraph*, August 10, 1875; and *Diamond News*, January 4, 1873; July 11, 1874; August 12 and September 7, 1876; September 4, 1877; February 5 and June 6, 1878; and February 7, 1879. For "Lucky Darkies" see *Diamond News*, July 17, 1879. Africans were also called "Jim Crows." J. W. Matthews, *Incwadi Yami; or, Twenty Years' Personal Experience in South Africa* (New York: Rogers and Sherwood, 1887), 193. There is some evidence suggesting the exchange of slurs was multidirectional, as one white minstrel in the British metropole called himself the "White-Eyed Kaffir." Douglass Lorimer, "Bibles, Banjoes and Bones: Images of the Negro in the Popular Culture of Victorian England," in *Search of the Visible Past: History Lectures at Wilfred Laurier University, 1973–1974*, ed. Barry Gough (Ontario: Wilfred Laurier University Press 1975), 43; Harry Reynolds, *Minstrel Memories: The Story of Burnt Cork Minstrelsy in Great Britain from 1836–1927* (London: Alston Rivers, 1928), 13–14.
8. Nelson Mandela, *A Long Walk to Freedom: The Autobiography of Nelson Mandela* (Boston: Little, Brown, 1994), 110; Peter Abrahams, *The Black Experience in the 20th Century: An Autobiography and Meditation* (Bloomington: Indiana University Press, 2000), 33; Sol Plaatje, *Native Life in South Africa* (Teddington, UK: Echo Library, 2007), 97. See also Peter Limb, ed., *The People's Paper: A Centenary History and Anthology of Abantu-Batho* (Johannesburg: Wits University Press, 2012), 62; and

Brian Willan, *Sol Plaatje: South African Nationalist, 1876–1932* (Berkeley: University of California Press, 1984), 120.

9. A local newspaper ran an advertisement for shoe polish with a minstrel caricature saying, "De Polish what am!" *Cape Times,* January 5, 1927. For other minstrel-inspired advertisements, see *Cape Argus,* January 7, 1913; and *Cape Times,* January 1, 1921; January 7, 1941; and January 3, 1958.
10. The city of Cape Town renamed the event "Minstrel Carnival" in the early 2000s so as to not alienate tourists who were offended by the word *coon.* Francesca Inglese, "Coloured Moves and Klopse Beats: Minstrel Legacies in Cape Town, South Africa" (PhD diss., Brown University, 2016), 31. In 2018 the event was renamed the "Cape Town Street Parade."
11. A "racial state" is a country that deploys government apparatuses (census counts, official histories, laws regulating immigration, citizenship status, zoning rights, and reproductive rights) to place citizens and noncitizens in racial categories, distribute resources and democratic rights along racial lines, and restrict first-class citizenship to one racial group. Jim Crow America and apartheid South Africa were primary examples of white racial states. For discussion on "racial states," see Michael Omi and Howard Winant, *Racial Formation in the United States,* 3rd ed. (New York: Routledge, 2015), 137–58; David Theo Goldberg, *The Racial State* (Malden, MA: Blackwell, 2002).
12. Robert C. Toll, *Blacking Up: The Minstrel Show in Nineteenth Century America* (Oxford: Oxford University Press, 1974), 67–68.
13. Frederick Douglass, *North Star,* October 27, 1848 (emphasis added). Douglass created a speaking persona in "contradistinction" to the conventions of blackface minstrelsy. Tavia Nyong'o, *The Amalgamation Waltz: Race, Performance, and the Ruses of Memory* (Minneapolis: University of Minnesota Press, 2009), 125–26.
14. Michael Pickering, *Blackface Minstrelsy in Britain* (Farnham: Ashgave, 2008), 124; Catherine Cole, *Ghana's Concert Party Theatre* (Bloomington: Indiana University Press, 2001), 25; Lott, *Love and Theft.*
15. Ralph Ellison, *Shadow and Act* (New York: Vintage, 1972), 49; Rogin, *Blackface, White Noise,* 37; Nathan Huggins, *Harlem Renaissance* (Oxford: Oxford University Press, 1971), 249.
16. My thinking about burnt cork nationalism is influenced heavily by Jill Lane's notion of "impersoNation," which she defines as "performances that link racial and gender impersonation to the development of racialized national discourses." ImpersoNation is different from burnt cork nationalism because it describes patriotic performances that do not require the use of blackface. Lane, *Blackface Cuba, 1840–1895* (Philadelphia: University of Pennsylvania Press, 2005), 16.
17. Marilyn Lake and Henry Reynolds, *Drawing the Global Colour Line: White Men's Countries and the Challenge of Racial Equality* (Cambridge: Cambridge University Press, 2008); Reginald Horseman, *Race and Manifest Destiny* (Cambridge, MA: Harvard University Press, 1981).

18. *Diamond News*, March 20, 1873.
19. Robert Ross, *Status and Respectability in the Cape Colony, 1750–1870: A Tragedy of Manners* (Cambridge: Cambridge University Press, 1999).
20. John Comaroff, "Reflections on the Colonial State, in South Africa and Elsewhere: Factions, Fragments, Facts and Fictions," *Social Identities* 4, no. 3 (1998): 325.
21. Catherine Cole, "American Ghetto Parties and Ghanaian Concert Parties: A Transnational Perspective on Blackface," in *Burnt Cork: Traditions and Legacies of Blackface Minstrelsy*, ed. Stephen Johnson (Amherst: University of Massachusetts Press, 2012), 224; David Harvey, *The New Imperialism* (Oxford: Oxford University Press, 2003), 137–12; Nyong'o, *Amalgamation Waltz*, 107–12.
22. Timothy Keegan, *Colonial South Africa and the Origins of the Racial Order* (Charlottesville: University Press of Virginia, 1996), 62.
23. George Liptsitz, *Possessive Investment in Whiteness* (Philadelphia: Temple University Press, 2006); Cheryl Harris, "Whiteness as Property," *Harvard Law Review* 106, no. 8 (1993): 1707–91. Harris first started developing her influential essay of critical race theory while in South Africa at an academic conference at the University of the Western Cape in 1991. Her conference paper "argued that American law had implicitly recognized a property interest in whiteness. The concept resonated in the South African context because of the similar and even more extreme patterns of white domination evident there" (1713n9). Relatedly, for Eric Lott, blackface minstrelsy represents the first moment in U.S. history when "black culture" became "property." Lott, *Love and Theft*, 39. Tavia Nyong'o relates: "Can we think of blackness as a property similarly stolen . . . that blackness, property, is constituted through theft?" Nyong'o, *Amalgamation Waltz*, 110.
24. *Cape Times*, January 8, 1931. See also *Cape Times*, January 6, 1931.
25. Katrina Thompson, *Ring Shout, Wheel About: The Racial Politics of Music and Dance in North American Slavery* (Urbana: University of Illinois Press, 2014), 69–98.
26. Nigel Worden, *The Making of Modern South Africa: Conquest, Apartheid, Democracy* 4th ed. (Hoboken, NJ: Wiley-Blackwell, 2007), 48.
27. William Beinart, *Twentieth Century South Africa* (Oxford: Oxford University Press, 2001), 124.
28. Worden, *Making of Modern South Africa*, 65–66. For a discussion on white poverty discourse in Cape Town in the late nineteenth century, see Vivian Bickford-Smith, *Ethnic Pride and Racial Prejudice in Victorian Cape Town: Group Identity and Social Practice, 1875–1902* (Cambridge: Cambridge University Press, 1995).
29. Rogin, *Blackface, White Noise*, 5; Toll, *Blacking Up*, 274.
30. LeRoy Ashby, *With Amusement for All: A History of American Popular Culture since 1830* (Lexington: University Press of Kentucky, 2006).
31. Rogin, *Blackface, White Noise*, 29. For blackface in early American cinema, see Arthur Knight, *Disintegrating the Musical: Black Performance and American Musical Film* (Durham, NC: Duke University Press, 2002); Donald Bogle, *Toms, Coons,*

Mulattoes, Mammies, and Bucks: An Interpretive History of Blacks in American Films, 4th ed. (New York: Continuum, 2001); Susan Gubar, *Racechanges: White Skin, Black Face in American Culture* (Oxford: Oxford University Press, 1997).

32. Nicholas Sammond, *The Birth of an Industry: Blackface Minstrelsy and the Rise of American Animation* (Durham, NC: Duke University Press, 2015); Christopher Lehman, *The Colored Cartoon: Black Representation in American Animated Short Films, 1907–1954* (Amherst: University of Massachusetts Press, 2007).
33. Karen Cox, *How the South Was Created in American Popular Culture* (Chapel Hill: University of North Carolina Press, 2011), 58–68; Melvin Ely, *The Adventures of "Amos 'n' Andy": A Social History of an American Phenomenon* (Charlottesville: University of Virginia Press, 2001).
34. For scholarship on transnational blackface minstrelsy, see chapter 1 and the afterword.
35. Michael Pickering, "Eugene Statton and Early Ragtime in Britain," *Black Music Research Journal* 20, no. 2 (2000): 151–80; James Dormon, "Shaping the Popular Image of Post-Reconstruction American Blacks: The 'Coon Song' Phenomenon of the Gilded Age," *American Quarterly* 40 (1988): 450–71; Waterhouse, *From Minstrel Show to Vaudeville*, 84–85, 89–91.
36. Matthew Wittmann, "Empire of Culture: U.S. Entertainers and the Making of the Pacific Circuit, 1850–1890" (PhD diss. University of Michigan, 2010), 15–16.
37. Gary Magee and Andrew Thompson, *Empire and Globalization: Networks of People, Goods and Capital in the British World* (Cambridge: Cambridge University Press, 2010); Alan Lester, *Imperial Networks: Creating Identities in Nineteenth Century South Africa and Britain* (London: Routledge, 2001).
38. Magee and Thompson, *Empire and Globalization*, 20–21; Lake and Reynolds, *Drawing the Global Colour Line*.
39. Ross, *Status and Respectability in the Cape Colony*, 43.
40. Bickford-Smith, *Ethnic Pride and Racial Prejudice;* Benjamin Kline, *Genesis of Apartheid: British African Policy in the Colony of Natal, 1845–1893* (Lanham, MD: University Press of America, 1988); William Worger, *South Africa's City of Diamonds: Mine Workers and Monopoly Capitalism in Kimberley, 1876–1895* (New Haven, CT: Yale University Press, 1987); Robert Turrell, *Capital and Labour on the Kimberley Diamond Fields, 1871–1890* (Cambridge: Cambridge University Press, 1987); Martin Legassick, "The Frontier Tradition in South African Historiography," in *Economy and Society in Pre-Industrial South Africa*, ed. Shula Marks and Anthony Atmore (London: Longman, 1980); David Welsch, *Roots of Segregation: Native Policy in Colonial Natal, 1845–1910* (Oxford: Oxford University Press, 1971).
41. A quote from Jacques Derrida, "Racism's Last Word," *Critical Inquiry* 12 (1985): 291. *Biopower* is a term that was coined by Michel Foucault, and it can be defined as state policies that attempt to manage human life. For a discussion of biopower and the apartheid state, see Achille Mbembe, "Necropolitics," *Public Culture* 15, no. 1 (2003): 11–40. As Frederick Cooper notes, much apartheid policy was designed

with the intention of controlling the movements and freedom of women. Cooper, *Africa since 1940: The Past to the Present* (Cambridge: Cambridge University Press, 2002), 55.

42. Leonard Thompson, *A History of South Africa* (New Haven, CT: Yale University Press, 2000), 190.
43. Immanuel Wallerstein, *World-Systems Analysis: An Introduction* (Durham, NC: Duke University Press, 2004).
44. James Campbell, "The Americanization of South Africa," in *Race, Nation, and Empire in American History*, eds. James Campbell, Matthew Guterl, and Robert Lee (Chapel Hill: University of North Carolina Press, 2007), 146–47. For a history of American investments in the apartheid economy, see Richard Hull, *American Enterprise in South Africa: Historical Dimensions of Engagement and Disengagement* (New York: New York University Press, 1990).
45. Campbell, "Americanization of South Africa," 131.
46. Several insightful comparative histories of the United States and South Africa have been published. See Ivan Evans, *Cultures of Violence: Racial Violence and the Origins of Segregation in South Africa and the American South* (Manchester: Manchester University Press, 2009); Pamela Brooks, *Boycotts, Buses, and Passes: Black Women's Resistance in the U.S. South and South Africa* (Amherst: University of Massachusetts Press, 2008); Anthony Marx, *Making Race and Nation: A Comparison of South Africa, the United States, and Brazil* (Cambridge: Cambridge University Press, 1998); John Cell, *The Highest Stage of White Supremacy: The Origins of Segregation in South Africa and the American South* (Cambridge: Cambridge University Press, 1982); and George Frederickson, *White Supremacy: A Comparative Study in American and South African History* (Oxford: Oxford University Press, 1981).
47. Here is a select list of sources I consulted to study African responses to blackface minstrelsy: Seetsele Modiri Molema with D. S. Matjia and Karen Haire, eds., *A Lover of His People: A Biography of Sol Plaatje* (Johannesburg: Wits University Press, 2012); Jeff Opland, ed., *Abantu Besizwe: Historical and Biographical Writings, 1902–1944* (Johannesburg: Wits University Press, 2009); Catherine Higgs, *The Ghost of Equality: The Public Lives of D. D. T. Jabavu of South Africa, 1885–1959* (Athens: Ohio University Press, 1996); Brian Willan, ed., *Sol Plaatje: Selected Writings* (Johannesburg: Wits University Press, 1996); Frieda Bokwe Matthews, *Remembrances* (Cape Town: Mayibuye Books, 1995); Phyllis Ntantala, *A Life's Mosaic: The Autobiography of Phyllis Ntantala* (Berkeley: University of California Press, 1993); Ellen Kuzwayo, *Call Me Woman* (San Francisco: Spinsters Ink, 1985); Tim Couzens, *The New African: A Study of the Life and Work of H. I. E. Dhlomo* (Johannesburg: Raven Press, 1985); Monica Wilson, ed., *Freedom for My People: The Autobiography of Z. K. Matthews: Southern Africa, 1901 to 1968* (Cape Town: David Philip, 1981); Noni Jabavu, *The Ochre People: Scenes from a South African Life* (New York: St. Martin's Press, 1963); Albert Luthuli, *Let My People Go* (New York: McGraw-Hill, 1962); and John Tengo Jabavu, *Life of John Tengo Javavu: Editor of "Imvo Zabantsundu," 1884–1921* (Lovedale, South

Africa: Lovedale Institution Press, 1922). I also consulted *Drum, Imvo Zabantsundu, Umthetheli Wabantu, Umteteli Wa Bantu,* and *Illanga Lase Natal.* A translator named Dingani Mthetwha transcribed Xhosa and Zulu newspaper articles that referenced minstrel lore into English. My research did not produce enough information for a chapter-long treatment of African responses to blackface minstrelsy.

48. The Centre for Popular Memory was previously called the Western Cape Oral History Project. The Centre for Popular Memory closed in 2013 and transferred its holdings to Special Collections at University of Cape Town Libraries.
49. For discussion on why song texts can be misleading for present-day researchers, see William Mahar, *Behind the Burnt Cork Mask: Early Blackface Minstrelsy and Antebellum American Popular Culture* (Urbana: University of Illinois Press, 1999), 16–17.
50. Jennifer Stoever's notion of a "sonic color line" that enabled nineteenth-century "listeners to construct and discern racial identities based on voices, sounds, and particular soundscapes" is very instructive. For Stoever, the racialization of sound is connected to civic participation, as white listeners learned to "hear themselves as 'normal' citizens." Matthew Morrison studies the ways in which blackface minstrelsy contributed to the racialization of sound. Although minstrel music combined European and African influences, it was still heard by many as a kind of "Blacksound." Ronald Radano's "insurgent textual listening" approach is also instructive. Stoever, *The Sonic Color Line: Race and the Cultural Politics of Listening* (New York: New York University Press, 2016), 11, 14; Morrison, "The Sound(s) of Subjection: Constructing American Popular Music and Racial Identity through Blacksound," *Women & Performance: A Journal of Feminist Theory* 27, no. 1 (2017): 13–24; Morrison, "Sound and the Construction of Race: From Blackface to Blacksound in Nineteenth-Century America" (PhD diss., Columbia University, 2014); Radano, *Lying Up a Nation: Race and Black Music* (Chicago: University of Chicago Press, 2003), 12.
51. *Port Elizabeth Telegraph*, September 27, 1862; *Cape Argus*, November 20, 1862, and September 2, 1865; *Natal Mercury*, October 14, 1865; *Cape Argus*, September 5, 1868; *Port Elizabeth Telegraph*, November 6, 1868; *Cape Argus*, April 22, 1869; *Port Elizabeth Telegraph*, October 2, 1874; *Eastern Province Herald*, April 3, 1877; *Cape Times*, July 21, 1883.
52. Bickford-Smith, *Ethnic Pride and Racial Prejudice*; Turrell, *Capital and Labour*; Worger, *South Africa's City of Diamonds*; Legassick, "Frontier Tradition."

CHAPTER 1: FOUNDATIONS

1. Dale Cockrell, *Demons of Disorder: Early Blackface Minstrels and Their World* (Cambridge: Cambridge University Press, 1997), 63; Alexander Saxton, "Blackface Minstrelsy," in *Inside the Minstrel Mask: Readings in Nineteenth-Century Blackface Minstrelsy*, ed. Annemarie Bean, James Hatch, and Brooks McNamara (Middletown, CT: Wesleyan University Press, 1996), 69; Hans Nathan, *Dan Emmettt*

and the Rise of Early Negro Minstrelsy (Norman: University of Oklahoma Press, 1962), 52; Carl Wittke, *Tambo and Bones: A History of the American Minstrel Stage* (Durham, NC: Duke University Press, 1930), 24–25. For a fictional portrayal of this exchange, see Wesley Brown, *Darktown Strutters: A Novel* (Amherst: University of Massachusetts Press, 2000).

2. Jenna Gibbs, *Performing the Temple of Liberty: Slavery, Theater, and Popular Culture in London and Philadelphia, 1760–1850* (Baltimore: John Hopkins University Press, 2014), 199.
3. Eric Lott, *Love and Theft: Blackface Minstrelsy and the American Working Class* (Oxford: Oxford University Press, 1993), 59.
4. Harry Reynolds, *Minstrel Memories: The Story of Burnt Cork Minstrelsy in Great Britain from 1836–1927* (London: Alston Rivers, 1928), 72–75. Eric Lott's comments are instructive: "This is probably the least trustworthy and most accurate account of American minstrel's appropriation of black cultural practices." Lott, *Love and Theft*, 19.
5. W. T. Lhamon, *Raising Cain: Blackface Performance from Jim Crow to Hip Hop* (Cambridge, MA: Harvard University Press, 1998); Cockrell, *Demons of Disorder.*
6. *Baltimore Sun*, 1837 (emphasis added), quoted in Tavia Nyong'o, *The Amalgamation Waltz: Race, Performance, and the Ruses of Memory* (Minneapolis: University of Minnesota Press, 2009), 122.
7. George Washington Dixon was another early contributor to the imaginary of burnt cork nationalism. However, Dixon did not enjoy the same amount of national or international fame as T. D. Rice. For a detailed study on Dixon, see Cockrell, *Demons of Disorder.*
8. Michael Omi and Howard Winant, *Racial Formation in the United States*, 3rd ed. (New York: Routledge, 2015), 141.
9. Brian Rouleau, *With Sails Whitening Every Sea: Mariners and the Making of an American Empire* (Ithaca, NY: Cornell University Press, 2014), 62–63.
10. Cockrell, *Demons of Disorder*, 62–65.
11. Ibid., 60; Lhamon, *Raising Cane*, 22; W. T. Lhamon, *Jump Jim Crow: Lost Plays, Lyrics, and Street Prose of the First Atlantic Popular Culture* (Cambridge, MA: Harvard University Press, 2003). In an earlier essay, Cockrell unequivocally criticizes the racism in the minstrel shows of the 1840s: "The entertainment took the form of derisive mimicking of the black man." Dale Cockrell, "Of Gospel Hymns, Minstrel Shows, and Jubilee Singers: Toward Some Black South African Musics," *American Music* 5, no. 4 (1987): 419.
12. Douglass Jones Jr., *The Captive Stage: Performance and the Proslavery Imagination of the Antebellum North* (Ann Arbor: University of Michigan Press, 2014), 68. Nyong'o describes that speech as "legibly pro-slavery and anti-black." Nyong'o, *Amalgamation Waltz*, 122.
13. Brian Roberts, *Blackface Nation: Race, Reform, and Identity in American Popular Music, 1812–1925* (Chicago: University of Chicago Press, 2017), 173.

14. Elizabeth Pryor, *The Colored Travelers: Mobility and the Fight for Citizenship before the Civil War* (Chapel Hill: University of North Carolina Press, 2016), 95.
15. Nathan, *Dan Emmett*, 113–42.
16. Ibram Kendi, *Stamped from the Beginning: The Definitive History of Racist Ideas in America* (New York: Nation Books, 2016), 214–15; Ian Binnington, *Confederate Visions: Nationalism, Symbolism, and the Imagined South in the Civil War* (Charlottesville: University of Virginia Press, 2013), 10–11.
17. Nathan, *Dan Emmett*, 117.
18. Lott, *Love and Theft*, 137.
19. Nathan, *Dan Emmett*, 120.
20. Nyong'o, *Amalgamation Waltz*, 107–12. Hans Nathan described the Virginia Minstrels as "primitive realism." Nathan, *Dan Emmett*, 151.
21. Saxton, "Blackface Minstrelsy," 69. E. P. Christy claimed his troupe predated the Virginia Minstrels. Nathan, *Dan Emmett*, 143–46.
22. Ken Emerson, *Doo-Dah: Stephen Foster and the Rise of American Popular Culture* (New York: Da Capo Press, 1997), 93.
23. Mel Watkins, *On the Real Side: A History of African American Comedy from Slavery to Chris Rock* (New York: Lawrence Hill Books, 1994), 89.
24. Robert C. Toll, *Blacking Up: The Minstrel Show in Nineteenth Century America* (Oxford: Oxford University Press, 1974), 140–45. For more discussion on the prima donna character, see Annemarie Bean, "Transgressing the Gender Divide: The Female Impersonator in Nineteenth-Century Blackface Minstrelsy," in *Inside the Minstrel Mask*, ed. Bean, Hatch, and McNamara, 245–65; Stephen Johnson, "Gender Trumps Race?," in *When Men Dance: Choreographing Masculinities across Borders*, ed. Jennifer Fisher and Anthony Shay (Oxford: Oxford University Press, 2009), 220–58. For misogyny in minstrel shows, see William Mahar, *Behind the Burnt Cork Mask: Early Blackface Minstrelsy and Antebellum American Popular Culture* (Urbana: University of Illinois Press, 1999), 268–328.
25. Robert Winans and Elias Kaufman, "Minstrel and Classic Banjo: American and English Connections, *American Music* 12 (Spring 1994): 1–30; Lott, *Love and Theft*, 92–100; Toll, *Blacking Up*, 43–50; Robert Cantwell, *Blue Grass Break Down: The Making of the Old Southern Sound* (Urbana: University of Illinois Press, 1984), 258; Nathan, *Dan Emmett*, 70–97, 159–88; Robert Winans, "The Folk, the Stage, and the Five-String Banjo in the Nineteenth Century," *Journal of American Folklore* 89, no. 354 (1976): 407–37.
26. Lhamon, *Jump Jim Crow*; Mahar, *Behind the Minstrel Mask*. For more discussion on European and African influences in early blackface minstrelsy, see Matthew Morrison, "Sound and the Construction of Race: From Blackface to Blacksound in Nineteenth-Century America" (PhD diss., Columbia University, 2014).
27. Lott, *Love and Theft*, 39.
28. Toll, *Blacking Up*, 32.
29. Mahar, *Behind the Burnt Cork Mask*, 2.

30. Toll, *Blacking Up*, 31.
31. White House Historical Association, "African American Performers at the White House," https://www.whitehousehistory.org/african-american-performers-at-the-white-house.
32. Stephen Johnson, "Juba's Dance: An Assessment of Newly Acquired Documentation," *Proceedings of the 26th Annual Conference of the Society for Dance History Scholars* (2003): 62–63; Brenda Dixon Gottschild, *Digging the Africanist Presence in American Performance: Dance and Other Contexts* (Westport, CT: Greenwood Press, 1996), 97–100; Marian Winter, "Juba and Blackface Minstrelsy," in *Inside the Minstrel Mask*, ed. Bean, Hatch, and McNamara, 224.
33. James Cook, "Master Juba, the King of All Dancers! A Story of Stardom and Struggle from the Dawn of the Transatlantic Culture Industry," *Discourses in Dance* 3, no. 2 (2006): 14. For more on William Henry Lane's impact in the United States, see Constance Hill, *Tap Dancing America: A Cultural History* (Oxford: Oxford University Press, 2010), 12; and Toll, *Blacking Up*, 43, 197–98.
34. Toll, *Blacking Up*, 197–98; Watkins, *On the Real Side*, 107.
35. For nineteenth-century "freak shows," see Linda Frost, *Never One Nation: Freaks, Savages, and Whiteness in U.S. Popular Culture, 1850–1877* (Minneapolis: University of Minnesota Press, 2005); Robert Bogdan, *Freak Show: Presenting Human Oddity for Amusement and Profit* (Chicago: Chicago University Press, 1990).
36. Saxton, "Blackface Minstrelsy," 76–77.
37. Douglass Jones Jr., "Black Politics but Not Black People: Rethinking the Social and 'Racial' History of Early Minstrelsy," *TDR: The Drama Review* 57, no. 2 (2013): 22 (see also Jones, *Captive Stage*); Nyong'o, *Amalgamation Waltz*, 8, 114–17; Saidiya Hartman, *Scenes of Subjection: Terror, Slavery, and Self-Making in Nineteenth-Century America* (Oxford: Oxford University Press, 1997), 32.
38. For more scholarship that adequately acknowledges the racial vitriol in early blackface minstrelsy, see Matthew Morrison, "The Sound(s) of Subjection: Constructing American Popular Music and Racial Identity through Blacksound," *Women & Performance: A Journal of Feminist Theory* 27, no. 1 (2017): 13–24; Mahar, *Behind the Burnt Cork Mask*; Lott, *Love and Theft*; David Roediger, *The Wages of Whiteness: Race and the Making of the American Working* (London: Verso, 1991); and Toll, *Blacking Up*.
39. James Burk, "Citizenship Status and Military Service: The Quest for Inclusion by Minorities and Conscientious Objectors," *Armed Forces and Society* 21, no. 4 (1995): 506.
40. Sam Dennison, *Scandalize My Name: Black Imagery in American Popular Music* (New York: Garland Publishing, 1982), 71.
41. Toll, *Blacking Up*, 120.
42. Mahar, *Behind the Burnt Cork Mask*, 93–95; Roediger, *Wages of Whiteness*, 125. For misogyny in minstrel shows, see Mahar, *Behind the Burnt Cork Mask*, 268–328.
43. Saxton, "Blackface Minstrelsy," 74; Lott, *Love and Theft*, 107.

44. Roediger, *Wages of Whiteness*, 119.
45. Toll, *Blacking Up*, 106.
46. Lott, *Love and Theft*, 203–7; Joseph Byrd, "Whitewashing Blackface Minstrelsy in American College Textbooks," *Popular Music and Society* 32, no. 1 (2009): 79.
47. Michael Pickering, *Blackface Minstrelsy in Britain* (Farnham, UK: Ashgave, 2008), 10, 9.
48. *Southern Australian*, July 23, 1841, quoted in John Whiteoak, "Demons of Discord Down Under: 'Jump Jim Crow' and Australia's First Jazz Band," *Jazz Research Journal* 8, nos. 1–2 (2015): 28.
49. Pickering, *Blackface Minstrelsy in Britain*, 18–24; Stephen Johnson, "Testimonials in Silk: Juba and the Legitimization of American Blackface Minstrelsy in Britain," in *Testimonial Advertising in the American Marketplace: Emulation, Identity, Community*, ed. Marlis Schweitzer and Marina Moskowitz (New York: Palgrave Macmillan, 2009), 23–49.
50. Richard Waterhouse, *From Minstrel Show to Vaudeville: The Australian Popular Stage, 1788–1914* (Kensington: New South Wales University Press, 1990), 12.
51. Laura Vorachek, "Whitewashing Blackface Minstrelsy in Nineteenth-Century England: Female Banjo Players in 'Punch,'" *Victorians: A Journal of Culture and Literature*, no. 123 (2013): 42.
52. Sarah Meer, *Uncle Tom Mania: Slavery, Minstrelsy, and Transatlantic Culture in the 1850s* (Athens: University of Georgia Press, 2005), 11–12, 19–50. See also Johnson, "Gender Trumps Race?," 236.
53. Meer, *Uncle Tom Mania*, 134.
54. Douglas Lorimer, "Bibles, Banjoes and Bones: Images of the Negro in the Popular Culture of Victorian England," in *In Search of the Visible Past: History Lectures at Wilfred Laurier University, 1973–1974*, ed. Barry Gough (Ontario: Wilfred Laurier University Press, 1975), 39.
55. Meer, *Uncle Tom Mania*, 133–60.
56. J. S. Bratton, "English Ethiopians: British Audiences and Blackface Acts, 1835–1865." *Yearbook of English Studies* 2 (1981): 133.
57. Reynolds, *Minstrel Memories*, 71.
58. John Blair, "Blackface Minstrels as Cultural Export," in *Yankee Go Home (& Take Me with U): Americanization and Popular Culture*, ed. George McKay (Sheffield: Sheffield Academic Press, 1997), 58.
59. Michael Pickering, "John Bull in Blackface," *Popular Music* 16, no. 2 (1997): 181.
60. Michael Pickering, "Mock Blacks and Racial Mockery: The 'Nigger' Minstrel and British Imperialism," in *Acts of Supremacy: The British Empire and the Stage, 1790–1930*, ed. J. S. Bratton (Manchester: Manchester University Press, 1991), 191.
61. Pickering, *Blackface Minstrelsy in Britain*, 112; Pickering, "Mock Blacks and Racial Mockery," 212.
62. Patrick Brantlinger, *Taming Cannibals: Race and the Victorians* (Ithaca, NY: Cornell University Press, 2011), 7. For scholarship on Victorian race thinking, see Edward

Beasley, *The Victorian Reinvention of Race: New Racism and the Problem of Grouping in the Human Sciences* (London: Routledge, 2012); Jennifer DeVere Brody, *Impossible Purities: Blackness, Femininity, and Victorian Culture* (Durham, NC: Duke University Press, 1998); Nancy Stepan, *The Idea of Race in Science: Great Britain, 1800–1960* (North Haven: Archon, 1982); Douglass Lorimer, *Colour, Class, and the Victorians: A Study of English Attitudes to the Negro in the Mid-Nineteenth Century* (New York: Holmes & Meier, 1978). For the eighteenth century, see Kathleen Wilson, *The Island Race: Englishness, Empire and Gender in the Eighteenth Century* (London: Routledge, 2014). For the Elizabethan era, see Kim Hall, *Things of Darkness: Economies of Race and Gender in Early Modern England* (Ithaca, NY: Cornell University Press, 1995).

63. Lorimer, *Colour, Class, and the Victorians*, 89, 63–64.
64. Matthew Wittmann, "Empire of Culture: U.S. Entertainers and the Making of the Pacific Circuit, 1850–1890" (PhD diss., University of Michigan, 2010), 15–16, 92–131; James Carr, *Hawaiian Music in Motion: Mariners, Missionaries, and Minstrels* (Urbana: University of Illinois Press, 2014), 126–58.
65. Waterhouse, *From Minstrel Show to Vaudeville*, 36, 40.
66. Ibid., 100, 38–39. For minstrel portrayals of Chinese people, see Krystyn Moon, *Yellowface: Creating the Chinese in American Popular Music and Performance, 1850s–1920s* (New Brunswick, NJ: Rutgers University Press, 2005); Robert Lee, *Orientals: Asian Americans in Popular Culture* (Philadelphia: Temple University Press, 1999). For more discussion on anti-Chinese prejudice in Australia, see Marilyn Lake and Henry Reynolds, *Drawing the Global Colour Line: White Men's Countries and the Challenge of Racial Equality* (Cambridge: Cambridge University Press, 2008), 15–48.
67. Timothy Keegan, *Colonial South Africa and the Origins of the Racial Order* (Charlottesville: University Press of Virginia, 1996), 41.
68. *Englishman & Military Chronicle*, March 3, 1838, quoted in Kellen Hoxworth, "Transoceanic Blackface, Imperial Whiteness: Performing 'Race' in the Global Nineteenth Century" (PhD diss., Stanford University, 2017), 210.
69. Bradley Shope, *American Popular Music in Britain's Raj* (Rochester, NY: University of Rochester Press, 2016), 29–30.
70. Harish Trivedi, "Performing the Nation: Dave Carson and the Bengali Babu," in *The Nation across the World: Postcolonial Literary Representations*, ed. Harish Trivedi et al. (Oxford: Oxford University Press, 2007), 250, 256.
71. Hoxworth, "Transoceanic Blackface," 319
72. Quoted in Shope, *American Popular Music in Britain's Raj*, 31–32. Waterhouse briefly mentions Carson in *From Minstrel Show to Vaudeville* (107). The most thorough discussion of Carson can be found in Hoxworth, "Transoceanic Blackface," 288–327.
73. Mahar, *Behind the Burnt Cork Mask*, 357–58.
74. Reynolds, *Minstrel Memories*, 90–92.

75. Waterhouse, *From Minstrel Show to Vaudeville*, 40.
76. The quote in the heading is from a Xhosa-language poem published by Nontsizi Mgqwetho in 1925. Nontsizi Mgqwetho, *The Nation's Bounty: The Xhosa Poetry of Nontsizi Mgqwetho*, ed. Jeff Opland (Johannesburg: Wits University Press, 2007), 332.
77. Nigel Worden, Elizabeth Van Heyningen, and Vivian Bickford-Smith, *Cape Town: The Making of a City* (Cape Town: David Philip, 1998).
78. Charles Feinstein, *An Economic History of South Africa: Conquest, Discrimination and Development* (Cambridge: Cambridge University Press, 2005), 22.
79. Nigel Penn, "Land, Labour and Livestock in the Western Cape during the Eighteenth Century," in *Class, Caste and Color: A Social and Economic History of the South African Western Cape*, ed. Wilmot James and Mary Simons (London: Transaction, 1992), 2–19.
80. Feinstein, *Economic History of South Africa*. Many San were never incorporated into the colonial system as the VOC embarked on several genocidal wars of extermination in the late 1700s. Mohamed Adhikari, *The Anatomy of a South African Genocide: The Extermination of the Cape San Peoples* (Athens: Ohio University Press, 2011).
81. Richard Elphick and Hermann Giliomee, "The Origins and Entrenchment of European Dominance at the Cape, 1652–1840," in *The Shaping of South African Society, 1652–1840*, ed. Richard Elphick and Hermann Giliomee (Middletown, CT: Wesleyan University Press 1989), 521–59. For slavery in the Cape, see Wayne Dooling, *Slavery, Emancipation and Colonial Rule in South Africa* (Athens: Ohio University Press, 2007); John Mason, *Social Death and Resurrection: Slavery and Emancipation in South Africa* (Charlottesville: University of Virginia Press, 2003); and Pamela Scully, *Liberating the Family: Gender and British Slave Emancipation in the Rural Western Cape, S. Africa, 1823–1853* (Portsmouth: Heinemann, 1997).
82. Keegan, *Colonial South Africa*, 291.
83. For several histories on Christian missions in South Africa, see Richard Elphick and Rodney Davenport, eds., *Christianity in South Africa: A Political, Social, and Cultural History* (Berkeley: University of California Press, 1997).
84. By the 1820s, many Dutch settlers in the Cape Colony were identifying as "Afrikaner." Herman Giliomee, *The Afrikaners: A Biography of a People* (Charlottesville: University of Virginia Press, 2003), 52.
85. Martin Meredith, *Diamonds, Gold, and War: The British, the Boers, and the Making of South Africa* (New York: PublicAffairs, 2008), 94.
86. On the location system in Natal, see Benjamin Kline, *Genesis of Apartheid: British African Policy in the Colony of Natal, 1845–1893* (Lanham, MD: University Press of America, 1988); David Welsch, *Roots of Segregation: Native Policy in Colonial Natal, 1845–1910* (Oxford: Oxford University Press, 1971).
87. D. Hobart Houghton, "Economic Development, 1865–1965," in *The Oxford History*

of South Africa, ed. Monica Wilson and Leonard Thompson (Oxford: Oxford University Press, 1971), 2:2.

88. A railway line connecting central Durban to a Natal harbor was built in 1860, but there was little incentive to build more railways during the decade. Bill Guest, "The KwaZulu-Natal Regional Economy in Retrospect and Prospect: A Brief Overview," *South African Historical Journal* 37 (November 1997): 70.
89. Feinstein, *Economic History of South Africa;* Houghton, "Economic Development."
90. Clifton Crais, *White Supremacy and Black Resistance in Pre-industrial South Africa* (Cambridge: Cambridge University Press, 1992), 47.
91. Keegan, *Colonial South Africa*, 35.
92. Keegan, *Colonial South Africa*, 289.
93. Alan Lester, *Imperial Networks: Creating Identities in Nineteenth Century South Africa and Britain* (London: Routledge, 2001), 183.
94. Elizabeth Elbourne, *Blood Ground: Colonialism, Missions, and the Contest for Christianity in the Cape Colony and Britain* (Montreal: McGill-Queen's University Press, 2002), 375.
95. For more on the Kat River settlement, see Robert Ross, *The Borders of Race in Colonial South Africa: The Kat River Settlement, 1829–1856* (Cambridge: Cambridge University Press, 2014).
96. Leonard Thompson, *A History of South Africa* (New Haven, CT: Yale University Press, 2001), 64–65.
97. For race thinking and the British settlers, see Vivian Bickford-Smith, *The Emergence of the South African Metropolis: Cities and Identities in the Twentieth Century* (Cambridge: Cambridge University Press, 2016); Lester, *Imperial Networks;* Keegan, *Colonial South Africa;* Vivian Bickford-Smith, *Ethnic Pride and Racial Prejudice in Victorian Cape Town: Group Identity and Social Practice, 1875–1902* (Cambridge: Cambridge University Press, 1995); and Crais, *White Supremacy and Black Resistance.*
98. John Blair makes a similar point in "First Steps toward Globalization: Nineteenth-Century Exports of American Entertainment Forms," in *Here, There and Everywhere: The Foreign Politics of American Popular Culture*, ed. Reinhold Wagnleitner and Elaine Tyler May (Hanover, NH: University Press of New England, 2000), 22.

CHAPTER 2: AN EMPIRE OF BURNT CORK

1. *Port Elizabeth Telegraph*, November 8, 1862.
2. W. T. Lhamon, *Raising Cain: Blackface Performance from Jim Crow to Hip Hop* (Cambridge, MA: Harvard University Press, 1998); Dale Cockrell, *Demons of Disorder: Early Blackface Minstrels and Their World* (Cambridge: Cambridge University Press, 1997).
3. *Diamond News*, July 21, 1881.

4. David Cannadine, *Ornamentalism: How the British Saw Their Empire* (Oxford: Oxford University Press, 2002).
5. Later in the 1870s, Harry Leslie performed with Dave Carson's Minstrels in India. Bradley Shope, *American Popular Music in Britain's Raj* (Rochester, NY: University of Rochester Press, 2016), 38.
6. I have chosen the names "Nish's Christy Minstrels," "Leslie's Christy Minstrels," and "Norton's Christy Minstrels" for the sake of convenience. Each troupe was simply listed as "Christy Minstrels" in the local press.
7. Kellen Hoxworth, "Transoceanic Blackface, Imperial Whiteness: Performing 'Race' in the Global Nineteenth Century" (PhD diss., Stanford University, 2017), 212–18; Dale Cockrell, "Of Gospel Hymns, Minstrel Shows, and Jubilee Singers: Toward Some Black South African Musics," *American Music* 5, no. 4 (1987): 420.
8. Although some scholars believe the Amateur Coloured Troupe was a group of coloured performers, I have come to a different interpretation. The Anglican names of the members of this troupe suggest they probably were British settlers: Joe Lyal, M. Clifton, E. Clifton, H. Burton, T. Grimes, J. France, and V. Buckley. I also used newspaper evidence to arrive at this speculation. Performances by nonwhite entertainers were a rare spectacle in the British colonies of South Africa. Newspapers were quick to describe the "nonnormative" racial position of the performers. Take, for example, the *Natal Mercury*'s description of a show that was carried out by the Kaffir Christy Minstrels: "a troupe of eight genuine natives, bones and all." *Natal Mercury*, December 28, 1880. In the 1890s, British settler newspapers constantly mentioned the racial identities of the members of Orpheus McAdoo's troupes. Nonwhite performers were a rare novelty worthy of mention in the settler press. By contrast, the race of the Amateur Coloured Troupe was never mentioned in the press. This is because they were British settlers and normative whiteness was not worthy of mention.
9. Michael Omi and Howard Winant, *Racial Formation in the United States*, 3rd ed. (New York: Routledge, 2015), 125.
10. *Cape Argus Supplement*, November 20, 1862. Another telling moment appeared in the June 12, 1872, edition of the *Diamond News*. A reviewer who described an amateur minstrel show was most interested in the visual presentation: "The company consisted of eight Christy's and their get-up was most creditable."
11. *Cape Argus*, August 21 and November 20, 1862, and November 23, 1865; *Eastern Province Herald*, September 19, 1865; *Natal Mercury*, October 7, 1865, quoted in Veit Erlmann, *African Stars: Studies in Black South African Performance* (Chicago: University of Chicago Press, 1991), 31.
12. *Friend of the Free State*, January 14, 1869.
13. *Port Elizabeth Telegraph*, November 6, 1868. A Natal review was less convinced: "[Norton's] [p]rima donna was natural and graceful, though slightly burlesque." *Natal Mercury*, April 13, 1869.
14. *Cape Argus*, April 22, 1869.

15. For advertisements listing the giant as part of the minstrel's program, see the *Eastern Province Herald*, September 5, 1865; and *Natal Mercury*, November 2, 1865. For the related issue of African representations in ethnological show business, see Bernth Lindfors, ed., *Africans on Stage: Studies in Ethnological Show Business* (Bloomington: Indiana University Press, 2000).
16. Mark Twain, *The Autobiography of Mark Twain*, ed. Charles Eider (New York: Harper and Row, 1959), quoted in Eric Lott, *Love and Theft: Blackface Minstrelsy and the American Working Class* (Oxford: Oxford University Press, 1993), 31; *Illustrated London News*, November 13, 1858; "The Coloured Opera Troupe," quoted in Michael Pickering, *Blackface Minstrelsy in Britain* (Farnham, UK: Ashgave, 2008), 99; *Natal Mercury*, October 7, 1865, quoted in Erlmann, *African Stars*, 31.
17. Hans Nathan, *Dan Emmett and the Rise of Early Negro Minstrelsy* (Norman: University of Oklahoma Press, 1962), 124; British review of the Ethiopian Serenaders from 1846, quoted in Nathan, *Dan Emmett*, 125.
18. *Cape Chronicle*, August 22, 1862.
19. *Eastern Province Herald*, November 6, 1868.
20. *The Original Christy Minstrel Song Book*, 41, National Library of South Africa Cape Town. "Tapioca" appears in several newspaper descriptions of minstrel shows: *Cape Argus*, August 6, 1864, September 22, 1868, and July 3, 1869; *Eastern Province Herald*, September 26 and 30, 1862; and *Port Elizabeth Telegraph*, October 1, 1862, August 5, 1863, and November 17, 1868.
21. *Christy's Bones and Banjo Melodist*, 1865, New York Public Library. "Down the River" was mentioned in *Natal Mercury*, November 2, 1865.
22. *Original Christy Minstrel Song Book*, 25, National Library of South Africa Cape Town. "Angelina Baker" was mentioned in *Cape Argus*, September 5, 1868, and September 11, 1869.
23. Peter Davis, *In Darkest Hollywood: Exploring the Jungles of Cinema's South Africa* (Johannesburg and Athens: Ravem and Ohio University Press, 1996), 7–12.
24. *Original Christy Minstrel Songbook*, National Library of South Africa Cape Town. "Beneath the Weeping Willow" was mentioned in *Port Elizabeth Telegraph*, October 4, 1862.
25. *Christy's Plantation Melodies*, New York Public Library. "Massa's in the Cold Ground" was mentioned in *Cape Argus*, October 24, 1868.
26. *Original Christy Minstrel Songbook*, National Library of South Africa. Cape Town. "I Long for My Old Kentucky Home" was mentioned in *Cape Argus*, August 24, 1864, and October 24, 1868.
27. "On Old Potomac's Shore," www.pdmusic.org/root-gf/gfr59g.txt. "Old Potomac Shore" was mentioned in *Cape Argus*, June 11, 1864.
28. Nigel Worden, Elizabeth Van Heyningen, and Vivian Bickford-Smith, *Cape Town: The Making of a City* (Cape Town: David Philip, 1998), 196.
29. Lott, *Love and Theft*, 32.
30. *Eastern Province Herald*, November 3, 1868.

31. W. T. Lhamon, *Jump Jim Crow: Lost Plays, Lyrics, and Street Prose of the First Atlantic Popular Culture* (Cambridge, MA: Harvard University, 2003), 46. *The Virginia Mummy* was mentioned in *Diamond News,* November 18, 1872; *Cape Argus,* November 25, 1865; *Port Elizabeth Telegraph,* September 15, 1865; and *Eastern Province Herald,* September 12 and 15, 1865.
32. *The Virginia Mummy,* 6–9, New York Public Library.
33. *Eastern Province Herald,* September 12, 1865; *Port Elizabeth Telegraph,* September 15, 1865.
34. Michael Bennett, *Union Jacks: Yankee Soldiers in the Civil War* (Chapel Hill: University of North Carolina Press, 2004), 176n146.
35. Lhamon, *Jump Jim Crow,* 46.
36. "Or Any Other Man" was mentioned in *Cape Mercantile Advertiser,* September 18, 1869; *Cape Argus,* August 25, June 23, and May 21, 1864; and *Port Elizabeth Telegraph,* October 1, 1862.
37. "Or Any Other Man," *Christy's New Songster and Black Joker,* New York Public Library. This stump speech used the conventions of a "mock political oration" speech. William Mahar, *Behind the Burnt Cork Mask: Early Blackface Minstrelsy and Antebellum American Popular Culture* (Urbana: University of Illinois Press, 1999), 59.
38. *Natal Mercury,* October 10, 1865.
39. *Natal Mercury,* October 7, 1865.
40. *Natal Mercury,* October 19, 1865.
41. *Natal Mercury,* November 4, 1865; Mahar, *Behind the Burnt Cork Mask,* 93–95.
42. *Cape Argus,* December 1, 1866.
43. "Who Stole the Chickens," New York Public Library. "Who Stole the Chickens" was mentioned in *Cape Argus,* August 7, 1869.
44. "The Sly Young Coon," *Christy and White's Ethiopian Melodies,* bk. 5, 28–29, New York Public Library. "The Sly Young Coon" was mentioned in *Cape Argus,* December 17, 1868.
45. Gary Engle, ed., *This Grotesque Essence: Plays from the American Minstrel Stage* (Baton Rouge: Louisiana State University Press, 1978), 17. "Challenge Dance" was mentioned in *Cape Argus,* August 7 and May 1, 1869; *Natal Mercury,* October 10, 1865; *Port Elizabeth Telegraph,* September 2, 1865.
46. "The Rival Lovers," 8–9, New York Public Library. "The Rival Lovers" was performed by the Amateur Coloured Troupe in 1870. *Cape Argus,* May 14, 1870.
47. "The Young Scamp," 4, New York Public Library. "The Young Scamp" was mentioned in *Cape Mercantile Advertiser,* September 18, 1869; *Eastern Province Herald,* November 27, 1868; *Cape Argus,* August 20, 1868, and November 18, 1865.
48. Ken Emerson, *Doo-Dah: Stephen Foster and the Rise of American Popular Culture* (New York: Da Capo Press, 1997), 14.
49. *Christy and White's Ethiopian Melodies,* bk. 2, 65, New York Public Library.
50. "The Coopers," New York Public Library. The play ends when Workman's ghost

disrupts the festivities by haunting the revelers and demanding his two-dollar debt: illogical blackness indeed. This play was performed in Cape Town by the YMI Amateur Christys. See *Cape Mercantile Advertiser*, September 25, 1869.

51. Saidiya Hartman, *Scenes of Subjection: Terror, Slavery, and Self-Making in Nineteenth-Century America* (Oxford: Oxford University Press, 1997), 30–31. Eric Lott's comments on minstrel violence are also instructive: "One might say that while such songs needed the recurring deaths of black people in order to exist, they also repeatedly wished away the existence of blacks altogether." Lott, *Love and Theft*, 189.
52. In 1925 Jessie Fauset made a similar point: "There is an unwritten law in America that though white may imitate black, black, even when superlatively capable, must never imitate white. In other words, grease-paint may be used to darken but never to lighten." Fauset, "The Gift of Laughter," in *The New Negro*, ed. Alain Locke (New York: Atheneum, 1992), 164. Some African American performers challenged minstrel conventions by "whiting up." See Marvin McAllister, *Whiting Up: Whiteface Minstrels and Stage Europeans in African American Performance* (Chapel Hill: University of North Carolina Press, 2011).
53. *The Virginny Cupids!* was performed in Port Elizabeth in 1874. See *Port Elizabeth Telegraph*, October 2, 1874.
54. Lhamon, *Jump Jim Crow*, 154. This sketch was based on the plot line of a popular minstrel song called "Coal Black Rose."
55. *The Virginia Mummy*, 9, New York Public Library.
56. Lhamon, *Jump Jim Crow*, 165.
57. *The Virginia Mummy*, 21, New York Public Library.
58. *Eastern Province Herald*, September 19, 1865 (emphasis added).
59. "The United States Mail," 16, New York Public Library.
60. Masters and Servants Act, quoted in Richard Elphick and Hermann Giliomee, eds., *The Shaping of South African Society, 1652–1840* (Middletown, CT: Wesleyan University Press, 1979), 168.
61. Clifton Crais, *White Supremacy and Black Resistance in Pre-industrial South Africa* (Cambridge: Cambridge University Press, 1992), 127–33.
62. Minstrel shows often portrayed hypersexual black caricatures. Lott, *Love and Theft*.
63. Alan Lester, *Imperial Networks: Creating Identities in Nineteenth Century South Africa and Britain* (London: Routledge, 2001); Timothy Keegan, *Colonial South Africa and the Origins of the Racial Order* (Charlottesville: University Press of Virginia, 1996); Robert Ross, *Beyond the Pale: Essays on the History of Colonial South Africa* (Middletown, CT: Wesleyan University Press, 1993); Crais, *White Supremacy and Black Resistance*; Benjamin Kline, *Genesis of Apartheid: British African Policy in the Colony of Natal, 1845–1893* (Lanham, MD: University Press of America, 1988); David Welsch, *Roots of Segregation: Native Policy in Colonial Natal, 1845–1910* (Oxford: Oxford University Press, 1971).
64. Ross, *Beyond the Pale*, 2.

65. Lhamon, *Jump Jim Crow*; Lhamon, *Raising Cane*; Cockrell, *Demons of Disorder.*
66. Mahar, *Behind the Burnt Cork Mask*, 25–27.
67. Stephen Johnson, "Testimonials in Silk: Juba and the Legitimization of American Blackface Minstrelsy in Britain," in *Testimonial Advertising in the American Marketplace: Emulation, Identity, Community*, ed. Marlis Schweitzer and Marina Moskowitz (New York: Palgrave Macmillan, 2009); Michael Pickering, *Blackface Minstrelsy in Britain* (Farnham, UK: Ashgave, 2008).
68. For more information on the Commercial Exchange, see Vivian Bickford-Smith, Elizabeth Van Heyningen, and Nigel Worden, *Cape Town: An Illustrated History* (Cape Town: David Philip, 1998).
69. *Cape Argus*, September 4, 1862.
70. "Old Joe," in *Queen and West's Popular Songster*, Harvard Theatre Collection.
71. Lily Wolpowitz, ed., *The Diaries of John Rose of Cape Town, 1848–1873* (Cape Town: Friends of the South African Library, 1990), 102.
72. *Natal Mercury*, October 3, 1865.
73. *Cape Argus*, November 14, 1865.
74. *Cape Argus*, April 21, 1869. In the Cape and Natal, *Christy* was often used synonymously with blackface minstrelsy.
75. *Cape Mercantile Advisor*, September 22, 1869.
76. *Grahamstown Journal*, December 12, 1862; *Grahamstown Journal*, December 16, 1862.
77. British migration to South Africa in the middle of the nineteenth century was relatively small when compared to the larger British settler colonies of New Zealand, Australia, and Canada. Gary Magee and Andrew Thompson, *Empire and Globalization: Networks of People, Goods and Capital in the British World* (Cambridge: Cambridge University Press, 2010), 67–72.
78. *Port Elizabeth Telegraph*, September 15, 1874.
79. *Port Elizabeth Telegraph*, September 22, 1865.
80. An advertisement published by Nish's Christy Minstrel included the following: "For Sale: The Book of Words from which the Songs for each performance are selected." *Grahamstown Journal*, October 4, 1862.
81. A music store advertised "Christy Minstrels Favourite songs" and "Buckley's American Melodies" in *Port Elizabeth Telegraph*, May 9, 1863. Another store sold "Christy and Buckley Songs," "Christy Minstrel Songs, with Choruses," and "Vocal Christy Minstrel Albums," *Cape Argus*, September 17, 1863. For additional examples, see *Cape Argus*, February 26 and May 29, 1869, February 26 and June 25, 1870, and February 2, 1871.
82. Joseph Roach, *Cities of the Dead: Circum-Atlantic Performance* (New York: Columbia University Press, 1996).
83. *Cape Chronicle*, November 7, 1862.
84. Michael Pickering, "John Bull in Blackface," *Popular Music* 16, no. 2 (1997): 181. Relatedly, the British settler press referenced several minstrel songs. The

Stephen Foster song "Hard Times Come Again No More" was referenced in *Diamond News,* January 9, 1886; January 9, 1883; July 29, 1876; *Cape Argus,* September 3, 1872; and *Port Elizabeth Telegraph,* July 15, 1863. The minstrel song "Medicine Jack" was referenced in *Diamond News,* February 22, 1877. The minstrel song "Whose Dat Knocking at de Door" was referenced in *Daily Independent,* June 26, 1877.

85. *Cape Chronicle,* November 14, 1862.
86. *Cape Argus,* September 5 (emphasis added) and September 23, 1865.
87. Nathan, *Dan Emmett,* 142–46.
88. Mahar, *Behind the Burnt Cork Mask,* 357–58. A year later, on June 21, 1866, the *Cape Argus* described an amateur minstrel scene as "a poor parody of Messrs. Leslie and Taylor's performance."
89. *Cape Argus,* June 2, 1864.
90. *Cape Argus,* November 1, 1870.
91. Several amateur troupes used the logic of surrogate authenticity. See the "Original South African Darkie Serenaders," *Cape Argus,* August 18, 1866; and December 19, 1865. See also "The Original Capetown Christys," *Diamond News,* May 28, June 5, and September 18 of 1872.
92. Lester, *Imperial Networks,* 46, 76.
93. *Eastern Province Herald,* October 10, 1862; *Port Elizabeth Telegraph,* October 11, 1862.
94. Worden, Heyningen, and Bickford-Smith, *Cape Town,* 190.
95. An African girl named Eliza saw the 1863 celebration of the marriage of Prince Albert firsthand. She was a student at a mission school in the Eastern Cape. She kept a diary in Xhosa that was translated into English by an Anglican missionary and published in a local newspaper: "[We] went to see white people smeared with soot." Quoted in Vivian Bickford-Smith, "Leisure and Social Identity in Cape Town, British Cape Colony, 1838–1910," *Kronos Journal of Cape History,* no. 25 (1998–99): 107.
96. Sarah Meer, *Uncle Tom Mania: Slavery, Minstrelsy, and Transatlantic Culture in the 1850s* (Athens: University of Georgia Press, 2005), 67.
97. *Cape Argus,* November 21, 1863.
98. *Cape Argus,* June 2, 1864.
99. *Cape Argus,* May 30, 1871; May 30 and 24, and April 29, 1869.
100. *Natal Mercury,* October 14, 1865.
101. *Port Elizabeth Telegraph,* September 5, 1865.
102. "Beautiful Isle of the Sea," in *Christy Minstrels Plantation Songster,* Harvard Theatre Collection.
103. *Natal Mercury,* October 19, 1865.
104. *Eastern Province Herald,* December 24, 1872.
105. Jill Bender, *The 1857 Uprising and the British Empire* (Cambridge: Cambridge University Press, 2016); "The Negro Outbreak in Jamaica," *Port Elizabeth Telegraph,* January 9, 1866.

106. In the 1860s, the British metropolitan government was reluctant to send economic support to a relatively underdeveloped economy with few natural resources to exploit. D. Hobart Houghton, "Economic Development, 1865–1965," in *The Oxford History of South Africa* eds. Monica Wilson and Leonard Thompson (Oxford University Press, 1971), 2:9.
107. Lester, *Imperial Networks,* 72–75.
108. *Cape Argus,* August 18, 1866.
109. Donald Akenson, *Occasional Papers on the Irish in South Africa* (Grahamstown: Grahamstown Institute of Social and Economic Research, Rhodes University, 1991), 53.
110. *Cape Argus,* November 23, 1865.
111. *Cape Argus,* September 10, 1869.
112. *Cape Argus,* April 14, 1870; "The Rival Lovers," 14, New York Public Library.
113. *Port Elizabeth Telegraph,* October 1, 1862; *Cape Argus,* September 9, 1868; March 26, 1870. "When Johnny Came Marching Home" was originally an American Civil War song. Norton's Christy Minstrels may have reinterpreted it. The *Cape Argus* on September 22, 1868, described "When Johnny Came Marching Home" as an "Irish comic" song.
114. *Eastern Province Herald,* November 6, 1868.
115. *Cape Argus,* November 19, 1872.
116. Here is another viable interpretation: the speakers described in the article might have been coloured. At this time, the Port Elizabeth population included more coloureds than Africans. For demographic information on Port Elizabeth, see Gary Baines, *A History of New Brighton, Port Elizabeth, South Africa, 1903–1953* (Lewiston, NY: Edwin Mellen Press, 2002), 14; A. J. Christopher, "Race and Residence in Colonial Port Elizabeth," *South African Geographical Journal* 69, no. 1 (1987): 3–20.
117. Lhamon, *Raising Cane.*
118. Michael Rogin, *Blackface, White Noise: Jewish Immigrants in the Hollywood Melting Pot* (Berkeley: University of California Press, 1998), 44.
119. *Grahamstown Journal,* September 13, 1862. For additional newspaper articles reporting on the international tours of the Christy Minstrel troupes who visited South Africa, see *Cape Argus,* July 16, 1864, July 13 and April 15, 1865, August 15, 1868, and May 3, 1870; *Cape Chronicle,* October 10, 1862; *Natal Mercury,* October 3, 1865; and *Port Elizabeth Telegraph,* June 3 and October 21, 1863, and July 23, 1864.
120. *Port Elizabeth Telegraph,* March 9, 1869.
121. *Diamond News,* May 6, 1879.
122. *Port Elizabeth Telegraph,* June 3 and October 21, 1863; July 21, 1864; *Cape Argus,* July 13, 1865; *Natal Mercury,* November 7, 1865; *Port Elizabeth Telegraph,* April 24, 1866; *Cape Argus,* April 19, 1866; August 15, 1868; May 1, 1869; *Port Elizabeth Telegraph,* April 5, 1869. According to a British newspaper, Norton's Christy Minstrels toured Bahia before going to London. *Era,* May 14, 1871, cited in Hoxworth, "Transoceanic Blackface," 263n157.
123. Magee and Thompson, *Empire and Globalization,* 67.

CHAPTER 3: DIAMONDS, DANDIES, AND DISPOSSESSION

1. J. K. Matthews, *Incwadi Yami; or, Twenty Years' Personal Experience in South Africa* (New York: Rogers and Sherwood, 1887), 192–93, referenced in Veit Erlmann, *African Stars: Studies in Black South African Performance* (Chicago: University of Chicago Press, 1991), 33.
2. Eric Lott, *Love and Theft: Blackface Minstrelsy and the American Working Class* (Oxford: Oxford University Press, 1993), 19.
3. David Harvey, *The New Imperialism* (Oxford: Oxford University Press, 2003), 137–82.
4. Tavia Nyong'o, *The Amalgamation Waltz: Race, Performance, and the Ruses of Memory* (Minneapolis: University of Minnesota Press, 2009), 107–12.
5. Vivian Bickford-Smith, *Ethnic Pride and Racial Prejudice in Victorian Cape Town: Group Identity and Social Practice, 1875–1902* (Cambridge: Cambridge University Press, 1995); Robert Turrell, *Capital and Labour on the Kimberley Diamond Fields, 1871–1890* (Cambridge: Cambridge University Press, 1987); William Worger, *South Africa's City of Diamonds: Mine Workers and Monopoly Capitalism in Kimberley, 1876–1895* (New Haven, CT: Yale University Press, 1987); John Cell, *The Highest Stage of White Supremacy: The Origins of Segregation in South Africa and the American South* (Cambridge: Cambridge University Press, 1982); Martin Legassick, "The Frontier Tradition in South African Historiography," in *Economy and Society in Pre-Industrial South Africa*, ed. Shula Marks and Anthony Atmore (London: Longman, 1980).
6. *Cape Argus*, April 17, 1875. This Australian performer was referencing the American Tom Thumb. For discussion on the American Tom Thumb's world tour in the 1870s, see Matthew Wittman, "Empire of Culture: U.S. Entertainers and the Making of the Pacific Circuit, 1850–1890" (PhD diss., University of Michigan, 2010), 132–90.
7. The decision to name the troupe the Georgia Minstrels is an interesting example of the ways in which cultural symbols change meanings while moving across national borders. In the United States after the Civil War, the term *Georgia Minstrels* was almost always applied to African American minstrel troupes. In contrast, the available evidence suggests the Georgia Minstrels troupe who performed in Cape Town were a group of white performers. The local press would have mentioned if they deviated from the racial norm.
8. Richard Waterhouse, *From Minstrel Show to Vaudeville: The Australian Popular Stage, 1788–1914* (Kensington: New South Wales University Press, 1990), 33–40.
9. Worger, *South Africa's City of Diamonds*, 114–15.
10. Turrell, *Capital and Labour*, 28.
11. Leonard Thompson, *A History of South Africa* (New Haven, CT: Yale University Press, 2001), 118.
12. Worger, *South Africa's City of Diamonds*, 97–98; Leonard Thompson, "The Subjection of the African Chiefdoms, 1870–1898," in *The Oxford History of South Africa*, ed.

Monica Wilson and Leonard Thompson (Oxford: Oxford University Press, 1971), 2:245–85.

13. Worger, *South Africa's City of Diamonds*, 109.
14. Donald Morris, *The Washing of the Spears: The Rise and Fall of the Zulu Nation* (New York: Da Capo Press, 1998); Thompson, "Subjection of the African Chiefdoms."
15. Bickford-Smith, *Ethnic Pride and Racial Prejudice*, 94.
16. Todd Cleveland, *Stones of Contention: A History of Africa's Diamonds* (Athens: Ohio University Press, 2014), 75–76.
17. *Cape Argus*, November 21, 1872. For other examples of "Grand Fashionable Night[s]," see *Cape Argus*, July 17 and May 18, 1886; and *Natal Mercury*, April 30, 1879.
18. Alan Lester, *Imperial Networks: Creating Identities in Nineteenth Century South Africa and Britain* (London: Routledge, 2001), 74.
19. *Diamond News*, March 20 and May 27, 1873.
20. *Eastern Province Herald*, December 24, 1872; *Cape Argus*, November 14, 1872.
21. *Standard and Mail*, November 5, 1872.
22. *Standard and Mail*, November 14, 1872.
23. *Diamond Field Advertiser*, August 8, 1874.
24. *Standard and Mail*, December 14, 1872.
25. *Cape Times*, March 6, 1879.
26. *Diamond News*, July 22, 1880.
27. Michael Pickering, *Blackface Minstrelsy in Britain* (Farnham: Ashgave, 2008); Harry Reynolds, *Minstrel Memories: The Story of Burnt Cork Minstrelsy in Great Britain from 1836–1927* (London: Alston Rivers, 1928).
28. *Diamond News*, October 24, 1883.
29. *Cape Argus*, December 21, 1876.
30. Thompson, "Subjection of the African Chiefdoms," 259.
31. *Cape Argus*, February 5, 1878.
32. *Cape Argus*, February 20, 1879.
33. *Cape Argus*, February 25, 1879.
34. *Cape Times*, March 6, 1879.
35. *Cape Argus*, May 27, 1879.
36. Morris, *Washing of the Spears*, 316.
37. *Diamond News*, November 2, 1883.
38. The date when the photograph was taken is unknown. This regiment was founded in Cape Town in 1855. They took the name Duke of Edinburgh's Own Volunteer Rifles in 1867. It's highly likely the picture was taken sometime between 1867 and the 1890s, a period when blackface minstrelsy was extremely popular among British settlers. For information on the Duke of Edinburgh's Own Volunteer Rifles, see Angus McKenzie, *The Dukes: A History of the Duke of Edinburgh's Own Rifles, 1855–1956* (Cape Town: Galvin and Sales, 1956). Relatedly, the band of the volunteer rifles performed at a minstrel fete in 1868. *Cape Argus*, February 22, 1868.

39. "Johnny Schmoker" was performed by the Harvey Minstrels in Cape Town. *Cape Argus,* February 2, 1874; November 22 and October 31, 1872. For "Tim Finagan's Wake," see *Port Elizabeth Telegraph,* November 25, 1873; and *Cape Argus,* November 30, 1872.
40. *Diamond News,* September 16, 1875, and August 23 and November 17, 1877.
41. "Billy Emerson's New Comic Songster," Harvard Theatre Collection, Songster Collection; *Cape Argus,* July 25, 1877.
42. *Cape Argus,* May 15, 1877.
43. *Diamond News,* July 31, 1877.
44. *Natal Mercury,* August 24, 1881; *Cape Argus,* May 1 and June 2, 1882.
45. *Cape Argus,* March 14, 1882.
46. *Cape Times,* August 25 and 24, 1883.
47. *Cape Argus,* July 26, 1886; *Daily Independent,* November 15, 1886.
48. *African Pictorial,* February 1903, 6–7.
49. *Cape Argus,* June 25, 1886.
50. *Cape Argus,* May 6, 1886.
51. Lott, *Love and Theft,* 18.
52. *Standard and Mail,* November 28, 1872.
53. *Port Elizabeth Telegraph,* October 28, 1873.
54. *Eastern Province Herald,* December 20, 1872.
55. *Standard and Mail,* December 14, 1872.
56. *Standard and Mail,* March 8, 1877.
57. *Diamond News,* December 17, 1881.
58. *Natal Mercury,* August 29, 1881.
59. Bickford-Smith, *Ethnic Pride and Racial Prejudice,* 77.
60. *Natal Mercury,* March 24, 1874; *Eastern Province Herald,* October 28, 1873; *Grahamstown Journal,* January 27, 1873; *Eastern Province Herald,* December 27, 1872.
61. *Diamond News,* March 27, 1873.
62. *Diamond Fields Advertiser,* July 15, 1874.
63. "Hemmed In," 4, New York Public Library.
64. Turrell, *Capital and Labour on the Kimberley Diamond Fields,* 27.
65. *Eastern Province Herald,* December 31, 1872.
66. *Standard and Mail,* December 5, 1872.
67. *Diamond News,* November 29, 1877.
68. *Cape Argus,* May 8, 1877.
69. *Cape Argus,* March 23, 1878. Benson may have been inspired by Ed Banker, a minstrel who performed alongside George Christy in the 1860s. He was credited as being the first minstrel performer to change "from black to white and back again in a few seconds." Edward Rice, *Monarchs of Minstrelsy: From "Daddy" Rice to Date* (New York: Kenny, 1911), 115.
70. Virginia Vaughan Mason, *Performing Blackness on English Stages, 1500–1800* (Cambridge: Cambridge University Press, 2005), 14.

71. *Cape Argus*, August 14, 1877. This minstrel show staged by children was not without precedent. In 1864 a troupe of amateur minstrels called the Juvenile Christy Minstrels performed in Cape Town. *Cape Argus*, June 11 and 23, 1864.
72. Barbara Fields relates, "Since race is not genetically programmed, racial prejudice cannot be genetically programmed either, but like race itself, must arise historically." Barbara Fields and Karen Fields, *Racecraft: The Soul of Inequality in American Life* (New York: Verso, 2014), 120.
73. One of the first colonial history textbooks was Alexander Wilmot's *History of the Cape Colony for Use in Schools* (Cape Town: J. C. Juta, 1871). This book taught children about the innate qualities of "Hottentots" and Xhosas. Vivian Bickford-Smith, *The Emergence of the South African Metropolis: Cities and Identities in the Twentieth Century* (Cambridge: Cambridge University Press, 2016), 49. The practice of segregated schooling helped British settler children learn about race. Cape Town English-language schools were almost exclusively white. Coloured children had to go to mission schools. Timothy Keegan, *Colonial South Africa and the Origins of the Racial Order* (Charlottesville: University Press of Virginia, 1996), 126. One headmaster of a British school in Grahamstown described British schools as "munitions factories" churning out patriotic human "munitions" for the imperial wars of the late nineteenth century. John Lampert, "'Munitions Factories . . . Turning Out a Constant Supply of Living Material': White South African Elite Boy's Schools and the First World War," *South African Historical Journal* 51 (2004): 66–86.
74. For example, a Cape Colony newspaper mentioned the Christy's Minstrel trip to the "sister colony" of Natal. *Cape Argus*, April 16, 1874. Kimberley papers did the same: "According to the colonial press the [Harvey Minstrels] entertainments at Cape Town, Port Elizabeth, and Grahamstown have been a continual round of success." *Diamond News*, February 1, 1873. Another *Diamond News* article of July 14, 1874, claimed the Harvey Minstrels "made the rounds to the best part of civilized South Africa."
75. "Ten Little Niggers," Harvard Theatre Collection, Sheet Music Collection. Relatedly, one patriotic poem written by a British settler "School-boy" included the following lines of verse: "Then with the seven-pounders they'll smash the niggers through. . . . Then when the war is over, and happy peace doth reign; Let us give them one more volley to scatter them again." *Diamond News*, June 6, 1878.
76. Another example was a "laughable farce" by the Harvey's Minstrels called "The Dead Nigger." *Port Elizabeth Telegraph*, July 29, 1874.
77. "Appetite and force" is a phrase Negritude writer Aimé Césaire used to describe Western colonial projects. Césaire, *Discourse on Colonialism* (New York: Monthly Review Press, 1972), 10.
78. Turrell, *Capital and Labour on the Kimberley Diamond Fields*, 28.
79. Worger, *South Africa's City of Diamonds*, 94–95.
80. Cell, *Highest Stage of White Supremacy*, 70.
81. Bickford-Smith, *Ethnic Pride and Racial Prejudice*, 91–92, 138–56.

82. James Campbell, "The Americanization of South Africa," in *Race, Nation, and Empire in American History*, ed. James Campbell, Matthew Guterl, and Robert Lee (Chapel Hill: University of North Carolina Press, 2007), 133.
83. In 1877 Rhodes wrote the following diary entry: "I contend that we are the first race in the world, and that the more of the world we inhabit the better it is for the human race. I contend that every acre added to our territory provides for the birth of more of the English race, who otherwise would not be brought into existence. Added to which the absorption of the greater portion of the world under our rule simply means the end of all wars. I will work for the furtherance of the British Empire, for the bringing of the whole civilized world under British rule, for the recovery of the United States, for the making of the Anglo-Saxon race into one empire. What a dream! But yet it is probable! It is possible!" Alan Sherwin, *Apartheid's Landscape and Ideas: A Scorched Soul* (Rochester, NY: University of Rochester Press, 2001), 265.
84. *Cape Argus*, May 5, 1874.

CHAPTER 4: "SLIPPING THE YOKE"

1. *Owl*, July 17, 1897.
2. Ralph Ellison, "Change the Joke and Slip the Yoke," in *Shadow and Act* (New York: Vintage, 1972), 45–59.
3. Robert Trent Vinson, *The Americans Are Coming! Dreams of African American Liberation in Segregationist South Africa* (Athens: Ohio University Press, 2012), 15–16.
4. Veit Erlmann, *African Stars: Studies in Black South African Performance* (Chicago: University of Chicago Press, 1991), 24.
5. Sandra Graham, *Spirituals and the Birth of a Black Entertainment Industry* (Urbana: University of Illinois Press, 2018), 48–81; Marti Newland, "Concert Spirituals and the Fisk Jubilee Singers," *American Music Review* 40, no. 1 (2010): 4–5, 14–15, 3.
6. *Cape Argus*, June 28, 1897.
7. Josephine Wright, "Orpheus Myron McAdoo: Singer, Impresario," *Black Perspective in Music* 4, no. 3 (1976): 320.
8. David Coplan, *In Township Tonight: South Africa's Black City Music and Theatre*, 2nd ed. (Chicago: University of Chicago Press, 2008); Vinson, *Americans Are Coming!*; Zine Magubane, *Bringing the Empire Home: Race, Class, and Gender in Britain and Colonial South Africa* (Chicago: University of Chicago Press, 2004); Lynn Abbot and Doug Seroff, *Out of Sight: The Rise of African American Popular Music, 1889–1895* (Jackson: University Press of Mississippi, 2002); Veit Erlmann, *Music, Modernity, and the Global Imagination: South Africa and the West* (Oxford: Oxford University Press, 1999); Veit Erlmann, *Nightsong: Performance, Power, and Practice in South Africa* (Chicago: University of Chicago Press, 1996); Christopher Ballantine, *Marabi Nights: Early South African Jazz and Vaudeville* (Johannesburg: Ravan Press, 1994); Erlmann, *African Stars*; Dale Cockrell, "Of Gospel Hymns, Minstrel Shows,

and Jubilee Singers: Toward Some Black South African Musics," *American Music* 5, no. 4 (1987): 417–32.

9. Mohamed Adhikari, *Not White Enough, Not Black Enough: Racial Identity in the South African Coloured Community* (Athens: Ohio University Press, 2005), 3.
10. Kevin Gaines, *Uplifting the Race: Black Leadership, Politics, and Culture in the Twentieth Century* (Chapel Hill: University of North Carolina Press, 1996), 67–99.
11. Graham, *Spirituals*, 73.
12. Andrew Ward, *Dark Midnight When I Rise: The Story of the Fisk Jubilee Singers* (New York: Amistad, 2001), 207, 115.
13. Marti Newland, "Concert Spirituals' Minstrel Inheritance" (master's thesis, Columbia University, 2007), 11 (emphasis added).
14. *Cape Argus*, July 1, 1895.
15. *Transvaal Advertiser*, February 4, 1891.
16. *Transvaal Advertiser*, February 2, 1891.
17. *Diamond Fields Advertiser*, July 30, 1895.
18. *Cape Times*, July 1, 1890.
19. *Freeman*, January 4, 1899, quoted in Erlmann, *African Stars*, 14.
20. *Graaff-Reneit Advertiser*, September 22, 1890.
21. *Cape Argus*, July 4, 1890.
22. Graham, *Spirituals*, 45.
23. *Natal Mercury*, November 17, 1890. McAdoo's troupe encountered the same problem in Sydney, Australia, as they were turned away from all the major hotels in the city. *Christian World*, October 1, 1886, Orpheus M. and Mattie Allen McAdoo Papers, Beinecke Library, Yale University, box 3, folder 22.
24. Fred Moten, *In the Breaks: The Aesthetics of the Black Radical Tradition* (Minneapolis: University of Minnesota Press, 2003).
25. *Natal Mercury*, November 17, 1890.
26. *Kaffarian Watchmen*, October 15, 1890.
27. *Natal Mercury*, November 19, 1890.
28. Daphne Brooks, *Bodies in Dissent: Spectacular Performances of Race and Freedom, 1850–1910* (Durham, NC: Duke University Press, 2006), 8.
29. *Cape Argus*, July 2, 1890.
30. *Daily Independent*, August 15, 1890.
31. *Daily Independent*, August 1, 1890.
32. *Cape Argus*, July 1, 1890.
33. *Natal Mercury*, November 15, 1890.
34. For more newspaper articles that described McAdoo's troupe as coloured, see *Natal Mercury*, November 22, 1890; *Natal Witness*, November 8, 1890; *Johannesburg Times*, September 10, 1895.
35. *Natal Mercury*, November 17, 1890.
36. *Transvaal Advertiser*, February 2, 1891 (emphasis added).
37. *Star*, March 7, 1898 (emphasis added).

38. *Cape Times,* July 2, 1890.
39. *Diamond Fields Advertiser,* July 29, 1895.
40. Letter from P. J. Joubert, American consul in Cape Town, to the state president of the Transvaal, July 9, 1890, Veit Erlmann Collection.
41. *Cape Argus,* October 8, 1896.
42. *Southern Workman,* November 1890, 120.
43. *Times of Natal,* March 30, 1898. For short articles describing the incident see *Natal Witness,* March 30, 1898.
44. *Southern Workman,* January 23, 1894, quoted in Wright, "Orpheus Myron McAdoo," 326.
45. Erlmann, *African Stars,* 46–50; Erlmann, *Music, Modernity, and the Global Imagination,* 62–63, 129–31, 144–64.
46. Brian Willan, *Sol Plaatje: South African Nationalist, 1876–1932* (Berkeley: University of California Press, 1984), 44–45.
47. Heather Hughes, *First President: A Life of John L. Dube, Founding President of the ANC* (Johannesburg: Jacana Media, 2011), 98–99.
48. Erlmann, *African Stars,* 159. For scholarship on *isicathamiya* choirs, see Coplan, *In Township Tonight;* Erlmann, *Music, Modernity, and the Global Imagination;* Erlmann, *Nightsong;* Ballantine, *Marabi Nights;* Cockrell, "Of Gospel Hymns, Minstrel Shows, and Jubilee Singers."
49. *Southern Workman,* February 1891, 146.
50. *Southern Workman,* February 1891, 147.
51. Vinson, *Americans Are Coming!,* 17.
52. *Leselinyana,* October 1, 1890, quoted in Erlmann, *African Stars,* 44.
53. *Imvo Zabantsundu,* October 16, 1890, quoted in Erlmann, *African Stars,* 44.
54. *Imvo-Zabantsundu,* March 11, 1897.
55. Bernard Peterson, *The African American Theatre Directory, 1716–1960: A Comprehensive Guide to Early Black Theatre Organizations, Companies, Theaters, and Performing Groups* (Westport, CT: Greenwood Press, 1997), 131. The "Georgia Minstrels" were a minstrel troupe that an African American manager named Charles Hicks brought to Australia in the late 1880s. This troupe was extremely successful, and McAdoo may have been trying to make potential theatergoers associate his troupe with Hick's troupe by using the name Georgia Minstrels.
56. *Transvaal Advertiser,* February 2, 1891.
57. Paul Gilroy, *The Black Atlantic: Modernity and Double-Consciousness* (Cambridge, MA: Harvard University Press, 1993), 55.
58. Graham, *Spirituals,* 44–45, 71–73.
59. Eric Lott, *Love and Theft: Blackface Minstrelsy and the American Working Class* (Oxford: Oxford University Press, 1993), 236.
60. Erlmann, *African Stars,* 36.
61. *Cape Times,* July 2, 1897.
62. *Natal Mercury,* August 25, 1897.

63. *Natal Mercury*, September 3 and September 2, 1897.
64. *Cape Argus*, July 28, 1897.
65. Robert Toll, *Blacking Up: The Minstrel Show in Nineteenth Century America* (Oxford: Oxford University Press, 1974), 198–99.
66. *Theatre Magazine* (supp.), August 1906.
67. *Transvaal Advertiser*, September 23, 1897.
68. *Standard News*, March 9, 1898.
69. *Press*, February 18, 1898 (emphasis added).
70. *Cape Times*, January 19, 1898.
71. *Eastern Province Herald*, July 23, 1897.
72. *Star*, March 7, 1898 (emphasis added).
73. *Transvaal Advertiser*, September 18, 1897.
74. *Cape Times*, January 17, 1898.
75. *Cape Times*, January 24, 1898. "I'se Gwine Back to Dixie," in *Tom Mcintosh Plantation Songster*, 14, Harvard Theatre Collection.
76. *Press*, September 25, 1897.
77. *Cape Times*, January 21, 1898. For another description of *Good Old Georgia in '49*, see *Eastern Province Herald*, December 13, 1897.
78. *Cape Times*, January 21, 1898.
79. *Natal Mercury*, November 17, 1890.
80. *Cape Argus*, June 28, 1897.
81. *Cape Times*, July 5, 1897.
82. *Cape Argus*, June 30, 1897.
83. Karen Sotiropoulos, *Staging Race: Black Performers in Turn of the Century America* (Cambridge, MA: Harvard University Press, 2006), 196.
84. *Press*, February 22, 1898; *Eastern Province Herald*, July 23, 1897; *Cape Times*, February 6, 1897; *Press*, September 20, 1897; *Transvaal Advertiser*, September 23, 1897; *Press*, February 21 and February 18, 1898.
85. *Cape Argus*, June 30, 1897.
86. *Press*, February 21, 1898; *Cape Times*, January 19, 1898; *Diamonds Field Advertiser*, November 18, 1897; *Natal Mercury*, August 25, 1897.
87. *Cape Times*, January 10, 1898. As Mahar demonstrates, it was fairly standard for early antebellum minstrel shows to include opera music. McAdoo's Minstrels were not the first. William Mahar, *Behind the Burnt Cork Mask: Early Blackface Minstrelsy and Antebellum American Popular Culture* (Urbana: University of Illinois Press, 1999).
88. *Cape Times*, January 10, 1898. At this time, Mattie E. Allen was married to Orpheus McAdoo and referred to in the press as Madame McAdoo.
89. *Diamond Fields Advertiser*, April 27, 1898.
90. *Cape Times*, July 5, 1897 (emphasis added).
91. *Cape Times*, July 5, 1897. For scholarship on the cakewalk, see Megan Pugh, *America Dancing: From the Cakewalk to the Moonwalk* (New Haven, CT: Yale University Press, 2015); and Brooks, *Bodies in Dissent*, 269–80.

92. *Cape Argus*, June 30, 1897.

93. *Natal Witness*, August 18, 1897.

94. Michael Pickering, "Eugene Statton and Early Ragtime in Britain," *Black Music Research Journal* 20, no. 2 (2000): 151–80; Richard Waterhouse, *From Minstrel Show to Vaudeville: The Australian Popular Stage, 1788–1914* (Kensington: New South Wales University Press, 1990), 84–85, 89–91.

95. *Natal Witness*, August 18, 1897; *Eastern Province Herald*, July 23, 1897; *Natal Mercury*, August 31, 1897.

96. *Transvaal Advertiser*, February 9, 1891. For a newspaper article in which McAdoo describes a conversation he had with Kruger, see *Cape Argus*, October 8, 1896.

97. For works on Afrikaner nationalism, see Hermann Giliomee, *The Afrikaners: Biography of a People* (Charlottesville: University of Virginia Press, 2009); Saul Dubow, "Afrikaner Nationalism, Apartheid and the Conceptualization of 'Race,'" *Journal of African History* 33 (1992): 209–37; Leonard Thompson, *The Political Mythology of Apartheid* (New Haven, CT: Yale University Press, 1985).

98. Jon Cruz, *Culture on the Margins: The Black Spiritual and the Rise of American Cultural Interpretation* (Princeton, NJ: Princeton University Press, 1999), 22.

99. In 2015 one theater critic used a "disengaged engagement" framework to critique David Kramer's musical *Orpheus in Africa*. The play enjoyed two successful runs at the Fugard Theater in 2015. The musical tells the story of McAdoo's troupe as they toured South Africa and Australia. The production is emblematic of David Kramer's approach to musical theater. Kramer consciously writes about "hidden history . . . the stories suppressed by the apartheid regime of [his] youth." David Kramer, email correspondence, May 13, 2014. *Orpheus in Africa* is one such story, and it received much praise from South African theater critics. See Steyn du Toit, "Kramer's High-Energy Orpheus," *Cape Times*, February 9, 2015; Peter Tromp, "'Orpheus' Is a Bold New Entry in the SA Musical Theatre Cannon," *Next 48 Hours*, no. 558 (February 13–19, 2015); Tracey Saunders, "Phenomenal Cast Makes 'Orpheus' Memorable," *Cape Times*, October 13, 2015. However, one review repeated the logic of "disengaged engagement" in order to critique the play: Lin Sampson's "Striking Black Gold," *Times*, February 13, 2015. At the tail end of a glowing review, Sampson said, "On the downside . . . the political point of how badly blacks are treated in South Africa is pushed into farce." This reviewer seems to want a musical theater experience that gives the audience a chance to engage black music but disengage from black politics. I commend David Kramer for refusing to create such a project. He forces audiences to engage the aesthetics and politics of black music, no matter how "uncomfortable" that may be. Those of us who are dedicated to the preservation of McAdoo's memory are greatly indebted to Kramer.

100. Relatedly, as several scholars have suggested, claims of racial hybridity often reinforce the very logics of pure and undiluted races. Tavia Nyong'o, *The Amalgamation Waltz: Race, Performance, and the Ruses of Memory* (Minneapolis: University

of Minnesota Press, 2009); Robert Young, *Colonial Desire: Hybridity in Theory, Culture and Race* (London: Routledge, 1995); David Theo Goldberg, *The Racial State* (Malden, MA: Blackwell, 2002), 24–35.

101. Gaines, *Uplifting the Race*, 20; Sotiropoulos, *Staging Race*, 195.
102. *Imvo Zabantsundu*, October 16, 1890.
103. *South African Citizen*, December 1, 1897, quoted in Erlmann, *African Stars*, 45.
104. *Transvaal Advertiser*, September 18, 1897.
105. *Cape Times*, June 16, 1898.
106. *Cape Argus*, June 16, 1898.

CHAPTER 5: BROWN-ON-BLACK MASQUERADE

1. For Malay Choirs and Christmas Bands, see Armelle Gaulier and Denis-Constant Martin, *Cape Town Harmonies: Memory, Humor and Resilience* (Cape Town: African Minds, 2017); Denis-Constant Martin, *Sounding the Cape: Music, Identity and Politics in South Africa* (Cape Town: African Minds, 2013); Sylvia Bruinders, "Parading Respectability: An Ethnography of the Christmas Bands Movement in the Western Cape, South Africa" (PhD diss. University of Illinois at Urbana-Champaign, 2012); and Denis-Constant Martin, *Coon Carnival: New Year in Cape Town, Past and Present* (Cape Town: David Philip, 1999).
2. Martin, *Sounding the Cape*, xvii, 82–83.
3. Martin, *Coon Carnival*, 135.
4. For scholarship on "moffies" in carnival, see Rosamond King, "Whither Transgression? The Disappearing Transvestite in Cape Town and Caribbean Carnivals," paper presented at American Studies Association, November 9, 2018; Gaulier and Martin, *Cape Town Harmonies*, 188–192; Francesca Inglese, "Coloured Moves and Klopse Beats: Minstrel Legacies in Cape Town, South Africa" (PhD diss., Brown University, 2016), 169–70; Bett Lacey, "The Emergence and Recognition of Moffies as Popular Entertainers in the Cape Minstrel Carnival," *South African Theatre Journal* 27, no. 2 (2014): 111–24; Jacqueline Maingard, "Bokkies/Moffies: Cinematic Images of Black Sexual Identity in Zonk (1950)," *Journal of African Cultural Studies* 16, no. 1 (2010): 25–43; Martin, *Coon Carnival*, 16–17; Peter Davies, *Darkest Hollywood: Exploring the Jungles of Cinema's South Africa* (Athens: Ohio University Press, 1996), 34–36; Shamil Jeppie, "Popular Culture and Carnival in Cape Town: The 1940s and 1950s," in *The Struggle for District Six: Past and Present*, ed. Shamil Jeppie and Crain Soudien (Cape Town: Buchu Books, 1990), 70, 80–82. Interview transcripts of carnival participants can be found in the holdings of the Centre for Popular Memory, currently stored at Special Collections at University of Cape Town Libraries. These transcripts mention "moffies" multiple times. According to the respondents, "moffies" were welcomed into the carnivals of the 1950s and 1960s and not treated with hostility. For *Drum* magazine articles that featured "moffies," see January 1954, January 1959, and January

1962. Advertisements announcing a "Coon and Moffee Carnival Concert" and "Coon and Moffee Carnival," respectively, appear in the *Cape Times*, January 5, 1940, and *Cape Standard*, January 3, 1939.

5. The published criticisms are too numerous to reference in total. For one example, see *Sun*, December 26, 1952. More examples can be found in opinion articles published in *Muslim News* during the 1960s, 1970s, and 1980s.
6. In January 1940, several coloured people published opinion pieces about the Coon troupes in the *Cape Standard*. See also the coverage of carnival from the *Muslim News*, especially the December 11, 1981, edition.
7. Inglese, "Coloured Moves and Klopse Beats," 91–94; Martin, *Coon Carnival*, 11–13. Relatedly, in 2009, most Klopse troupes were prohibited by the city from marching in the Bo-Kaap, largely because of the noise complaints of gentrifying residents. Klopse successfully petitioned the city government to remove the ban in 2011. Inglese, "Coloured Moves and Klopse Beats," 105–6.
8. John Mason, *One Love, Ghoema Beat* (Charlottesville: University of Virginia Press, 2010), 20; Amy Jephta, "On Familiar Roads: The Fluidity of Cape Coloured Experiences and Expressions of Migration and Reclamation in the Performances of the Kaapse Klopse in Cape Town," in *Performing Migrancy and Mobility in Africa: Cape of Flow*, ed. Mark Fleishman (London: Palgrave Macmillan, 2015), 165; Inglese, "Coloured Moves Klopse Beats," 115.
9. Martin, *Coon Carnival*, 13–16.
10. Inglese, "Coloured Moves and Klopse Beats," 218 (for more on women in the carnival, see 202–51); Gaulier and Martin, *Cape Town Harmonies*, 21–23; Martin, *Coon Carnival*, 18–20; Jeppie, "Popular Culture," 82–86. For interviews with seamstresses who made outfits for Klopse, see Fagmiejah Jansen, interview with Lisa Baxter, Western Cape Oral History Project, May 24, 1995; and Faldiela Isaacse, interview with Western Cape Oral History Project, May 17, 1995. Relatedly, according to the *Cape Times*, Mrs. Jariya Mitchell played a "leading" role organizing the Cape Peninsula Coloured Carnival Board. *Cape Times*, December 29, 1951.
11. For a history of the American origins of the racial slur *coon*, see David Roediger, *Wages of Whiteness: Race and the Making of the American Working* (London: Verso, 1991), 97–100.
12. See *Cape Standard*, January 1940.
13. *Sun*, December 31, 1948. For more information on the *Sun* and *Cape Standard*, see Gavin Lewis, *Between the Wire and the Wall: A History of South African "Coloured" Politics* (New York: St. Martin's Press, 1987), 155–56, 184.
14. *Cape Times*, January 4, 1954.
15. Mike Norton, "Crazier than a Coon," *Drum*, January 14, 1968. A similar example can be found in the *Outspan*, November 25, 1949.
16. *Cape Times*, January 5, 1967. Later, in the 1990s, several carnival goers mentioned "raccoon" when telling academic researchers about the origins of the word. Martin, *Coon Carnival*; Lisa Baxter, "History, Identity and Meaning: Cape Town's

Coon Carnival in the 1960s and 1970s" (master's thesis, University of Cape Town, 1996). Baxter reports, "Interviewees are dismissive of the negative racial connotations of the word [*coon*]. One informant insisted the term had "nothing" to do with race but came from the practice of blackening the face and whitening the eyes "like a raccoon." He failed, however, to speculate on the implications of this "blackening-up" (xi).

17. For academic works on carnival corroborating this point, see Inglese, "Coloured Moves and Klopse Beats"; Chanell Oliphant, "The Changing Faces of the Klopse: Performing the Rainbow Nation during the Cape Town Carnival" (master's thesis, University of the Western Cape, 2013); Martin, *Coon Carnival;* and Baxter, "History, Identity and Meaning."
18. Gaulier and Martin, *Cape Town Harmonies,* xxiv; Martin, *Coon Carnival,* 4.
19. Martin, *Coon Carnival,* 151–52.
20. Mohamed Adhikari, *Not White Enough, Not Black Enough: Racial Identity in the South African Coloured Community* (Athens: Ohio University Press, 2005), 165–67; Vivian Bickford-Smith, Nigel Worden, and Elizabeth van Heyningen, *Cape Town in the Twentieth Century: An Illustrated Social History* (Cape Town: David Philip, 1998), 132.
21. Gerald Stone was a linguist who specialized in Afrikaans. Here is his definition: "The Afrikaans term for Coons, 'Klopse,' derives from 'Klubbe' (clubs)." Stone, "The Coon Carnival," unpublished paper, University of Cape Town, Abe Bailey Institute of Interracial Studies, 1971, 2.
22. "The annual festival of the "klops" [*sic*], as the troops are generally called by their members." *Cape Times,* January 1, 1934. "We still find the Coloured people of the Cape referring in Afrikaans to the coon bands as 'klopse' or clubs and the word 'coon' is seldom, if ever, used." *Cape Times,* January 12, 1957.
23. Jeppie, "Popular Culture," 69; Baxter, "History," 82–96.
24. Robert Rydell and Rob Kroes, *Buffalo Bill in Bologna: The Americanization of the World, 1869–1922* (Chicago: University of Chicago Press, 2005); Reinhold Wagnleitner and Elaine Tyler May, eds., *Here, There, and Everywhere: The Foreign Politics of American Popular Culture* (Hanover, NH: University Press of New England 2000); Philip Bell and Roger Bell, eds., *Americanization and Australia: Australian Experience* (Sydney: University of New South Wales Press, 1998); Rob Kroes, *If You've Seen One, You've Seen the Mall: Europeans and American Mass Culture* (Urbana: University of Illinois Press, 1996); Richard Kuisel, *Seducing the French: The Dilemma of Americanization* (Berkeley: University of California Press, 1993).
25. Zimitri Erasmus, "Introduction: Re-imagining Coloured Identities in Post-Apartheid South Africa," in *Coloured by History, Shaped by Place: New Perspectives on Coloured Identities in Cape Town,* ed. Zimitri Erasmus (Cape Town: Kwela Books, 2001), 13–28.
26. David Kramer and Taliep Petersen, *District Six: The Musical,* DVD (Stage Productions, 2007).

27. *South African Commercial Advertiser*, December 6, 1834, referenced in Denis-Constant Martin's "Chronicles of the Kaapse Kloppse," https://criticalworld.net/cw_medias/U7d3zo_DCM_Chronicles.pdf. Although several scholars claim that documented proof of the festivities can be found as early as 1823, my reading of available sources traced the origins of this idea to an uncorroborated statement made by the *Cape Times* on December 28, 1949. Some documentation from 1823 could help substantiate this claim.
28. Nigel Worden, Elizabeth Van Heyningen, and Vivian Bickford-Smith, *Cape Town: The Making of a City* (Cape Town: David Philip, 1998), 194.
29. *Cape Times*, December 2, 1885, quoted in Vivian Bickford-Smith, "Meanings of Freedom: Social Position and Identity among Ex-Slaves and Their Descendants in Cape Town, 1875–1910," in *Breaking the Chains: Slavery and its Legacy in the Nineteenth-Century Cape Colony*, ed. Nigel Worden and Clifton Crais (Johannesburg: Witwatersrand University Press, 1994), 298.
30. Stone, "Coon Carnival," 3; *Drum*, March 1957; *Cape Times*, December 28, 1949.
31. *Cape Times*, December 30, 1979; Stone, "Coon Carnival"; *Cape Herald*, December 20, 1969; *Drum*, March 1957.
32. Desmond Desai, "An Investigation into the Influence of the 'Cape Malay' Child's Cultural Heritage upon His Taste in Appreciating Music; With a Proposed Adaptation of the Music Curricula in South African Schools to Reflect a Possible Application of 'Cape Malay' Music Therein" (master's thesis, University of Cape Town, 1983), 124.
33. Gerald Hoberman, *Kaapse Klopse: Cape Town Minstrel Carnival* (Cape Town: Gerald and Marc Hoberman Collection, 2009), 12; Michael Hutchinson, *Bo-Kaap: Colourful Heart of Cape Town* (Cape Town: David Philip, 2006), 99.
34. *Cape Chronicle*, July 8, 1870; *Cape Times*, February 15, 1877.
35. *Cape Times*, August 3, 1877.
36. Martin, *Sounding the Cape*, xvii, 82–83.
37. *Sun*, January 3, 1941.
38. Inglese, "Coloured Moves and Klopse Beats," 142.
39. M. Cassiem D'Arcy, *The Coon* (Johannesburg: Viva Books, 1999), 19. Originally written in Afrikaans, the book was later translated to English. For a brief biography on D'arcy, see Hein Viljoen and Chris van der Merwe, *Beyond the Threshold: Explorations of Liminality in Literature* (New York: Pieterlen Peter Lang, 2007), 86.
40. I use the phrase "Coloured Carnival" to refer to the 1907 carnival because this is how it was advertised in local newspapers. Beginning in 1928, the phrase "Coon Carnival" began showing up in press announcements.
41. Michael Pickering, *Blackface Minstrelsy in Britain* (Farnham, UK: Ashgave, 2008), 32–47.
42. *Cape Times*, November 9, 1906.
43. Gaulier and Martin, *Cape Town Harmonies*, 17; Inglese, "Coloured Moves and Klopse Beats," 188.

44. For the cakewalk in early carnivals, see *Cape Argus,* January 8 and January 2, 1908; January 4, 1907; *Cape Times,* January 3, 1907. A picture titled "Cake Walk (Princess Escort)" from the 1907 carnival can be found in the *Cape Times* Collection of the National Library of South Africa, Cape Town.
45. The 1907 carnival included one additional competition category inspired by minstrel shows but not mentioned in the planning meeting: the "Buck and Wing" dance. *Cape Argus,* January 4, 1907.
46. *Cape Times,* January 3, 1907.
47. *Cape Times,* January 3, 1908.
48. *Cape Times,* January 8, 1908.
49. *Cape Times,* December 29, 1933.
50. Achmat Levy, interview with Western Cape Oral History Project, June 3, 1990, 15. For a profile on Levy, see *Cape Herald,* December 15, 1973.
51. *SA News,* January 3, 1908.
52. *Cape Times,* January 12, 1939. For contemporaneous and less patronizing observations regarding the large amount of American musical influence, see *Cape Standard,* January 10, 1939; and *Cape Times,* December 29, 1938.
53. Martin, *Sounding the Cape,* 117. Relatedly, when asked if the songs of Coon troupes were rendered in Afrikaans, Achmat Levy, responded, "No . . . was mostly based . . . on the American songs . . . English songs." Levy, interview, 7.
54. Mason, *One Love, Ghoema Beat,* 10–11.
55. I found one exception. A newspaper article on Cape Town carnival music from 1948 mentioned Malay Choirs who sang "ghommaliedjies" [*sic*]. *Ghoemaliedjies* translates to English as "drum songs." These folks songs are musical predecessors to "moppies." However, Malay Choirs were and are very different from Klopse troupes. Thus, the articles' statement about Malay Choirs singing "ghommaliedjies" [*sic*] cannot be interpreted as evidence of ghoema beats among the Klopse. George Aschman, "Cape's Unique New Year Carnival of Music," *Cape Times,* December 29, 1948. For ghoemaliedjies, see Martin, *Sounding the Cape,* 112–13.
56. Gaulier and Martin, *Cape Town Harmonies,* 141.
57. I found no evidence of nineteenth-century minstrel troupes advertising their shows by parading through Cape Town. Later, when Bing Crosby's "Dixie" was released to international audiences in 1944, Klopse were exposed to minstrel street-parade imagery.
58. A description of coloured holiday revelers in 1886 included the phrase "beating the drum." *Cape Times,* January 4, 1886. According to Coplan and Martin, nineteenth-century Klopse bands included ghoema drums. See Martin, *Sounding the Cape,* 84; and David Coplan, *In Township Tonight: South Africa's Black City Music and Theatre,* 2nd ed. (Chicago: University of Chicago Press, 2008), 51.
59. *Cape Times,* January 4, 1909; December 19, 1908.
60. Several coloured carnival enthusiasts who were interviewed in the 1990s

observed that ghoema drums contributed to carnival music during the 1960s and 1970s: Janet Matthews, interview with Lisa Baxter, Western Cape Oral History Project, September 1995, 3; Barty Daniels, interview with Lisa Baxter, Western Cape Oral History Project, July 1995, 2; Ibrahim Ishmael, interview with Western Cape Oral History Project, date unknown, 2; Adiel Mohammed, interview with Western Cape Oral History Project, date unknown, 2. For more discussions on the ghoema beat, see Gaulier and Martin, *Cape Town Harmonies*, 154–71; Inglese, "Coloured Moves and Klopse Beats," 95–101; Martin, *Sounding the Cape*, 347–54; Bruinders, "Parading Respectability." The following documentary is also instructive: Angela Ramirez, Sara Gouveia, and Calum Macnaughton, dir., *Mama Goema: The Cape Town Beat in Five Movements*, DVD (Paris: Windrose, 2011).

61. The last quote is from *Cape Times*, January 4, 1886.
62. This interpretation was first offered by Denis-Constant Martin in *Coon Carnival*, 65–76. See also Inglese, "Coloured Moves and Klopse Beats," 15–16; Nadia Davids, "'It is Us': An Exploration of 'Race' and Place in the Cape Town Minstrel Carnival," *TDR: The Drama Review* 57, no. 2 (2013): 88, 92.
63. *SA News*, January 3, 1908.
64. *Cape Standard*, December 28, 1936; January 8, 1937; *Sun*, January 8, 1937; *Cape Times*, January 5, 1937; January 4, 1938; January 4, 1939.
65. *Sun*, January 5, 1940; January 6, 1950; *Cape Times*, January 3, 1946; January 4, 1950; January 3, 1956; January 3, 1957; January 3, 1952.
66. Eric Lott, *Love and Theft: Blackface Minstrelsy and the American Working Class* (Oxford: Oxford University Press, 1993), 148.
67. Noor Ebrahim, *Noor's Story: My Life in District Six* (Cape Town: District Six Museum Foundation, 2007), 38–42.
68. *Cape Times*, January 3, 1907; *SA News*, January 3, 1908; *Cape Times*, January 8, 1908; January 5, 1937.
69. D'arcy, *The Coon*, 23; George Manuel, *I Remember Cape Town* (Cape Town: Don Nelson, 1977), 73; *Cape Times*, January 20, 1951.
70. *Cape Times*, January 3, 1948.
71. Jansen, interview, 3.
72. Daniels, interview, 12 (emphasis added).
73. One recipe published in the *Cape Herald* on January 10, 1970, taught people how to make "Carnival Faces" cookies. The last ingredient was chocolate icing.
74. *Cape Times*, January 3, 1907.
75. *SA News*, January 3, 1908.
76. *Cape Times*, January 3, 1925.
77. *Cape Times*, December 28, 1949. A picture of "Spanish Cavaliers" from the *Cape Times* includes no whiteface makeup. *Cape Times Supplement*, June 1, 1931, National Library of South Africa: Cape Times Collection, Cape Town.
78. *Cape Times*, January 12, 1957.
79. *Cape Argus*, January 4, 1921.

80. *Cape Times*, January 4, 1927.
81. *Cape Times*, November 9, 1906.
82. *Cape Argus*, January 4, 1907 (emphasis added).
83. *Cape Times*, December 31, 1921.
84. *Cape Times*, December 29, 1933.
85. *Cape Times*, December 27, 1946, and December 29, 1950.
86. *Cape Times*, January 3, 1923.
87. *Cape Times*, January 10, 1930.
88. *Cape Times*, January 4, 1933.
89. *Cape Times*, January 4, 1937 (emphasis added). For another article describing a wide range of masquerades, see *Cape Times*, January 3, 1928.
90. Denis-Constant Martin, "The Burden of the Name: Classifications and Constructions of Identity. The Case of 'Coloureds' in Cape Town (South Africa)," *African Philosophy* 13, no. 2 (2000): 99–124.
91. I excluded troupes whose names did not directly mention black identity. For example, troupes such as the Sunshine Coons, Incubator Coons, or the Famous Happy Victory Coons probably included many members who were consciously portraying diasporic blackness, but because the word *Coon* alone cannot be read as a reference to blackness, I did not include them on the list.
92. *Cape Times*, December 27, 1947.
93. Lawrence Green, *Grow Lovely, Growing Old: The Story of Cape Town's Three Centuries—The Streets, The Houses, The Characters, The Legends, The Tradition and Folk-Lore, the Laughter and Tears* (Cape Town: Howard Timmins, 1951), 193.
94. *Cape Argus*, January 26, 1956.
95. *Drum*, March 1957. Another *Drum* article claimed, "Yes, this is Coon-time. . . . A medley of song and dance in many languages sprung out from the Negro troupe that visited Cape Town over fifty years ago." *Drum*, January 1954.
96. George Manuel, "Coon Custom's Roots in Slavery," *Cape Times*, December 30, 1980. In some accounts, "Dantu Brothers" is spelled "Dante Brothers."
97. David Coplan advanced a similar perspective: "While local oral tradition [claimed] it was the street minstrel marches of the . . . Dante Brothers performed during Queen Victoria's Jubilee celebrations in Cape Town in 1887 that led to the famous Cape Coon Carnival, the Christy Minstrels must rather be credited as the original influence for this tradition." Coplan, *In Township Tonight*, 50.
98. *Cape Times*, December 29, 1948.
99. *Cape Times*, January 8, 1959.
100. Levy, interview, 20.
101. Martin, *Coon Carnival*, 94.
102. Karen Cox, *Dreaming of Dixie: How the South was Created in American Popular Culture* (Chapel Hill: University of North Carolina Press, 2011), 32.
103. *Drum*, January 1953.

104. Levy, interview, 16.
105. Toll, *Blacking Up*, 19; Pickering, *Blackface Minstrelsy in Britain.*
106. Denis-Constant Martin, "An Imaginary Ocean: Carnival in Cape Town and the Black Atlantic," in *Africa, Brazil and the Construction of Transatlantic Black Identities*, ed. Livio Sansone, Elisée Soumonni, and Boubacar Barry (Trenton, NJ: Africa World Press, 2008), 71–72.
107. Davids, "'It is Us,'" 97.
108. Michelle Stephens, *Black Empire: The Masculine Global Imaginary of Caribbean Intellectuals in the United States, 1914–1962* (Durham, NC: Duke University Press, 2005).
109. Robert Trent Vinson, *The Americans Are Coming! Dreams of African American Liberation in Segregationist South Africa* (Athens: Ohio University Press, 2012), 72–80.
110. Jacqueline Maingard, "Cinemagoing in District Six, Cape Town, 1920s to 1960s: History, Politics, Memory," *Memory Studies* 10, no. 1 (2016): 17–34; Shamil Jeppie, "Popular Culture," 67.
111. Martin, *Coon Carnival*, 115.
112. *Cape Times*, January 3, 1951.
113. Martin, *Coon Carnival*, 146, image 1, "A programme for the Hi-Note Tour."
114. Daniels, interview, 20.
115. *Drum*, January 1954.
116. Coco Fusco, "Who's Doin' the Twist: Notes towards a Politics of Appropriation," in *English Is Broken Here: Notes on Cultural Fusion in the Americas* (New York: New Press, 1995), 68.
117. *Drum*, January 1955.
118. Martin, *Coon Carnival*, 127.
119. *Cape Times*, January 9, 1926.
120. Grant Farred, *Midfielder's Moment: Coloured Literature and Culture in Contemporary South Africa* (Boulder, CO: Westview, 2000); 12; Erasmus, *Coloured by History*, 13.
121. For discussion on archival silencing, see Michel-Rolph Trouillot, *Silencing the Past: Power and the Production of History* (Boston: Beacon Press, 1997).
122. Gerald Stone, interview with Western Cape Oral History Project, April 13, 1996, 14.
123. Richard Humphries, "Administrative Politics and the Coloured Labour Preference Policy During the 1960s," in *The Angry Divide: Social and Economic History of the Western Cape*, ed. Wilmot Godfrey James and Mary Simons (Cape Town: University of Cape Town, Centre for African Studies), 169–79; Ian Goldin, *Making Race: The Politics and Economics of Coloured Identity in South Africa* (London: Longman, 1987), 65–73.
124. For more scholarship on coloured identity, see Mohamed Adhikari, ed., *Burdened by Race: Coloured Identities in South Africa* (Cape Town: Juta Academic, 2009); Farred, *Midfielder's Moment*; Vivian Bickford-Smith, *Ethnic Pride and Racial Prejudice in Victorian Cape Town: Group Identity and Social Practice, 1875–1902*

(Cambridge: Cambridge University Press, 1995), 186–209; R. du Pre, *Separate but Unequal: The "Coloured" People of South Africa- A Political History* (Johannesburg: Jonathan Ball, 1994); Mohamed Adhikari, "The Sons of Ham: Slavery and the Making of Coloured Identity," *South African Historical Journal* 27 (1992): 95–112; and R. van der Ross, *The Rise and Decline of Apartheid: A Study of Political Movements among the Coloured People of South Africa, 1880–1985* (Cape Town: Tafelberg, 1986).

125. Adhikari, *Not White Enough*, 12.
126. Ibid., 11.
127. Ibid., 12.
128. John Western, *Outcast Cape Town* (Berkeley: University of California Press, 1996), 34–35.
129. Ibid., 336.
130. Ibid., 337.
131. Goldin, *Making Race.*
132. *Cape Times*, January 3, 1907.
133. *Cape Times*, January 9, 1926.
134. *Cape Times*, January 5, 1939.
135. Martin, *Coon Carnival*, 103. Shamil Jeppie offers another interpretation. He argues that spatial apartheid is the main factor explaining the lack of an African presence in carnival, as the apartheid state consciously separated the coloured and African populations from one another. Jeppie, "Popular Culture," 73.
136. Robert Cantwell, *Blue Grass Break Down: The Making of the Old Southern Sound* (Urbana: University of Illinois Press, 1984), 265; Roediger, *Wages of Whiteness*, 153–54.
137. Michael Rogin, *Blackface, White Noise: Jewish Immigrants in the Hollywood Melting Pot* (Berkeley: University of California Press, 1998); Susan Gubar, *Racechanges: White Skin, Black Face in American Culture* (Oxford: Oxford University Press, 1997), 73.
138. *SA News*, January 3, 1908. The song "She's Getting More like the White Folks Every Day" was published by Bert William and George Walker in 1901, https://levysheetmusic.mse.jhu.edu/collection/149/088.
139. Martin, *Coon Carnival*, 111–12.
140. Ibid., 112.
141. Joseph Roach, *Cities of the Dead: Circum-Atlantic Performance* (New York: Columbia University Press, 1996); George Lipsitz, *Dangerous Crossroads: Popular Music, Postmodernism, and the Poetics of Place* (New York: Verso, 1994).
142. Some Africans have also reinterpreted the word *darkie*. One contemporary South African fashion label is called Darkie Clothing. Founder Themba Mngomezulu explains: "In South Africa . . . [darkie] represents someone who is dark and also the lifestyle of someone who lives a rebellious culture." Kevin Mwanza, "Cape Town Designers Build Fashion Brands That Speak to the Youth," *AFKInsider*, http://afkinsider.com/98514/cape-town-designers-build-fashion-brands-that-speak-to-the-youth/.

143. Vincent Kolbe, interview with Shamil Jeppe, Western Cape Oral History Project, unknown date, 60.
144. Mikhail Bakhtin, *Rabelais and His World* (Bloomington: Indiana University Press, 1984).
145. *Cape Times*, January 8, 1957.
146. Rob Nixon, *Homelands, Harlem and Hollywood: South African Culture and the World Beyond* (New York: Routledge, 1994), 43–76.
147. *Cape Standard*, January 10, 1939.
148. Cheryl Harris, "Whiteness as Property," *Harvard Law Review* 106, no. 8 (1993): 1707–91.
149. For pictures of recent carnival masks, see Mason, *One Love, Ghoema Beat;* Hoberman, *Kaapse Klopse;* Ashraf Hendricks, "The Making of the Minstrels," *GroundUp*, January 3, 2017, www.groundup.org.za/article/making-minstrels/.
150. Martin, *Coon Carnival*, 175.
151. Davids, "'It Is Us,'" 89.
152. Complicating the nonracialism reading is the fact that Atjas carnival characters who portray Native Americans are still a part of postapartheid carnival. Also worthy of mention is the fact that one 2010 troupe chose the orange, white, and blue of the Nationalist Party flag during the era of apartheid. This decision celebrates apartheid-era race thinking.
153. Here is Inglese's list: Parkwood Youth Development, Original Famous Wild Apachees, Bonteheuwel Superstars, Miami Dolphins, Rainbow Nation Entertainers, Woodlands Youth Development Entertainers, Bishop Lavis Community Entertainers, D6 Hanover Minstrels, Nokia All Stars, Fabulous Woodstock Starlites, New Year Entertainers, Carnival Boys, Olympic Superstars, Son Seawinds, Cape Town Hawkers, V&A Minstrels, Sherwood Youth Development, African Dolphins Minstrels, Holly Hoods Entertainers, Manenberg Superstars, Ken Fac Entertainers, Ohio Hotshots Development, Penny Pincher T.V. Stars, Lentegeur Community Entertainers, Santam District Six Entertainers, Shoprite Pennsylvanians, Juvie Boys, DFS Woodstock Starlites, Heideveld Entertainers, Play Boys Youth Development, Down Town New Edition, Vangate Community Entertainers, Spes Bona, Lavender Superstars, Pick N Pay Lentegeur, Atlantis Community Entertainers, Salt River Community Entertainers, Cape Flats Minstrels, Fabulous Star Spangles, Burger Happy Boys, 20th Century, Dolphins Community Minstrels, Eindhoven African Zonks, Golden Dixies, Kalksteen Youth Development, and Dubai World Entertainers. Francesca Inglese, email, August 8, 2014.
154. Gerald Hoberman, *Kaapse Klopse: Cape Town Minstrel Carnival* (Cape Town: Gerald and Marc Hoberman Collection, 2009),19. Furthermore, a 2005 list of troupe names for the Kaapse Klopse Carnival Assosiasie does not mention racial slurs. I must thank Leonard Benjamin for giving this list to me.
155. Inglese, "Coloured Moves and Klopse Beats," 5.

156. Martin, *Coon Carnival*, 160–61; Richard O. Dudley, interview with Lisa Baxter, Western Cape Oral History Project, September 1995, 2.
157. Bickford-Smith, *Ethnic Pride and Racial Prejudice*, 188.
158. Banjoes are often used to play ghoema beats. Gaulier and Martin, *Cape Town Harmonies*, 98; Inglese, "Coloured Moves and Klopse Beats," 14, 188–89; Martin, *Sounding the Cape*, 351.
159. Gaulier and Martin, *Cape Town Harmonies*, 141–42. Boeta Achmat Sabera is a skilled ghoema drum maker whose technological innovations probably helped increase the popularity of ghoema drums in Klopse bands. In the 1970s, he found ways to make lighter ghoema drums that were easier to march with. Boeta Achmat Sabera, interview with Western Oral Cape History Project, November 10, 1995, 1. For more on Boeta Achmat Sabera, see Inglese, "Coloured Moves and Klopse Beats," 96n31, 103, 278; Mason, *One Love, Ghoema Beat*, 54–55.
160. *Cape Herald*, January 5, 1984.
161. *Cape Times* pictures of 2001 carnival, Special Collections Library, National Library of South Africa, Cape Town.
162. Karriem Thompson and Radifa Thompson, interview with Lisa Baxter, Western Cape Oral History Project, June 8, 1995, 9–10.
163. Adhikari, *Not White Enough.*
164. *Argus*, January 2, 1996.
165. Quoted in Baxter, "History, Identity and Meaning," iv.
166. Nelson Mandela, *A Long Walk to Freedom: The Autobiography of Nelson Mandela* (Boston: Little, Brown, 1994), 110.
167. Christian DuComb, *Haunted City: Three Centuries of Racial Impersonation in Philadelphia* (Ann Arbor: University of Michigan Press, 2017); Roediger, *Wages of Whiteness*, 106.
168. For a history of the *Amos 'n' Andy* show, see Melvin Ely, *The Adventures of "Amos 'n' Andy": A Social History of an American Phenomenon* (Charlottesville: University of Virginia Press, 2001). Ely offers a detailed and nuanced discussion of *Amos 'n' Andy*. He also describes a humor that is very similar to burnt cork nationalism: "The show also conveyed some of those countless messages emanating from the white America of my youth [in Jim Crow Virginia] that taught me to laugh at black striving, at Afro-Americans *as* Afro-Americans" (257).
169. On neoliberalism, see Joseph Stiglitz, *Globalization and Its Discontents Revisited: Anti-globalization in the Era of Trump* (New York: W. W. Norton, 2017); Patrick Bond, *Elite Transition: From Apartheid to Neoliberalism in South Africa*, rev. ed. (London: Pluto Press, 2014); Vijay Prashad, *The Poorer Nations: A Possible History of the Global South* (New York: Verso, 2014); Anne-Maria Makhulu, "The Question of Freedom: Post-emancipation South Africa in a Neoliberal Age," in *Ethnographies of Neoliberalism*, ed. Carol Greenhouse (Philadelphia: University of Pennsylvania Press, 2010), 131–45; David Harvey, *A Brief History of Neoliberalism* (Oxford: Oxford University Press, 2007).

AFTERWORD: GLOBAL BLACKFACE

1. Commodore Perry quoted in Victor Fell Yellin, "Mrs. Belmont, Matthew Perry, and the 'Japanese Minstrels,'" *American Music* 14, no. 3 (1996): 265.
2. Joseph Boskin, *Sambo: The Rise and Demise of an American Jester* (Oxford: Oxford University Press 1986), 76–77.
3. Yellin, "Mrs. Belmont," 266.
4. Brian Rouleau, *With Sails Whitening Every Sea: Mariners and the Making of an American Empire* (Ithaca, NY: Cornell University Press, 2014), 48.
5. Rouleau, *With Sails Whitening Every Sea*, 43–73; Michael Bennett, *Union Jacks: Yankee Soldiers in the Civil War* (Chapel Hill: University of North Carolina Press, 2004), 174–76. After leaving Japan, Perry's crew presented minstrel shows in Hong Kong, Shanghai, and Canton. Rouleau, *With Sails Whitening Every Sea*, 50–52.
6. Catherine Cole, "American Ghetto Parties and Ghanaian Concert Parties: A Transnational Perspective on Blackface," in *Burnt Cork: Traditions and Legacies of Blackface Minstrelsy*, ed. Stephen Johnson (Amherst: University of Massachusetts Press, 2012), 224.
7. For more on Perry's Minstrels, see Peter Booth Wiley, *Yankees in the Land of Gods: Commodore Perry and the Opening of Japan* (New York: Viking, 1990), 368–69; and Emily Roxworthy, *The Spectacle of Japanese American Trauma: Racial Performativity and World War II* (Honolulu: University of Hawai'i Press, 2008), 27–28. For a fictional novel on Perry's Minstrels, see Richard Wiley, *Commodore Perry's Minstrel Show* (Austin: University of Texas Press, 2007).
8. W. T. Lhamon, *Raising Cain: Blackface Performance from Jim Crow to Hip Hop* (Cambridge, MA: Harvard University Press, 1998), 58.
9. Kellen Hoxworth, "Transoceanic Blackface, Imperial Whiteness: Performing 'Race' in the Global Nineteenth Century" (PhD diss., Stanford University, 2017), 210–12; Richard Waterhouse, *From Minstrel Show to Vaudeville: The Australian Popular Stage, 1788–1914* (Kensington: New South Wales University Press, 1990), 28.
10. Stephen Johnson, "Testimonials in Silk: Juba and the Legitimization of American Blackface Minstrelsy in Britain," in *Testimonial Advertising in the American Marketplace: Emulation, Identity, Community*, ed. Marlis Schweitzer and Marina Moskowitz (New York: Palgrave Macmillan, 2009), 46–47n21.
11. Ibid., 31–34.
12. Stephen Johnson, "Gender Trumps Race?," in *When Men Dance: Choreographing Masculinities across Borders*, ed. Jennifer Fisher and Anthony Shay (Oxford: Oxford University Press, 2009), 239n2; Johnson, "Testimonials in Silk," 32.
13. Michael Pickering, *Blackface Minstrelsy in Britain* (Farnham, UK: Ashgave, 2008), 20. See also Stephen Johnson, "Death and the Minstrel," in *Burnt Cork: Traditions and Legacies of Blackface Minstrelsy*, ed. Stephen Johnson (Amherst: University of Massachusetts Press, 2012), 73–103.

14. Robert Toll, *Blacking Up: The Minstrel Show in Nineteenth Century America* (Oxford: Oxford University Press, 1974), 199–200.
15. Pickering, *Blackface Minstrelsy in Britain,* 28.
16. Scholarship on blackface minstrelsy in England is relatively robust. See Laura Vorachek, "Whitewashing Blackface Minstrelsy in Nineteenth-century England: Female Banjo Players in *Punch,*" *Victorians: A Journal of Culture and Literature* 123 (2013): 31–51; Robert Nowatzki, *Representing African Americans in Transatlantic Abolitionism and Blackface Minstrelsy* (Baton Rouge: Louisiana State University Press, 2010); Pickering, *Blackface Minstrelsy in Britain;* Nathalie Rosset, "The Birth of the 'African Glen': Blackface Minstrelsy between Presentation and Representation," *Rethinking History* 9, no. 4 (2005): 415–28; Michael Pickering, "Eugene Statton and Early Ragtime in Britain," *Black Music Research Journal* 20, no. 2 (2000): 151–80; Jennifer Devere Brody, *Impossible Purities: Blackness, Femininity, and Victorian Culture* (Durham, NC: Duke University Press, 1998); Simon Featherstone, "The Blackface Atlantic: Interpreting British Minstrelsy," *Journal of Victorian Culture* 3, no. 2 (1998): 234–51; Michael Pickering, "John Bull in Blackface," *Popular Music* 16, no. 2 (1997): 181–201; Robert Winans and Elias Kaufman, "Minstrel and Classic Banjo: American and English Connections," *American Music* 12, no. 1 (1994): 1–30; Michael Pickering, "Mock Blacks and Racial Mockery: The 'Nigger' Minstrel and British Imperialism," in *Acts of Supremacy: The British Empire and the Stage, 1790–1930,* ed. J. S. Bratton (Manchester: Manchester University Press, 1991); Michael Pickering, "'A Jet Ornament to Society': Black Music in Nineteenth-Century Britain," in *Black Music in Britain: Essays on the Afro-Asian Contribution to Popular Music,* ed. Paul Oliver (Milton Keynes: Open University Press, 1990); Thomas Riis, "The Experience and Impact of Black Entertainers in England, 1895–1920," *American Music* 4, no. 1 (1986): 50–58; J. P. Green, "*In Dahomey* in London in 1903," *Black Perspectives in Music* 11, no. 1 (1983): 22–40; J. S. Bratton, "English Ethiopians: British Audiences and Blackface Acts, 1835–1865," *Yearbook of English Studies* 2 (1981): 127–42; George Rehin, "Blackface Street Minstrels in Victorian London and Its Resorts: Popular Culture and Its Racial Connotations as Revealed in Polite Opinion," *Journal of Popular Culture* 15 (1981): 19–38; Tony Barker, "Eugene Stratton," *Music Hall* 12 (April 1980): 107–17; Barry Anthony, "Early Nigger Minstrel Acts in Britain," *Music Hall* 12 (1980): 118–23; and George Rehin, "Harlequin Jim Crow: Continuity and Convergence in Blackface Clowning," *Journal of Popular Culture* 9 (1975): 682–701.
17. Even before the 1860s, several British troupes went to Dublin. Douglass Riach, "Blacks and Blackface on the Irish Stage, 1830–60," *Journal of American Studies* 7, no. 3 (1973): 231–41.
18. For blackface minstrelsy in India, see Hoxworth, "Transoceanic Blackface"; Bradley Shope, *American Popular Music in Britain's Raj* (Rochester, NY: University of Rochester Press, 2016), 4; and Harish Trivedi, "Performing the Nation: Dave Carson and the Bengali Babu," in *The Nation across the World: Postcolonial Literary Representations,* ed. Harish Trivedi et al. (Oxford: Oxford University Press, 2007).

19. Waterhouse, *From Minstrel Show to Vaudeville*, 40.
20. Matthew Wittman, "Globalization and Jim Crow: American Minstrelsy in Oceania, 1850–1880" (conference paper, American Studies Association, 2005). See also Matthew Wittman, "Empire of Culture: U.S. Entertainers and the Making of the Pacific Circuit, 1850–1890" (PhD diss., University of Michigan, 2010.
21. Waterhouse, *From Minstrel Show to Vaudeville*, 65.
22. Melisa Bellanta, "Leary Kin: Australian Larrikins and the Blackface Minstrel Dandy," *Journal of Social History* 42, no. 3 (2009): 677–95.
23. Geoffrey Ward, *Unforgivable Blackness: The Rise and Fall of Jack Johnson* (New York: Alfred A. Knopf, 2004), 85.
24. Waterhouse, *From Minstrel Show to Vaudeville*, 100. For more scholarship on blackface in Australia, see John Whiteoak, "Demons of Discord Down Under: 'Jump Jim Crow' and Australia's First Jazz Band," *Jazz Research Journal* 8, nos. 1–2 (2015): 23–51; and Jon Stratton, "The Jackson Jive: Blackface Today and the Limits of Whiteness in Australia," *Journal of the European Association for Studies on Australia* 2, no. 2 (2011): 22–41.
25. James Revell Carr, *Hawaiian Music in Motion: Mariners, Missionaries, and Minstrels* (Urbana: University of Illinois Press, 2014), 138, 137. Wittman also talks about Hawaii in "Empire of Culture." For amateur minstrel shows on several Pacific islands, including Tahiti, Fiji, and New Zealand, see Rouleau, *With Sails Whitening Every Sea*, 55–70.
26. Stephen Johnson, "'Shield Us from This Base Ridicule': The Petitions to Censor Blackface Circus Clowns, Toronto, 1840–43," in *Canadian Performance Histories and Historiographies*, ed. Heather Davis-Fisch (Toronto: Playwrights Canada Press, 2017), 254–79.
27. William Mahar, *Behind the Burnt Cork Mask: Early Blackface Minstrelsy and Antebellum American Popular Culture* (Urbana: University of Illinois Press, 1999), 2.
28. Stephen Johnson, "Uncle Tom and the Minstrels: Seeing Black and White on Stage in Canada West prior to the American Civil War," in *(Post)Colonial Stages: Critical & Creative Views on Drama, Theatre & Performance*, ed. Helen Gilbert (London: Dangaroo Press, 1999), 55–63; Lorraine Le Camp, "Racial Considerations of Minstrel Shows and Related Images in Canada" (PhD diss., University of Toronto, 2005), 327, 344.
29. Kelly Best, "'Making Cool Things Hot Again': Blackface and Newfoundland Mummering," *Ethnologies* 302 (2008): 215–48.
30. Joan Nicks and Jeannette Sloniowski, "Entertaining Niagara Falls, Ontario: Minstrel Shows, Theatres and Popular Pleasures," in *Covering Niagara: Studies in Local Popular Culture*, ed. Joan Nicks and Barry Keith Grant (Waterloo, Ontario: Wilfrid Laurier University Press, 2010), 293.
31. Le Camp, "Racial Considerations of Minstrel Shows," iv–ix.
32. Errol Hill, *The Jamaican Stage, 1655–1900: Profile of a Colonial Theatre* (Amherst: University of Massachusetts Press, 1992), 90.

33. Hill does not mention Washington Norton. Hoxworth's account fills in this detail. Hoxworth, "Transoceanic Blackface," 48n80.
34. Hill, *Jamaican Stage*, 269.
35. Hollis Liverpool, *Rituals of Power and Rebellion: The Carnival Tradition in Trinidad & Tobago, 1763–1962* (Chicago: Research Associates School Times Publications / Frontline Distribution International, 2001), 267; Donald Hill, *Calypso Calalloo: Early Carnival Music in Trinidad* (Gainesville: University Press of Florida, 1993), 157.
36. Liverpool, *Rituals of Power and Rebellion*, 267–68. See also John Cowley, *Carnival, Canboulay and Calypso: Traditions in the Making* (New York: Cambridge University Press, 1996), 62–63, 113–15, 183.
37. Jill Lane, *Blackface Cuba, 1840–1895* (Philadelphia: University of Pennsylvania Press, 2005), 239n7; Robin Moore, *Nationalizing Blackness: Afrocubanismo and Artistic Revolution in Havana, 1920–1940* (Pittsburgh: University of Pittsburgh Press, 1997), 248n3.
38. Lane, *Blackface Cuba*, 15, 90–99, 147–48. See also Christina Civanto, "Race/Class/Language: 'El Negro' Speaks Cuban Whiteness in the Teatro Bufo," *Latin American Theatre Review* 39, no. 1 (2005): 49–70. For a discussion on present-day Cuban American comedians who continue Teatro Bufo traditions by blacking up on Miami-based Spanish-language television shows, see Albert Laguna, *Diversión: Play and Popular Culture in Cuban America* (New York: New York University Press, 2017).
39. Yiedy Rivero, *Tuning Out Blackness: Race and Nation in the History of Puerto Rican Television* (Durham, NC: Duke University Press, 2005), 28, 38.
40. Gladys Jiménez-Muñoz, "The Black-Face of Puerto Rican Whites: Race and Representation in Postwar Puerto Rico," *Latino Review of Books* (2002): 102.
41. Rivero, *Tuning Out Blackness*, 104.
42. John Chasteen, *National Rhythms, African Roots: The Deep History of Latin American Popular Dance* (Albuquerque: University of New Mexico Press, 2004), 59. For a brief account of an American minstrel troupe who performed in Peru in 1860 and Buenos Aires in 1868, see Isabel Aretz, "Music and Dance in Continental Latin America, with the Exception of Brazil," in *Africa in Latin America: Essays on History, Culture, and Socialization*, ed. Manuel Fraginals (New York: Holmes and Meir, 1984), 222.
43. Chasteen, *National Rhythms*, 62.
44. Matthew Karusch, "Blackness in Argentina: Jazz, Tango and Race before Perón," *Past and Present*, no. 216 (August 2012): 220–21.
45. Chasteen, *National Rhythms*, 62. Later, in the twentieth century, a famous Argentinian film actor named Luis Sandrini also performed in blackface. Gladys Jiménez-Muñoz, email to the author, August 24, 2017.
46. George Andrews, "Remembering Africa, Inventing Uruguay: Sociedades de Negros in the Montevideo Carnival, 1865–1930," *Hispanic American Historical Review* 87, no. 4 (2007): 707.
47. Ibid., 723–25.

48. James Dormon, "Shaping the Popular Image of Post-Reconstruction American Blacks: The 'Coon Song' Phenomenon of the Gilded Age," *American Quarterly* 40 (1988): 453.
49. Pickering, "Eugene Stratton," 155–56.
50. Waterhouse, *From Minstrel Show to Vaudeville,* 89–90.
51. *New York Dramatic Mirror,* August 25, 1900.
52. On Golliwogs, see "Hamleys Joins Queen's Estate in Banning Golliwogs," *Guardian,* February 5, 2009; Donna Varga and Rhoda Zuk, "Golliwogs and Teddy Bears: Embodied Racism in Children's Popular Culture," *Journal of Popular Culture* 46, no. 3 (2013): 647–71; Jan Pieterse, *White on Black: Images of Africa and Blacks in Western Popular Culture* (New Haven, CT: Yale University Press, 1995), 156–58. On blackface-inspired imagery in material culture, see Patricia Turner, *Ceramic Uncles and Celluloid Mammies: Black Images and Their Influence on Culture* (Charlottesville: University of Virginia Press, 1994).
53. Daphne Brooks, *Bodies in Dissent: Spectacular Performances of Race and Freedom, 1850–1910* (Durham, NC: Duke University Press, 2006), 207–12.
54. Camille Forbes, *Introducing Bert Williams: Burnt Cork and the Story of America's First Black Star* (New York: Basic Civitas Books, 2008), 121, 298.
55. For other works on Bert Williams in transnational contexts, see Theresa Saxon, "*In Dahomey* in England: A (Negative) Transatlantic Performance Heritage," *Atlantic Studies* 13, no. 2 (2016): 265–81; Louis Chude-Sokei, *The Last "Darky": Bert Williams, Black-on-Black Minstrelsy, and the African Diaspora* (Durham, NC: Duke University Press, 2006); and Thomas Riis, ed., *The Music and Scripts of In Dahomey* (Madison, WI: A-R Editions, 1996).
56. Cathy Wagner, "Blackface Minstrelsy and Ethnic Identity as Globalized Market Commodities," in *Imagined Identities: Identity Formation in the Age of Globalization,* ed. Gönül Pultar (Syracuse, NY: Syracuse University Press, 2014), 127.
57. David Ciarlo, *Advertising Empire: Race and Visual Culture in Imperial Germany* (Cambridge, MA: Harvard University Press, 2011), 213–23.
58. Petrine Archer-Straw, *Negrophilia: Avant-Garde Paris and Black Culture in the 1920s* (New York: Thames and Hudson, 2000), 40–42.
59. Andy Fry, *Paris Blues: African American Music and French Popular Culture, 1920–1960* (Chicago: University of Chicago Press, 2014), 29–79. Harry Reynolds, interlocutor for the Mohawk minstrels and amateur historian, claimed that Canfield and Booker were the first minstrels to visit France. He did not provide a year or source. Harry Reynolds, *Minstrel Memories: The Story of Burnt Cork Minstrelsy in Great Britain from 1836–1927* (London: Alston Rivers, 1928), 23. In the 1990s, historians Leora Auslander and Thomas Holt saw a life-size "Sambo" statue with "exaggeratedly red lips, servile smile, and bulging eyes" while walking the streets of Paris. Auslander and Holt, "Sambo in Paris: Race and Racism in the Iconography of the Everyday," in *The Color of Liberty: Histories of Race in France Peabody,* ed. Sue Stovel and Tyler Stovel (Durham, NC: Duke University Press, 2003), 147.

60. Robert Rydell and Rob Kroes, *Buffalo Bill in Bologna: The Americanization of the World, 1869–1922* (Chicago: University of Chicago Press, 2005), 131

61. This scene can be found on YouTube. The comments section is an interesting study, and one statement from 2017 is especially notable: "Obama cabinet meeting! #MAGA?." Burnt cork nationalism provides a set of common symbols and references that racist people can use to disparage the concept of black citizenship and rally behind the white racial state. https://www.youtube.com/watch?v=R4v_yRFf4-Y.

62. Susan Gubar, *Racechanges: White Skin, Black Face in American Culture* (Oxford: Oxford University Press, 1997), 58.

63. Michael Hammond, "'A Soul-Stirring Appeal to Every Briton': The Reception of 'The Birth of a Nation' in Britain (1915–1916)," *Film History* 11, no. 3 (1999): 355.

64. Brian Ward, "Music, Musical Theater, and the Imagined South in Interwar Britain," *Journal of Southern History* 80, no. 1 (2014): 44.

65. Brian Willan, "Cinematographic Calamity' or 'Soul-Stirring Appeal to Every Briton': *Birth of a Nation* in England and South Africa, 1915–1931," *Journal of Southern African Studies* 39, no. 3 (2013): 623–40.

66. Kristin Thompson, *Exporting Entertainment: America in the World Film Market, 1907–1934* (London: British Film Institute, 1985), 78–79.

67. Willan, "Cinematic Calamity," 624.

68. Rydell and Kroes, *Buffalo Bill in Bologna*, 133.

69. Melvyn Stokes, "Race, Politics, and Censorship: D. W. Griffiths *The Birth of a Nation in France*, 1916–1923," *Cinema Journal* 50, no. 1 (2010): 19–38.

70. Willan, "'Cinematographic Calamity' or 'Soul-Stirring Appeal to Every Briton.'"

71. Kerry Wallach, *Passing Illusions: Jewish Visibility in Weimar Germany* (Ann Arbor: University of Michigan Press, 2017), 81–85.

72. Ibid., 84.

73. Valerie Weinstein, *Anti-Semitism in Film Comedy in Nazi Germany* (Bloomington: Indiana University Press, 2019).

74. Eric Sundquist, *Strangers in the Land: Blacks, Jews, Post-Holocaust America* (Cambridge, MA: Harvard University Press, 2005), 184–85.

75. Catherine Cole, *Ghana's Concert Party Theatre* (Bloomington: Indiana University Press, 2001), 26.

76. For more on blackface performance in Ghana, see Efua Sutherland, *The Original Bob: The Story of Bob Johnson, Ghana's Ace Comedian* (Accra: Anowuo Educational Publications, 1970); Edmund John Collins "Jazz Feedback to Africa," *American Music* 5, no. 2 (1987): 176–93. One concert-party troupe toured Nigeria. Oyekan Owomoyela, *Visions and Revisions: Essays on African Literatures and Criticisms* (New York: Peter Lang, 1991), 199–201.

77. Robert Irwin, "Memín Pinguín, Rumba, and Racism: Afro-Mexicans in Classic Comics and Film," in *Hemispheric American Studies*, ed. Caroline Levander and Robert Levine (New Brunswick, NJ: Rutgers University Press, 2007), 253.

78. Mónica Figueroa and Emiko Tanaka, "'We Are Not Racists, We Are Mexicans': Privilege, Nationalism and Post-racial Ideology in Mexico," *Critical Sociology* 42, nos. 4–5 (2016): 517, 515–16.
79. Theressa Delgadillo, "Singing 'Angelitos Negros': African Diaspora Meets Mestizaje in the Americas," *American Quarterly* 56, no. 2 (2006): 415.
80. Irwin, "Memín Pinguín, Rumba, and Racism," 259.
81. Miguel Becerra, "Stereotypes of Afro-Peruvians through the Media: The Case of the Peruvian Blackface," in *Converging Identities: Blackness in the Modern African Diaspora*, ed. Julius Adekunle and Hettie Willims (Durham, NC: Carolina Academic Press, 2013), 289. See also Marîa Ximena Plaza, "What's New in South America? Blackface Is Okay in Peru," *Africa Is a Country*, February 22, 2013, http://africasacountry.com.
82. Michael Pickering, "Race, Gender and Broadcast Comedy: The Case of the BBC's *Kentucky Minstrels*," *European Journal of Communication* 9, no. 3 (1994): 311–33.
83. Ibid., 161. Interestingly enough, Jon Stratton speculates that *The Black and White Minstrel Show* might have been "just as popular in Australia" as England. Stratton, "Jackson Jive," 25–26.
84. A recent biography focuses on George Mitchell, one of the producers of *The Black and White Minstrel Show*. Eleanor Pritchard, *Minstrel Magic: The Story of the George Mitchell Choirs* (Mamhilad: Saron, 2017) .
85. Fry, *Paris Blues*, 29.
86. Danielle Roper, "Inca Drag Queens and Hemispheric Blackface: Contemporary Blackface and Drag Performance from the Andes to Jamaica" (PhD diss., New York University, 2015). For a very different example of blackface in Columbia, see Andrés Duque, "Blackface at Bogota Pride + Latin American Pride, 2006," *Blabbeando*, July 3, 2006, http://blabbeando.blogspot.com/2006/07/blackface-at-bogota-pride-latin.html, referenced in Cole, "American Ghetto Parties," 253.
87. Roper, "Inca Drag Queens and Hemispheric Blackface," 6. Roper's updated definition of "hemispheric blackface" will appear in a forthcoming journal article, "Blackface at the Andean Fiesta: Performing Blackness in the *Danza de Caporales*," *Latin American Research Review* (Spring 2019). For another example of contemporary blackface in Peru, see the debates regarding a blackface character named "El Negro Mama." Becerra, "Stereotypes of Afro-Peruvians," 290–97. For Brazil, see Ron Conner, "Brazilian Blackface: Maracatu Cearense and the Politics of Participation" (master's thesis, University of California–Riverside, 2009).
88. Katrin Sieg, "Race, Guilt and Innocence: Facing Blackfacing in Contemporary German Theater," *German Studies Review* 38, no. 1 (2015): 131. For another essay on contemporary blackface in Germany, see Jonathan Wipplinger, "The Racial Ruse: On Blackness and Blackface Comedy in 'Fin-de-Siècle' Germany," *German Quarterly* 84, no. 4 (2011): 457–76.
89. Philip Howard, "On the Back of Blackness: Contemporary Canadian Blackface and the Consumptive Production of Post-racialist, White Canadian Subjects,"

Social Identities 24, no. 1 (2018): 1–17; Philip Howard, "A Laugh for the National Project: Contemporary Canadian Blackface Humour and Its Constitution through Canadian Anti-Blackness," *Ethnicities* (2018): 1–26. For blackface in contemporary Canadian theater, see Robin Breon, "Blackface: Thoughts on Racial Masquerade," *Canadian Theatre Review* 98 (Spring 1999): 60–62. For discussion on the challenges of teaching the history of blackface minstrelsy in Canadian universities, see Natalie Alvarez and Stephen Johnson, "Minstrels in the Classroom: Teaching, Race, and Blackface," *Canadian Theatre Review* 147 (Summer 2011): 31–37.

90. Gil-Soo Han, "K-Pop Nationalism: Celebrities and Acting Blackface in the Korean Media," *Continuum* 29, no. 1 (2015): 2–16.
91. John Russell, "Consuming Passions: Spectacle, Self-Transformation, and the Commodification of Blackness in Japan," *Positions* 6, no. 1 (1998): 113–77. For more on contemporary Japanese blackface, see Michelle Ho, "Consuming Women in Blackface: Racialized Affect and Transnational Femininity in Japanese Advertising," *Japanese Studies* 37, no. 1 (2017): 49–69; Marvin Sterling, *Babylon East: Performing Dancehall, Roots Reggae, and Rastafari in Japan* (Durham, NC: Duke University Press, 2010); Ian Condry, *Hip-Hop Japan: Rap and the Paths of Cultural Globalization* (Durham, NC: Duke University Press, 2006); Joe Wood, "The Yellow Negro," in *Giant Steps: The New Generation of African American Writers*, ed. Kevin Young (New York: Harper Perennial, 2000), 310–33; Nina Cornyetz, "Fetishized Blackness: Hip-Hop and Racial Desire in Contemporary Japan," *Social Text* 41 (1994): 113–39.
92. Douglass McGill, "Colgate to Rename a Toothpaste," *New York Times*, January 27, 1989.
93. Jane Perlez, "With Blackface and Monkey Suit, Chinese Gala on Africa Causes Uproar," *New York Times*, February 16, 2016.
94. Siyuan Liu, *Performing Hybridity in Colonial Modern China* (New York: Palgrave Macmillan, 2013); Alexander Huang, *Chinese Shakespeares: Two Centuries of Cultural Exchange* (New York: Columbia University Press, 2009); Claire Conceison, *Significant Other: Staging the American In China* (Honolulu: University of Hawaii Press, 2004).
95. David Theo Goldberg, "Racism in Orange: Afterword," in *Dutch Racism*, ed. Philomena Essed and Issabel Hoving (Amsterdam: Rodopi, 2014), 412–13.
96. Emily Raboteau, "Who Is Zwarte Piet?," *Virginia Quarterly Review* 90, no. 1 (2014): 152.
97. Sacha Hilhorst and Joke Hermes, 'We Have Given Up So Much': Passion and Denial in the Dutch Zaarte Piet (Black Pete) Controversy," *European Journal of Cultural Studies* 19, no. 3 (2016): 218–33; Goldberg, "Racism in Orange: Afterword"; Pieterse, *White on Black*, 163–65.
98. Jeroen Rodenberg and Pieter Wagenaar, "Essentializing 'Black Pete': Competing Narratives Surrounding the Sinterklaas Tradition in the Netherlands," *International Journal of Heritage Studies* 22, no. 9 (2016): 716–28; Koen Lemmens, "The Dark

Side of 'Zwarte Piet': A Misunderstood Tradition or Racism in Disguise? A Legal Analysis," *International Journal of Human Rights* 21, no. 2 (2017): 120–41.

99. Micah Garen, Marie-Helene Carleton, and Justine Swaab, "Zwarte Piet: Black Pete Is 'Dutch Racism in Full Display,'" *Al-Jazeera*, November 27, 2018, www.aljazeera.com; Zack Newmark, "Zwarte Piet Protestors: 'The System Has Failed'; Dozens Arrested at Sinterklaas Events," *NL Times*, November 19, 2018, https://nltimes.nl.
100. Chude-Sokei, *Last "Darky,"* 141.
101. *Diamond News*, October 24, 1883; *Natal Mercury*, October 3, 1865.
102. Johnson, "Death and the Minstrel," 77. Frank Hussey probably brought copies of *New York Clipper* to Kimberley to use as promotional material.
103. Mike Pearson, "'No Joke in Petticoats': British Polar Expeditions and Their Theatrical Presentations," *TDR: The Drama Review* 48, no. 1 (2004): 44–59.
104. Rouleau, *With Sails Whitening Every Sea*, 73.
105. Hoxworth, "Transoceanic Blackface."
106. Kellen Hoxworth, email to the author, November 19, 2018. To access the Trove collection, see http://trove.nla.gov.au/. To access the "Papers Past" collection, see https://paperspast.natlib.govt.nz/. For information on the World Newspaper Archive, see www.readex.com/content/world-newspaper-archive.
107. https://images.hollis.harvard.edu/primo-explore/search?vid=HVD_IMAGES&sortby=rank&lang=en_US.
108. https://www.utm.utoronto.ca/~w3minstr/.
109. Hoxworth, "Transoceanic Blackface," 346n80.

INDEX

abolitionists, 3, 17, 19, 23, 26, 125, 188–89
Abrahams, Peter, 2
accumulation by dispossession, 5, 74–75, 94
Adhikari, Mohamed, 98–99, 163–64
Adventures of Two Dutch Dolls and a Golliwogg, The (Upton), 194
advertisements, blackface in, 2, 8, 68–69, 138, 184, 196, 204–6
Africa, British views of, 195–96
African Americans: and blackface masks, 201; and *Coon*, as term, x; and Coon Carnival, 138, 152–58, 163; idealized by British settlers, 40, 54–55; and K-pop stars, 206; performers, 231n52; and racial uplift politics, 99, 119–20; spirituals of, 97, 100, 110, 113, 124–25, 154; touring the Atlantic world in the nineteenth century, 113–14
African choirs, 110
African National Congress (ANC), 164, 178–79, 182
Afrikaans (language), 67, 132, 136, 143, 246nn21–22, 248n53
Afrikaner nationalism, 124
Afrikaners: and apartheid, 10; British settler conflict with, 124; Dutch settlers identifying as, 226n84; emigration from Cape Colony, 32–33; and English-language minstrel shows, 214n10–11; and exclusionary racial order, 108–9, 124–25; off limits for masquerade, 175, 179; portrayed in minstrel shows, 67–68, 85; race thinking of, 98, 129; and South African racial categories, 15; and the Virginia Jubilee Singers, 124–25, 128; Voortrekkers, 33, 124, 175, 179; and Zulu people, 82
Afro-diasporic music, dance, and folklore: emotional response to, 124–25; and McAdoo's troupes, 97–98, 101, 110, 114, 154; and minstrel culture, 21, 56, 156–57; Rice's exposure to, 16–17
Afro-diasporic nationalism, 158–59, 176
afterpiece, 21
Alabama (ship), 138
Alabama Coons, 151
Albert, Prince, 25, 64–65, 233n95
Alexandra of Denmark, 64–65
alien citizens, vii, 213n1
aliens, blacks as: and blackface mask, 3–5, 11, 123; and burnt cork nationalism, 5–7, 11, 17, 91; and citizenship, 5–7, 123, 181; and minstrel humor, 48–49, 89
"Alladin" (minstrel sketch), 85
Allen, Jimmy, 154–55
Allen, Mattie, 106–7, 119, 121
Always Sunny in Philadelphia (TV show), 204
Amagama abantu (Zulu song collection), 110

"Amaqabuqabu" (Innovations; Zulu song), 110
amateur blackface minstrelsy: and black illogics humor, 48–49; and British royal family, 65; and British soldiers, 83–84; in Canada, 189; elite participation and marketing, 57–58; and failed-facade humor, 52–53; and "Jump Jim Crow," 184; and mixed-race crowds, 139; newspaper reviews of, 228n10, 233n88; popularity of, 38–39, 58–60; and racial identities of performers, 228n8; and surrogate authenticity, 60–64, 233n91; war songs and patriotism, 82
Amateur Coloured Troupe, 38–39, 49, 57, 67–68, 228n8
American Colonization Society, 195
American Sporting Club, 149
Amos 'n' Andy Show (radio and TV show), 7, 180–81, 254n168
Anderson, Susan B., 120–21
Andrews, George, 193
"Angelina Baker" (song), 44
Angelitos Negros (film), 202
Anglo-American folklore, 21
Anglo-American Minstrels, 75, 81, 83, 85, 139
Anglo-colonial minstrel circuit, 9, 28–31, 33–34, 71, 186
Anglo-Saxon empire, 94, 239n83
Anglo-Zulu War (1879), 82–83
Angulo, Liliana, 204
animation industry, 7
Antarctica, 210
antiapartheid activists, vii–viii, 2, 133, 164, 178–79, 182
anti-Chinese sentiment, 29, 188, 207
anticolonial resistance, 167, 177, 191
antimiscegenation statutes, 11, 168
antiracism, vii, 27, 181–82, 204, 208, 212
anti-Semitism, 200–201
antislavery activists. *See* abolitionists
Antwerp, Netherlands, 208
apartheid South Africa: carnivals during era of, 2–3, 133–37, 157–63, 166, 168, 177, 252n135; and coloured racial identity, 164–66, 174–75; and control of women, 218–19n41; Jim Crow America compared to, x; labor laws and control, 92–93; and minstrelsy contribution to race thinking, 55, 93–94; racial projects and path toward, 130; as racial state, 216n11; social control policies during, 168, 174; U.S. support for, 10–11
Archer-Straw, Petrine, 196
Argentina, 192–93, 198, 258n42, 258n45
Arno, Siegfield, 200
Ashante Dwarf Minstrels and Punch and Judy, 75
Athlone Cottonfield Darkies, 167
Atjas carnival characters, 149, 253n152
"Aunt Chloe's lecture on the rights of woman" (minstrel stump speech), 48
Auslander, Leora, 259n59
Australia: and Anglo-colonial circuit, 9, 28–30, 36, 38, 186; and *Birth of a Nation*, 198; British settlers in, 232n77; Christy Minstrels in, 71, 186; coon-song craze in, 8, 194; Georgia Minstrels in, 187; Larrikins, 187–88; McAdoo and troupes in, 97, 112–13, 194, 240n23, 241n55; mineral rushes in, 75; minstrel troupes from, 184; and Pacific circuit, 9, 28–29, 187–88; race relations in, 29; and second wave of minstrel globalization, 186–88, 209
Australian Variety Company, 75, 84, 139

Baby Benson (minstrel performer), 75, 84–85, 89–90, 237n69
Backus Minstrels, 28, 188
Bahia, 234n122
Baker, Josephine, 196
Bakhtin, Mikhail, 167, 174
Baltimore, Maryland, 17–18
Bamboozled (film), 196, 204
banjoes, 186, 254n158
Banker, Ed, 237n69
Bantustans, 10
Barkly, Henry, 76, 78–79
Baron, D., 150
Basutoland, 77
Batavia, 9
Beaconsfield Darkies, 167
Beast Is the B2ST, 206
"Beautiful Isle of the Sea" (song), 65–66, 79
Bellanta, Melisa, 187–88
"Beneath the Weeping Willow" (song), 45
"benevolent" slave masters, 44–45, 117–18, 161–62
Bengalee Baboo, 30
Benson, Tom, 87
Benson American Troupe, 75, 84–85, 89–90, 139, 237n69

Berlin, Germany, 196, 205
Bethune, Thomas Greene (Blind Tom), 22
Bickford-Smith, Vivian, 87, 93
biopower, 10, 218–19n41
Birth of a Nation (film), 7–8, 197–99
black, as term, 14–15
black African response to minstrel shows, 68–69, 233n95
Black and White Minstrel Show, The (TV show), 203, 261n83
"black boom," 206
"Black Brigade" (song), 23
"Black DJ English," 206
blackface clown circus character, 188
blackface lore cycles, 69
blackface masks: absent from postapartheid carnivals, 175–79; and African Americans, 201; and blacks as aliens, 3–5, 11, 123; burnt cork nationalism symbolized by, 3–5, 181; and coloured racial identity, 166; and Coon troupes, 139, 146–48, 152; in England, pre-America, 215n2; as figure of ambivalence, 176; and hyperbolic blackness, 42–43, 146; Jolson's, 201; in Mummers Parade, 179–80; power dynamics of, 192; racial meanings behind, 23, 141, 152, 157; rejection of, 122–23, 154, 185, 194; in South America, 192–93; and Williams, Bert, 195–96
blackface minstrel globalization, 7–9, 183–212; fifth-wave, 8–9, 184, 203–8; first-wave (1836–48), 8, 25–26, 184–86, 189; fourth-wave, 8, 148, 184, 197–203, 208; and maritime culture and imperialism, 183–84; second-wave (1850–80), 8–9, 28–31, 75, 184, 186–88, 190, 209; third-wave (1890–1915), 8, 99, 184, 189, 193–97; and transatlantic conversation, 208–9
blackface minstrelsy, American: and American popular culture, 1–2, 7–8, 180–81, 184; during antebellum era, 17–25, 29, 55, 86, 242n87; black performers in, 22, 185–87, 231n52, 235n7; class orientation of, 55–58; and Coon Carnival, 142–43; and distancing of middle groups from Africans, 166; export of, vii, 1–2, 25–28, 86, 183–84; and first wave of minstrel globalization, 185–86; radical progressivism narrative, viii–x, 18–19, 23, 55–56; and Rice's "Jim Crow," 17–19, 214n2; and second wave of minstrel globalization, 186–87; songs, 1, 214n11; three-part shows, 20–21; traveling, 1, 18–21, 25, 28–31, 36, 38, 184–89; two-section structure of, 3; white ethnicities portrayed in, 67; and white nationalism, vii–viii
blackface minstrelsy, Australian, 184
blackface minstrelsy, British: audience for, 56; in Australia, 186–87; and Coon Carnival, 141; imported from the United States, 25–28, 86; in Ireland, 256n17; late nineteenth century, and music, 157; minstrel shows in South Africa evoking, 80–81; and second wave of minstrel globalization, 186–87; traveling, 1, 28–31, 36, 38, 184, 186–87; white nationalism and, vii, x
blackface minstrelsy in South Africa: academic interpretations of, ix–x, 57–58; arrival of, 35, 56; black African response to, 68–69, 233n95; child performers in, 90, 238n71; as export of American popular culture, vii, 1–2, 86; and imperialism, 74–75; and multiracial audiences, 139–40; and racial slurs, 2, 215n7; and second wave of minstrel globalization, 8–9, 30–31, 75; songs and sketches, 12, 60, 70–71; white ethnicities portrayed in, 67–68, 84–86. *See also* British settlers in South Africa; Coon Carnival; McAdoo, Orpheus; mineral revolution in South Africa; preindustrial period in South Africa; *specific colony and city names*
black illogics humor, 46–50, 87–88, 180, 230–31n50
black lives, devaluation of, 91–92, 238n76
black modernity, 136–37, 158, 163, 176, 177
black music. *See* Afro-diasporic music, dance, and folklore
black nationalism, 112
blackness: "authentic," portrayed by minstrels, 87, 89, 116; comic book portrayals of, 202; Coon troupe names referencing, 152, 169–74, 176, 250n91; and Cuban Teatro Bufo, 190–91; expropriation of, 5–6, 13, 20, 68–69, 74, 91, 217n23; and failed-facade humor, 51–53, 88; hyperbolic, 42–44, 146–48, 166, 178–79, 207, 249n73; Larrikins' association with, 187–88; and minstrel portrayals of Irish people, 68; parodies of, 22, 44, 204–5
Black Pete traditions, 207–8

Blacksound, 220n50
Black Star Line Coons, 158–59
Blue Danube Troubadours, 151
Bohee, George, 186
Bohemian Girl (opera), 121
Bokomo Cornfields Darkies, 167
Bolivia, 198
Bombay, India, 29
Bones (minstrel character), 20–21, 25, 43–44, 96, 129
Bosko (cartoon character), 7
Boston, Massachusetts, 19, 21
Bowery Amphitheater, New York City, 19–20
Bowery Amphitheater Circus, 189
Braham's Empire Minstrels, 139
Brantlinger, Patrick, 27
Brazil, 72
"Brian O'linn or the Irish Mormon" (minstrel sketch), 85
British Broadcasting Company (BBC), 195, 203
British Colonial Office, 76
British Empire: Cape Colony acquired by, 33; imperial networks, 9; Jim Crow mania in, 1–2; minstrel performances celebrating war victories of, 83; minstrel tours of, 28–31; Natalia Republic annexed by, 33; progressive changes in South Africa, 32; resource war with Transvaal Republic, 124; uprisings by subject peoples in, 66. *See also* blackface minstrelsy, British
British folk music, 21, 25–26, 41
British metropole: blackface minstrelsy popularized in, 25–28; British settler connection to, 9, 13, 61, 63–64, 69, 79–81, 86; and burnt cork nationalism, 58; diamonds and investment in South Africa by, 13, 75–77; fashion trends from, 79; fear of abandonment by, 66, 234n106; and hyperbolic blackness, 43; and Indian trading networks, 29; Jim Crow mania in, 1–2; slave trade ban, 32. *See also* blackface minstrelsy, British; England; Great Britain
British missionaries, 32, 35
British national identity, 26–27
British nationalism, 10
British royal family: birthday celebrations, 13, 63, 65–66, 79; and Coon Carnival, 160–63; King Edward VII (formerly Prince), 186, 195; and minstrel show advertisements, 57; Prince Albert, 25, 64–65, 233n95; Prince Charles, 160–61; Prince Edward (later King Edward VIII), 1; Prince of Wales, 69, 79, 101; Queen Victoria, 63, 65, 79, 101; Queen Victoria's Jubilee, 153–54, 250n97; songs celebrating, 65–66, 79, 86, 195; and the Virginia Jubilee Singers, 101
British settlers in South Africa: accumulation and dispossession ideology of, 5; Afrikaner conflict with, 124; amateur minstrels, 38–39, 48–49, 58–62, 228n8; and apartheid, 10; British metropole connection to, 9, 13, 61, 63–64, 69, 79–81, 86; clashes with colonized peoples, 34–35, 66; economic issues of, 33–35; and exclusionary racial order, 4–5, 108–9; and expropriation of blackness, 5–6; identity and blackface minstrelsy, 13, 61, 64–72, 79, 85–86; and logics of empire, 37; and minstrel music, 12; minstrelsy adaptations for, 56–58, 65; minstrelsy popularity with, 2; numbers compared to other British colonies, 232n77; professional minstrelsy linking settlements of, 69–72, 91, 238n74; and royal family, 1; and South African racial categories, 15; and surrogate authenticity, 61–64; and the Virginia Jubilee Singers, 101–2, 105–6, 113, 125, 128. *See also* race thinking and discourse of British settlers
British soldiers and amateur minstrelsy, 83–84
Broadway, 195
Broadway Gentlemen Singing Coons, 151
Brooks, Daphne, 104
Brower, Frank, 19
Brown, Joe, 38, 41
brownface, 200
Bubble Sisters, 206
Buck and Wing dance, 248n45
Buckley, V., 228n8
Buenos Aires, Argentina, 192, 198, 258n42
Buffalo, New York, 20
Bugs Bunny (cartoon character), 7
burlesque European operas and Shakespeare plays, 21, 65
"Burlesque History of England" (minstrel stump speech), 48, 66
Burns, Tommy, 188

burnt cork nationalism: adaptability of, 26–27, 30, 58; and *Birth of a Nation*, 198, 260n61; blackface masks as symbol of, 3–5, 181; and blacks as aliens/noncitizens, 5–7, 11, 17, 91; and British settler identity, 64, 69, 71–72, 79, 91; in Canada, 205; in Cape and Natal Colonies, 35, 38, 72; and Dixon, 221n7; as gendered discourse of exclusionary citizenship, 23–25; and impersoNation, 216n16; and Independence Day break-ins, 19; and Klopse racial impersonations, 166; and land, 25; McAdoo's challenge to, 98–99, 114; and minstrel patriotism, 82, 208; origin narrative, 17–18; and parodies of blackness, 22, 44; patriarchal nature of, 23–24; and Rice, 17–19, 221n7; taught to children, 89–90, 238nn72–73; and violence, 89

Burton, H., 228n8

cakewalk (dance), 115, 121, 141–42, 154, 195

cakewalk craze, 196

Calcutta, India, 2, 29, 184

Caledon Codes (1809), 32

California, 9, 21, 75

California gold rush, 25

Calypso Calaloo (D. Hill), 190

Canada, 184, 188–89, 198–99, 205, 232n77

Canadian Observer, 198

candombes, 192–93

Canfield and Booker, 259n59

Canton, China, 255n5

Cape Argus, 42, 56, 62, 71, 121–22, 150, 153, 233n84, 233n88

Cape Chronicle, 61–62, 139

Cape Colony, South Africa: and Afrikaners, 32–33, 124, 226n81; amateur blackface minstrelsy in, 38–39, 48–49, 52–53, 57–65; and apartheid roots, 10; arrival of minstrelsy in, x, 35–36; British settler anxiety in, 66–67; and British settler identity, 64–66, 72, 79, 85–86; *Christy* synonymous with blackface minstrelsy in, 232n74; and expropriation of blackness, 5–6; first decade of professional minstrelsy in, 37–38, 40–41, 69–72; founding and early history of, 31–36; during mineral revolution years, 73, 75–78; minstrel caricatures in, 4–5, 41–44, 46, 48–49, 54–55; minstrel character names in, 37; and minstrel circuits and imperial networks, 9, 31; minstrelsy popularity in, vii, 2; and minstrel tour reports, 238n74; racial concepts taught to children in, 89–90, 238nn72–73; racial segregation in, 93–94; Rhodes as prime minister of, 94; white ethnicities in, 67–68, 85–86

Cape Herald, 249n73

Cape Peninsula Coloured Carnival Board, 245n10

Cape Peninsula Coon Carnival Board, 143

Cape Slave Codes, 77–78

Cape Standard, 135, 145

Cape Times, 6, 83, 87, 117, 121, 135, 138–39, 141–43, 145–47, 149, 151, 152–53, 155, 162–63, 245n10, 249n77

Cape-to-Cairo train line, 94

Cape Town, South Africa: amateur blackface minstrelsy in, 38–39, 52–53, 57, 63–65, 82, 231n50; and Anglo-colonial circuit, 30, 93; Bo-Kaap neighborhood, 132, 134, 245n7; District Six neighborhood, 132–34, 140, 146, 155, 167; Eastern Cape African migrations to, 163; formation of, 31; Green Point neighborhood, 132, 134; holiday traditions of coloured people in, 131–32; "Johnny Schmoker" performed in, 237n39; "Juanita" performed in, 71; Juvenile Christy Minstrels in, 238n71; and Leslie's Christy Minstrels, 38, 57, 62–63, 139; London Minstrels in, 82–83; McAdoo in, 95–97, 104, 107–8, 138; during mineral revolution years, 73; minstrel shows for children in, 67, 89–90; minstrel shows for elite audiences in, 78–79; and minstrel tour reports, 238n74; music stores in, 38, 60, 143, 156; newspapers in, 2, 62–63, 71, 214n11, 216n9; Nish's Christy Minstrels in, 30, 38, 56, 61, 69–70, 139, 186; Norton's Christy Minstrels in, 38, 71–72, 139; pass system in, 106; Plantation Ball in, 6–7; racial segregation in, 93; school segregation in, 238n73; and surrogate authenticity, 61–63; and the Virginia Jubilee Singers, 125. *See also* Coon Carnival; *specific newspaper names*

Cape Town Gentleman Jazz Singers, 167

Cape Town Hawker Coons, 143, 167

Cape Town Minstrel Carnival Association, 176

Cape Town's Famous Checker Coons, 167

Cape Town Street Parade, 178, 216n10. *See also* Coon Carnival
Caribbean, 189–92, 199, 204–5
carnivalesque, 167–68, 174–75
"Carnival Face" cookies, 249n73
Carr, James Revell, 188
Carson, Dave, 29–30, 212, 228n5
Catholic Young Men's Society Christy Minstrels, 38–39
Cattle Killing (1857), 34
Cell, John, 93
Césaire, Aimé, 238n77
Cetshwayo kaMpande, 82
"Challenge Dance" (minstrel sketch), 50
Chasteen, John, 192
Chatham Street Chapel, New York City, 19
Cheever's and Kennedy's Great American Entertainment Troupe, 84
Chile, 198
China, 9, 71, 206–7, 255n5
Chinese Australians, 187–88
Chinese caricatures, 29, 85
Christianity, 35
Christmas Bands (Christmas Choirs), 132
Christy, Edwin Pearce (E. P.), 20, 62–63, 222n21
Christy, George (Harrington), 20, 22, 237n69
Christy Minstrels: and black illogics, 47–48; British colony tours, 28–31, 38–42; in Buenos Aires, 192; and Coon Carnival origin narrative, 140, 250n97; McAdoo's troupes compared to, 113, 116–17; newspaper reports of, 69–72, 238n74; original, in the United States, 20, 22, 222n21; songbooks, 38, 60, 232nn80–81; and surrogate authenticity, 61–63; troupe names, 228n6. *See also* amateur blackface minstrelsy; *specific troupe names*
Chude-Sokei, Louis, 208–9
circum-Atlantic cultures, 60–61
citizenship: black, and racial uplift politics, 98–99, 122–23; black, in *Birth of a Nation*, 198, 260n61; and blackface minstrel conventions, 181; and blacks as aliens, 5–7, 123, 181; and coloured racial identity, 164, 166; and gender, 23–25, 46
citizen-soldier ideal, 23
civil rights movement, vii, 8, 180–81
Civil War and Reconstruction eras, 23, 33, 103, 115, 197–98, 234n113
Clansmen, The (play), 197
Clay, Cassius, 48
Clifton, E., 228n8
Clifton, M., 228n8
closed-compound system, 93
"Coal Black Rose" (minstrel song), 231n54
Cockrell, Dale, 18, 55, 221n11
Cold War, 10
Cole, Catherine, 5, 7, 201
Cole, C. J., 138
Colgate, 206
Collins, Dick, 109
Colón, Ángel Amílcar, 202
colonial expropriation. *See* expropriation, colonial
colonialism, Western, 5, 31–36, 159, 177, 238n77
colonial states and extractive logics, 5–6
coloured, as term, 15, 99, 104–5, 112–13, 115–16, 163
Coloured Labour Preference Policy, 163
coloured modernity, 177
Coloured Opera Troupe, 26
Coloured Petes, 208
coloured racial identity: and Coon Carnival, 137, 163, 165–68, 174–75, 177; history of, 163–64; and McAdoo, 104–10, 112–15, 125–28; as middle racial category, 98–99; and 1994 elections, 164–65, 178–79; and racial logics, 243n100; and racism toward Africans, 164–65
Columbia, 204
comic books, 184, 201–3
Commercial Exchange, Cape Town, 56–57
compound system, 93
Confederacy, 19, 197
Congress of Racial Equality, 180
contemporary blackface, 8–9, 204–8, 261n87
Cook, James, 22
Coon, as term: and African Americans, x, 155, 157; as American racial slur, 155, 157, 216n10, 246n16; in Australia, 188; in Cape Town, 134–36, 245–46n16; and *Klopse*, as term, 131. *See also* Klopse/Coon troupes
Coon, The (D'arcy), 140
Coon Carnival, 131–82; during apartheid era, 2–3, 133–37, 157–63, 166, 168, 177, 252n135; blackface mask removed from, 11; blackness referenced in troupe names, 152, 169–74, 176, 250n91; and coloured racial identity, 137, 163, 165–68,

174–75, 177; early carnivals, 131–33, 137–48, 247n27, 247n40, 248n45; and Jolson, 147, 159–61, 201; and local cultural traditions, 143–44; minstrel influences on, 141–43, 144–48, 150–51, 157–58, 175, 177–78, 248n45; names for, 2–3, 131, 136, 178, 216n10, 247n40; origin narratives, 137–40, 152–57, 247n27, 250n95, 250n97; photo (1937), 142; photo (1949), 160–61; photo (1957), 160; postapartheid, 134–36, 175–80, 253nn152–54, 254nn158–59; Privateer troupes, 148–50; racial masquerading, 141, 150–52, 163, 165–67, 174–75
coon-song craze, 8, 122, 193–94
Cooper, Frederick, 218–19n41
"Coopers, The" (minstrel sketch), 50, 230–31n50
Coplan, David, 250n97
Correll, Charles, 180
Cox's Christy Minstrels, 139
Coyle, Norman, 38
creolization, 144, 177
critical race theory, 6, 217n23
crooked gluttony humor, 49, 89, 145
Crosby, Bing, 156, 159, 163, 248n57
Cruz, Jon, 125
Cuba, 25, 190–91
Cuff (in Rice's story), 16
Cuff (minstrel character), 51
cultural appropriation, 157, 162
cultural assimilation, 164
Curry, Mr. M., 82

Dahomey Coon Troupe, 165–66
Daily Independent, 105, 233n84
Dantu family, 153, 250n97
D'arcs Marionetts, 75, 139
D'arcy, M. Cassiem, 140, 146
darkie, as term, 152, 167, 179, 252n142
Darkie Clothing, 252n142
Darkie Toothpaste, 206
Darwinist logic, 126–28
"Das Klein Niggergirl" (minstrel song), 196
Dave Carson's Minstrels, 228n5
Davejee Carsonbhoy, 30
Davids, Nadia, 158
Davy Crockett folktales, 21
Dawn Darkies, 151
Day of the Kings carnival, 193
"Dead Nigger, The" (minstrel sketch), 238n76
De Beers Consolidated Mines, 94
Delgadillo, Theresa, 202
Democratic Party, 23
DeVere's Comedy Company, 75
Diamond, John, 22
diamond industry, 73–79, 88–89, 92–94
Diamond News, 70–71, 73, 79, 209, 228n10, 233n84
diamond theft, accusations of, 88–89, 92
Dickens, Charles, 185
Dick K. Knowles (photo), 4
digital archives, 210–12
Dilward, Thomas, 22
Diplo (blackface character), 191–92
disengaged engagement, 125–26, 243n99
Dishcover Minstrel Troupe, 210
District Six (musical), 137–38
Dixie (film), 148, 156, 159, 163, 248n57
"Dixie" (song), 1, 19, 155–56
Dixon, George Washington, 221n7
Doctor Quash (minstrel character), 50
Dougherty, Huey, 79–80, 87–89
"Dougherty Beaten" ("Lawks"), 88
Douglass, Frederick, 3, 19, 28, 216n13
"Down among the Dead Men" (song), 79
"Down the River" (song), 44
Dramático-Musical Society Los Negros, 192
Drum, 135, 153, 159, 250n95
Dube, John, 110
Dublin, Ireland, 256n17
Duke of Edinburgh's Own Volunteer Rifles, 83–84, 236n38
Durban, South Africa, 33, 38, 41, 103–4, 159, 227n88
"Dutch Broom Girl, The" (minstrel song), 85
Dutch East India Company, 31–32, 36, 134, 177, 226n80
Dutch settlers in South Africa. *See* Afrikaners
Du Toit's Pan mine, 73

Eastern Cape, South Africa, 37, 163, 233n95
Eastern Province Herald, 41, 47
ebony, as term, 115
Ebrahim, Noor, 146
Edward, Prince (later King Edward VIII), 1
Edward VII, King (formerly Prince), 186, 195
Edwin Browne's Minstrel and Novelty Company, 190
86th Royal Downshire Minstrels, 38–39
Ellis, A. B., 27–28

Ellison, Ralph, 3, 96
"El negro bueno" (Cuban anticolonial anthem), 191
El Negro Mama (blackface character), 261n87
Ely, Melvin, 254n168
Emmett, Dan, 19–20, 159
England: Africa, views of, in, 195–96; and Anglo-colonial circuit, 9, 28–30, 36, 71; and *Birth of a Nation*, 198; blackface masking in, 215n2; coon-song craze in, 8, 194; diamonds and investment in South Africa by, 76; economy of, South African integration with, 76; fashion trends from, 79; Golliwog character in, 194–95; imperial wars in South Africa, 77; Jim Crow mania in, 1–2; Lancashire Cotton Famine in, 64; minstrel shows and connection to, 80–81, 86; racism in, 27–28; Rice's travel to, 17–18, 25, 185; scholarship on blackface minstrelsy in, 256n16; *Uncle Tom's Cabin* in, 26; Virginia Minstrels in, 19, 25; and waves of minstrel globalization, 8, 185, 186. *See also* blackface minstrelsy, British; British metropole; Great Britain
Erasmus, Zimitri, 137
Erlmann, Veit, 114
"Essence of Old Virginia, The" (song), 41
Ethiopian Serenaders, 8, 25, 185
ethnological show business, 42
European operas, burlesque, 21
Exhibition March Past, 144
expropriation, colonial: of black labor, 68–69; of blackness, 5–6, 13, 20, 68–69, 74, 217n23; of land and resources, 6, 13, 31, 34, 92, 94; minstrelsy's contribution to, 83–84, 94

Fabulous Woodstock Starlets, 140
failed-facade humor, 51–53, 88, 119, 231n52
fashion trends from England, 79, 86
Fauset, Jessie, 231n52
Felix the Cat (cartoon character), 7
femininity, 46, 204
Fernandez, Leopoldo, 191
Fields, W. C., 195
Fisk Jubilee Singers (Loudin's), 97, 100
Fisk Jubilee Singers (original), 97, 100, 103, 113–14, 129
Fisk University, 97, 112
Flower of Hawaii, The (film), 200
folk music of the British Isles, 21, 25–26, 41
folk spirituals, African American. *See under* African Americans
Forbes, Camille, 195
Foster, Stephen, 20, 23, 25, 233n84
Foucault, Michel, 218n41
France, 18, 196, 199, 259n59
France, J., 228n8
freak shows, 22
free blacks, 31–32
free burghers, 31–32
Freeman Journal, 102
French Ministry of Foreign Affairs, 199
frenetic corporality minstrel trope, 43, 59, 87, 145–46, 157
Fritz! Our Cousin German (minstrel play), 85
Fry, Andy, 196, 204
Fusco, Coco, 159

Gaines, Kevin, 99, 126
"Gal Wid the Blue Dress On" (song), 50
Gario, Quinsy, 207–8
Garvey, Amy Ashwood, 158
Garvey, Marcus, 158
gender hierarchy in South Africa, 46, 75
genocide, 226n80
George, South Africa, 63, 65
Georgia Minstrels, 75, 139, 187, 196, 235n7
Georgia Minstrels and Alabama Cake Walkers, 112–13, 123, 241n55
German settlers in South Africa, 85
Germany, 196, 199, 200–201, 205
Ghana, 201
ghoema beat, 143–44, 177–78, 248n55, 248n58, 248–49n60, 254nn158–59
ghoemaliedjies, 248n55
Ginger Blue (minstrel character), 41, 46–47, 49, 51–52
globalization of blackface minstrelsy. *See* blackface minstrel globalization
"God Bless the Prince of Wales" (song), 66, 79
"God Save the King" (song), 195
"God Save the Queen" (British national anthem), 66, 79
Goldberg, David, 207
Goldin, Ian, 165
gold rushes, 9, 25, 28, 98
Golliwog, 194–95
Gone with the Wind (film), 7, 156

Good Old Georgia in '49 (drama), 118–19
Goomah Dance, 144
Gosden, Freeman, 180
Grahamstown, South Africa, 38, 58, 61, 110, 238nn73–74
Grahamstown Journal, 58, 69–70, 127–28
Graham's Town Minstrels, 61–62
Grand Fashionable Nights, 78–79, 86
Grand March Past, 144
Great Britain, 26–28, 185, 203. *See also* blackface minstrelsy, British; British metropole; England
Great Depression, 6–7
Great Trek, 33
Green, Lawrence, 153
Greensboro, North Carolina, 96–97
Grey, George, 34
Griffith, D. W., 198
Grimes, T., 228n8
Griqualand West, 77, 92–93
Group Areas Act (1950), 168, 174
gunboat diplomacy, 183

Hague, Sam, 186
Hague's Slave Troupe, 186
Halifax, Nova Scotia, 199
Hamburg, Germany, 196
"Hamfat Man" (minstrel song), 86
Hamleys toy shop of London, 194–95
Hampton Institute, 97, 102–3, 108–9, 111–12
Happy Little Darkies Masquerading Troupe, 152
happy-worker minstrel trope, 40, 44, 54, 118, 145
"Hard Times Come Again No More" (minstrel song), 233n84
Harris, Cheryl, 217n23
Hartman, Saidiya, 23, 50
Harvey, David, 5, 74
Harvey, E. H., 86–87, 89
Harvey-Doughertly-Leslie-Brahim Minstrels: black lives devalued by, 238n76; Cape and Natal Colonies toured by, 75; in Cape Town, 139; disrupted performance of, 94–95; elites entertained by, 78–79; *Johnny Schmoker* performed by, 84, 237n39; in Port Elizabeth, 68; tour reports of, 238n74
Harvey's Ethiopian Opera Troupe, 139
Harvey's Grotesques, 75
Harvey's New English Company, 139
Harvey's Variety Troupe/Company, 82, 85, 139
Havana, Cuba, 190
Haverly, J. H., minstrel troupe of, 186
Haverly's Mastodon Minstrels, 196
Hawaii, 9, 28, 188, 200, 257n25
Hawley and Hazel Chemical Company, 206
hemispheric blackface, 204–5, 261n87
Hicks, Charles, 187, 194, 196, 241n55
Highborn Coons, 132, 140
High Class Coloured American Minstrel Vaudeville Company (McAdoo's Minstrels): benevolent slave master songs, 117–18; blackface makeup rejected by, 122–23, 139, 154, 194; and black modernity, 112; and cakewalk, 141; and coloured racial identity, 114–15; and Coon Carnival origin narratives, 138, 152–55; coon-song craze rejected by, 122, 194; McAdoo's formation of, 97–98; name changed, 112–13; newspaper reviews of, 96, 116–17, 129; race thinking challenged by, 98, 129–30; and racial authenticity, 115–16; and racial uplift politics, 96–99, 119–22, 194; stump speeches rejected by, 194
high imperialism, 194
Hill, Donald, 190
Hill, Errol, 189–90
History of the Cape Colony for Use in Schools (Wilmot), 238n73
Hitler, Adolf, 201, 208
Hoberman, Gerald, 176
Holliday Street Theater, Baltimore, 17–18
Hollywood, 8, 148, 156, 184, 197–200
Holt, Thomas, 259n59
Hong Kong, China, 9, 206, 255n5
Honolulu, Hawaii, 9, 28, 188
Hoxworth, Kellen, 210–12, 258n33
Huggins, Nathan, 3–4
Hughes, Heather, 110
Hussey, Frank, 190, 209, 263n102
hyperbolic blackness, 42–44, 146–48, 166, 178–79, 207, 249n73
hypersexuality, 53–54, 191, 193, 231n62

"I Long for My Home in Kentucky" (song), 46
Il Trovatore (opera), 102–3
"Imitation Dance," 22
"I'm Leaving Thee in Sorrow, Annie" (minstrel song), 83

Immorality Act (1950), 168
imperial expansion, 25, 74–77, 82, 92
imperialism: and accumulation by dispossession, 5; coon songs and high imperialism period, 194; English, and Afrikaner people, 124; and minstrel performances, 29, 74–75, 79, 83, 184; and minstrel tours, 9, 31; and racial hierarchy, 27
imperial ornamentation, 37
impersoNation, 216n16
Imvo Zabantsundu (newspaper), 112, 127–28
In Dahomey (musical), 195
Independence Day break-ins, 19
India: and Anglo-colonial circuit, 9, 29–30, 38, 71, 186; at center of British Empire, 29–30; Dave Carson's Minstrels in, 228n5; enslaved workers from, 31; and race relations, 29; and second wave of minstrel globalization, 186; workers recruited from, 34
Indian Mutiny (1857), 66
Indonesia, 31
Inglese, Francesca, 134, 176, 253n153
instruments, 21
insurgent textual listening, 220n50
International Monetary Fund (IMF), 11, 182
Ireland, 256n17
Irish Australians, 187–88
"Irish Farce" (minstrel sketch), 85
Irish jig dance, 21–22
"Irish Lilt, The" (minstrel song), 68
Irish minstrel performers, 166
Irish Princes, 149
Irish settlers in South Africa, 67–68, 85, 234n113
"Irish Tutor, The" (minstrel sketch), 68
Irwin, Robert, 202
Isandlwana, 82–83
"I'se Gwine Back to Dixie" (minstrel song), 117–18
isicathamiya, 110–11
Italian Life Guards, 149

Jabavu, John Tengo, 112, 127–28
Jackson, Andrew, 23
Jacobs, Moeniel, 140
Jamaica, 66, 189–90
Jamaican Stage, The (E. Hill), 189–90
Japan, 183–84, 206
Japanese American internment/concentration camps, vii
Japanese minstrels, 183
"Japanese Tommy," 22
jazz music, 200–201
Jazz Singer, The (film), 7, 148, 159–61, 200–201
Jephta, Amy, 134
Jeppie, Shamil, 252n135
Jewish identity, 200
Jewish minstrel performers, 166
"Jim Brown" (song), 23
Jim Crow, as term, 19
Jim Crow America, vii–viii, x, 11, 199, 216n11, 254n168
"Jim Crow in London" (burlesque), 189
Jim Crow mania in British Empire, 1–2, 25, 37, 80
Jim Crow's Alphabet, 25
Jiménez-Muñoz, Gladys, 191–92
Johannesburg, South Africa, 1, 69, 98, 106, 109, 199
John Bull (personification of England), 27
Johnny Schmoker (minstrel play), 84, 237n39
Johnson, Bob, 201
Johnson, Jack, 188
Johnson, Stephen, 185, 189, 212
Jolly Coons Masquerading, 141
"Jolly Irish couple" (minstrel sketch), 84
"Jolly Irishman, The" (minstrel song), 84–85
Jolson, Al, 147, 159–61, 200–201, 206
Jones, Douglass, Jr., 18–19
"Juanita" (song), 70–71
juba dancing, 22
"Juba Project" (S. Johnson), 212
jubilee singing, 97, 99
"Jump Jim Crow" (song and act): British version, 27; and early minstrelsy in United States, 18–19; in Jamaica, 189; and Jim Crow mania, 1–2; in Mexico, 18; and "More Perfect Union," viii; popularized in British metropole, 25, 184; and Rice, viii, 1–2, 16–19, 25, 80, 214n2; translated into Afrikaans, 214n11
Juvenile Christy Minstrels, 38–39, 238n71

Kaapse Klopse (Clubs of the Cape) carnivals. *See* Coon Carnival
Kaffir Christy Minstrels, 228n8
Kaffir Employment Bill, 34
kaffirs, 108–9, 164, 179
Kamehameha IV, King, 188
Karusch, Matthew, 192
Kat River Rebellion, 35

Keegan, Timothy, 32
Kemble, Charles, 17
Kentucky Minstrels, The (radio program), 203
Khoekhoe herders, 15, 31, 35, 53–54
Khoisan people, 15, 31–32, 98, 163
Kikuyu people, 167
Kikuyu Warriors, 151
Kimberley, South Africa: Anglo-American minstrels in, 83; and Australian Variety Company, 84; coloured people in, 128; diamond industry in, 73–74, 76–77, 88–89, 94; Harvey-Doughertly-Leslie-Brahim Minstrels in, 79; labor control in, 92–93; McAdoo's cultural influence in, 110; and minstrel tour reports, 238n74; *New York Clipper* in, 209, 263n102; pass system in, 106; Phillips's variety show in, 80–81; racial slurs in, 2, 215n7; telegraph office in, 70–71; "Uncle Tom's Cabin" (building) in, 37; and the Virginia Jubilee Singers, 125; whiteface performance in, 4
Klopse, as term, 131, 136, 246nn21–22
Klopse/Coon troupes, 131–32, 245nn7–8. *See also* Coon Carnival; *specific troupe names*
Knowles, Dick K., 4
Kolbe, Vincent, 167
Korea, 205–6
K-pop industry, 205–6
Kramer, David, 100, 111, 113, 137–38, 243n99
Kruger, Paul, 107, 124–25
Ku Klux Klan, 197–98, 205

labor coercion, 40, 75–77, 93
labor laws and control, 53–54, 76–79, 92–93
Lancashire Cotton Famine, 64
Lane, Jill, 190–91, 216n16
Lane, William Henry, 22, 185–86
Lantern, 87
Lanyon, Colonel, 92–93
La Revue Nègre, 196
Larrikins, 187–88
Latin America, 204–5. *See also specific Latin American countries*
"Lawks" (pen name of British settler), 88
Lee, Spike, 196, 204
Le Roux, J. D., 175
Leslie, Harry: and Dave Carson's Minstrels, 228n5; and failed-facade humor, 52; as Ginger Blue, 41, 47; photo of, 39; and whiteness, 67. *See also* Leslie's Christy Minstrels
Leslie's Christy Minstrels: and black illogics, 47–48; in Cape Town, South Africa, 38, 57, 62–63, 139; elite patrons listed by, 57; international touring circuit of, 209; and minstrel caricatures, 41–42; South Africa toured by, 38, 62, 70–71; and surrogate authenticity, 62–63, 233n88
Lester, Alan, 64, 79
Levy, Achmat, 143, 155–56, 248n53
Lhamon, W. T., viii–ix, 18, 55, 69, 184, 212
Littlest Rebel, The (film), 156
Liverpool, England, 19
Liverpool, Hollis, 190
Livingston, David, 79
location systems, 33, 92–94, 226n86
Loftus, Victoria, 87
London, England: American blackface acts in, 184–86; first Christy's Minstrel performance in, 30; Golliwog dolls sold in, 194–95; *In Dahomey* performed in, 195; and minstrel show advertisements, 63, 80–81; minstrel troupes based in, 26–30, 56; Rice in, 18; and traveling minstrel troupes, 36; Virginia Minstrels in, 19
London Hawker Jubilee Coons, 151
London Minstrels, 75, 80, 82–83, 139
Lord Nelson's Escorts, 149
lore cycles, blackface, 69
Lott, Eric, 20, 74, 86, 145–46, 217n23, 221n4, 231n51
Loudin, Frederick, 97
Louisville, Kentucky, viii, 16, 18
Love, Louis, 119
Lovedale Institute, 110
Lyal, Joe, 228n8

Macbeth (burlesque performances), 65
Madagascar, 31
Mad Men (TV show), 204
Magubane, Zine, 2
Mahar, William, 242n87
Malay Choirs, 132, 248n55
Malay people, 139–40, 153
Malaysia, 206
"Malingo Hoy, the Cape Town Coolie" (minstrel song), 67–68
Maltabella Plantation Darkies, 167
Mambo Negrita (2006 exhibit), 204
Mandela, Nelson, vii–viii, 2, 179
Manhattan, New York City, 17, 19–21, 55–56
manifest destiny, 25

Manila, Philippines, 9
Mannenberg Entertaining Minstrels, 167
Manuel, George, 146, 149, 153
Maori uprisings in New Zealand, 66
Mardi Gras, New Orleans, 134, 138, 167
Martin, Denis-Constant, ix–x, 136, 140, 158, 160, 176, 212
masculinity, 46, 167, 193
Mason, John, 134
masquerade, racial, 141, 150–52, 163, 165–67, 174–75, 190
Massachusetts, 19, 21
"Massa's in the Cold Ground" (minstrel song), 45, 117, 161–62
"Master Juba." *See* Lane, William Henry
Masters and Servants Act (1856), 53–54
Masters and Servants Act (1873), 77
Masters and Servants Ordinance (1841), 53
Matabele people, 124, 167
Matabele Warriors troupes, 166
Matthews, Melvin, 176
Mauritius, 71
Mbongwe, Titus, 111
McAdoo, Eugene, 110
McAdoo, Orpheus, 95–130; death of, 194; and educational exchange, 111; as jubilee singer, 97, 99–114, 153–54; newspapers and racial identities of troupe members, 228n8; in photo with M. Allen, 107; and proslavery logics, 161; and racial uplift politics, 98–99, 102–5, 111–12, 119–22, 126–30; use of coloured racial identity by, 104–10, 112–15, 125–28. *See also* Georgia Minstrels and Alabama Cake Walkers; High Class Coloured American Minstrel Vaudeville Company; *Orpheus in Africa*
McAdoo's Minstrels. *See* High Class Coloured American Minstrel Vaudeville Company
measles outbreak, 93
Mechanic's Hall, New York City, 20
"Medicine Jack" (minstrel song), 233n84
Melba, Nellie, 120–21
Melbourne, Australia, 28–29
Melbourne, Elizabeth, 35
Melvyn (minstrel performer), 38
Memín Pinguín (comic book character), 201–3
Merchant of Venice, The (burlesque performances), 65
Mérida, Mexico, 18
Merikey (minstrel character), 50
mestizaje, 191, 202
Mexican Outlaws, 149
Mexico, 25, 201–3
Mickey Mouse (cartoon character), 7
Millionaire Darkies, 151
mineral revolution in South Africa (1872–89), 73–95; antebellum-style racial imagery during, 86–87; British settler identity during, 79, 85–86; and diamond industry, 73–79, 88–89, 92–94; imperialism and imperial expansion during, 74–77, 82–84; minstrel caricatures and race thinking during, 87–90; minstrel portrayal of white ethnicities during, 84–85; minstrel shows and connection to British metropole during, 79–81; minstrel shows for elites during, 78–79; patriotism during, 82–84, 92; power relations between black and white workers during, 73–78; social changes during, 98–99; social functions of minstrelsy during, 91–92
minstrel caricatures, 40–55; belief in accuracy of, 40–42, 53–55, 86–87, 89; and black illogics humor, 46–50, 87–88, 230–31n50; of black politicians, 104; and British settler identity, 13, 64; and burnt cork nationalism imaginary, 38, 44–45; and comedic violence, 49–50; and Coon Carnival, 157–58; and crooked gluttony humor, 49; failed-facade humor, 51–53; and fifth-wave blackface minstrelsy, 204, 206; and fourth-wave blackface minstrelsy, 198, 201; and hyperbolic blackness, 42–44; and hypersexuality, 53–54, 231n62; and masculinity, 46; and minstrel shows for children, 89–90; and race thinking and discourse, 41–55, 87–90; and sentimentalism, 46; and third-wave blackface minstrelsy, 193–96
Minstrel Carnival, 2, 216n10. *See also* Coon Carnival
minstrel progressivism. *See* radical progressivism narrative
minstrel sadism, 50, 59–60, 91–92, 119, 231n51, 238n75
minstrel songs and sketches, 1, 12, 49, 214n11. *See also specific song and sketch names*

minstrel stump speeches: "Aunt Chloe's lecture on the rights of woman," 48; and black illogics, 47–49, 87–88; "Burlesque History of England," 48, 66; and imperialism, 79; McAdoo's rejection of, 104, 121–22, 194; "Or Any Other Man," 48, 230n37
miscegenation, 11, 168, 197, 201–2
misogyny, 203, 222n24
missionaries, 32, 35, 125
Mississippi Nigger Minstrels, 152
Mitchell, A. B., 143
Mitchell, Jariya, 245n10
Mixed Marriages Commission, 11
mixed-race former slaves, 98, 163
mixed-race identity. *See* coloured racial identity
mixed-race marriage, 168. *See also* miscegenation
Mngomezulu, Themba, 252n142
mock political oration speeches, 48, 230n37
modernity, 136–37, 158–59, 163, 166, 176–77
"moffies," 132, 244n4
Mohawk Minstrels, 141, 186, 259n59
Montevideo, Uruguay, 192–93
Moore and Burgess Minstrels, 80–81, 122, 186
moppies, 143–44, 248n55
Morant Bay Rebellion (1865), 66
Moreland, Mantan, 196
morenas, 193
"More Perfect Union" (Obama's speech), viii
Moritz Makes His Fortune (film), 200
Morrison, Matthew, 220n50
multiracialism and multiracial democracy, 176–77, 181–82
Mummers of Newfoundland, 189
Mummers Parade, Philadelphia, 179–80
"My Old Kentucky Home" (song), 1

Napoleon Hemmed In (minstrel sketch), 88
Natal Colony, South Africa: amateur blackface minstrelsy in, 38–39, 48–49, 57–59, 64–65, 184; and apartheid roots, 10; arrival of minstrelsy in, x, 35–36; British settler anxiety in, 66; and British settler identity, 64–66, 72, 79, 85–86; *Christy* synonymous with blackface minstrelsy in, 232n74; disrupted minstrel show in, 94–95; and expropriation of blackness, 5–6; first decade of professional minstrelsy in, 37–38, 62, 70; founding and early history of, 33–36; location system in, 33, 93–94, 226n86; during mineral revolution years, 73, 75–77; minstrel caricatures in, 42–43, 48–49, 54–55; and minstrel circuits and imperial network, 9, 13; minstrelsy popularity in, vii, 2; and minstrel tour reports, 238n74; pass system and discrimination in, 106, 109; patriotic minstrel shows in, 82–83; railway line, 227n88; Transvaal annexed to, 82; and the Virginia Jubilee Singers, 125; white ethnicities in, 67–68, 85–86; Zulus, relationship with, 82
Natalia Republic, 33
Natal Mercury, 48, 71, 104, 119, 209, 228n8, 228n13
Nathan, Hans, 43, 222n20
National Association for the Advancement of Colored People (NAACP), 180, 98
nationalism, Afrikaner, 124
nationalism, Afro-diasporic, 158–59, 176
nationalism, British, 10
nationalism, white, vii–viii, x, 3, 27, 208
Nationalist Party, 164–65, 168, 178, 253n152
National Library of South Africa, 156
Native Americans, 135, 149–50, 167, 253n152
Naturalization Act (1790), 17–18
Nazi Party, 200–201
negro, as term, 104–6, 109, 115–16
"negro lubolo" (carnival character), 193
"Negro Minuet," 115, 121
negro racial identity, 115, 126
Negro Utópico (2003 exhibit), 204
neoliberalism, 182, 206
Netherlands, 207–8
New WORLD Theater, vii, 213n2
New Year's Day Coloured Carnival Board, 150
New Year's Eve, 132
New York City, 17, 19–21, 55–56
New York Clipper, 209, 263n102
New York Serenaders, 28–29, 188
New Zealand, 66, 198, 232n77
Ngai, Mae, 213n1
Niagara Falls, Canada, 189
"Niggermania" (British minstrel song), 27, 61
nigger or *nigga*, as term, 152, 167, 179, 188

Nish, Anthony, and Nish's Christy Minstrels: amateur minstrelsy following tour of, 58, 61–62; and Anglo-colonial circuit, 30–31, 93, 186; in Australia, 71; in Cape Town, 30, 38, 56, 61, 69–70, 139, 186; and Lancashire relief fund, 64; and minstrel caricatures, 41; newspaper reviews of, 69–70; and second wave of minstrel globalization, 186; songbooks sold by, 38, 232n80; South Africa toured by, 38, 40, 70; upper-class audiences of, 56–57
nonracialism, 177, 253n152
normative whiteness, 42, 68, 84–85, 228n8
Norton, Washington, 38, 40–42, 75, 139, 228n13
Norton's Christy Minstrels: and amateur minstrels, 60; Bahia toured by, 234n122; "Beautiful Isle of the Sea" performed by, 65; in Cape Town, 38, 71–72, 139; in Jamaica, 190, 258n33; and minstrel caricatures, 41–42, 228n13; South Africa toured by, 38, 70–72; and "When Johnny Came Marching Home," 68, 234n113
nouveau-rich racism, 206
Nyon'go, Tavia, 5, 23

Obama, Barack, viii–ix, 205, 260n61
"Oh! Susanna" (Foster's song), 25, 50
OIO Christy Minstrels, 62–63
"Old Black Joe" (minstrel song), 89
"Old Folks at Home, The" (minstrel song), 1
"Old Joe" (minstrel song), 56
"Old Mother Gum" (minstrel song), 89
"Old Negro Dying" (minstrel song), 89–90
"Old Potomac Shore" (minstrel song), 46
olio, 21
Omi, Michael, 39
opera music, 102–3, 121, 242n87
operas, burlesque, 21
Orange Free State, 33, 108–9, 124
"Or Any Other Man" (minstrel stump speech), 48, 230n37
Ordinance 50, 32
Oregon, 25
Original California Minstrels, 188
Original Cape Town Christys, 38–39
Original Christy Minstrel Song Book, The, 156
Original Georgia Minstrels, 190
Origin of Jim Crow, The, 25
Orpheus in Africa (Kramer), 100, 111, 113, 243n99
Othello (burlesque performances), 65
"Other Side of Jordan, The" (minstrel song), 65
Our Gang (film and comic franchise), 202

Pacific minstrel circuit, 9, 28–29, 71, 187–88
Pan-African Historical Theatre Festival, 201
pan-Atlantic working-class culture, 37
Panic of 1837, 18–19
Paris, France, 18, 196, 199, 259n59
Pariscope, 204
pass systems, 32, 106–9
Pedi people, 77
Pelham, Richard, 19, 189
Pell, George, 8, 185
Perry, Matthew, 183–84, 206, 210, 255n5
Peru, 198, 202–5, 258n42, 261n87
Petersen, Davey, 155
Peterson, Taliep, 135, 137–38
Phewa, Thembinkosi, 110–11
Philadelphia, Pennsylvania, viii, 21, 180
Phillips, Bertie, 80–81
pickaninnies, 189
Pickering, Michael, 27, 185, 194, 203
Pierce, Earl, 30
Pietermaritzburg, South Africa, 110
Pittsburgh, Pennsylvania, 16
Plaatje, Sol, 2, 110, 198
plantation, sentimentalism for, 46
Plantation Ball, 6–7
plantation songs and material, 6, 12, 20–21, 25, 29–30, 40–41, 53
Poincaré, Raymond, 199
Poor Paddy (minstrel sketch), 85
Population Registration Act (1950), 168
Port Elizabeth, South Africa: amateur minstrel troupes in, 60; and black illogics, 47; coloured population in, 234n116; expropriation of blackness and black labor in, 68–69; and failed-facade humor, 52; "God Bless the Prince of Wales" performed in, 66; and hyperbolic blackness, 44; and minstrel tour reports, 238n74; professional minstrel troupes in, 38, 60, 62, 68; Rice's popularity in, 37
Port Elizabeth Telegraph, 47, 65, 70–71, 232n81, 233n84
Porter, Maggie, 100
Portuguese Guards, 149
postapartheid era, 134–36, 175–82, 253nn152–54, 254nn158–59

postracialism, 205
preindustrial period in South Africa (before the mid-1870s), 37–72; amateur blackface minstrelsy during, 38–39, 48–49, 52–53, 57–65, 228n8, 228n10, 233n88; black African response to minstrel shows during, 68–69, 233n95; British settler anxiety in, 66–67; British settler identity during, 64–66, 72; minstrel caricatures and British settler discourse, 40–55; professional blackface minstrelsy during, 37–39; professional minstrelsy linking British settlements during, 69–72; racial projects, 39–40, 54–55, 76; surrogation and authenticity, 60–64, 233n91; white ethnicities in, 67–68. *See also* burnt cork nationalism
Pretoria, South Africa, 1, 69, 98, 101, 106, 129
prima donna character, 21, 41–42, 228n13
primitivism, 166, 200
primitivist accumulation, 5, 20, 74
Princess Escort Masquerading Troupe, 148–49
Privateer carnival troupes ("Privates"), 148–50
"Proclamation 14," 76, 92
progressivism. *See* radical progressivism narrative
Prohibition of Mixed Marriage Act (1949), 168
proletarianization, 31, 34
proslavery sentiment and logics, 17–19, 23, 117–18, 127, 158, 161–62
Pryor, Elizabeth, 19
Puerto Rico, 191–92
Pumpkin Darkies, 132, 140
Putnam's Monthly, 2

Quebec, 205
"Queen's Letter, The" (British minstrel song), 65
Queenstown, South Africa, 79
Queen Victoria's Jubilee, 153–54, 250n97
quick changes in theater performances, 90

race, as term, 14
race thinking and discourse of British settlers, 40–55; belief in accuracy of minstrel caricatures, 40–42, 53–54, 86–87, 89; and black illogics humor, 46–50, 87–88, 230–31n50; and burnt cork nationalism, 35, 38, 44–45; and failed-facade humor, 51–53; in the *Grahamstown Journal*, 127–28; and hyperbolic blackness, 42–44; and masculinity, 46; and McAdoo's troupes, 98, 127–30; and minstrel caricatures, 41–55, 87–90; and minstrel sentimentalism, 46; and minstrel shows for children, 67, 89–90; minstrelsy's contribution to, and apartheid, 55, 93–94; and minstrel violence, 49–50, 59–60, 231n51, 238n75; and racial capitalism, 54; and racial projects, 39–40, 54–55, 92–95; stereotypes dominating, 53–54
racial and ethnic hierarchy: African, British at the bottom of, 68–69; and Afrikaners, 124–25; in the Cape Colony, 31–32; and coloured identity, 104–5, 163–67; and Coon Carnival, 162–63, 165–67; and imperialism, 27; and minstrel violence, 50; and performance culture, 55, 75; and racial uplift politics, 126–28; taught to children, 91; of whiteness, 67–68
racial authenticity, 115–16
racial capitalism, 54
racial hybridity, 243n100. *See also* coloured racial identity
racialization of sound, 220n50
racial masquerade, 141, 150–52, 163, 165–67, 174–75, 190
racial nationalism. *See* white nationalism
racial projects, 39–40, 54–55, 92–95, 126–28, 130
racial segregation: blackface minstrelsy's contribution to, 93–94; at Coon Carnivals, 133; and McAdoo's Minstrels, 128; and measles outbreak in Cape Town, 93; and mineral revolution, 75; in railroad cars in the United States, 19; residential, in South Africa, 33, 92–94, 168, 174; in schools in South Africa, 238n73. *See also* apartheid South Africa; Jim Crow America
racial slurs, 2, 29, 162, 176–77, 179, 215n7, 253nn153–54
racial states: Afro-diasporic nationalism and freedom from, 159, 163; blackface minstrelsy and power relations in, 179; and burnt cork nationalism, 3, 5, 11; Confederacy, 19; continuation of, 181–82; defined, 216n11; South Africa, 6–7, 10–11, 75, 94, 181–82, 208, 216n11; transition to multiracial states, 181; United States, 10–11, 18, 162, 181–82, 208, 216n11; Western colonies as, 31–36

racial uplift politics: and African choirs, 110–11; Fisk Jubilee model of, 100, 113–14, 129; and McAdoo, 98–99, 102–5, 111–12, 119–22, 126–30; and minstrelsy, 113–23, 128–29; problems of, 126; of Virginia Jubilee Singers, 100–114, 126–28
racism: and apartheid, 10, 11; in blackface minstrel shows, 2, 8–9, 12, 18, 22–23, 145, 185; and Canadian postracialism, 205; in Cape Town newspaper articles, 87; in China, 207; and coloured racial identity, 164–65; and Coon Carnival, 137, 145, 176; and high imperialism period, 194; in the Netherlands, 208; and Rhodes, 94, 239n83; and Rice, 17–19; in South Korea, 205–6; structural, in diamond fields, 76; taught to British settler children, 89–90, 238nn72–73; in Teatro Bufo, 190–91; in the United States, vii–x, 2, 11, 155–56. *See also* antiracism
Radano, Ronald, 220n50
radical progressivism narrative, viii–x, 18–19, 23, 55–57
Rainbow Nation, 176
Rainer's Original Ethiopian Serenaders, 28
Rainford, T., 38
Raising Cane (Lhamon), 184, 212
"Raw Recruits" (cover art for song), 23–24
Rayner (minstrel performer), 38
Raynor, J. W., 30
Republican Party, 182
Retief, Piet, 124
Reynolds, Harry, 259n59
Rhodes, Cecil, 94, 239n83
Rice, Thomas Dartmouth (T. D.): and burlesque Shakespeare plays, 65; and burnt cork nationalism, 17–18; and first wave of blackface minstrel globalization, 8, 184; Jim Crow act, viii, 1–2, 16–18, 25, 80, 214n2; popularity among British colonists, 37; proslavery speech of, 17–19; *The Virginia Mummy*, 41, 46–47, 49, 51–52; *The Virginny Cupids!*, 51
Rio de Janeiro, Brazil, 72
Rituals of Power and Rebellion (Liverpool), 190
"Rival Lovers, The" (minstrel sketch), 50, 68
Rivero, Ramón, 191–92
Rivero, Yeidy, 191–92
Roach, Joseph, 60–61
Robertson's (British company), 194
Robinson, Jeannie, 121
Roediger, David, 180
Rogin, Michael, 3, 7
Romeo and Juliet (burlesque performances), 65
Roper, Danielle, 204–5, 261n87
Rorke's Drift, battle of, 83
Rose, John, 56–57
"Rose of No Man's Land" (song), 151
Ross, Robert, 10, 55
Rouleau, Brian, 210
Rover Minstrels, 139
"Runaway Zulu, The" (minstrel song), 83
Russell, John, 206

Sabera, Boeta Achmat, 254n159
Sahabodien, Solly, 156
S. A. Independent Darkies, 167
Sambo (minstrel character), 23, 140, 207, 259n59
sambo, as term, 150–51, 176
Sambo Johnson (minstrel character), 50–51, 231n54
Sambos con Sentimiento y Devotion, 204–5
Sampson, Lin, 243n99
Sandrini, Luis, 258n45
San Francisco, California, 28–29, 188
San Francisco Minstrels, 28–30, 212
San hunter-gatherers, 15, 31, 226n80
Sarah Silverman Program, The (TV show), 204
Saxton, Alexander, 23
school segregation, 237n73
Schreiner, W. P., 199
Scott, Robert Falcon, 210
Scottish songs, 85
segregation. *See* racial segregation
self-aware blackface, 8, 184, 203–4
Semouse, Josiah, 112
Seven Steps Darkies, 167
Shakespeare plays, burlesque, 21, 65
Shanghai, China, 206, 255n5
Sharpeville Massacre, 10–11
"Shaughraun, The" (minstrel sketch), 85
Shepstone, Theophilus, 33, 82
Shepstone System, 33
Siamese Twins (minstrel sketch), 88
Sieg, Katrin, 205
Simmons, Lew (member of London Minstrels), 81
Singapore, 9, 206
Singing Fool, The (film), 200
Slagtersnek rebels, 124

slave consciousness, subtle, 163
slavery: abolished in South Africa, 32, 34, 53, 55, 131; and African American music, 124–25; in Cape Town, 143–44; celebrations of emancipation from, 131, 137–38, 163, 176–78
slave trade ban (1807), 32
"Sly Young Coon, The" (song), 49
Smith, Elizabeth Oakes, 24
sonic color line, 220n50
Sotho people, 77, 124
Sotiropoulos, Karen, 120, 126
South Africa: Afro-diasporic cultural formations and exchange, 98, 110, 114; and Anglo-colonial circuit, 9, 29–31, 33–34, 186; and *Birth of a Nation*, 199; Dutch settlers/Afrikaners in, 10, 15, 32–33, 214n10–11; Jim Crow laws imported into, 11; Jolson, and performance culture in, 201; as minstrel nexus, 9; 1994 elections in, 164–65, 178–79; Prince Edward's tour of, 1; and second wave of minstrel globalization, 186; white population in, x, 6–7, 10, 214n10–11. *See also* apartheid South Africa; blackface minstrelsy in South Africa; British settlers in South Africa; McAdoo, Orpheus; mineral revolution in South Africa; preindustrial period in South Africa; race thinking and discourse of British settlers; racial segregation; *specific city and colony names*
South African Citizen, 128
South African film, 45
South America, 192–93
Southern Workman, 111
South Korea, 205–6
southwestern frontier humor, 21
Spanish Cavaliers, 149, 249n77
spatial apartheid, 252n135
spectacular opacity, 104–6, 114–15, 126
Spes Bona Nigger Minstrels, 155, 160
Spirit, The (comic series), 202
Standard News, 116
Stanley, Henry, 79
steam-engine technology, 9, 72, 187
Steele, Charles, 38, 63
Stephens, David, 159–60
Stewart (minstrel performer), 38
St. Helena, 72
St. James Hall, London, 63, 80
St. James Theatre, London, 30
Stoever, Jennifer, 220n50
Stokes, Melvyn, 199
Stone, Gerald, 163, 246n21
Stowe, Harriet Beecher, 26, 28
Stratton, Eugene, 194
Stratton, Jon, 261n83
stump speeches. *See* minstrel stump speeches
Sun, 135, 140, 145
surrogation and authenticity, 60–64, 233n91
swart gevaar redux, 164
Sydney, Australia, 2, 184, 188
Sydney Truth, 188

Tahiti, 9, 28
Taiwan, 206
Tambo (minstrel character), 20–21, 25, 86–87, 96, 129
"Tapioca" (song), 44, 229n20
Taylor, J. R., 38, 63, 233n88
Teatro Bufo, 190–91, 203, 258n38
"Ten Little Niggers" (minstrel song), 90–91, 238n75
Thailand, 206
Thatcher, Carol, 195
Thayer, James, 47
Theatre Magazine, 115–16
30 Rock (TV show), 204
Thompson, Karriem, 178
Thompson, Leonard, 76
Those German Emegrants (minstrel play), 85
"Tim Finagan's Wake" (minstrel song), 84
Tokugawa Shogunate, 183
Toll, Robert, 22, 115, 157
Tom Thumb, American (circus performer), 22, 235n6
Tom Thumb, Australian (minstrel performer), 75, 235n6
Topsy (minstrel character), 87
Toronto, Canada, 188–89, 198
Totten's Harmoneons, 28
transnational circulation of minstrel shows, 1–3, 7
transnational minstrelsy studies, ix, 5, 7–8, 184, 208–12
"Transoceanic Blackface, Imperial Whiteness" (Hoxworth), 210–11
Transvaal Advertiser, 116
Transvaal Republic, 33, 82, 98, 106–9, 124–25
"Trilby's Wedding; or, Life on the Mississippi," 115

Trinidad, 190
Tropic Thunder (film), 204
Tuning Out Blackness (Y. Rivero), 191
Tutu, Desmond, 176
Twain, Mark, 43
Tweede Nuwe Jaar, 131, 162, 178
Twenty-Fourth Regiment, 83

Uncle O'brieans (minstrel play), 85
"Uncle-Tom Mania," 26
"Uncle Tom's Cabin" (building), 37
Uncle Tom's Cabin (dramas), 18, 26
Uncle Tom's Cabin (film), 7
Uncle Tom's Cabin (minstrel rendition), 87
Uncle Tom's Cabin (Stowe), 26, 48
Underground Railroad, 97
Union of South Africa, 10
United States: and apartheid government, 10–11; and Coon Carnival culture, 158, 162; coon-song craze in, 8, 194; and Coon troupe names, 152; McAdoo's early life in, 96–97; minstrel dolls in, 194; naturalized citizenship in, 17–18; popular culture in, 1–2, 7–8; racial projects in, 54–55; racial segregation in, 19; racial uplift politics in, 99; racism in, vii–x, 2; Rice's performances in, 16–18; slavery in, 17–18, 26, 96–97; and Teatro Bufo, 190–91; tourists from, in France, 199. *See also* blackface minstrelsy, American; Jim Crow America
"United States Mail, The" (sketch), 52–53
Universal Negro Improvement Association (UNIA), 159
Upton, Florence Kate, 194
urban dandy character (zip coon): and black illogics humor, 48, 87; Carson's reinterpretation of, 30; and Coon Carnival, 175, 177; and coon songs, 122, 193; and Larrikins, 187; and minstrel sadism, 50; racial messaging of, 21
Uruguay, 192–93, 198

Vagrancy Ordinance (1834), 53
Valencia Burgos, Sixto, 202
vaudeville, 7–8, 115–16, 184, 193–95, 197
Vaughn, Virginia Mason, 90
Vereenigde Oostindische Compagnie (VOC), 31–32, 226n80
Versatile Eight, 201
Very Black Show, The (film), 204
Victoria, Queen, 63, 65, 79
Victoria Loftus Troupe, 75, 85, 87, 139, 197
Victorian culture, 27, 60
violence: against African workers, 88–89; and apartheid, 94; colonial, 84, 92; in minstrel shows, 49–50, 59–60, 91–92, 119, 231n51, 238n75; of slavery, 119
violoncello, 57
Virginia Jubilee Singers (Virginia Concert Company), 97, 100–114, 124–30, 153–54, 240n23
Virginia Minstrels, 19–20, 25, 43, 159, 222nn20–21
Virginia Mummy, The (minstrel play), 41, 46–47, 49, 51–52, 88
Virginny Cupids!, The (minstrel play), 51, 88, 231n54
Voorlopers, 132–33
Voortrekkers, 33, 124, 175, 179

Wales, Prince of, 69, 79
walkaround, 20
Walker, George, 115–16, 120, 195
Wallach, Kerry, 200
Warriors of Mahratta, 149, 151
Washington, Booker T., 102
Washington Consensus, 182
Washington Norton and the Merrymakers, 75, 139
Waterhouse, Richard, 28–29, 187, 209
Watkins, Mel, 20
wealth, uneven distribution of, 181–82
Weinstein, Valerie, 200
wench (minstrel character). *See* prima donna character
Western, John, 164–65
Western Cape, South Africa, 56, 61, 65–66, 152, 163–65
Western Cape Archives, 83
Western Cape Oral History Project (Centre for Popular Memory), 147
Western colonialism, 5, 31–36, 159, 177, 238n77
Western Province Coloured Carnival Board, 150
Western Province Jubilee Carnival Board, 154
Wheeler, Frank, 85
Wheeler Comedy Company, 75, 85, 139
"When Johnny Came Marching Home" (minstrel song), 68, 234n113
"Whistling Coon, The" (coon song), 194

white, as term, 15
White, Charles, 51
White, Frank, 81
White, George, 100
white American tourists, 199
"White-Eyed Kaffir," 215n7
whiteface makeup/whiting up, 231n52, 249n77
White House, 21–22
white identity politics, 23. *See also* burnt cork nationalism
white modernity, 159
white nationalism, vii–viii, x, 3, 27, 208
whiteness: British settler hierarchy of, 67–68; and coloured racial identity, 164, 166; and dispossession, 94; as exclusive property, 6, 175, 217n23; and failed-facade humor, 52–53; and Klopse troupes, 159–60, 166; and minstrel characters and imagery, 42, 69, 84; minstrel representations of, 119; normative, 42, 68, 84–85, 228n8
"Whiteness as Property" (Harris), 6, 175, 217n23
white poverty, 7
white supremacy, viii–ix, 6, 11, 94, 239n83
Whitlock, Billy, 19
"Whose Dat Knocking at de Door" (minstrel song), 233n84
"Who Stole the Chickens" (minstrel sketch), 49
Wicklow Wedding (minstrel play), 85
Wild American Masqueraders, 149
Willan, Brian, 110, 199
Williams, Bert, 115–16, 120, 195–96
Williams, Gardner, 94
Wilmot, Alexander, 238n73
Wilson, Woodrow, 197–98
Winant, Howard, 39
Wittman, Matthew, 187, 257n25
Witwatersrand, South Africa, 98
Wodehouse, Governor and Mrs., 57
women, men cross-dressing as: moffies, 132, 244n4; mummers wench, 180; prima donna character, 21, 41–42, 228n13
women, representation of: in blackface movies, 202; in British minstrel troupes, 26; in Chinese comedy sketch, 207; in Coon Carnival, 134; in *The Kentucky Minstrels*, 202; in McAdoo's troupes, 105–7, 119, 121, 123; in minstrel sketches, 50, 52–53; in minstrel songs, 44, 50, 85, 196; in minstrel stump speeches, 23–25, 48; in Rice's plays, 46, 51; in self-aware antiracist blackface, 204. *See also* Baby Benson
women's rights lectures, parodies of, 23–25
Wood, Jerry, 84
Woodstock Mohawk Minstrels, 141, 167
Worger, William, 77, 92–93
working-class carnival troupes, 134, 193
working-class culture, 18, 37, 55–58, 126, 182, 185, 191
working-class people, black, 76, 165, 192–93
working-class people, coloured, 158, 164–65
working-class people, white, 19, 23, 76, 180
World Bank, 11, 182
Wright, Josephine, 98

Xhosa people, 34–35, 40, 53–54, 66, 77, 82, 233n95

YMI Amateur Christys, 231n50
Young Louisiana Coons, 151, 160–63
Young Men's Institute Christys, 38–39
"Young Scamp, The" (minstrel sketch), 50

zip coon character. *See* urban dandy character
Zonk Coon troupe, 159
Zululand, 82
Zulu people, 33, 45, 77, 82–83, 110–11, 124, 167
Zulu Warriors troupes, 166

CHINUA THELWELL earned his PhD from the American studies program at New York University in 2011. His essays have appeared in *Safundi: The Journal of South African and American Studies* and *TDR: The Drama Review,* among other venues. His edited collection, *Theater and Cultural Politics for a New World,* was published by Routledge in 2016. He is assistant professor of history and Africana studies at the College of William and Mary.